Developments in Central
East European Politics

Developments titles available from Palgrave Macmillan

Alistair Cole, Sophie Meunier and Vincent Tiberj (eds)
DEVELOPMENTS IN FRENCH POLITICS 5

Maria Green Cowles and Desmond Dinan (eds)
DEVELOPMENTS IN THE EUROPEAN UNION 2

Richard Heffernan, Philip Cowley and Colin Hay (eds)
DEVELOPMENTS IN BRITISH POLITICS 9

Erik Jones, Paul M. Heywood, Martin Rhodes and
Ulrich Sedelmeier (eds)
DEVELOPMENTS IN EUROPEAN POLITICS 2

Stephen Padgett, William E. Paterson and Gordon Smith (eds)
DEVELOPMENTS IN GERMAN POLITICS 5*

Gillian Peele, Christopher J. Bailey, Bruce Cain and B. Guy Peters (eds)
DEVELOPMENTS IN AMERICAN POLITICS 6

Stephen White, Paul G. Lewis and Judy Batt (eds)
DEVELOPMENTS IN CENTRAL AND EAST EUROPEAN
POLITICS 5*

Stephen White, Richard Sakwa and Henry E. Hale (eds)
DEVELOPMENTS IN RUSSIAN POLITICS 7*

If you have any comments or suggestions regarding the
above or other possible *Developments* titles, please write to
Steven Kennedy, Palgrave Macmillan, Houndmills,
Basingstoke, RG21 6XS, UK, or e-mail s.kennedy@palgrave.com

* Rights world excluding North America

Developments in Central and East European Politics 5

Edited by

Stephen White
Paul G. Lewis
and
Judy Batt

palgrave
macmillan

First published 2013 by
PALGRAVE MACMILLAN

Palgrave Macmillan in the UK is an imprint of Macmillan Publishers Limited,
registered in England, company number 785998, of Houndmills, Basingstoke,
Hampshire RG21 6XS.

Palgrave Macmillan in the US is a division of St Martin's Press LLC,
175 Fifth Avenue, New York, NY 10010.

Palgrave Macmillan is the global academic imprint of the above companies
and has companies and representatives throughout the world.

Palgrave® and Macmillan® are registered trademarks in the United States,
the United Kingdom, Europe and other countries

ISBN 978–1–137–26299–8 hardback
ISBN 978–1–137–26298–1 paperback

This book is printed on paper suitable for recycling and made from fully
managed and sustained forest sources. Logging, pulping and manufacturing
processes are expected to conform to the environmental regulations of the
country of origin.

A catalogue record for this book is available from the British Library.

A catalog record for this book is available from the Library of Congress.

Contents

List of Tables and Figures

Tables

Figures

Preface

The dramatic changes of the late 1980s brought an end to the division of Europe and – at least in its original form – to communist rule. The changes took a variety of forms, and governments changed more quickly than forms of ownership, still less the political culture that had developed over forty years of communist rule (and sometimes rather longer). But by the early years of the new century, the Central and East European countries were facing very similar sets of challenges. Could they balance effective leadership, often through an elected presidency, with participation and accountability? Could they reverse the economic decline of the late communist years? And how would these changes affect the wider society – young and old, males and females, rich and poor – whether or not their country had joined an expanding European Union?

These are just some of the issues that are addressed in this collection, which (like its predecessors) brings together a group of leading specialists from both sides of the Atlantic. We begin with a chapter that seeks to define this elusive half-continent, and then move on to consider the patterns of change that have taken place in individual groups of countries. The remaining chapters focus on the framework of politics – leaderships, parliaments, parties and electoral systems – and the place of the countries of the region between the EU and a still-powerful Commonwealth of Independent States. We also consider the process of politics on a more comparative basis, including participation, protest and social movements, the politics of economic neoliberalism, social change, and the nature of the post-communist system. There is a guide to further reading at the end of the book, and a bibliography of all the publications that are cited in earlier chapters.

The politics of Central and Eastern Europe have been changing, and so has this book. Nominally a fifth edition, it is, in fact, a substantially new book. The entire text has been rewritten, several of the contributors are new to this or any previous edition, and the chapter structure itself has been reconsidered. But our objective has not changed, which is to provide a clear, well-informed and sometimes challenging guide to the common patterns as well as individual variety of a group of states that were formerly modelled on the Soviet Union, but which are now a distinctive and varied presence within a continent that has been redefining its own boundaries and values. We hope not only our students, but also colleagues and a wider public, will find something of value in the result.

STEPHEN WHITE
PAUL G. LEWIS
JUDY BATT

Notes on Contributors

Judy Batt holds a Jean Monnet Ad Personam Chair in the European Integration of Southeast Europe. She has lectured at the Universities of Birmingham and Leicester, and held research fellowships at the EU Institute for Security Studies, the Royal Institute for International Affairs, the Robert Schumann Centre at the the EUI in Florence, and at FRIDE in Madrid. She currently works for the European Fund for the Balkans in a training programme on EU affairs. Her publications include *Region, State and Identity in Central and Eastern Europe* (co-edited with Kataryna Wolczuk, 2002); *The Western Balkans: Moving On* (editor, 2004); and *The Question of Serbia* (2005).

Sarah Birch is a Professor of Politics at the University of Glasgow and was formerly at the University of Essex, UK. Her research interests include electoral systems and electoral conduct in democratizing and semi-democratic states, with a particular focus on Central and Eastern Europe. Her most recent book is *Electoral Malpractice* (2011). She has also written *Electoral Systems and Political Transformation in Post-Communist Europe* (2003) and *Full Participation: A Comparative Study of Compulsory Voting* (2009).

Nathaniel Copsey is Reader in Politics and Co-Director of the Aston Centre for Europe at Aston University, UK. He is also co-editor of the *Journal of Common Market Studies Annual Review* and a Visiting Professor at both Sciences-Po, Rennes, France, and the European Studies Institute of MGIMO-University in Moscow, Russia. His study of *Public Opinion and the Making of Foreign Policy in the 'New Europe': A Comparative Study of Poland and Ukraine* was published in 2009.

Terry Cox is Professor of Central and East European Studies at Glasgow University in the UK, and Editor of *Europe-Asia Studies*. His recent research has focused on the politics and sociology of post-communist transformations and state–society relations in Central and Eastern Europe. His publications include *Communication and Consultation in Public Space* (co-authored, 2002); *Challenging Communism in Eastern Europe: 1956 and its Legacy* (2008), and

Reflections on 1989 in Eastern Europe (2012, both edited); and *Reinventing Poland: Economic and Political Transformation and Changing National Identity* (2008, co-edited).

Rick Fawn is Senior Lecturer in International Relations at the University of St Andrews in the UK and a past director of its Centre for Russian and Central and East European Studies. He works generally on international relations and on the politics, foreign relations and security of post-communist countries. Among his recent publications are *Globalising the Regional, Regionalising the Global* (as editor, 2009), and *The Historical Dictionary of the Czech State* (as co-author, 2010), and he is completing a book entitled *International Organizations and Internal Conditionality: When Norms are Not Enough*.

Tim Haughton is Reader in European Politics and Director of the Centre for Russian and East European Studies at the University of Birmingham, UK. He is the author of *Constraints and Opportunities of Leadership in Post-Communist Europe* (2005), the editor of *Political Parties in Central and Eastern Europe: Does EU Membership Matter?* (2011), and the co-editor of the *Journal of Common Market Studies'* Annual Review of the European Union. He is currently working on domestic politics in Slovakia, Slovenia and the Czech Republic and has embarked on a project examining the role of the past in the politics of the present.

Krzysztof Jasiewicz is currently the William P. Ames, Jr. Professor and Head of the Department of Sociology and Anthropology at Washington and Lee University in Lexington, Virginia. In the 1990s, he was the founder and first director of electoral studies at the Polish Academy of Sciences. His recent publications include articles in *East European Politics and Societies, Journal of Democracy, Communist and Post-Communist Studies, Problems of Post-Communism*, and the *European Journal of Political Research*, as well as chapters in edited volumes in English, Polish, and French.

Paul G. Lewis is Emeritus Professor of Politics at the Open University in the UK. His books include *Central Europe since 1945* (1994), *Political Parties in Post-Communist Eastern Europe* (2000), and (co-) edited works on *Party Development and Democratic Change in Post-Communist Europe* (2001), *The European Union and Party Politics in Central and Eastern Europe* (2006) and *Europeanising Party Politics?* (2011). His main research interests concern the continuing development of political parties in Central and Eastern Europe and EU influences in this area.

Frances Millard is Professor Emerita, University of Essex, UK. She has written widely on communist and post-communist political and social developments, particularly in Poland. Her publications include *Embodying Democracy: Electoral System Design in Post-Communist Europe* (with others, 2002). *Elections, Parties, and Representation in Post-Communist Europe* (2004) and *Democratic Elections in Poland, 1991–2007* (2010). She is currently writing a book on transitional justice in Poland.

David M. Olson is Senior Research Fellow in the Center for Legislative Studies, and Professor Emeritus of Political Science, University of North Carolina at Greensboro, USA. He is the author *Democratic Legislative Institutions: A Comparative View* (1994), and has co-edited *Committees in Post-Communist Democratic Parliaments: Comparative Institutionalization* (with William E. Crowther, 2002), and *Post-Communist Parliaments: Change and Stability in the Second Decade* (with Gabriella Ilonszki, 2012). He is past co-chair of the Research Committee of Legislative Specialists of the International Political Science Association.

Mitchell A. Orenstein is Professor and Chair of the Department of Political Science at Northeastern University in Boston, MA, USA. His research in international politics has focused on the political economy of transition in Central and Eastern Europe, pension privatization worldwide, and the role of policy paradigms in economic reform. His books include *Out of the Red: Building Capitalism and Democracy in Postcommunist Europe* (2001), *Pensions, Social Security, and the Privatization of Risk* (edited, 2009) and *Privatizing Pensions: The Transnational Campaign for Social Security* (2010). The assistance of Andrew Bergmanson is gratefully acknowledged.

Andrew Roberts is Associate Professor of Political Science at Northwestern University in Illinois, USA. He is the author of *The Quality of Democracy in Eastern Europe: Public Preferences and Policy Choices* (2010) and *From Good King Wenceslas to the Good Soldier Švejk: A Dictionary of Czech Popular Culture* (2005). He has published articles in the *British Journal of Political Science*, *Comparative Political Studies*, and *Legislative Studies Quarterly* among other journals. He is currently studying inequalities in democratic responsiveness in post-communist Europe.

Ray Taras has served as Willy Brandt Professor at Malmö University in Sweden, Visiting Fellow at the European University Institute in Florence, Italy, and Professor of Politics at Tulane University in New Orleans, USA. His recent books include *Liberal and Illiberal Nationalisms* (2002), *Democracy in Poland* (with Marjorie Castle, second edn, 2002), *Europe Old and New: Transnationalism, Belonging, Xenophobia* (2009), *Xenophobia and Islamophobia in Europe* (2012), and *Russia's Identity in International Relations* (edited, 2012).

Stephen White is James Bryce Professor of Politics at the University of Glasgow in the UK, and is Visiting Professor at the Institute of Applied Politics in Moscow; he has also held recent visiting appointments at the Johns Hopkins Bologna Center and Grinnell College, Iowa, and co-edits the *Journal of Eurasian Studies*. His recent books include *Understanding Russian Politics* (2011) and *Russia's Authoritarian Elections* (with others, 2011); he is presently completing a study of relations between Russia, Ukraine, Belarus and 'Europe' with Valentina Feklyunina of Newcastle University.

Andrew Wilson is Reader in Ukrainian Studies at University College in London, UK. In 2008–10 he was a Senior Policy Fellow at the European Council on Foreign Relations (www.ecfr.eu). His latest book *Belarus: The Last European Dictatorship* was published in 2011. His other recent books include *The Ukrainians: Unexpected Nation* (third edn, 2009), *Ukraine's Orange Revolution* (2005) and *Virtual Politics: Faking Democracy in the Post-Soviet World* (2005).

List of Abbreviations

ALDE	Association of Liberals and Democrats for Europe
AWS	Solidarity Electoral Action
BiH	Bosnia-Herzegovina
BSEC	Organization for Black Sea Economic Cooperation
BSP	Bulgarian Socialist Party
BTI	Bertelsmann Transformation Index
CBSS	Council of the Baltic Sea States
CDPP	Christian-Democratic People's Party
CDR	Democratic Convention of Romania
CEE	Central and Eastern Europe
CEFTA	Central European Free Trade Agreement
CEI	Central European Initiative
CIS	Commonwealth of Independent States
CME	coordinated market economy
CMEA/Comecon	Council for Mutual Economic Assistance
CPI	Corruption Perception Index
CSSD	Social Democrats
DANCEE	Danish Cooperation for Environment in Eastern Europe
DME	dependent market economy
EaP	Eastern Partnership (of the EU)
EFA	European Greens–European Free Alliance
EP	European Parliament
EPP–ED	European People's Party–European Democrats
EU	European Union
EVS	European Values Survey
FDI	foreign direct investment
Fidesz	Young Democrats (Fidesz-MPSz from 2003)
FKGP	Independent Smallholders Party
FYROM	Former Yugoslav Republic of Macedonia
GDR	German Democratic Republic (GDR)
GUAM	Alliance of Georgia, Ukraine, Azerbaijan and Moldova
GUE-NGL	European United Left
HDI	Human Development Index
HZDS	Movement for a Democratic Slovakia

ICTY	International Criminal Tribunal for the former Yugoslavia
IDEA	International Institute for Democracy and Electoral Assistance
IMF	International Monetary Fund
IND/DEM	Independence and Democracy
IVF	International Visegrad Fund
KDU-CSL	Czech Christian Democrats
KSCM	Communist Party of Bohemia and Moravia
LME	liberal market economy
LPR	League of Polish Families
MDF	Hungarian Democratic Forum
MEP	Member of European Parliament
MIEP	Justice and Life Party
MSzP	Hungarian Socialist Party
NATO	North Atlantic Treaty Organization
NDSV	National Movement Simeon II
NGO	non-governmental organization
NS/SL	New Union–Social Liberals
ODA	Civic Democratic Alliance
ODS	Civic Democratic Party
OECD	Organisation for Economic Co-operation and Development
OSCE	Organization for Security and Cooperation in Europe
OSI	Open Society Institute
PCA	Partnership and Cooperation Agreement
PCRM	Communist Party of the Republic of Moldova
PES	Group of European Socialists
PiS	Law and Justice Party
PLC	Parliamentary Leadership Council
PO	Civic Platform
PPP	parliamentary party groups
PPP	purchasing power parity
PR	proportional representation
PRM	Party of Great Romania
PSL	Polish Peasant Party
RCC	Regional Cooperation Council
RMDS/UDMR	Democratic Alliance of Hungarians in Romania
SAA	Stabilization and Association Agreement
SdPl	Polish Social Democracy
SDS	Christian-Democratic Union of Democratic Forces
SEE	South-Eastern Europe

SEECP	South-East European Cooperation Process
SFRY	Socialist Federal Republic of Yugoslavia
SLD	Democratic Left Alliance
SMD	single-member district
Smer-SD	Direction-Social Democracy
SNS	Slovak National Party
SO	Self-Defence
SSR	Soviet Socialist Republic
STV	single transferable vote
SzDSz	Free Democrats
UEN	Union for Europe of the Nations
UNDP	United Nations Development Programme
UP	Labour Union (Poland)
US	Freedom Union (Czech Republic)
UW	Freedom Union (Poland)
WSI	Military Intelligence Services
WVS	World Values Study

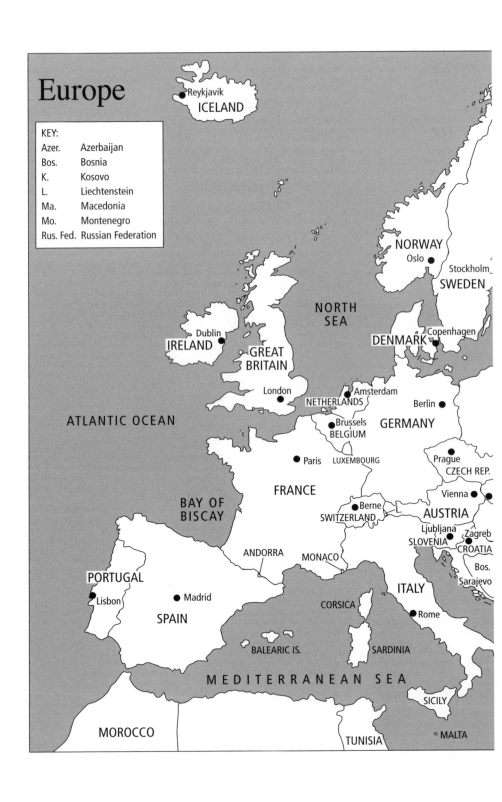

Europe

KEY:
Azer.   Azerbaijan
Bos.   Bosnia
K.   Kosovo
L.   Liechtenstein
Ma.   Macedonia
Mo.   Montenegro
Rus. Fed. Russian Federation

Reykjavik
ICELAND

NORWAY
Oslo
Stockholm
SWEDEN

NORTH SEA

DENMARK
Copenhagen

Dublin
IRELAND
GREAT BRITAIN

London
Amsterdam
NETHERLANDS
Berlin
Brussels
BELGIUM
GERMANY

ATLANTIC OCEAN

Paris
LUXEMBOURG
Prague
CZECH REP.

FRANCE

Vienna

Berne
L.
AUSTRIA
SWITZERLAND

BAY OF BISCAY

Ljubljana
Zagreb
SLOVENIA
CROATIA

ANDORRA
MONACO

Bos.
Sarajevo

PORTUGAL
ITALY

Lisbon
Madrid
CORSICA
Rome

SPAIN

BALEARIC IS.
SARDINIA

MEDITERRANEAN SEA

SICILY

MOROCCO

TUNISIA
° MALTA

Chapter 1

Introduction: Defining Central and Eastern Europe

Judy Batt

This book covers a wide range of European countries that emerged from the collapse of communism in the years 1989 to 1991. From this common starting point, they embarked, with varying degrees of commitment and success, on the 'transition to democracy'. Many of them, in fact, first acquired or recovered independent statehood as part of this process. Their democratic transition was, moreover, profoundly affected by the international context: the end of the Cold War and the east–west division of Europe, followed by the enlargement of the European Union and NATO to embrace many of the states of this region. These countries thus provide political scientists with an unprecedentedly rich testing ground for comparative theorizing on many questions of key importance for our understanding of the workings of democracy: what are the conditions for the establishment of democracy? How does the heritage of the communist past, or the existence of a strong and cohesive national identity, or geographical proximity to Western Europe affect the process? Where do new parties come from, and why do some succeed and others fail? To what extent can 'institutional engineering' – for example, the choice of electoral system and the formal 'rules of the game' set out in the constitution – contribute to the stabilization of new democracies? How important are political culture and the strength or weakness of independent civil society to the establishment of democracy, and what is the impact of the complete overhaul of the economic system and the reshaping of the basic structure of social interests and classes that are simultaneously taking place?

The richness of this region as a testing ground for political science provides a justification for treating all together in one book the politics of the Central and Eastern European states. Yet that very richness is due to its enormous complexity and diversity, which often challenge the very notion of Central and Eastern Europe as a distinctive and

1

coherent region. As the Czech novelist Milan Kundera (1984) has put it, this is a 'condensed version of Europe in all its cultural variety', made up 'according to one rule: the greatest variety within the smallest space'. This amorphous region spans states as diverse as tiny Slovenia in the far south-west, a cohesive nation of just under two million, with a standard of living approaching that of the West European average, and a lifestyle that has much in common with its Alpine neighbours Austria and Italy; and, in the east, vast Ukraine sprawling across the steppes, with a population of 46 million, a state that, having emerged almost by accident in 1991upon the collapse of the Soviet Union, has been struggling ever since with uncertainty as to its national identity and place in the world, with profound economic decline, mass impoverishment, and poor government by more or less corrupt, politically inept elites. The peoples of Central and Eastern Europe, their languages, religions and cultures, are extremely diverse (see Tables 1.1 and 1.2). Linguistic proximity, for example, among the largest, Slavonic language group, is cross-cut by the religious divide between the mainly Roman Catholic Poles, Czechs and Slovaks (the latter two also including Protestant minorities) and the Orthodox Russians, Belorussians and Ukrainians (the latter also including a significant minority of 'Greek' Catholics, practising Orthodox rites while accepting the Pope in Rome as spiritual leader). Speakers of Serbo-Croat, once (but no longer) regarded as a single language within the South Slavonic sub-group, comprise four separate and mutually mis-

Table 1.1   *Major languages spoken in Central and Eastern Europe*

INDO-EUROPEAN GROUP		NON-INDO-EUROPEAN GROUPS	
Slavonic		*Uralic*	
West:	Polish, Czech, Slovak	Finnic:	Estonian
East:	Russian, Ukrainian,	Ugric:	Hungarian
	Rusyn, Belorussian		
South:	Serbo-Croat, Slovene,	*Altaic*	
	Bulgarian, Macedonian	Turkish	
		Gagauz	
Germanic			
German, Yiddish			
Baltic			
Latvian, Lithuanian			
Italic (Latin-based)			
Romanian (including Moldovan)			
Albanian			

Table 1.2   *Religious traditions in Central and Eastern Europe*

MAINLY ROMAN CATHOLIC	MAINLY ORTHODOX
Poles	Russians
Lithuanians	Bulgarians
Slovenes	Serbs
German 'Schwabs' in Hungary, Romania and former Yugoslavia	Montenegrins
	Macedonians
Croats	Moldovans
	Gagauzi
MAJORITY CATHOLIC WITH SIGNIFICANT PROTESTANT MINORITY	**MUSLIMS**
Czechs	Bosnian Muslims
Slovaks	Turkish Muslims
Hungarians	Sandzhak Muslims in Serbia
MAINLY PROTESTANT	**MAINLY MUSLIM WITH CATHOLIC AND ORTHODOX MINORITIES**
Latvians	Albanians
Estonians	
German 'Saxons' in Romania (Transylvania)	JEWS: mainly urban dwellers throughout Central and Eastern Europe; much reduced by assimilation in the nineteenth century and the Holocaust in the Second World War.
MAJORITY ORTHODOX WITH SIGNIFICANT UNIATE (GREEK-CATHOLIC) MINORITY	The ROMA throughout Central and Eastern Europe have tended to adopt the majority religion of the locality in which they live. But many recently have joined various Christian sects and the Seventh Day Adventists.
Ukrainians	
Rusyns	
Romanians	

trustful nations – Serbs, Montenegrins, Croats, and Bosniaks – primarily identified by their respective Orthodox, Catholic and Muslim traditions. Romanians, who speak a Latin-based language, are by religion mainly Orthodox, with a sizeable Greek-Catholic minority; while Hungarians, whose language falls outside the Indo-European group, share with their Central European neighbours both the Western Catholic and Protestant religious traditions.

The *diversity* that is the hallmark of Central and Eastern Europe – within countries as much as between them – has often been a source of political tension. Although the region's history has also been marked by long periods of peaceful inter-ethnic coexistence, the prevailing

Western perception is one of chronic fragmentation and conflict between states and peoples. When we come to look for a common identity, as the commentator Timothy Garton Ash has written:

> we shall at once be lost in a forest of historical complexity – an end-lessly intriguing forest to be sure, a territory where peoples, cultures, languages are fantastically intertwined, where every place has several names and men change their citizenship as often as their shoes, an enchanted wood full of wizards and witches, but one which bears over its entrance the words: 'Abandon all hope, ye who enter here, of ever again seeing the wood for the trees.' (Garton Ash, 1989a: 47)

A first stop in the search for commonalities would be the fact that all the states covered in this book experienced several decades of commu-nist rule until the dramatic changes of 1989–91. The communist system was a unique form of dictatorship that was characterized not only by the monopoly of political power in the hands of a single party, but also by far-reaching expropriation of private property and the direct subordination of the economy and society to political control. Communist ideology was universalist, in the sense that it predicted a common destiny for all mankind, a utopia of equality and justice tran-scending class and national divisions. The communist politico-eco-nomic system, pioneered by the Soviet Union, was justified as a universally valid 'model' that all peoples would follow on the path to this utopia. Communism was thus an experiment in enforcing con-formity to this model upon the highly diverse region of Central and Eastern Europe. When it failed, all these countries faced broadly similar challenges in unscrambling its legacies and building anew: establishing new multi-party systems; holding competitive elections for the first time in decades; transforming parliaments from puppet the-atres in which the communists pulled all the strings into working arenas for debate and legislation; dismantling the pervasive networks of the political police; as well as re-privatizing their economies and establishing functioning market economies virtually from scratch.

However, when we dig deeper into the communist past, we dis-cover that communism took on markedly different forms across the states of Central and Eastern Europe. This started with Yugoslavia's breakaway in 1948 from the 'bloc' of countries under the control of the Soviet Union. The Yugoslav communists soon realized that in order to stabilize and consolidate their control without external help from the Soviet Union, they needed to develop their own 'road to socialism', more in conformity with their own conditions. They bolstered their independence by attacking the centralist form of communism imposed throughout the Soviet bloc as a 'bureaucratic deformation', and in its place they proposed a decentralized model of 'self-management'. The Yugoslav economic system was transformed into what became known as 'market socialism'. Central planning was abolished, enterprises were no longer controlled by the state but by their own employees, and market forces were allowed considerable latitude. The political system was federalized, and the six national republics and two autonomous provinces came to enjoy a large measure of political and economic autonomy. For many years the Yugoslav economy appeared to flourish, bolstered by growing ties with the West (including financial support), and by remittances sent home by large numbers of Yugoslavs allowed to work abroad in Western Europe.

Diversification also began among the countries remaining within the Soviet bloc after the death in 1953 of the Soviet leader Stalin, who had brought communism to the region at the end of the Second World War. Revolts and attempted revolutions in East Berlin in 1953, Hungary and Poland in 1956, Czechoslovakia in 1968 and Poland in 1980–1 demonstrated the fragility of the centralized Soviet model, its lack of genuine roots in the societies and cultures of the region, and its inability to provide the promised superior economy and standard of living to that provided by Western capitalism. Although these revolts were all put down by force, and Soviet-style 'normalization' quickly re-imposed, it was clear that some leeway had to be granted to the different countries to respond more flexibly to national conditions. In the cases of Poland and Hungary, communist governments experimented with economic reforms, some aspects of which were similar to the Yugoslav experiment. The aim was to make the economy more flexible and dynamic, and so to buy popularity for the communist system, without weakening the communist party's monopoly of power. Nevertheless, reforms did lead to a significantly less oppressive political atmosphere in these countries than, for example, in the German Democratic Republic (GDR, or Eastern Germany) and Czechoslovakia (after 1968), which stuck to a rigid form of barely modified Stalinist centralism, as did Romania. However the latter, in contrast to the GDR and Czechoslovakia, the Soviet Union's staunchest allies, pursued an independent foreign policy, cultivating ties with the Soviet Union's chief 'enemies', China, Israel and the West. This did not mean political relaxation at home: in fact the Ceausescu regime was the most repressive of all, culminating in a personalized dictatorship that recalled inter-war fascist glorification of the Leader, drawing heavily on Romanian nationalist symbols to appeal to the masses, backed up by all-pervading secret police intimidation. However, by the end of the communist period, all of the countries of Central and Eastern Europe faced profound economic crisis. So when in 1989 the then Soviet leader Gorbachev took the momentous decision to withdraw from Central and Eastern Europe, these communist regimes collapsed in rapid succession. This culminated in the Soviet Union itself in 1991, when the Baltic republics, Ukraine and other former Soviet republics broke away to form new independent states.

Although all states faced challenges of post-communist political and economic transformation, they each did so in their own specific way. Precisely what had to be unscrambled when communism collapsed, and what material and human resources were available on which to build, varied widely. Hungary, Poland and Yugoslavia were all saddled with crippling debts and high inflation resulting from their failed reform experiments; but at least their elites contained political pragmatists and technocrats having some understanding of the market economy, and their peoples had had a chance over the previous decades to engage in small-scale private entrepreneurship. Travel to the West, or at least access to information about it, was quite widespread. Yugoslavia, however, squandered these initial advantages when its crisis-ridden federation broke down in more than a decade of inter-ethnic war. One of the Yugoslav republics, Slovenia, did manage to escape unscathed, and having established its independence, joined the group of seven other Central European states that forged ahead in political and economic transformation and in May 2004 joined the European Union. Romania and Bulgaria lagged behind, their economic transformation burdened by impoverishment inherited from communist misrule, the ambiguities of their post-communist elites about change, and the political weaknesses and inexperience of alternative non-communist elites. But still, in January 2007, their reforms were deemed sufficiently advanced to allow them to enter the EU.

The end of communism reopened questions of statehood that had long been assumed settled in post-Second World War Europe. The GDR disappeared altogether after unification with the Federal Republic in 1991, which ensured its radical economic and political transformation by a unique process of absorption into another state (and also its exclusion from this volume). Czechoslovakia too disappeared by 1993, fractured into two independent states as a result of long-submerged national differences between Czechs and Slovaks that resurfaced after 1989. Nearly 70 years of common statehood and 40 years of communist centralism have not prevented the two new Czech and Slovak states from taking on quite different profiles. The same is even more obvious in the cases of former Soviet republics: the Baltic republics' experience of independent statehood in the inter-war period – albeit brief – seems to have given them a head-start over Ukraine and

Moldova, both of which have been teetering on the brink of an economic and political abyss for most of the period since independence. In
Belarus, on the other hand, independent statehood for this former
Soviet republic has seen the consolidation of an unreformed commu-
nist-style regime, heavily dependent on Russia.

Thus the diversity that was already becoming apparent in the communist period has further deepened since the end of communism,
hence the question with which we started remains to be answered.
What justifies treating together these highly disparate states? If we take
a longer historical view, we can identify some broad, recurrent themes
that have shaped – and continue to shape – the political development
of the region and its interactions with the wider Europe.

The 'Lands in Between': a geopolitical predicament

Central and Eastern Europe often seems easier to define by what it is
not, than by what it is. It is an area, without clear geographical
borders, that stretches from the Baltic Sea in the north to the Adriatic
in the south, and south-eastward to the Black Sea. In the north, it comprises part of the Great European Plain that extends to the west across
northern Germany and the Low Countries and to the east deep into
Russia. In the centre is the upland plateau of the Czech lands and the
Danubian Basin spreading out between the Alps and the Carpathian
mountains. Further south still is the mountainous, often remote and
inaccessible region of the Balkans, and to the south-east the land
stretches away into the steppes of Ukraine. These are sometime called
the 'Lands in Between', a broad frontier zone between Russia and
Germany, Europe and Asia, East and West.

This indeterminate location has had a fundamental impact on the
shaping of political identities throughout the region. The lack of
natural borders exposed the region to successive waves of migration
over the centuries, while inaccessibility and economic marginalization
helped preserve distinctive local traditional cultures, languages and
dialects – hence the region's ethnic diversity. An enormous variety of
peoples came to settle here, not for the most part (until the twentieth
century) in consolidated and clearly defined territories, but intermin-
gled in a complex ethnic patchwork. As a result of its geopolitical
exposure, the region has been chronically vulnerable to invasion by
larger and stronger powers to the west, east and south. Between the fifteenth and seventeenth centuries, when in Western Europe the foundations of modern nation-states were being laid, Central and Eastern
Europe fell under the control of large multinational empires. The

Balkans and most of Hungary were conquered by the Ottoman Empire, and were thus isolated from the West in a formative period when the cultural influences of the Renaissance and Reformation took hold. Rump Hungary depended on the Habsburg Empire, and after the imperial forces drove the Ottomans out of its territory at the end of the eighteenth century, Hungary fell under the rule of Vienna. Meanwhile, the Russian Empire in the seventeenth and eighteenth centuries expanded its might southwards to the Black Sea and captured the southern shore of the Baltic in the north from the Swedes. In the late eighteenth century, Poland was partitioned between Russia, Prussia and Habsburg Austria.

The establishment of the various empires promoted (or forced) further migrations of the peoples of the region as some groups fled before one imperial army to seek protection under another, others moved in to fill their place, and new ruling groups were brought from far-away imperial capitals to run the local administration. Along with ethnic diversity and intermingling, imperial rule promoted and entrenched complex patterns of ethnic stratification. Typically, the landowning nobility was of a different language and/or religion from the peasants who worked their estates, and different again from the administrative elites, commercial and professional classes in the towns. Thus, for example, in Hungary, Magyar nobles lorded it over Slovak or Romanian peasants; in Austrian Galicia, Polish nobles did the same over Ukrainians and Rusyns; in the Baltic, it was Germans and Swedes who dominated the Estonian and Latvian masses. Servicing the bureaucratic and military needs of empire brought fresh influxes of German speakers to the eastern towns of the Habsburg Empire, to join long-settled communities of German craftsmen. Russians came to govern the cities of Ukraine, Moldavia and that part of Poland, which had fallen under Russian control at the end of the eighteenth century. Greeks came from Constantinople in order to take on that role on behalf of the Ottomans in much of the Balkans. Throughout the region, Jews constituted a significant proportion of the urban population occupied in trade and commerce, petty crafts and the professions. Ethnic stratification was exploited by imperial rule, which favoured some ethnic groups over others, such as the Germans in imperial Russia's Baltic provinces, or Slavic converts to Islam in parts of the Balkans under Ottoman control. Challenges to the central imperial authorities were thus fended off by a strategy of 'divide and rule' whose consequences are still being felt in inter-ethnic relations in the region today.

The lack of defensible territorial borders had led, by the late eighteenth century, to the whole of Central and Eastern Europe being swallowed up between rival multinational empires that, in the course of the nineteenth century, began to look increasingly ramshackle. Autocratic rule and socio-economic stagnation blocked the development of dynamic modern civil societies. The intermingling of peoples did not lead to a 'multicultural' paradise or the emergence of an integrated, coherent 'body politic' capable of calling the state to account. The very absence of clear territorial bases for the exercise of political power led rather to the accentuation of language and religion as key markers of social group formation.

'Catching up' with Europe

In the course of the nineteenth century, the challenge of cultural, political and economic modernization posed by the example of more developed and dynamic nation-states in Western Europe began to make itself felt among the peoples of the dynastic empires of Central and Eastern Europe. Defeat in war made the rulers of the region aware that the economic backwardness of their empires was a major source of military weakness. In the late nineteenth century, state-promoted industrialization drives were launched, but proceeded unevenly, in fits and starts. 'Take-off' into sustained growth was held back by rigidly conservative political and social institutions, chief among which was the preservation of a feudal-type agricultural system in which peasants remained tied to the land as serfs. Despite, or rather, because of this social and economic backwardness, the ideas of individual liberty, social emancipation and national self-determination proclaimed by the French Revolution had an enormous impact on educated elites throughout the region, who came to see 'catching up' with the mainstream of Western Europe as the key goal for their societies. The ideal of the 'nation-state', a political order in which the state was held to be accountable to the 'People', provided would-be reformers with the intellectual ammunition with which to attack autocracy, feudal privilege, ossified conservative traditions and social injustice in the name of the European liberal ideals of individual freedom, equal rights, the rule of law, and constitutional government.

But problems arose with the redefinition of the state as representative of the 'nation'. In the French context, the 'nation' had been conceived as the whole 'People' inhabiting the existing state's well-established historical territory, a free association of individual citizens with equal rights. Transformation of the Central and East European empires along the same lines was blocked not only by the entrenched resistance of the old regimes but also by lack of consensus on who precisely constituted 'the People' to whom the state was to be made accountable. By the early nineteenth century, under the influence of German Romanticism and especially of Johann von Herder, a native of the Baltic province of East Prussia, the idea of the 'nation' in the Central and East European context began to depart from the state-centred French concept, which defined 'citizens' in terms of residence on the state's territory, and moved towards a definition which drew political borders along cultural and linguistic lines. Thus the demand for 'national self-determination' was raised on behalf of ethnic communities, and implied the creation of new states for the respective ethnic communities on whatever territory they claimed as their homeland. Effectively this meant that the multinational Central and East European empires could only be transformed into 'nation-states' by redrawing territorial borders and breaking them up. But further, because most of the empires' constituent territories contained more than one ethnic nation, and because of the extensive intermingling of peoples that had in the meanwhile taken place, competing claims were laid by the various ethnic nations to the various parts of the imperial territories.

The collapse of the Ottoman, Russian and Habsburg empires, culminating at the end of the First World War, left the victorious Western Powers with the task of implementing the principle of 'national self-determination' as promised by the American President Woodrow Wilson (see Macmillan, 2001). The way seemed open for the peoples of the region finally to acquire their own sovereign nation-states and so to reach political modernity on the pattern already laid down by their neighbours in the West. The disintegration of the Russian Empire into the chaos of revolution in 1917 and civil war in the following years allowed the Estonians, Latvians and Lithuanians to break free and form their own states. The simultaneous demise of the Habsburg Empire and the defeat of Germany paved the way for a united independent Poland to reappear on the map of Europe. The Czechs and Slovaks formed a new common state of Czechoslovakia, while the South Slavs of Austria–Hungary united with Serbia in the Kingdom of Serbs, Croats and Slovenes, later Yugoslavia. Romania, which like Serbia had wrested independence from Ottoman control in the late nineteenth century, acquired from Hungary to its west and Russia to its east extensive new territories where Romanians formed local majorities. Other nations were less successful, notably, the Ukrainians, who remained divided between the Soviet Union in the east and Poland in the west; and the Hungarians, who gained independence from Austria only to lose two-thirds of their historic territory to Romania, Czechoslovakia and Yugoslavia.

The new nation-states of Central and Eastern Europe faced enormous internal and external challenges in the inter-war period. The heritage of history and the endemic problem of geopolitical vulnerability did not melt away overnight. First of all, the new states did not, for the most part, inherit ready-made administrations and integrated political communities of citizens. These had to be built almost from scratch on the territories inherited from various former rulers. So, for example, the Polish leader Piłsudski faced a huge task in 1918:

> Piłsudski had to weld together different economies, different laws and different bureaucracies. He had to rationalise nine separate legal systems. He had to reduce five currencies to one, and he did not even have the means to print banknotes. Railways were a nightmare, with 66 different kinds of rails, 165 types of locomotives and a patchwork of signalling systems. (Macmillan, 2001: 220)

The new Czechoslovak Republic, comprising Bohemia–Moravia, a province formerly ruled from Vienna, and Slovakia, which had been part of a semi-independent Hungary, had no rail link from its capital, Prague, in the west, to Kosice, the main city at its eastern end. Rail routes ran towards either Vienna or Budapest, which meant that in the early days of the republic one actually had to leave the country in order to get from one end of it to the other.

Most important of all, most states were not 'nation-states' in the sense in which their new rulers had expected – states of and for a single, united 'nation' in ethnic terms – but contained sizeable minorities, more or less aggrieved at the changes in borders that had taken place over their heads. Thus Poland, reborn in its pre-partition borders, contained large minorities of Ukrainians and other east Slavic, Orthodox peoples who identified more closely with kinsfolk over the border in the Soviet Union than with their Polish fellow-citizens; Germans, who found it hard to accept their diminished status in a state dominated by Poles whom they tended to disdain; and Jews, who were regarded as alien by their devoutly Catholic Polish neighbours. Both Czechoslovakia and Yugoslavia rested on unresolved questions of whether the aim was to construct a unified nation-state resting on a single composite political identity, or whether in fact they were multinational states that should give institutional recognition to their constituent national groups. The dismantling of historic Hungarian territory to the benefit of neighbouring Czechoslovakia, Romania and Yugoslavia transferred large minorities of Hungarians to rule by the peoples whom they had previously dominated, and who regarded them as 'foreigners' rather than fellow-citizens. Moreover, many individuals were of two (or more) minds as to their ethnic identity and how it related to the new political order, as the inter-war writer Odon von Horvath explained:

> If you ask me what is my native country, I answer: I was born in Fiume, I grew up in Belgrade, Budapest, Pressburg, Vienna and Munich, and I have a Hungarian passport: but I have no fatherland. I am a very typical mix of old Austria–Hungary: at once Magyar, Croatian, German and Czech; my country is Hungary, my mother tongue is German. (Quoted in Rupnik, 1990: 250)

The strategy adopted by state-builders across Central and Eastern Europe was to impose from above a centralized state apparatus in order to enforce maximum uniformity within tightly controlled borders. This accorded with their perception of the French republican model, and fitted well with their objectives of securing the sovereignty and hegemony of the majority nation in whose name the state had been founded. But it was to prove a recipe for internal instability and external conflict. First, nationalistic policies of building up state strength by economic protectionism exacerbated the economic difficulties caused by the fragmentation of previously relatively open, large markets of the imperial territories, and made the whole region peculiarly vulnerable to the economic crisis of the late 1920s and 1930s. This was combined with the explosive fact that most states were multinational. On one side stood the 'nationalizing' elites, bent on entrenching the hegemony of the majority by means of centralized political and administrative structures, ostensibly in the name of modernization, efficiency and civic equality. On another side stood the national minorities, for whom this represented just another form of bureaucratic pressure for assimilation and subjection to the untrammelled 'tyranny of the majority'. Often too there was a third side, a neighbouring state aggrieved by the outcome of the peace settlement, which took upon itself the role of 'protector' of minorities abroad where these were ethnic kinsfolk, and aimed at eventual revision of the new borders (see Brubaker, 1996).

Bearing the brunt of European power politics

All of these tensions were exacerbated by the external threats posed in the inter-war period by the resurgence of Germany in the west and Soviet Russia in the east. By the early 1930s, these rival powers were set upon expansion into the Central and East European territories they had 'lost' at the end of the First World War, and promoted their aims in the name of the radically opposed and profoundly illiberal ideologies of fascism and communism. Most of the new states in Central and Eastern Europe, by contrast, were small in size, economically weak, and deficient in military organization and capacities. Moreover, mutual mistrust among them obstructed any move toward common defence against the looming threats. The peace settlement had failed to provide an overarching security framework and structures to promote regional cooperation, without which 'national self-determination' was to be precarious and short-lived. This point was not lost on more perceptive individuals in the region, such as the Hungarian Oszkar Jaszi, who early recognized the unsustainability of the situation:

> The only possible cure for Europe's ills is a democratic confederation of democratic peoples, the extirpation of rigid and selfish national sovereignty, peaceful and rational cooperation between all countries for the good of all. The fundamentals of this system are to be found in two basic institutions: one, free trade between all parties to the confederation; the other, a system of honest national and cultural autonomy for all national minorities living within the boundaries of the confederation. Under such conditions political frontiers would slowly become mere demarcations of administrative divisions. (Jaszi, 1923: 280–1)

Voices such as Jaszi's were not heeded at the time. Instead, Central and East Europe fell prey to a new round of imperial conquest, more brutal and oppressive than anything experienced before. After 1939, Nazi Germany and the Soviet Union redrew the map of Europe by carving up the lands in between them. Poland once again disappeared, partitioned between the rival powers. Poles became forced labourers for the Nazi war machine, their military elite massacred by the Soviet army advancing from the east, and their country reduced to the site of the major death camps into which Jews from the whole of Europe were herded and exterminated. The Baltic republics were invaded first by Germany, then forcibly incorporated into the Soviet Union. Divisions among the Central and East Europeans themselves were ruthlessly exploited: Czechoslovakia and Yugoslavia were dismembered, and Nazi-backed puppet states were formed in breakaway Slovakia and Croatia. Axis ally Italy seized the Dalmatian coast and ran an enlarged Albania, while Hungary seized the opportunity to regain lost lands in southern Slovakia, north-western Romania and northern Serbia. As Great Power rivalry was being fought out over their heads, bitter ethnic wars meanwhile broke out on the ground between Poles and Ukrainians, Hungarians and Romanians, Serbs, Croats and Bosnian Muslims; and Jews and gypsies suffered at the hands not only of the Nazi invaders but also of their own neighbours.

The peace that eventually came to the region at the end of the Second World War was bought at an exceptionally heavy price with the advance westward of the Soviet Army, by now in alliance with the Western Powers. 'Liberation' from Nazi control by Soviet forces was rapidly followed by the installation of temporary governments stacked with local communist recruits and fellow-travellers. For the Western Allies, preoccupied with the final defeat of Germany and Japan, keeping Stalin on side in the last months of the war was the priority. By the time they turned their attention to the situation in Central and Eastern Europe at the end of the war, the Western Allies' national capacities and will to intervene to avert the consolidating Soviet grip over the region were exhausted. The main result of belated efforts on the part of the new US administration under Truman to 'roll back' communism in Europe was to prompt Stalin to seal off the Central and East European states that his troops had occupied behind an 'Iron Curtain'. Thereafter, all remaining non-communist parties and politicians were ousted from government, and the local communist parties were tightly bound into a communist international system that enforced uniformity and subordination to the dictates of Moscow.

The states of Central and Eastern Europe thereafter found themselves set on a new course of 'socialist construction' following the Soviet model. This was a project of 'catching up' with the West, but one explicitly designed in opposition to the capitalist path re-launched in Western Europe with US support in the 'Marshall Plan'. The continent was divided into two opposing blocs, and Central and Eastern Europe became once again the front line of East–West superpower rivalry. Although the project of 'catching up and overtaking' the West presented by communist rule held some attractions for the peoples of the region insofar as it promised rapid social and economic modernization, communist rule was regarded as politically alien, a new form of imperialism that suppressed their political freedom, their religions, and above all their national identity. For centuries, it had been Western Europe, not Russia that they had regarded as the model to emulate and the centre of their cultural gravitational field. Although communist ideology was certainly a Western import into Russia, when it was forcibly imposed from the east onto Central and Eastern Europe, it was experienced as a form of 'Asiatic despotism' with which only a narrow minority could ever identify. The subsequent failure of communist regimes to deliver the promised economic and social progress only exposed the acute fragility of these regimes in the region, which explains why they all collapsed so quickly in 1989–91.

The 'return to Europe'

The slogan that best encapsulated popular understanding of the meaning of the revolutions of 1989–91 in Central and Eastern Europe was the 'Return to Europe'. Of course, geographically, they had never moved but, meanwhile, Western Europe had surged ahead. Post-war recovery was followed by decades of economic growth and radical technological innovation; unprecedentedly prosperous societies enjoyed the additional security of extensive state welfare provision; and the problem of German power seemed to have been resolved by binding its larger western part, the Federal Republic, into political and economic integration within the European Community (later European Union) and military integration in NATO. Buoyed up by self-confidence and not a little complacency, the western side of the Iron Curtain had come to regard itself as 'Europe'. In 1989, it awoke to find long-forgotten neighbours clamouring to join in. For what the Central and East Europeans recognized in the 'Europe' represented by the EU and NATO was precisely that 'democratic confederation of democratic peoples' that Jaszi, among others, had envisioned: an overarching framework for the weak, small and divided peoples of the region to overcome their geopolitical predicament and achieve the security and prosperity without which the long-cherished goal of 'national self-determination' would remain unfulfilled. 'Returning to Europe' held the promise of a replicating a tried-and-tested formula that would allow them finally to 'catch up' with the West.

Western observers have often remarked on the apparent contradiction in the revolutions of 1989, seeking simultaneously to recover national independence and to join in West European processes of deepening political, economic and military integration that unquestionably affect key aspects of the traditional sovereignty of nation-states. The end of communist rule in Central and Eastern Europe saw an upsurge of nationalist rhetoric, leading not only to a revival of the sort of tensions between ethno-national majorities and minorities that had fatefully afflicted the stability of the region in the inter-war period, but also to the break-up of the three multinational communist states – the Soviet Union, Yugoslavia and Czechoslovakia – to form a whole set of new nation-states. The temptation is to regard this as a symptom of some endemically recurrent Central and East European disease that sets apart this part of the continent from the West, and raises the question of whether history has so shaped this region as to preclude its ever being fully integrated into the mainstream of modern Europe. Enlargement of the EU and NATO, from the Western perspective, could thus seem a profoundly risky undertaking. It threatened to overwhelm these elaborately constructed and highly valued European institutions with an influx of states whose fragile new political and administrative structures seemed unready to play by the established Western 'rules of the game', whose ruined economies would be heavily dependent on Western support for decades to come, and who seemed more likely to consume than to contribute to common security.

For Central and East Europeans, the contradiction between 'national self-determination' and joining the EU and NATO is much less obvious, for reasons that this chapter has sought to make clear. The notion of 'returning to Europe' usefully captures an essential fact of life in this region: the inseparability of the internal and external dimensions of politics. Establishing and consolidating democracy and the rule of law, overcoming inter-ethnic tensions, nationalistic rivalries and mistrust, creating flourishing and competitive economies all largely depend on a stable external environment, free of the threat of imperialist domination, in which borders can be freely crossed by people, products and capital. The EU, for all its shortcomings, has proved a markedly successful model in the West, where similar challenges were faced at the end of the Second World War. Integration into pan-European structures can now provide practical support for Central and East Europeans to stay the course of difficult, painful reforms and the wrenching social upheavals they may bring. Reciprocally, political stabilization and economic revival in Central and Eastern Europe offers Western Europe its best guarantee of security in a new era: 'Fortress Europe' ceased to be an option once the Iron Curtain came down and the balance-of-terror system of the Cold War collapsed. Security must be now rebuilt on the bases of intense cooperation with neighbours, and of explicit recognition that the benefits will be mutual and self-reinforcing. Arguments such as these in favour of EU and NATO enlargement eventually won out over Western scepticism. In 1993, the EU explicitly recognized enlargement into Central and Eastern Europe as a goal; eight states from the region acceded to EU membership in May 2004, and Romania and Bulgaria followed in January 2007. NATO took the first decision to expand into the region in 1996. Three new members (Poland, Hungary and the Czech Republic) were admitted in 1999, and several others have since been invited to join.

The process of EU and NATO enlargement, however, raises new questions for the definition of our region. Many of the states covered in this book will only join the EU after several more years, if at all. In

2003, an EU summit at Thessaloniki confirmed the EU's commitment to bringing all the states of the Western Balkans in, but a combination of 'enlargement fatigue' that took hold in several member states after 2004, slow implementation of reforms in the Balkans, and more recently, the almost overwhelming economic, financial and political crisis that has beset the EU since 2008 all conspire against early fulfilment of the 'Thessaloniki promise', except for Croatia. Meanwhile, the EU has steadfastly refused even to discuss the prospect of membership with the East Europeans, Ukraine and Moldova.

These distinctions have important consequences, because the new borders they set up between 'ins', 'pre-ins' and 'outs' cut across a region that is only just emerging from the damaging divisions imposed by communist rule to rediscover shared history and to identify strongly with the idea of a united Europe. The point was dramatically demonstrated in 1999, when, just three weeks after taking in the new CEE members, NATO launched its bombardment of Serbia. For the Czechs, with strong historic sympathies for their fellow Slavs the Serbs, and for Hungary, with some 400,000 ethnic kin living over their southern border in Serbia, this proved an unexpected wrench of their loyalties. More generally, exclusion from enlargement has a demoralizing psychological impact. Because EU membership in particular has become equated with 'being European', and because, in Central and Eastern Europe, being 'European' has come to mean much the same as being 'civilized' and 'modern', exclusion from EU enlargement can be a national humiliation that may provoke a resentful backlash. Differentiation can also revive tensions and rivalries between states, as was the case in the 1990s, when Romania sometimes expressed the fear that if Hungary joined the EU before itself, Hungary would exploit its position on the 'inside' to secure concessions from Romania as regards treatment of their still large and somewhat restive Hungarian minority. In the event, this did not happen, and both states worked to rebuild a more constructive relationship. But similar tensions may arise and will need to be managed when, for example, Croatia joins the EU several years ahead of Serbia. Another point is that those states that join the EU first will benefit from full access to the single market and to substantial transfers from the EU's structural funds, far exceeding what is delivered in the various EU pre-accession funds for the Western Balkans and 'neighbourhood' assistance programmes for the East Europeans. This could further accelerate the divergence in economic performance between states of the region.

Moreover, EU widening has taken place alongside accelerated deepening of EU integration in key fields. One result is that while nation-state borders are becoming less significant between member states, the

EU's external border is becoming an ever more salient line demarcating the unified economic, monetary and trading space within from those on the outside. The EU's external border is also taking on the security and policing functions formerly exercised at national borders by member states. The EU now has a common visa regime, and is developing common policies on immigration and asylum, a common arrest warrant, and closer cooperation among member states' intelligence and security forces in the fight against terrorism. These have divisive implications for the Central and East European region. For example, once the CEEs joined, they had to implement to EU's common visa regime *vis-à-vis* the East Europeans and the Western Balkans states, which they did not previously need. Although the EU is working gradually towards visa liberalization and visa-free access for citizens of neighbouring states, in the meanwhile the 'Europeanization' of the region, insofar as it is taking place in stages, seems likely to become as much a factor for further diversification within the region as for its unification.

In the chapters that follow, we pursue the themes of convergence and divergence within the region, from the 'starting point' of decay and collapse of communist regimes through the ensuing two decades of transition, in chapters covering groups of states – Chapters 2 and 3 on the eight 'new Europeans' that are now EU members, Chapter 4 on the Western Balkans, and Chapter 5 on the East Europeans, Ukraine, Belarus and Moldova. Variations in national patterns of democratization can be explained by reference to the histories of individual countries, to the specific legacies of communist rule, and to the external influences exerted by inclusion in or exclusion from the processes of EU and NATO enlargement. Even those furthest advanced in their 'return to Europe', such as Poland, Hungary, the Czech Republic and Slovakia, continue to face the challenges of underpinning their democratic institutions with popular confidence, efficient administrative practices and habitual respect for the rule of law. Political developments in all four have, at times, raised questions about how far 'democratic consolidation' had actually gone, and many have expressed worries about whether Romania and Bulgaria were really ready for EU membership in 2007. Although much progress has been made since 2000 in post-war reconstruction and the stabilization of fragile states of the Western Balkans, with the exception of Croatia, one cannot yet say with confidence that this region has finally turned the corner. A credible perspective of eventual EU membership is now recognized as essential to support these states. Closer EU engagement is also seen as a vital factor in sustaining the motivation for reform in Ukraine and Moldova. As we see in Chapter 6, since the 2004 EU enlargement, the rejection of the EU Constitutional treaty in the French and Dutch referendums in 2005, and the eruption of the crisis in the eurozone after 2008, there is room for concern about whether the EU itself is ready to play its part. West European public opinion seems to have lost its enthusiasm for extending the benefits of integration further to the east and south-east, being more preoccupied with illegal immigration, the penetration of international organized crime, increased competition on labour markets from workers from new member states, and the generally more insecure global environment. Western democracies themselves are confronting challenges of political disaffection among citizens, social fragmentation and exposure to global economic pressures. The 'Europe' to which the CEEs are 'returning' is itself in a state of flux and uncertainty, and Western political leaders have not yet shown the capacity for collective leadership necessary to confront the increasingly complex internal problems of their societies and the rising demands on the EU as a major international actor with particular responsibility for the stability and prosperity of the continent as a whole.

Chapter 2

The Czech Republic, Hungary and Poland

Frances Millard

From the outset, the Czech Republic, Hungary and Poland were among the front-runners in building democracy and capitalism in post-communist Europe. These countries made the task of democratization seem easy: peaceful regime change marked by free elections, the construction of new institutions, and a subsequent process of continuing democratic consolidation. They moved rapidly to reorient their economic and foreign policy away from the former Soviet Union, signalled by growing links with Western Europe, the break-up of the Warsaw Pact, and the withdrawal of Russian troops. The dissolution of the Czechoslovak federation was also both swift and peaceful: in January 1993, the decree absolute for the 'Velvet Divorce' added two new states, the Czech Republic and Slovakia, to the map of Europe. In 1997, Poland, Hungary, and the Czech Republic passed the European Union's 'democracy test'; in 1999, they became the first new members of NATO; and in 2004 they became fully fledged EU members.

Yet along the way perturbations and crises continued to punctuate the processes of multi-faceted change. Turbulence and uncertainty did not disappear, and patterns that emerged in the 1990s shifted in the second decade of the new century. Though the achievements appeared indisputable, acute problems remained in many spheres of political and social life. Some spoke of a post-EU malaise following the period in which so much elite energy had been expended on the demands of membership. The 'transition consensus' was less relevant, and global economic crisis meant new challenges after 2008. 'Transition issues' remained, particularly in Hungary after 2010, where the new governing party Fidesz sought to undo the settlement established by Hungary's 'negotiated exit' from communism in 1989. Political parties did not maintain 'core electorates' and new parties continued to enter parliament at successive elections. In 2005 in Poland, in 2006 in the Czech Republic, and in 2010 in Hungary the centre-left lost power;

and in Poland and Hungary the once powerful Social Democrats, the communist-successor parties, were discredited and saw wholesale electoral collapse. Along with the policy battles of 'normal politics' these dimensions continued to make Central Europe rather different from its West European neighbours.

The structures of government

Institutionally these three countries resembled typical parliamentary systems of government, based on the responsibility of government to parliament with adjudication of conflicts by constitutional courts. New constitutions were promulgated in the Czech Republic in 1992 and in Poland in 1997. Hungary made numerous and piecemeal amendments to the old 'communist' constitution until its controversial fundamental revisions in 2011. While Poland and the Czech Republic were bicameral, Hungary retained its single-chamber parliament. Poland had the strongest and (up to 2013, when Milos Zeman became president of the Czech Republic) the only directly elected president, though the 1997 Constitution shifted it from its earlier 'semi-presidential' model. In Hungary and Poland prime ministers were strengthened by the 'constructive vote of no confidence', requiring agreement on an alternative candidate before the prime minister could be dismissed. All constitutions enumerated civil liberties and introduced mechanisms to safeguard individual rights.

Constitutions were not set in stone, though as the 'supreme law' they were deliberately difficult to alter; only in Hungary was the Fidesz government strong enough to dictate a new constitutional settlement after its 2010 electoral victory. (Cross-party consensus characterized the Czech introduction of direct presidential elections.) Ironically, Hungary, with its piecemeal jumble of a Constitution, had seen the greatest stability, with routine elections at four-year intervals and strong majority governments. Fidesz passed a controversial new Constitution, in force from January 2012, seen as a final break with the communist past and a reaffirmation of Hungary's national and Christian values, but – along with 32 areas specified as 'cardinal laws' requiring a two-thirds majority – it also represented a shift away from the traditional notion of the separation of powers. The Constitution and the new cardinal laws affected the judiciary, the media, the central bank, local government, the status of churches, national minorities, and the electoral system, among many other areas.

Parliament was reduced in size from 386 to 199 and chosen by a still more majoritarian electoral law. But the judiciary was the main focus of concern for domestic opposition and international bodies, including the EU and the Council of Europe. The number of judges on the Constitutional Court was increased, and access to the Court was made more difficult, while the Court lost the capacity to adjudicate on tax and budgetary matters for 'as long as state debt exceeds half of the Gross Domestic Product' (Art. 37). The retirement age of ordinary judges was lowered from 70 to 62 years; and the president of the National Judicial Office (NJO), elected by parliament, gained the right to appoint judges, transfer them, and allocate them to particular cases. The changes were seen as offering Fidesz the potential to entrench its supporters and enhance its electoral prospects in a new, single-party hegemony. Critics saw extending the terms of office for the head of the NJO, the public prosecutor, and the heads of the state audit office, the media board and the budget council in this light – as well as the new electoral law.

The nature of government

Unlike Hungary, with only a brief period of minority government in 2008–10, the Czech Republic experienced recurring political deadlock, with minority or wafer-thin majority governments. The centre-left government of 2002–6 saw three prime ministers. In 2006 government formation was protracted because the 'left' and the 'right' each commanded 100 seats in parliament. The Czechs also saw two periods of non-partisan caretaker government, in 1997 and again in 2009. From April 2012, the Necas government maintained a small, insecure majority after the coalition broke up. By the latter part of the year, with 100 seats, it had lost its narrow majority.

Poland, once the most turbulent of the three – with more numerous elections (parliamentary and presidential), frequent changes of government, and problematic periods of 'cohabitation' between governments and presidents of different political persuasions – settled into a period of greater calm after the 2007 elections. After President Lech Kaczynski perished in the Smolensk air disaster in April 2010, along with many parliamentarians and prominent public office-holders, the political institutions functioned smoothly, including the election of a new president. In 2011 the major governing party, Civic Platform, was the first to win a second term and its continuing coalition with the Polish Peasant Party provided a measure of continuity.

We can see the differences between the three countries clearly in Table 2.1, which shows changes of prime minister and the status of their governments. Coalition government was the norm, but minority governments were common in Poland and the Czech Republic, whose majority coalitions were also fractious. The period between 2005 and 2007 in Poland saw frequent coalition reconfiguration, as Law and Justice (PiS) shared power with the radical populist Self-Defence (SO) and the radical clerical-nationalist League of Polish Families (LPR). In some cases prime ministers changed but their coalitions remained intact; in other cases the prime minister remained to head a new governing coalition.

Elections were the major reason for changes of government. Sixteen elections saw the defeat of twelve sitting governments. In Poland all governments suffered defeat until 2011. Up until 2005 power oscillated between groups that had their origins in the Solidarity opposition movement and the Social Democrats, the transformed Communist Party. Governments became very unpopular during their terms of office and, in 2001, the two Solidarity parties that had governed after 1997 failed to win seats in the new parliament. Hungary saw similar electoral shifts between former-opposition parties and the successor party, the Hungarian Socialist Party (MSzP). This changed only in 2006, when the Socialists won a successive victory. But in Poland and Hungary corruption scandals weakened the successor parties and they were no longer major parties from 2005 and 2010 respectively.

In the Czech Republic the position differed because the Communist Party (KSCM) remained 'unreformed' and it was not seen as a viable coalition partner for any other party. The historic Czech Social Democratic Party (CSSD) took over the political space occupied by the successor parties in Poland and Hungary. Power oscillated, but not at successive elections. Klaus's Civic Democratic Party (ODS) was returned to power in 1996. The Social Democrats were the largest party in 1998 and in 2002. They were overtaken again by ODS in 2006. In 2010 they were the largest party, but they could not form a government.

Euro-elections also proved important. The first elections to the European Parliament in 2004 were a disaster for all three then-governing social democratic parties. In Poland Leszek Miller resigned just before the elections, leaving a vacuum in government and, following their Euro-losses, prime ministers Peter Medgyessy and Vladimir Spidla resigned in Hungary and the Czech Republic. Loss of their own parties' confidence and difficult coalition relations were the key to their departures.

Nine governments changed because of the resignation of the prime minister (including those of Medgyessy and Spidla), with three more toppled by no-confidence votes. In the Czech Republic scandals brought the resignations of Vaclav Klaus and Stanislav Gross. Klaus's

Table 2.1   *Governments in Hungary, the Czech Republic and Poland to 2012*

Prime minister	Period served	Nature of government	Leaning of government	Reason for change
Hungary				
Antall	1990–93	Majority coalition	Centre-right	Death of PM
Boross	1993–94	Majority coalition	Centre-right	Election
Horn	1994–98	Majority coalition	Centre-left	Election
Orban	1998–02	Majority coalition	Right	Election
Medgyessy	2002–04	Majority coalition	Centre-left	Resignation of PM
Gyurcsany	2004–06	Majority coalition	Centre-left	Election
Gyurcsany	2006–08	Majority coalition	Centre-left	Collapse of coalition
Gyurcsany	2008–09	Single-party minority	Centre-left	Resignation of PM
Bajnai	2009–10	Single-party minority	Centre-left	Election
Orban	2010–	Single-party majority	(Centre)right	
Czech Republic				
Klaus	1996–97	Minority coalition	Centre-right	Resignation of PM
Tosovsky	1997–98	Caretaker	'Expert'	Election
Zeman	1998–02	Single-party minority	Centre-left	Election
Spidla	2002–04	Majority coalition	Centre-left	Resignation of PM
Gross	2004–05	Majority coalition	Centre-left	Resignation of PM
Paroubek	2005–06	Majority coalition	Centre-left	Election
Topolanek	2006–09	Majority coalition	Centre-right	No confidence
Fischer	2009–10	Caretaker	'Expert'	Election
Necas	2010–12	Majority coalition	Centre-right	Withdrawal of one coalition partner
Necas	2012–	Majority coalition	Centre-right	
Poland				
Olszewski	1991–92	Minority coalition	Right	No confidence

coalition was rocked by party-financing illegalities. Gross was the only prime minister to resign because of allegations of personal wrongdoing (he was never charged with an offence). The 2010 Czech coalition looked rocky from the start, but Petr Necas survived its first two years despite extensive corruption scandals, including its anti-corruption junior coalition partner Public Affairs. Hungary's president Schmidt resigned in 2012 over allegations of plagiarism in his doctoral thesis.

Scandals also affected political leadership in Poland. The most bizarre case was that of Jozef Oleksy, forced from office in 1995 after (never substantiated) allegations of spying for Russia. Oleksy's case was part of a wider conflict between President Wałesa of Solidarity and the coalition of communist-successor parties. Prime Minister Pawlak had also resigned earlier after relentless pressure from Walesa. After

Table 2.1   *continued*

Prime minister	Period served	Nature of government	Leaning of government	Reason for change
Poland *continued*				
Suchocka	1992–93	Minority coalition	Centre-right	No confidence
Pawlak	1993–95	Majority coalition	Centre-left	Resignation of PM
Oleksy	1995–96	Majority coalition	Centre-left	Resignation of PM
Cimoszewicz	1996–97	Majority coalition	Centre-left	Election
Buzek	1997–00	Majority coalition	Centre-right	Break-up of coalition
Buzek	2000–01	Minority coalition	Right	Election
Miller	2001–03	Majority coalition	Centre-left	Break-up of coalition
Miller	2003–04	Minority coalition	Centre-left	Resignation of PM
Belka	2004–05	Minority coalition	Centre-left	Election
Marcinkiewicz	2005–06	Single-party minority	Right	Formation of coalition
Marcinkiewicz	May-July 2006	Majority coalition	Right- populist-nationalist	Resignation of PM
J. Kaczynski	July-Sept. 2006	Majority coalition	Right- populist-nationalist	Break-up of coalition
J. Kaczynski	Sept.–Oct. 2006	Minority coalition	Right- populist-nationalist	Re-formation of coalition
J. Kaczynski	Oct. 2006–	Majority coalition	Right- populist-nationalist	Early election
Tusk	2007–11	Majority coalition	Centre-right	Election
Tusk	2011–	Majority coalition	Centre-right	

Note: A government changes with (a) a new parliamentary term, (b) a change in the prime minister, or (c) a change in the composition of the governing coalition.

2001, Leszek Miller came under huge pressure from persistent allegations of high-level corruption, leading to tensions within his own social democratic party (SLD) and to plummeting government popularity.

The negative experience of 'cohabitation' between a 'Solidarity' president and social democratic governments was a major reason for reducing the president's powers in the 1997 Constitution. The president's veto was made slightly easier to override, and the president lost his power to name three key government ministers. It was Walesa's outgoing man at the Interior Ministry who levelled spying charges against Oleksy after Walesa lost the presidential election. President Kwasniewski 'cohabited' uneasily with the Solidarity government from 1997 to 2001. After 2005 President Kaczynski openly served the interests of his party, Law and Justice (PiS), thwarting the legislative programme of Civic Platform (PO) after PiS's electoral defeat in 2007.

After PiS and PO failed to form the coalition promised to the electorate in the 2005 elections, a minority government followed; then PiS negotiated a coalition with two hitherto marginalized parties. Andrzej Lepper's Self-Defence (SO) and the League of Polish Families (LPR) had previously been regarded as unacceptable coalition partners by all other parties. Bringing them into government (May 2006) marked the end of the Solidarity-successor divide in Polish politics. Jaroslaw Kaczynski became prime minister, making Poland once again distinctive: twins occupied the key executive posts of president and prime minister. Kaczynski ejected the troublesome Lepper from the coalition in September, only to restore him to government one month later. Coalition tensions did not dissipate, and Kaczynski chanced his arm (and failed) with early elections in late 2007.

After 1991, when two minority governments were defeated on confidence votes, the constructive vote of no confidence (1992) safeguarded prime ministerial tenure. Thus Buzek and Miller remained in office after their coalitions collapsed because the opposition could not agree on an alternative candidate – as did Gyurcsany in Hungary after the Free Democrats withdrew in 2008. In the Czech Republic relations within governing coalitions were difficult and their majorities (if any) were tiny. Governments could often rely on non-governing deputies, and Social Democrat prime ministers often benefited from communist support while denying them a role in government. However, in 2009, Prime Minister Topolanek fell on a vote of no confidence, with four members of his own side voting with the opposition. In April 2012 the scandal-ridden Public Affairs (VV) split, leading to the collapse of the coalition; the government survived with the support of a VV splinter group, LIDEM.

Political parties and party systems

This brief survey indicates why political parties are central to explanations of government formation and government stability. Parties are the main aggregators of policies into the manifestos offered to the electorate. They negotiate to form governments and their relations affect government stability. Parties also structure parliaments into government and opposition (we discuss matters of this kind at greater length in Chapter 11).

Because of these party functions, much of the routinization of democratic politics in parliamentary systems depends on the nature of parties, including their cohesion, discipline, and willingness to cooperate with other parties in coalition. The development of party systems – stable patterns of party interaction – proved variable in Poland, Hungary, and the Czech Republic. Even where some parties proved durable and their interactions predictable, unexpected changes could and did ensue. The collapse of the Social Democrats in Poland and Hungary meant far-reaching changes in inter-party relations.

In Hungary, the number of parliamentary parties gradually fell and a highly polarized two-bloc system emerged. In 1990, five new parties entered the first democratic parliament. The clear victor was the Hungarian Democratic Forum (MDF), which won 42.5 per cent of the seats. The newly reconstituted successor party, now the Hungarian Socialist Party (MSzP), registered a small but loyal following. These six parties maintained their presence in 1994; but the MSzP's fortunes had risen (Agh, 1995) and it gained an absolute majority of seats (54.2 per cent), though it chose to govern with the liberal Free Democrats (SzDSz). Party splits and the unpopularity of its government had drastically reduced the Forum's parliamentary strength (9.8 per cent) by 1994. The Forum's weakness provided an opening effectively exploited by the Young Democrats (Fidesz, from 2003 Fidesz-Hungarian Civic Union, Fidesz-MPSz – *Fidesz–Magyar Polgári Szövetség*), who began to recast their image. Abandoning its youthful radical liberalism, Fidesz moved steadily to appropriate the Hungarian centre-right space (Kiss, 2002; Fowler, 2004; Enyedi and Toka, 2007). When it emerged victorious in 1998, Fidesz had already effectively incorporated the Christian Democrats, as well as elements of the Forum and the Smallholders (FKGP). The Smallholders became a junior partner in the coalition, but splits, scandals, and leadership disputes took their toll. In that parliament, the extreme-right Justice and Life Party (MIEP), an offshoot of the Forum, also gained seats; neither entered parliament in 2002.

By 2002, the Hungarian party system had coalesced around the Hungarian Socialist Party and Fidesz, with two small parties, the Free Democrats and the Forum. The Socialists and the Fidesz-Forum joint lists gained 83 per cent of the vote. Fidesz won the most seats in 2002, but the strategy of fielding joint lists meant that it had no coalition partner. The Free Democrats were Fidesz's implacable enemies and again formed a coalition with the MSzP. In 2006 the two-bloc line-up was identical: the giant Fidesz and the small Forum (which now stood separately) versus the giant Socialists and the small Free Democrats. The 2002 campaign was bitter and closely fought, with a clear divide between two camps offering different versions of 'identity politics' based on conservative nationalism and secular cosmopolitanism (Fowler, 2002). This was also the case in 2006, when the deep divisions reflected 'two irreconcilable visions of the world, with two moral orders, with two visions of right and wrong battling in a "cold civil war"' (Schopflin, 2006). The Socialists gained ten seats more than in 2002 and, for the first time in Hungary, a sitting government returned to power.

Table 2.2 shows this process of consolidation. The party system gradually acquired a measure of coherence with a '2 and 2 halves'

Table 2.2   *Election results of major winning parties in Hungary, 1990–2010*

	1990		1994		1998		2002		2006		2010	
Party	*List vote %*	*Seats*	*List vote %*	*Seats*	*List vote %*	*Seats*	*List vote %*	*Seats*	*List vote %*	*Seats*	*List vote %*	*Seats*
Hungarian Socialist Party (MSzP)	10.9	33	33.0	209	32.9	134	42.1	178	43.2	186	19.3	59
Alliance of Free Democrats (SzDSz)	21.4	92	19.7	69	7.6	24	5.6	19	6.5	18	–	–
Fidesz	9.0	21	7.0	20	29.5	113	Joint with MDF	Joint with MDF	42.0	164	52.7	262
Fidesz-MDF joint candidates						50	41.1	188	–	–	–	–
Hungarian Democratic Forum (MDF)	24.7	164	11.7	38	2.8	2	Joint with Fidesz	Joint with Fidesz	5.0	11	–	–
Independent Smallholders (FKGP)	11.7	44	8.8	26	13.2	48	0.8	–	–	–	–	–
Christian Democratic People's Party (KDNP)	6.5	21	7.0	22	–	–	–	–	–	with Fidesz		
Justice and Life (MIEP)	–	–	–	–	5.5	14	–	–	–	–	–	–
Movement for a Better Hungary (Jobbik)	–	–	–	–	–	–	–	–	–	–	16.7	47
Politics Can Be Different (LMB)	–	–	–	–	–	–	–	–	–	–	7.5	16

Sources: www.essex.ac./elections; results for 2006 and 2010 from www.election.hu. Independents and parties with single seats are excluded. In 2006 six candidates stood jointly for MSzP and SzDSz.

format. Electoral volatility declined markedly in 2006, as voters cemented their allegiance to the two major parties. However, shortly after the 2006 election things began to unravel. A tape revealed Prime Minister Gyurcsany admitting to 'lying day and night' and using 'hundreds of little tricks' to hide the disastrous state of the Hungarian economy from the electorate. Fidesz's fortunes rose still further when the global financial crisis hit Hungary, with the MSzP government forced to seek a loan from the International Monetary Fund. Although Gyurcsany's replacement Gordon Bajnai earned international plaudits for his handling of the crisis, he could not stem the tide of anti-socialist feeling. The Socialist vote fell below 20 per cent in 2010, the Free Democrats disappeared, and Fidesz won a majority of seats. The extreme-right Movement for a Better Hungary (Jobbik) entered parliament for the first time, along with the new Green party Politics Can Be Different (LMB).

Political parties in the Czech Republic also showed a marked degree of initial stabilization. Table 2.3 shows the election results, indicating the reduction in the number of parliamentary parties and the changing relative strengths of the four survivors, but also the arrival of new parties in 1998, 2006, and 2010. As in Hungary, two large parties of right and left came to dominate the political landscape. The Civic Democrats (ODS), led by Vaclav Klaus until the launch of his successful bid for the presidency (February 2003), were the largest party resulting from the break-up of the umbrella opposition formation Civic Forum. From 1992 to 1997, ODS was the major force in Czech politics and the linchpin of its 1992–97 centre-right coalitions. Its main thrust was economic liberalism, with Klaus himself the main architect of Czech economic transformation. In 1997, ODS's party-financing scandals and Klaus's personal style caused acute tensions within the minority coalition and a split in his party, resulting in the emergence of the Freedom Union. ODS lost in 1998 to the Social Democrats (CSSD), who had emerged as its major challenger in 1996. Although the former governing parties and the new Freedom Union (US) had a majority of parliamentary seats, anti-Klaus sentiment in the US was too strong for the reconstruction of the former coalition. Nor was the more nationalist, Euro-ambivalent message of ODS's 2002 election campaign a success. The electoral alliance the 'Coalition' of Christian Democrats and Freedom Union (now tied to the small Democratic Union) preferred a coalition with the Social Democrats. Unlike the Free Democrats in Hungary, the Czech Christian Democrats (KDU-CSL) were eager to play a pivotal role, capable of allying in coalition with either ODS (1992–97, 2006–10) or the CSSD (2002–06). In 2006, ODS's new leader Topolanek steered ODS to its highest-ever share of

Table 2.3 Results for parliamentary parties in Czech elections, 1992–2010

Party	1992[1] Vote %	Seats	1996 Vote %	Seats	1998 Vote %	Seats	2002 Vote %	Seats	2006 Vote %	Seats	2010 Vote %	Seats
Civil Democratic Party (ODS)	29.7	76	29.6	68	27.7	63	24.5	58	35.9	81	22.2	53
Coalition (KDU-CSL + US-DEU)	–	–	–	–	–	–	14.3	31	–	–	–	–
Freedom Union (US)	–	–	–	–	8.6	19	Combined in Coalition	(9)	–	–	–	–
Christian Democratic Union–Czechoslovak People's Party (KDU-CSL)	6.3	15	8.1	18	9.0	20	Combined in Coalition	(22)	7.2	13	–	–
Civic Democratic Alliance (ODA)	5.9	14	6.4	13	–	–	–	–	–	–	–	–
Czech Social Democratic Party (CSSD)	6.5	16	26.4	61	32.3	74	30.2	70	32.3	74	22.1	56
Communist Party (KSCM)	14.1[2]	35	10.3	22	11.0	24	18.5	41	12.8	26	11.3	26
Republicans (SPR-RSC)	6.0	14	8.0	18	–	–	–	–	–	–	–	–
Moravia & Silesia Society–Movement for Self-Governing Democracy (HSD-SMS)	5.9	14	–	–	–	–	–	–	–	–	–	–
Liberal Social Union (LSU)	6.5	16	–	–	–	–	–	–	–	–	–	–
Green Party (SZ)	–	–	–	–	–	–	–	–	–	–	–	–
Public Affairs (VV)	–	–	–	–	–	–	–	–	–	–	10.9	24
TOP09	–	–	–	–	–	–	–	–	–	–	16.7	41

Notes: [1] to Czech National Council (Czechoslovakia); [2] as part of Left Bloc.

Sources: www.essex.ac.uk/elections; www.volby.cz (2006, 2010).

the vote, but unlike Fidesz, ODS failed to consolidate the whole of the centre-right. ODS, the Christian Democrats, the Social Democrats, and the Communists were enduring features of the political scene until 2010, when the Christian Democrats fell below the electoral threshold.

The 2006 campaign was particularly brutal (Plecita-Vlachova and Stegmaier, 2008). Its outcome created complex problems for the political parties and highlighted some perennial problems of government formation. Together the ODS, the Christian Democrats, and the new parliamentary party, the Greens (more right-wing than their West European counterparts), held exactly half the seats. The Social Democrats and the Communist Party also held half. But the Communists were still excluded from coalition calculations; since 1995 the Social Democrats had explicitly rejected the possibility of coalition with the Communists. Thus, unlike Poland and Hungary, the Czech Republic had a strong non-successor social democratic party, with historic roots in the inter-war period of Czechoslovak democracy. It also had a Communist Party which retained its radical edge (Grzymala-Busse, 2002; Hanley, 2001).

The problem of unacceptable coalition partners was not new. In 1996, the Communists and the extreme-right Republicans occupied one-fifth of parliament's seats. Their exclusion from government meant that a minority coalition was the only political solution. However, the radical right faded, as the Republicans split and failed to enter subsequent parliaments. Although elections still showed high levels of volatility, it was also the case that parties retained a core following of loyal voters (Vlachova, 2001). Parties also became increasingly institutionalized and more stable; only two deputies left their parties in the 2002–06 parliament.

Things changed with the 'earthquake election' of 2010 (Bakke, 2012; Haughton *et al.*, 2011), when frustrated Czech voters deserted the two major parties; together they gained only 42 per cent of the vote, down from 68 per cent in 2006. Almost 20 per cent of the vote was 'wasted' on parties that did not cross the electoral threshold. ODS lost votes – and its dominance of Prague – to TOP09. The unpopularity of CSSD leader Paroubek gave credibility to former prime minister Zeman's new party SPOZ, which drew its votes (4.3 per cent) mainly from the CSSD. The Greens failed to win seats, but two new right-wing parties entered parliament. Tradition, Responsibility, Prosperity (TOP09), led by foreign minister Karel Schwartzenberg, brought together one wing of the Christian Democrats and local politicians. Public Affairs (VV) was an 'anti-corruption' party (in fact, it had close links to the private security agency ABL), which gained popularity when the popular investigative journalist Radek John formally assumed the leadership. Both TOP and Public Affairs entered government, but VV began to unravel almost immediately. In April 2012 its founder and effective leader Vit Barta was convicted on corruption charges, and the party split, leaving a rump in the coalition.

Poland's story was similar in some ways but markedly different in others. The centre-right remained fragmented, while until 2005 the communist-successor party, the SLD, dominated the centre-left. Three aspects are important here. First, until 2005, the oscillation of power noted in Hungary also characterized Poland. Power shifted from 'Solidarity' governments to 'successor' governments. Only in 2005 was this mould broken, when the SLD crumbled; non-Solidarity parties with dubious democratic credentials formed a coalition with one strong Solidarity party, and the main axis of competition was between parties of Solidarity provenance.

Second, from 1991 to 2001, the SLD gained votes with each successive election. No contender seriously challenged its position on the centre-left. At the same time, Solidarity's heirs remained fissiparous and failed to consolidate a strong party. The unity of Solidarity Election Action (AWS), which won in 1997, was all too brief. AWS arose after savage defeats of post-Solidarity parties in 1993 and the 'loss' of the presidency to the Social Democrat Kwasniewski. AWS gathered an array of small Solidarity parties and groupings under the auspices of the Solidarity trade union. Although it aspired to create a unified party of the right, AWS imploded under the weight of internal dissensions among its constituent elements, the ineptitude of the AWS government, and the ignominious performance of the Solidarity trade union leader Marian Krzaklewski in the 2000 presidential election. In 2001, neither the rump of the badly splintered AWS nor the (also riven) Freedom Union crossed electoral thresholds.

The disintegration of AWS brought three new self-styled right-wing parties into the Sejm, joining the SLD and the peasant party PSL. Civic Platform (PO) was a liberal–conservative formation drawn from the liberal wing of the UW and conservative elements of AWS. Law and Justice (PiS), a 'law and order' party, came largely from AWS and the personal following of the Kaczynski twins. The League of Polish Families (LPR) assembled elements of AWS and small extra-parliamentary nationalist and clerical formations. Self-Defence (SO), known for its propensity for direct action, also entered parliament for the first time in 2001.

These parties were also present in the 2005 Sejm (see Table 2.4). But the SLD was now a shadow of its former self. Beleaguered by corruption scandals, the haemorrhage of its 2001 vote was massive, from over 40 per cent to just 11 per cent. In March 2004, the SLD had split,

Table 2.4 *Victorious parties in the Polish Sejm, 2001 to 2011*

Election	2001			2005			2007			2011		
Party/grouping	Vote %	Seats	Seats %	Vote %	Seats	Seats %	Vote	Seats	Seats	Vote	Seats	Seats
Alliance of the Democratic Left (SLD)[1]	41.0	216	47.0	11.3	55	12.0	stood as part of LiD			8.2	27	5.9
Civic Platform (PO)	12.7	65	14.1	24.1	133	28.9	41.5	209	45.4	39.2	207	45
Self-Defence (SO)	10.2	53	11.5	11.4	56	12.2	–	–	–	–	–	–
Law and Justice (PiS)	9.5	44	9.6	27.0	155	33.7	32.1	166	36.1	29.9	157	34.1
Polish Peasant Party (PSL)	9.0	42	9.1	7.0	25	5.4	8.9	31	6.7	8.4	28	6.1
League of Polish Families (LPR)	7.9	38	8.3	8.0	34	7.4	–	–	–	–	–	–
German Minority (MN)*	0.4	2	0.4	0.3	2	0.4	0.2	1	0.2	0.2	1	0.2
'Left and Democrats' (LiD)	–	–	–	–	–	–	13.2	53	11.5	–	–	–
Palikot Movement (RP)	–	–	–	–	–	–	–	–	–	10.2	40	8.7

Notes: [1] in 2001 in alliance with the Labour Union (UP); [2] exempt from national threshold.
Source: www. pkw.gov.pl.

but its new offshoot, Polish Social Democracy (SdPl), failed to make an impression. While the left splintered, Civic Platform (PO) and Law and Justice (PiS) prospered and the distance between them eroded. PO retained its economic liberalism, and this divided the two parties; but its social conservatism closely mirrored that of PiS. However, in 2005, PO and PiS failed to keep their electoral promise to form a coalition government. PiS unexpectedly emerged as the largest party in parliament (34 per cent of the seats) with PO a close second (29 per cent). Their relations had deteriorated badly during the overlapping election campaigns for parliament and president. PO and PiS provided the main presidential contenders, concentrating their fire on one another. Lech Kaczynski of PiS triumphed, and PiS fully exploited its new advantage. PiS's determination to dominate key posts and the personal bitterness that spilled over from the campaign hampered negotiations, and PO chose the path of opposition.

Thus the 2005 parliament saw two strong antagonistic right-wing parties, both claiming to be heirs of Solidarity, facing a badly weakened SLD on the left, and no party of the centre ground. After a brief spell of minority government, PiS, SO and LPR formed a coalition in May 2006 and Jaroslaw Kaczynski became prime minister in July. Difficult coalition relations strengthened Civic Platform (PO). In 2007, PO pushed PiS into second place, the SLD remained weak, and the Families and Self-Defence failed to cross the electoral threshold. PO governed for four years with the Polish Peasant Party and won re-election in 2011.

Although the 2011 elections maintained the dominant position of PO and PiS, while the SLD shrunk further, the surprise element was the success of the new Palikot Movement (RP), centred on the extravagant maverick Janusz Palikot, entrepreneur, showman, and former deputy for Civic Platform. Much of RP's electorate was young, drawn by Palikot's anti-clerical stance and his cosmopolitan pluralism – a stark contrast to the other political parties. RP's parliamentary party included Poland's first transgender and openly gay deputies.

Party evolution: a summary

Hungary developed from multi-partism to an oscillating two-party-plus system and then into one of a dominant party hegemony, with Fidesz strong enough to entrench its position at least in the medium term. With the decline of the Socialists and the emergence of the extreme-right Jobbik, the Hungarian political spectrum had shifted firmly to the right. In the Czech Republic ODS and CSSD remained the two strongest parties but failed to consolidate their vote in 2010. Given its association with severe austerity measures and perpetual coalition crisis, the position of ODS was particularly tenuous; it was polling only 11 per cent in April 2012 (Centrum pro vyzkum verejneho mineni, 2012). Poland moved from a dominant Solidarity-successor divide to an open mode of party competition with a conservative–populist–nationalist alliance of 2005–07 followed by a liberal–conservative–peasant alliance after 2007, with two large right-wing parties and three other small parties.

Although the terms 'left' and 'right' were widely used, the dividing lines between parties were rather different. In Hungary, Fidesz was a party of the 'right' by virtue of its social conservatism and its nationalist and religious orientation. By the late 1990s its economic and social policies differed little from those of the Socialist Party, and it was just as amenable to state economic intervention.

In Poland too, the labels of 'left' and 'right' centred less on pro-market or pro-interventionist stances but more on historical, social, and moral issues. With the SLD impotent, however, divisions within the right became more important. PiS resembled Fidesz in many respects. Its animosity to Civic Platform arose not because of social issues, where they largely agreed, nor because PiS was more economically interventionist. The most important dimension of the relationship was Kaczynski's insistence on the fundamental illegitimacy of Civic Platform's governance. Kaczynski had long argued that Civic Platform was part of the network of intrigue that allowed the Communists to retain key positions of power after 1989. To this he added his belief in Prime Minister Tusk's complicity (with the Russians) in the 'coup' of the Smolensk air disaster ('I have a feeling that Lech Kaczynski was murdered'; Kaczynski, 2012). Poland and Hungary contrasted with the Czech Republic, where economic divisions were salient and moral–cultural issues played only a secondary role compared with issues of redistribution. Even with its rather anomalous new parties in 2010, Czech parties fit into the familiar left–right divisions and 'party families' of Western Europe (Deegan-Krause, 2006; Hanley, 2007).

How can we explain these divergent paths of party-system development? The historical legacy, the institutional context, the character of new political elites, and social responses to the dislocations of transition interacted in different ways in these three countries. In Hungary, the fragmentation of the opposition in 1989 generated new political parties from the outset, while the reform-oriented Communist Party was the first to position itself as a modern European democratic party. Parliamentary parties gained media visibility and political resources. The distinctive mixed Hungarian electoral system played a role because the complex interactions of its three tiers stimulated party organization and favoured larger parties, though they did not preclude the emergence of new parties in 2010. The decline in the Forum was at least partly due to the impact of 'transition', permitting the Socialist Party to consolidate its position, while the charismatic Victor Orban shaped an effective organizational and electoral strategy that enabled Fidesz to absorb smaller parties of the Right.

In the Czech Republic, the two major parties mirrored the central economic divide of Czech politics. The apparent ease of economic transformation helps explain why ODS was the major beneficiary of the split in Civic Forum and its electoral victory in 1992. Its leader Klaus propagated an image as a tough reformer generating painless transition in the Czech lands (if not in Slovakia). It was only in the mid-1990s that the consequences of delayed enterprise restructuring led to a serious economic downturn, with a leftward shift of the electorate's attitudes evident in 1996 (Mateju and Rehakova, 1997). The CSSD benefited from the unreformed character of the Communist Party, which maintained a small loyal electorate, buttressed by dissatisfied protest voters. Both ODS and CSSD took organization and ideology seriously. Electoral thresholds also played a role in excluding small parties (though the number of electoral challengers remained large, with 28 'parties' contesting the election in 2002, 16 in 2006, and 26 in 2010). However, contingent factors were the key to the ructions of 2010: the calm of Jan Fischer's caretaker government after unedifying party infighting, the scandals surrounding former ODS leader Topolanek, the unpopularity of CSSD leader Paroubek, and the charisma of TOP's von Schwartzenberg.

In Poland, Solidarity split into multifarious elements as the shock therapy of the first Solidarity government bit hard. Although the dislocations of the move to capitalism were apparent throughout the region, the initial impact – deep industrial recession, coupled with high inflation and emerging unemployment – was more savage than in either Hungary or the Czech Lands of Czechoslovakia. The timing of early party formation appears to be a major factor in party development, and in this respect Poland paid the price for holding its first democratic election during the worst economic upheavals. It is also the case that party elites squandered the opportunities offered by the creation of AWS in 1996. SLD leaders similarly wasted the advantages of their dominant position. They overestimated the solidity of their electoral support, and they failed to respond to growing concerns with corruption. In 2005, PiS captured right-wing voters with its social conservatism and demand for moral revolution and it attracted former left voters with promises of a massive welfare cushion. In 2007, Civic

Platform capitalized on the fact that it was 'not PiS'. Albeit with no coherent ideological narrative to match that of PiS, Civic Platform's emphasis on stability and continuity led it to a second victory in 2011.

The voters and the public

Continuing electoral volatility thus plagued party-system development. Indeed, nowhere did post-communist voters come to love their parties. Trust in political parties and politicians remained abysmally low in all the new EU accession states, including Poland, Hungary and the Czech Republic (Rose, 2004: 6; European Social Survey, 2010). In Poland in 2011, most (86–90 per cent) poll respondents saw political parties as power-hungry agents of conflict (CBOS, 2011). The head of the Czech polling agency STEM said, 'people think that politics is a dirty business and that the majority of politicians are crooks... So they are not all that surprised by corruption scandals and nepotism in Czech politics. What is relatively new is that people are starting to see political elites as professionally incompetent' (Lazarova, 2012). This supports the work of Margot Tavits, who saw the success of new parties largely as a function of the failures of new political elites (Tavits, 2008b).

Mishler and Rose (2001) have linked levels of trust in political parties (and political institutions) to evaluations of their economic and political performance, mediated by individual values. Economic crisis was clearly a factor in attitudes to governing parties in recent elections: Hungary was among the hardest hit countries in the region, while Poland was the only EU member to maintain positive economic growth. Corruption also played a significant role in voter assessments, with the transfer of ownership from state to private hands providing wide opportunities for corrupt practices. Serious scandals linked to privatization plagued all three countries from 1990 onwards. After 1997, the EU's increasing concern with the impact of corruption on the rule of law and the quality of democracy increased the salience of this issue; but corruption, especially in public procurement, remained widespread and informal and clientelistic practices were ingrained. Kornai (2012) noted reports of 'shadow empires' associated with Fidesz. Transparency International's 2011 Corruption Perception rankings rated the Czech Republic 57th and Hungary 54th, both 'highly corrupt', while Poland at 41st was just on the right side of 'clean' (Transparency International, 2012). TI's National Integrity Study of the Czech Republic identified legal and institutional changes that 'facilitated corruption rather than combating it' (Transparency International, 2011).

We saw above that dubious practices brought down two prime ministers in the Czech Republic and contributed to the resignations of Miller and Gyurcsany. Corruption and integrity were themes in virtually every election campaign, including the most recent. In Poland in 2005, PiS promised a 'moral revolution', with a full-scale attack on the corruption that linked all post-communist elites after 1989. After 2010, Kaczynski sought to regain the high ground by using the Smolensk air crash as a symbol of Tusk's 'betrayal' of the nation.

Corruption allegations dominated the nasty Czech election of 2006, including a report asserting links between prime minister Paroubek and the criminal underworld. In 2010, Public Affairs owed much of its success to its anti-corruption message, but it soon became bogged down in scandal. In Hungary, the leaking of Gyurcsany's 'confession tape' sparked outraged, sometimes violent, protest. Following the controversy, Fidesz achieved a comprehensive victory in the 2006 local government elections, a prelude to its landslide victory in 2010. All in all, it is not difficult to sympathize with the public's yearning for 'clean hands'.

Current issues

From 2007, economic issues dominated the political agenda. Following a deep recession at the start of the 1990s the region grew rapidly. After accession, EU funds provided an added economic boost. Then the crisis struck. Poland, with large domestic demand and modest levels of debt (Leven, 2011), was the only EU country to maintain a positive growth rate, though reduced growth created its own problems for the public finances. The budget deficit, the main immediate economic challenge, was expected to stand at about 5.6 per cent of GDP in 2011, well above the EU's ceiling. After his re-election, Tusk announced measures intended to reduce the deficit to just 1 per cent by the end of the current parliament.

The Czech Republic, as a small, export-oriented country, was vulnerable to external influences, and a fall in demand for its exports led to a decline in GDP and an increase in the unemployment rate. The resumption of growth was slower than expected, and the dramatic fiscal tightening programme of the Necas government was one reason for the successive weakening of the coalition in 2012.

The position of the Hungarian economy remained extremely serious, as successive governments had failed to deal with underlying structural problems. When the global crisis struck, Hungary (with Latvia) was hit hardest. Credit was closed off, foreign capital and investment ceased, the forint plummeted, and the economy went into reverse. Bajnai's stabilization programme was received positively by the international community (Marer, 2010); but after 2010, Fidesz's constitutional changes and economic policies – in the context of Europe's sovereign debt crisis – put Hungary on a collision course with the EU and the IMF, while Hungary's credit rating was downgraded to junk status in November 2011 (see Chapter 13).

Social policy issues, long a political thorn in the sides of government, were common to all three countries and were obviously linked to economic conditions. The health service, welfare benefits and pensions remained persistent sources of dispute. Most CEE countries moved in the 1990s to insurance-based, contract-based health systems modelled on the perceived successes of the Bismarckian model of Germany and Austria. Not surprisingly, changing the health-funding system did not prove the magic bullet that many had anticipated. Citizens remained deeply unhappy with access to, and the quality of, health care provision. Health workers often expressed their discontent over pay and working conditions with strikes and protest actions. Doctors threatened mass resignations and refused to sign new contracts. Governments struggled to respond. The OECD classed the health status of the Polish population as 'relatively poor' (Boulhol *et al.*, 2012: 2) and noted the 'relatively limited effectiveness of the health care system' in Hungary (Eris, 2012: 10). In May 2012, the Czech Health Forum concluded that the government deserved a 'near failing grade' for its work on health care (Radio Prague, 2012).

Pension changes were a source of recent political conflict. In Hungary, Orban's 'pensions grab' forced citizens to choose between turning their private pension funds over to the government or giving up their state pensions (this reduced the budget deficit but merely delayed renewed requests for international support). In Poland, the Tusk government reduced the proportion of salary that could be paid into a private fund and transferred the difference to the state social security system. Raising the retirement age to 67 proved particular controversial in Poland in 2012; massive public protest and disagreement within the coalition forced the prime minister to compromise on the timing and staging of implementation.

Although the ombudsman was viewed as a successful institution and the basic rights of free association, expression and conscience were secured, civil liberties issues were not absent (and the new media law raised concerns about government control in Hungary). The Roma population experienced continuing social, economic, and political marginalization, especially in the Czech Republic and Hungary. Jobbik's parliamentary success in Hungary risked giving credibility to its vicious anti-Roma rhetoric. Conservative attitudes to women were widespread, and women were underrepresented in the political sphere. Abortion and IVF remained contentious issues in Poland. In Hungary, the new Constitution protected 'embryonic and foetal life' from the moment of conception. (Art II). Only in the more secular Czech Republic did the concept of civil partnerships find favour.

Such issues are the normal stuff of politics. Yet wider systemic issues did not disappear. In Hungary and Poland, the right-wing parties Fidesz and PiS questioned the very legitimacy of the opposition Social Democrats and the 'round table settlements' of 1989. In both countries their actions in government aroused anxieties about the security of democracy itself. PiS's conflict with Civic Platform dominated politics after 2005, when PiS deemed PO complicit with an alleged conspiracy of ex-communists, liberals, and secret police agents. The interpretation of history again became an instrument of politics, and old debates about de-communization gained fresh currency. Determined to root out vested interests, PiS introduced measures to dilute the independence of the National Bank, to secure a more compliant judiciary, and to install party-loyal functionaries in public broadcasting and the civil service. After 2007, Civic Forum moved to undo many such 'reforms'. But in Hungary Fidesz celebrated its 'ballot-box revolution' by entrenching similar measures in the new Constitution and in special super-majority laws, as well as some contentious history: the Declaration of National Cooperation stated that with the 2010 election 'Hungary regained the right and ability of self-determination', lost after 1944 (Political Declaration, 2010). The Constitution branded the former Communist Party a criminal organization and designated the opposition Socialist Party as its legal successor. Freedom House reduced Hungary's 'national governance' and 'independent media' scores in its 2011 report. In January 2012, the European Commission launched accelerated infringement proceedings against Hungary over the independence of its central bank and data protection authorities and measures affecting the judiciary. In March the Venice Commission of the Council of Europe also criticized the new Constitution. George Schopflin, Fidesz MEP and political scientist, accused the international media of transmitting the left's narrative of Hungarian politics in a 'manifest failure to grapple with Hungarian realities' with a 'readiness to rely on convenient clichés' (Schopflin, 2012). Others, like the economist Janos Kornai, feared a 'descent into autocracy' (Kornai, 2012).

Foreign policy matters remained the province of the executive, with little public engagement. The Czech president Klaus remained an outspoken Eurosceptic. The Czech government, with the United Kingdom, refused to sign the EU's agreed fiscal pact in May 2012. Aside from its problems with the EU, Fidesz maintained its concern with Hungarians in neighbouring states, risking conflict with Slovakia in particular. In Poland, however, Donald Tusk adopted a far more pro-EU stance; he hastened to reverse Poland's inward turn under PiS, when relations with both Germany and Russia had deteriorated.

Conclusion

Following their 'exit from communism', Poland, Hungary, and the Czech Republic followed their own distinct trajectories of political, social, and economic change. Yet we have identified similarities as well as differences in their development and the unexpected changes of recent years. Hungary had the most stable governments and – until 2010 – the most stable party system. Poland was the most turbulent, with greater stability emerging only after 2007. Both countries had successful social democratic successor parties throughout the 1990s; but in neither did they retain their position as strong parties of the centre-left. The Czech Republic continued to experience chronic problems of coalition politics, with ODS unable to consolidate the centre-right as Fidesz did so successfully in Hungary. New parties emerged in all recent elections. Nor had any country resolved its welfare system, including health. Recurring problems of corruption and civic alienation continued to plague all three. In Poland and Hungary there was a worrying tendency for parties to question the legitimacy of their opponents, as Fidesz did with the Socialists and PiS did with Civic Platform and the Social Democrats. The intensity of this confrontational discourse went beyond mere campaigning hyperbole. Poland, Hungary, and the Czech Republic had completed their successful transition to democracy when tested by their capacity to weather crises; but the democracy-building project could not be regarded as complete.

Chapter 3

The Other New Europeans

Tim Haughton

The magnitude of the changes accomplished by the states of Central and Eastern Europe (CEE) following the 1989 revolutions should not be underestimated. In addition to creating democracies, market economies and, in the case of many countries in the region, new states, these countries undertook the long, time-consuming and at times rocky road of integration into the European Union and other Western clubs. For much of the decade and a half following the collapse of the communist regimes, politics was dominated by, or at least couched in, the language of these broad themes.

By the time the seven countries covered in this chapter (Bulgaria, Estonia, Latvia, Lithuania, Romania, Slovakia and Slovenia) entered the latter half of the second post-communist decade, they appeared to be faced with a series of more manageable tasks thanks, in no small part, to high and sustained levels of growth in the early to mid-2000s. Economic growth, however, came to a shuddering halt in 2009, a consequence of the global credit crunch sparked by the collapse of Lehman Brothers the previous September. Difficulties persisted into the new decade thanks to the general malaise engulfing the European economy due to a significant degree to the eurozone debt crisis. CEE, therefore, began the third post-communist decade embroiled in an era of austerity, replete with cuts, painful reforms and associated resentments. Whilst the depth, duration and resultant consequences of the harsh financial winds varied significantly across the seven countries covered in this chapter, all experienced tougher economic times.

This chapter seeks to highlight the salient themes shaping contemporary politics in the seven countries under consideration. Whilst they do not form as coherent a group as the collections of countries covered by other contributions to this volume, there are sufficient commonalities to justify treating them together. All have grappled with the challenges of exiting communist rule, building new democracies and market economies and coming to terms with the past; a set of tasks exacerbated – and at times – smoothed by European Union accession and membership. With the exceptions of Slovenia and Lithuania, which like Poland and the Czech Republic do not have large ethnic minorities, the cocktail of tasks facing the states covered in this chapter has been made more potent by tensions between titular ethnic groups and others in the state. Moreover, in contrast to Poland, which likes to see itself as a member of the club of 'big' EU member states, and Hungary, which in many respects is still grappling with the post-First World War reality of a 'much diminished Hungarian state incongruously matched to the cultural and psychological borders of the larger Hungarian nation' (Waterbury, 2010: 30), with the occasional exception of Romania, for obvious geographical reasons, these seven states tend to see themselves as 'small' in the European context and act accordingly. Nonetheless, the seven states cannot be considered in an undifferentiated way. As we saw in Chapter 1, thanks to different historical experiences, and linguistic, cultural and religious differences, diversity is the 'hallmark' of Central and Eastern Europe. Indeed, the themes of diversity and commonality in the region run not only through this chapter, but the study of CEE as a whole.

Given the focus later in this volume on specific aspects of political development, such as political parties, social policy, the nature of executive leadership, and mechanisms of representation and accountability, this chapter provides an introduction to the politics of the seven countries by shining a spotlight on their connecting threads. These themes reflect, reinforce, shape and animate party competition, battles over policy choice and conflicts between presidents and prime ministers, legislatures and executives. The chapter argues that with the challenges of post-communism (democratization, marketization, state-building and integration) having largely been met, politics in the region entered a new era. Many of the themes of politics, such as how to flourish economically as an EU member-state in an increasingly competitive world economy, and more recently the task of coping with the travails of the eurozone, were new. Other themes, however, such as corruption and policies towards ethnic minorities and former imperial masters, were variations on old, perennial themes.

Before embarking on a comparative analysis of the salient themes of politics in the seven countries covered in this chapter – including EU membership, the age of austerity, the role of the past in the politics of the present, values, minorities, corruption and the fluidity of party politics – we begin with a brief overview of recent political history.

Meeting the challenges of post-communism

Following the end of communist rule in 1989–91, the seven countries embarked on the process of marketization with varying degrees of enthusiasm. Whilst Estonia, for example, blazed a Thatcherite trail, introducing a radical liberalization package early in the 1990s, other states were reform laggards. Bulgaria and Romania, for instance, only began to undertake significant economic reform towards the end of the 1990s. Their initial reluctance has been ascribed to the success of the former communists in the first free elections (Fish, 1998), but the reasons go deeper. Not only were economic developments during the communist period viewed more favourably in those countries, but they also lacked ambitious, reform-minded politicians along the lines of Estonia's Mart Laar or Czechoslovakia/Czech Republic's Vaclav Klaus. Moreover, Estonia's drive to a market economy was motivated, in part, by a desire to distance the country from its Soviet past and demonstrate its perceived rightful place among the European mainstream.

Equally, there were striking differences in the process of democratization in the region. Both Slovakia and Slovenia, for example, not only had to build new democracies, but they also faced the challenges of building the apparatus of a new state. Whereas the latter made a relatively easy transition to democracy, the former experienced a more troubled transition (Harris, 2002; Fisher, 2006). In the mid-1990s under Prime Minister Vladimir Meciar's government, Slovakia appeared to be veering away from democracy. Indeed, following *demarches* (strong diplomatic notes) issued by the EU deploring developments in Slovakia, the European Commission's 1997 opinion (*avis*) highlighted concerns about the treatment of minorities, the behaviour of the government towards key institutions such as the Presidency and Constitutional Court and, more broadly, the government's unwillingness to play by the rules and conventions of democratic politics (Henderson, 1999). Following the 1998 elections, however, a broad-based coalition under the leadership of the new prime minister Mikulas Dzurinda, returned Slovakia to the path of liberalism and restored its image, which reaped international dividends.

Despite the great strides achieved by the seven states in creating, institutionalizing and consolidating democracies over the past two-and-a-half decades, we should add a note of caution. Indeed, a few developments in more recent times have cast doubts on how deeply rooted democratic norms are across the region (for instance, some of the developments in Hungary discussed in the previous chapter). Whilst tensions between different organs of government are part and parcel of the functioning of a democracy, the vicious power struggle between Romanian Prime Minister Victor Ponta and the country's president Traian Basescu, which followed Ponta's elevation to the premiership in May 2012, overstepped the boundaries of the usual battles between a president and a prime minister in a democracy. Ponta used decrees to force the suspension of Basescu, who had long courted controversy due to his interventionist style, which had provoked an earlier conflict with another prime minister, Calin Popescu-Tariceanu. Accusations of overstepping his constitutional role and suspicious acts in his past had led to Basescu's impeachment in April 2007; a scenario which was repeated five years later when Ponta instigated a referendum designed to remove the president from power. Although the overwhelming majority of those who cast their ballots in July 2012 voted for impeachment, Basescu survived due to a low turnout. Both sides emerged from the events with their legitimacy weakened, but more importantly it appeared to illustrate the lack of a deeply rooted commitment to democratic norms and procedures.

The seven countries under consideration entered the new millennium at different stages along the road to EU membership, in part a product of their relative progress towards consolidated democracies and market economies. Estonia and Slovenia were ahead of the rest of the pack, having been invited to begin accession negotiations at the Luxembourg European Council in 1997, but the rest were given their much sought-after present at the Helsinki summit just before Christmas 1999, beginning their negotiations early the following year.

EU accession played an important role in the politics of all seven states, especially from the mid-1990s onwards (see Chapter 6). Although the EU was not always the key driver of domestic change, the requirements of joining the club were significant in shaping the contours of politics. Much debate was couched in terms of meeting requirements. As EU membership was a widely shared goal advocated by the major parties in all the countries under consideration, the issue of EU membership became largely an issue of competence, that is, who was best placed to ensure entry into the EU was achieved. Although this tendency was noticeable in the politics of the 2004 entrants, especially Slovakia, it was more significant in recent times in the cases of Bulgaria and Romania, which joined in 2007. Indeed, for these two states securing EU entry became, in the words of Romanian journalist Adrian Lungu, 'a trophy'.

All accession states were required to jump through a complex series of hoops including the laborious task of incorporating the body of EU law known as the *acquis communautaire* into domestic law. The process of integration, however, was not fully complete when the countries joined the EU. Estonia, Latvia, Lithuania, Slovakia and Slovenia joined Europe's border-free Schengen zone in December 2007. Given that one of the most acutely felt grievances of communist times was travel restrictions, the opening of the Schengen zone to embrace the 2004 CEE entrants was a hugely symbolic moment. Partly due to their later entry into the EU, but also fuelled by the concerns and preferences of the older EU member states, not least in part a product of the unsatisfactory progress made in implementing reforms in the field of justice and home affairs, Romania and Bulgaria remained outside the Schengen zone.

In addition to joining the Schengen zone, the states were also treaty-bound to join the single currency. Progress varied significantly across the region. Whilst for Bulgaria and Romania, membership of the single currency was more of an aspiration than a goal, Estonia, Lithuania and Slovenia targeted entry in January 2007, but concerns emerged during the course of 2006 over a sudden burst of energy-related inflation in the two Baltic candidates, leaving Slovenia as the only one of the trio to join on target. Slovakia followed two years later. Moreover, amid the turmoil besetting the single currency, Estonia joined the single currency on 1 January 2011. To mark the occasion, alongside his counterparts from Latvia and Lithuania, the Prime Minister Andrus Ansip replete with beaming smile withdrew euro notes from an ATM in the Estonian capital Tallinn, providing a modest vote of confidence in the single currency, and highlighting that even in the midst of a crisis small states, such as the Baltics, can realize the apparent benefits of being inside the eurozone.

The demands of EU entry, at times, were onerous, but it would be incorrect to see the EU as the main driver of politics in the region either before or after entry. The EU's influence has been more significant at particular stages of the process, especially during the decision phase when the Union decided whether or not to open accession negotiations (Haughton, 2007). Moreover, in certain areas, such as policies towards ethnic minorities, the EU's influence may have helped change formal policy, but frequently there was a large gap between the declared policies and actual policy implemented on the ground (Rechel, 2009).

Opportunities and constraints of EU membership

Membership, as opposed to accession, accords states much more room for manoeuvre. The seven states are no longer merely objects of EU decision-making, but rather have become political subjects with the ability to shape EU policy from the inside: an adjustment some have found easier than others. Nonetheless, there are limits to any country's power in a union of more than two dozen members, especially if the new member state is small and relatively poor. Thanks in part to their civil servants' limited experience of dealing with European institutions, the new member states from CEE initially had little impact on EU decision-making (Malova *et al.*, 2010). The only apparent exception was foreign policy, especially when it came to the EU's policies towards its new eastern neighbours. Driven by their national priorities and trumpeting their intimate knowledge of the region, Lithuanian politicians, for instance, alongside counterparts from Poland, were active during Ukraine's Orange Revolution helping to push the issue of the EU's relations with the east higher up the Union's agenda.

With a few years of membership under their belt, the CEE states became more assertive, demonstrating both their willingness to stand up to some of the older member states and defend their national interests. Along with Poland, Lithuania for instance blocked progress on EU–Russia relations in 2007 and 2008 and, in July 2011, stood up to Austria in a dispute surrounding the extradition of an ex-Soviet official. Moreover, Slovenia – which had championed enlargement to the Western Balkans as one of its key priorities when it held the EU rotating presidency in 2008 (Kajnc, 2009) – was willing to stand alone blocking accession negotiations with Croatia over a border dispute. Latterly, Slovenia threatened to refuse to ratify Croatia's EU accession treaty due to unresolved disputes stemming from the break-up of Yugoslavia.

With nearly a decade of membership behind them the seven states are much more aware of the opportunities and constraints of EU membership, their role in shaping the EU's policies and general direction, and how to play the EU game. As relatively small and poor states, despite a desire to influence developments in a whole range of areas, there is an increasing awareness that at times their clout is limited, although it can be augmented by allying with like-minded states. The Baltic States, for example, have joined their Nordic neighbours in such bodies as the Nordic Defence Cooperation and the Nordic-Baltic-Eight where their relatively weak single voices become enhanced as part of a larger ensemble.

Nonetheless, despite sticking out their necks on some issues, all of the states covered in this chapter have generally not been awkward and problematic member states. Away from the headline-grabbing disputes between member states, research shows that compliance in the new member states has been surprisingly good. Indeed, analysis of Commission infringement decisions highlights that the five 2004 entrants in particular achieved a higher rate of compliance than the EU average, with Lithuania the star performer (Sedelmeier, 2012).

Although EU membership has had a profound influence on certain policy areas, its impact on party competition has been limited (Lewis and Mansfeldova, 2006; Lewis and Markowski, 2011; Haughton,

2011b). Whilst the difficulties of the eurozone provided the context for recent elections, even in those states which belong to the single currency, such as Slovakia and Slovenia, European issues were peripheral in the campaigns beyond discussion of the dangers of the 'Greek' route, the need to be on the safe side of any divide and the articulations of resentments of poor states subsidizing the mistakes of richer one (Krasovec and Haughton, 2012; Haughton and Deegan-Krause, 2012).

Their later entry into the EU and the decision to impose an additional element of post-accession conditionality in the form of the Cooperation and Verification Mechanism (CVM) placed Bulgaria and Romania in a different category of membership. The CVM was not an empty threat. In 2008, for instance, the European Commission suspended structural funds earmarked for Bulgaria worth 500m euros over rampant corruption and organized crime. Nevertheless, whilst the CVM and the previous threat of postponing entry into the EU were designed to improve the countries' performances in the fields of justice and home affairs, there was 'stagnation and regression' in the fight against high-level corruption (Mendelski, 2012: 33). More broadly, in terms of government effectiveness, regulatory quality, rule of law and corruption, the 2007 entrants lagged behind the 2004 entrants (Spendzharova and Vachudova, 2012).

The EU has, at various times, been a source of inspiration, a driving force for change and a scapegoat for unpopular policies across the seven countries, but one point on which both proponents and critics of the EU in the region agree is that for relatively poor states, the EU offers the prospect of EU funds. The EU might at times be regarded as a 'cash cow' for poorer member states, but the existence of such funds has been at the heart of some of the most egregious cases of corruption in the region. Moreover, money is not offered without strings attached, especially in the management of such funds. Indeed, Romania in 2012 had the lowest absorption rate (7.4 per cent) of EU funds in the 27-member Union. Nevertheless, despite the millions of euros on offer in EU funds, it was the billions of euros involved in the bailouts which became a more prominent theme of politics in more recent times.

Boom, bailouts and austerity

With the necessary reforms needed to secure EU membership undertaken, the seven states could start to focus on facing up to the challenge of flourishing economically in the increasingly competitive world economy. In the boom years of the early to mid-2000s, driven by an ideological belief in the free market and armed with a set of policy pre-scriptions inspired by the World Bank, states such as Slovakia imple-mented a series of radical reforms in health care, pensions and fiscal policy (Fisher *et al.*, 2007). A central component of the reforms was the much-vaunted 19 per cent flat-rate tax. Although the Baltic States had had a flat tax in place since the mid-1990s, the Slovak govern-ment's decision provoked a new wave of fiscal reform with no fewer than 21 post-communist states having adopted a flat tax by the end of 2011, including Romania and Bulgaria in 2005 and 2008 respectively, in a process of 'competitive emulation' (Frye, 2010: 13; Appel and Orenstein, 2013). Even in Slovenia where an attempt to introduce a flat tax in 2005 was halted in part due to effective mobilization by opposition groupings including trade unions (Fink-Hafner, 2006), there was a flattening of the tax rate.

Initially, such policies appeared to reap rewards. In Slovakia, for instance, the government's economic policies helped to transform the country's image and encouraged the inflow of large amounts of foreign investment, most notably in the automotive industry from manufac-tures such as Kia, Volkswagen and Peugeot. Although lower rates of taxation were popular, the thrust of the government's neoliberal package, especially in healthcare and welfare reform, fuelled discontent and led to the government's defeat in the 2006 elections. Despite being elected on a platform criticizing his predecessor's reforms and promises to reverse some of the more unpopular elements introduced between 2002 and 2006, the new left-leaning Prime Minister Robert Fico left much of the neoliberal package intact (Gould, 2009). Nevertheless, by the time Fico returned as prime minister for a second time in 2012, one of his government's first steps was to end the flat tax.

In the six years since Fico had previously been sworn in as Slovak premier much had changed in the international economic climate. The global credit crunch and associated recession hit the seven states hard, especially the Baltic States. As Table 3.1 shows, the Baltics experienced a severe growth reversal. After seven years of growth averaging around 8 per cent, in 2009 their economies contracted by around 15 per cent in a single year. Between 2008 and 2010, Latvia's GDP, for instance, plunged by 25 per cent and unemployment rose over 20 per cent. The severity of the downturn in the Baltics owed much to the global credit crunch. As credit dried up in 2008, house prices, which had ballooned in recent years fuelling a 'feeling of growing prosperity', crashed by 30 per cent in Estonia and 50 per cent in Latvia in 2009 (Connolly, 2011: 261). In echoes of 'shock therapy' in CEE in the early 1990s, the Latvian government responded to the economic crisis with a package of austerity, including cuts of 30 per cent in public sector wages

Table 3.1   *Boom and bust: GDP growth in CEE, 2000–11*

	Annual GDP growth 2000–07 (%)	Change in GDP in 2009	Change in GDP in 2010	Change in GDP in 2011*
Bulgaria	5.5	–5.5	0.2	2.2
Estonia	8.4	–14.3	2.3	8.0
Latvia	8.8	–17.7	–0.3	4.5
Lithuania	7.5	–14.8	1.4	6.1
Romania	5.7	–6.6	–1.9	1.7
Slovakia	5.6	–4.9	4.2	2.9
Slovenia	4.4	–8.0	1.4	1.1
EU average	2.6	–4.2	2.0	1.6

* Estimated.
Sources: Connolly 2012; Hodson, 2012.

(Hudson and Sommers, 2012). Unsurprisingly, anger at the economic slump in the Baltics provoked a series of protests. In the Lithuanian capital Vilnius the mood turned ugly as a protest morphed into a riot in front of the parliament building. Perhaps the most disturbing statistics were those which indicated that citizens of the Baltics saw their futures elsewhere. Not only did the most recent census conducted in 2010–11 highlight that 200,000–300,000 people (around 10 per cent of the population) had emigrated from Latvia over the preceding decade, but a Eurobarometer poll in 2010 indicated nearly a quarter of Lithuanians were planning to leave the country permanently within the following decade (Auers, 2012; Krupavicius, 2011).

Mass protests also greeted the introduction of austerity measures in Romania. In a similar vein to the Baltic States and Bulgaria, Romania's pre-crisis boom was primarily associated with a rapid expansion of investment and a credit-fuelled expansion of private consumption. The Romanian situation was exacerbated by its flexible exchange rate regime, which saw its currency depreciate by nearly a third in the space of two years (2007–09). Not surprisingly, Romania was forced to seek external help. The combined forces of the EU, the European Investment Bank, the European Bank for Reconstruction and Development, the IMF and the World Bank duly obliged, providing 20 billion euros, but imposed constraints on the government's ability to shape its response. The 2009–11 balance of payments assistance programme was successful completed, but the government's austerity-induced policies came at a price. Sparked by a dispute over health reforms, but fuelled by the swingeing cuts imposed on Romanians in

June 2010, including 25 per cent cuts in the salaries of public servants and 15 per cent cuts in unemployment, child and other welfare benefits (Stan and Zaharia, 2011: 1110), Romanians protested and rioted in early 2012. The ire of ordinary citizens was not just a product of the impact of austerity measures, but also disgust at widespread cronyism and corruption in Romanian politics.

New versions of old themes

The politics of the past

Coping with the credit crunch-induced contraction and subsequent eurozone woes were new challenges, but many of the salient themes of politics were new variations on old themes, intimately tied into the legacies of history. Indeed, the past, in both its communist and pre-communist variants, continued to play a role in the politics of the region. Central to debates surrounding the communist period in CEE as a whole was whether there had been a sufficient reckoning with the past. Who did what to whom during communist times still animated some politicians, although the communist period was increasingly less significant in shaping the contemporary politics of the seven countries under consideration than others in CEE, such as Poland. Moreover, debates about the communist past became increasingly muddied by debates about who benefited politically and economically from the early post-communist years.

Nonetheless, the past continues to matter. The twentieth century saw two significant periods of redrawing of borders in CEE: in the aftermath of the First World War and after the collapse of the communist regimes. On both occasions, the three Baltic republics became independent states. The absorption into the Soviet Union in the 1940s was viewed by Baltic politicians as an illegal act, with knock-on implications for constitutional settlements and policies towards ethnic minorities in the post-1991 period (see below). But the history of incorporation into two Russian-dominated empires and the existence of a large Russian-speaking minority in Latvia and Estonia who had moved to the Baltics during Soviet times caused frictions, not least in the attitudes towards Russia.

History had taught the titular ethnic groups in the Baltic States to view Russia with suspicion, whereas the ethnic Russians viewed their ethnic motherland in a far more favourable light. The salience of history was well illustrated by the 'War of Monuments' in Estonia, particularly the relocation of the statue of a bronze soldier in a

Second World War Red Army uniform in April 2007, which pro-voked riots. For ethnic Estonians, the Second World War is seen as years 'synonymous first and foremost with suffering at the hands of the Soviet regime', whereas for most of Estonia's Russian-speaking population, the same war is 'remembered as a victorious struggle against a Nazi German invader that inflicted immense suffering on the peoples of the USSR' (Smith, 2008: 420). The sensitivity of links with Russia were highlighted more recently when, in December 2010, widely reported allegations were made against the Mayor of Tallinn and Centre Party leader Edgar Savisaar of soliciting illegal funds for his party from Russia (Sikk, 2011). Whilst some of his opponents were keen to use the allegations to attack Savisaar, ironically they may actually have helped him win more support from Russian-speaking voters.

Both Slovenia and Slovakia became independent states in the early 1990s, but the legacies of being part of large multi-ethnic empires con-tinued to play a role in contemporary politics. Despite generally good relations, tensions have flared up periodically between Slovenia and its former federal partner Croatia over fishing rights and the exact demar-cation of land and sea border points, which even led to Slovenia blocking Croatia's EU accession negotiations in 2008–09. In a different vein, Slovakia's relations with Hungary have been shaped by imperial history, new citizenship laws and the injudicious remarks of some nationalist Hungarian politicians providing fuel for the fire of Slovak nationalists.

Policies towards minorities

Given historical experiences, especially imperial subjugation and the redrawing of borders, states' policies towards minorities have long been a salient feature of the politics of the region. In the 1990s, inter-national bodies such as the EU devoted much attention to the treat-ment of minorities in states such as Estonia and Latvia, where such groups live in significant numbers. Indeed, it was the very size of these minorities (the Russian minority amounted to around a third of the population in both Estonia and Latvia) which fuelled the demand for more exclusionary new citizenship laws (Mole, 2012). As mentioned above, the Baltic States were incorporated into the Soviet Union in the 1940s. For many from the titular ethnic groupings (i.e. Estonians and Latvians) incorporation into the Soviet Union in the 1940s was viewed as an illegal takeover. The collapse of the Soviet Union and the emer-gence of independent states in the Baltics provoked questions of nationality, citizenship and loyalty to the state. In Estonia, for instance, the 'new' state was defined as the legal continuation of the inter-war republic and the post-war years were seen as an illegal Soviet occupation. In consequence, ethnic Russians who had moved to the then Soviet Republic of Estonia were now not automatically classified as citizens, resulting in them not being accorded the same rights as ethnic Estonians (Mole, 2012).

Discrimination against ethnic Russians in the Baltics provoked international bodies to criticize the governments in Tallinn and Riga. Pressure from the Council of Europe and the European Union was significant in ensuring some changes in the 1990s. With EU accession conditionality at an end, however, the power of the EU to affect domestic policy in this area appeared to diminish. Indeed, less than two years after entry, changes were proposed to the citizenship laws making the language requirement for Latvian citizenship much stricter. Three years after joining the EU, there were still 392,816 non-citizens (17 per cent of the population) and 41,439 aliens registered in Latvia (Sasse, 2009).

Throughout the region, relations between titular ethnic groups and ethnic minorities with a kin state, such as ethnic Hungarians, ethnic Russians and ethnic Turks, have ebbed and flowed in recent years. A number of parties representing ethnic minorities, such as the ethnic Turks' Movement for Rights and Freedom in Bulgaria, the Democratic Alliance of Hungarians in Romania (RMDS/UDMR) and the Party of the Hungarian Coalition (SMK) in Slovakia, have participated in governments in the post-communist years. Opinion is frequently split amongst the titular ethnic groups about these parties and their leading politicians. Such ethnically based parties tend to focus their attention on improving the position of their ethnic minority, but using their political muscle to achieve these aims can cause tensions with the titular ethnic groups and provide ammunition for nationalists. Although his party was out of the Slovak parliament by 2011, SMK leader Jozef Berenyi's announcement of his decision to file a request for Hungarian citizenship, for instance, according Slovak nationalists the opportunity to question his and his party's commitment to the state.

Although ethnicity is likely to remain one of the perennial themes of politics in CEE, the form it takes may vary. Ethnic questions may begin to become more integrated into mainstream party politics as the development of the Centre Party in Estonia or the creation of the party Most-Hid (using the word for bridge in both Slovak and Hungarian) in Slovakia illustrates. But as the electoral success of Jobbik and the increased use of national rhetoric on the part of the governing party Fidesz in Hungary underline, nationalist appeals remain a quick and easy resource for politicians in CEE.

Whilst there is some hope that with the passage of time the strained relations caused by the travails of history might recede, the challenges associated with the Roma (often referred to as gypsies) look set to persist. Although by no means a homogenous ethnic group, taking the Roma as whole, they constitute the most marginalized minority in the region (for example, Rechel, 2009; Vermeersch, 2006). Large numbers of ethnic Roma live in Bulgaria, Romania and Slovakia, constituting around 5–10 per cent of the population, although the reported totals vary significantly. Discrimination against the Roma is widespread. Most of them are in the lowest socio-economic strata of society, frequently unemployed and living in dilapidated and overcrowded accommodation. Conditions in some Roma settlements are often more akin to rural Africa than twenty-first century Europe. Many Roma's life chances are limited by discrimination in education where Roma children are frequently either segregated into special schools or separate classes.

Treatment of the Roma became a salient issue during EU accession, helping to change policy and ensuring the allocation of funds to tackle exclusion, but the results of the policies were limited. Lack of progress was blamed by the Roma on ill-conceived projects and a lack of genuine commitment on the part of the governments to tackle Roma exclusion, unemployment and discrimination. In contrast, titular ethnic groups laid the blame partly on the Roma's lack of organization and diligence. Treatment of the Roma was rarely a significant issue in domestic party politics, in part because strong Roma parties did not exist, nevertheless their considerably higher birth rate raised concerns about the future implications of current demographic trends for domestic politics. Given perceptions among titular ethnic groups and demography, criticism of the Roma is an even easier tool for nationalist politicians to use, as the Slovak National Party's 2010 election posters illustrate well in which a picture of a tattooed Roma was accompanied by the slogan, 'we don't feed those who don't want to work'.

Values and lifestyle

Across CEE as a whole there is a discernible streak of political opinion which laments what they see as the lack of moral values in post-communist societies. Although this has fed into debates about the future of the EU, particularly what is seen to be the social liberal bias of Brussels, conservative opinion has predominantly directed its fire at the domestic audience calling for a return to more traditional Christian values, focusing in particular on the issues of abortion and same-sex marriage.

Gay pride marches have been a notable focal point for both advocates and opponents of homosexual rights. In 2008, Bulgaria's first pride march was marred by the throwing of petrol bombs at the marchers, although four years later the annual parade passed off without incident. The 2005 parade in Latvia's capital Riga provoked a large-scale counter-demonstration and violence leading in part to the following year's parade being banned on security grounds. Thanks to a particular interaction of religion, national identity and the party system, Latvia has pursued some of the most fervently anti-gay policies (O'Dwyer and Schwartz, 2010). In 2005, for instance, it became the first European country to enact an anti-gay marriage constitutional amendment and in the following year the parliament voted against a sexual orientation amendment required to bring Latvian law in line with the EU-mandated anti-discrimination directive. Elsewhere in the region, however, the social liberal agenda proved much less controversial. Nonetheless, the values agenda mattered not just in terms of rallying support to a party's cause, but also in identifying a party's values, and it continues to have political ramifications. In the 2011 Slovene elections, for example, opposition to a liberal Family Law, which included the possibility of adoption by same-sex couples, helped the conservative New Slovenia party rally enough support to return to parliament (Krasovec and Haughton, 2012).

Corruption, disillusionment with politicians and the fluidity of party politics

Corruption has been a prominent theme of politics in the seven states and has arguably become more prominent in recent times, playing a significant role in the removal from office of dominant political parties and providing a rallying cry for new entrants. Allegations and investigations acted as a corrosive on once powerful political entities such as the Slovak Democratic and Christian Union-Democratic Party (SDKU-DS) led by Mikulas Dzurinda, which had been at the helm of coalitions from 1998–2006 and from 2010–12. Elsewhere, corruption prosecutions produced prominent headlines such as when former Romanian prime minister Adrian Natase was rushed into hospital in June 2012 to undergo surgery following an apparent suicide attempt after being jailed for corruption.

Allegations of corruption were easy to make and found a receptive audience among ordinary citizens, especially in countries like Romania where venal, corrupt and untrustworthy politicians appeared to be the norm. Nevertheless, even when politicians sought to follow through on anti-corruption promises such as Romanian President Traian Basescu, who was elected in 2004 on a strong anti-corruption platform, it was easy for his opponents to paint the president's actions as all just politically motivated.

Whilst many of the corrupt activities in the first post-communist decade were inextricably linked to privatization and state-building, a large slice of the more recent less than angelic behaviour was intimately linked to party financing (especially of newer parties) – what Malova and Ucen (2011: 1126) dubbed the 'Achilles heel' of politics in CEE – but also to EU funds. Although the seven states received less money than they had hoped for in the EU's 2007–13 financial perspective, unprecedented amounts of cash were earmarked to help agriculture, regional development and infrastructure projects. Being in power, or proximity to those in power, therefore, had its pecuniary advantages, helping to explain, for example, why all too frequently shady businessmen and politicians made such happy bedfellows.

Widespread feelings that politicians frequently put their own (material) interests and those of their associates before the interests of their countries, combined with the perceived lack of competence of incumbent politicians, proved to be fertile ground for the emergence of a succession of 'new' parties, which used their novelty as an asset (Sikk, 2012). Although the extent of change varied markedly across the region (Deegan-Krause and Haughton, 2012), Bulgaria illustrates well the role anti-corruption plays in domestic party politics.

The National Movement Simeon II (NDSV) in Bulgaria garnered no fewer than 42.7 per cent of the votes in its first parliamentary elections in 2001. The party's identity and appeal cannot be divorced from the man whose name appears in the party's moniker. Expelled by the communist authorities in 1946 at the age of nine, the former Tsar only revealed his political ambitions in 2001 and quickly set about forming a party for the impending elections. Bulgarian politics had been dominated for much of the 1990s by the communist-successor Bulgarian Socialist Party (BSP) and the Union of Democratic Forces (SDS), albeit often as part of broader coalitions. The latter had come to power in 1997 in the midst of an economic crisis caused largely by the policies of the former. The SDS's tough economic measures, plus accusations of corruption and clientelism, which dogged the party throughout its time in office, allied to the BSP's unwillingness to change, created space for a new party. NDSV carefully positioned itself as the antidote to both BSP and SDS and built on Simeon's reputation as a noble and honest man unsullied by the dirty deals of the 1990s.

Such claims of competence and clean hands are easy to invoke, but harder to sustain. Although NDSV's economic package promised to transform Bulgaria in 800 days, many ordinary citizens failed to feel any significant benefits. Moreover, the government led by the NDSV proved not to be whiter than white. As support for NDSV began to wane, the anti-corruption mantle was taken up Boyko Borisov and his party GERB (Citizens for the European Development of Bulgaria). Highlighting the corrupt deals of the NDSV, BSP and the Movement for Rights and Freedom (DSP), GERB's popularity rose, propelling Borisov into the prime ministership in 2009.

Conclusion: a tale of three elections

Elections well encapsulate political developments. They tend to highlight the dynamics of party politics and the issues which animate politics. Three recent parliamentary elections underline the motors and brakes of politics across CEE: Latvia in September 2011, Slovenia in December 2011 and Slovakia in March 2012.

The 2011 Latvian elections were held after President Valdis Zatlers' television address to the nation calling a referendum on early elections. Zalters complained that Latvia was under the 'almost absolute control' of three tycoons: Aivars Lembergs, Andris Skele and Ainars Slesers (Auers, 2012: 1). Latvian voters backed Zatlers' proposal in July, with parliamentary elections taking place two months later. The results did diminish the powerful position of parties associated with the three tycoons, but despite wanting his party to signal a new beginning in Latvian politics, parliamentary arithmetic meant, in the end, Zatlers formed a coalition which allowed Valdis Dombrovskis to be the first prime minister in Latvia's history to lead three successive governments.

Corruption and the desire to punish the established parties was also central to the 2011 elections in Slovenia where two new parties, the Zoran Jankovic List-Positive Slovenia and the Civic List of Gregor Virant, both established just two months prior to the elections, managed to win 37 per cent of the vote. The government led by Borut Pahor, which took power in Slovenia on almost the same day in 2008 as the collapse of Lehman Brothers, saw its popularity sink under the weight of unpopular reforms, coalition infighting and corruption allegations. But the stain of corruption was not just the preserve of the governing parties. The main opposition party, the Slovene Democratic Party (SDS), was embroiled in a long-running saga surrounding alleged bribes to a Finnish defence contractor. Given the cocktail of corruption scandals, low levels of trust in government and difficult economic times, the ground was fertile for new political parties. Riding a wave of discontent with the existing parties and building on his business experience and tenure as mayor of the capital city Ljubljana, Zoran

Jankovic's party won the election. Nevertheless, he struggled to form a coalition and much to the chagrin of many left-leaning voters who had rallied behind Ljubljana's mayor, the leader of the centre-right SDS Janez Jansa returned to the prime ministership he had held from 2004–08. The election highlighted that winning an election is only half the battle; victory lies in forming a government, which requires a different set of skills and personal attributes.

Slovakia's four party centre-right coalition, which had taken power in June 2010, collapsed thanks to a dispute over the euro bailout. Complaining that a poor state such as Slovakia should not be bailing out a richer member of the eurozone such as Greece, one of the junior coalition partners, Freedom and Solidarity, refused to back prime minister Iveta Radicova's position of solidarity with fellow eurozone members in October 2011, even when she tied support to a confidence motion in parliament. Radicova's government duly fell, but before elections were held Slovak politics became dominated by the Gorilla scandal, so called after the leak of the eponymously named police file purportedly highlighting intimate links and lucrative mutually beneficial deals between financial groups and politicians during the 2002–06 government led by Mikulas Dzurinda. Gorilla led to a significant drop in support for Dzurinda's party, but ultimately produced little change. Indeed, polling data suggested that Robert Fico was already set for a return to power just weeks after Radicova's government took power. Delving deeper into Slovak party politics, we see that frequent changes in party and government obscure a remarkable degree of stability within the four key electoral blocs: left, right, Hungarian nation and Slovak national (those of Slovak ethnicity for whom ethnicity is particularly important) (Haughton and Deegan-Krause, 2012).

All three of these elections were called early, highlighted the salience of the issues of corruption and competence, and all illustrate the dilemmas and dynamics of coalition formation and maintenance. In a political atmosphere infused with disappointment with politicians seen to be corrupt and incompetent, and with governments struggling in tough economic times, new parties offered voters a breath of fresh air and a semblance of hope. Nevertheless, despite the changes in the menus of parties on offer to the electorate and the rise and fall of individual politicians, even in these landmark elections where much appeared to change on one level, at a deeper level much remained the same.

Chapter 4

The Western Balkans

Judy Batt

The 'Western Balkans' is a term invented by the European Union in 1999 to cover a heterogeneous group of countries, mainly from the former Yugoslavia that had been wracked by war for almost a decade, and that the EU had now decided to draw together into a 'Stabilization and Association Process'. The group included most of the states that had emerged from the defunct Socialist Federal Republic of Yugoslavia (SFRY), except for Slovenia, which having extricated itself early from the Yugoslav quagmire, managed to rebrand itself as an 'Alpine Republic' and join the EU in May 2004. The Western Balkans group also includes Albania (which had not been part of SFRY, and had taken no part in the wars). The political fragmentation of the former Yugoslav space continued up to 2008, with the independence of Kosovo, formerly a province of Serbia. So today the group comprises: Albania (3.2 million); Bosnia and Herzegovina (BiH, est. 4 million); Croatia (population: 4.4 million); Kosovo (est. 2.5 million); Macedonia (internationally known as the Former Yugoslav Republic of Macedonia, FYROM, 2.1 million); Montenegro (620,000); and Serbia (7.1 million).

The externally imposed origin of the name of this region is symptomatic of an important feature of its politics: the extent to which political developments in the region have been driven by external intervention, and political institutions in some cases have even been imposed from outside. The wars of the 1990s were only brought to an end by NATO's armed intervention; peace processes entailed heavy involvement by the UN, and a plethora of international organizations installed themselves on the ground for many years. Both BiH and Kosovo are still today in a sense semi-sovereign international protectorates. The EU's aim in launching the Stabilization and Association Process in 1999 was to kick-start long delayed political and economic reform in this region (see Lehne in Batt, 2004) by offering the perspective of EU membership (something which is not on offer to the East European 'neighbours', treated in Chapter 5). The expectation was that once the wars were over, the region could be induced to move on and follow the same trajectory followed by the Central Europeans after 1989. At the Thessaloniki European Council in June 2003, the EU made its commitment to the region unambiguous: 'The future of the Balkans is within the European Union'. Progress towards this end has, however, been slower than expected and uneven. The West Balkans, always a very diverse group of countries, has become more so as time goes on.

Croatia, never happy with the 'Balkans' label with its negative associations, made strenuous efforts to distance itself from the region. After 2000, the government accelerated domestic reforms so that by 2006, it was judged ready to begin accession negotiations with the EU. These were completed in June 2011; the Treaty of Accession was signed the following December, and ratified by Croatia after the January 2012 referendum. Once the EU's member states had also ratified, Croatia was able to become the 28th member state in July 2013. However, it seems likely that several years will pass before any of the others will be able to follow.

There are two mutually reinforcing factors in this delay. On the one hand, many questions remain about the readiness of the rest of the region for EU membership. Many – both in the EU and in the region – are frustrated by the slow pace of change, the continuing fragility of many states, and the lingering sense of precariousness that hovers over the region's stability. What is often loosely called 'political will' – the capacity to generate strong *internal* drivers of reform – seems to be deficient here. On the other hand, questions can be raised about the EU's commitment to the region, which has seemed to fluctuate as it succumbed to bouts of 'enlargement fatigue' and internal crisis in recent years. Moreover, the conditions it has set for would-be new members have become much more onerous, and are much more stringently applied and monitored today than they were for the Central Europeans in the 1990s. In some cases, individual EU member states have blocked the progress of Western Balkans countries towards EU membership, even where they were actually ready to move forward to the next stage. The Western Balkans has simply not been a high priority for the EU. This is not the place to review the successes and failures of the EU's enlargement strategy; the key point is that precisely because of the region's heavy dependence on the external driver of the EU, the EU factor has to be included in any assessment of the political dynamics of the states of the region.

This chapter approaches the question not so much through case-by-case analysis of political institutions, party systems, electoral dynamics as by drawing broad comparisons with the Central European experience. How far are the challenges of transition that these countries face really comparable to those surmounted by the Central Europeans after 1989? Is it a question merely of delayed transition, starting ten years late after the wars of the 1990s were brought to an end? Are we being too impatient, forgetting just how uncertain things looked in Central Europe in the mid-1990s, at a comparable point in their transitions? Or are the circumstances of transition in the countries of the Western Balkans 'special', burdened by some peculiar historical and structural inheritance? Three main possible factors that could explain divergence from Central European patterns can be identified: political culture; problems of statehood; and the impact of war on transition.

Political culture shaped by strategic uncertainties

The Western Balkans region – with the exception of Croatia –wholly comprises territory that, historically, was shaped by the Ottoman Empire. This invites one to ask whether the legacies of that historical experience set the region apart from Central Europe, and account for Croatia's 'exceptionalism' within the region. Croatia's southern border was once the southern border of the Habsburg empire, and today this border marks it off from the rest of the Western Balkans group. This border does indeed more or less coincide with one of Samuel P. Huntington's 'civilizational dividing lines' – between the Habsburg world of Western Christendom and the 'eastern' former Ottoman domain (Huntington, 1996). Westerners have traditionally identified 'the Balkans' with a peculiarly intractable mix of characteristics including political fragmentation and bitter 'tribal' feuding, archaic social structures, chronic economic backwardness and sloppy, corrupt administrative habits (see Jezermik, 2004; Todorova, 1997). The question of whether this region is 'really part of Europe' is not new, and many would ask whether, therefore, it can ever be successfully assimilated into the Europe of the EU. Such sceptics might also point to the erratic performance of other Balkan countries – Romania, Bulgaria and Greece – as EU members.

However, we must avoid the trap of historical determinism. Why should the heritage of empires that collapsed a century ago still be decisive? Radical change has been as salient a feature of this region as continuity. We should not forget that many in Western Europe were equally sceptical of the capacity of post-communist 'Eastern' Europe (as Poland, Hungary, Czechoslovakia and others were known in 1989) to 'return to Europe' – and yet these countries proved able to execute a radical break with the past, firmly detaching themselves from the former Soviet space, establishing functional democracies, and implementing radical reforms. In principle, change is an option for any society if its leaders can mobilize national consensus and the necessary political will.

The political weaknesses conventionally attributed to the 'Balkans' as a region are by no means immutable; nor are such defects unique to this region. Benign 'Habsburg legacies' have often been invoked in recent years to explain the superior performance of the 2004 accession countries by comparison with the 'laggards', Romania and Bulgaria – and are regularly hinted at by Croats to emphasize their superior 'European' credentials. But some 'Habsburg legacies' that one could cite are far from benign: one has only to recall the exposure of Habsburg social, political and bureaucratic pathologies in the nightmarish works of the Austrian novelists Franz Kafka and Robert Musil. Moreover, one could well argue that ethno-linguistic 'tribal' nationalism was quintessentially a 'Habsburg' product, subsequently exported to the Ottoman world – whose own record in cultural coexistence was for much of its history somewhat better than that of most of Europe (see Mazower, 2000).

What was characteristic of Central European states and societies after 1989 was – for all their political fractiousness – a basic national consensus that they rightfully belonged to the 'European family', and this generated a strong will for change and reform in order to prove their 'European' credentials. Underpinning their determination was a deeply felt strategic imperative of escaping forever from the external domination of the then Soviet Union. Today, opinion polls in the Western Balkans show levels of popular support for European integration that are comparable, and in some cases exceed, those found in Central Europe as it prepared for EU accession. What ordinary people in the Western Balkans region appear to want from the EU is no different from what the Central Europeans wanted in the 1990s: first, an overarching security framework to guarantee their newly won independence; second, a decisive stimulus towards social and economic modernization; and third, a powerful anchor for democratic governance and the rule of law to constrain corrupt and rapacious political elites.

Yet what is striking about the political culture of the Western Balkans today is the ambivalence and lack of self-confidence in their 'European vocation'. While clearly wanting EU integration, people have absorbed the negative Western stereotypes of 'the Balkans' and worry that the special 'Balkan' character of their states and societies means they may not be up to the challenge. As one Bosnian journalist lamented as the war broke out, 'Thus, instead of being an integral part of Europe, we are again becoming the Balkans, we are sinking into it equally in Ljubljana as well as in Zagreb, in Belgrade, Stara Pazova and Foca, in Velika Kladusa, Pristina and Skopje' (quoted in Todorova, 1997: 53). One poll in Serbia is typical: asked what were the reasons for Serbia's lagging economic performance, a clear majority placed political instability and lack of consensus among the parties, corruption and poor quality legislation at the top of the list, followed (at some distance) by the 'mentality' of the people – laziness, disorganization, bad habits (Marten Board International, 2004). People from the region often ruefully confess, 'If I were the EU, I wouldn't let us in.'

An important factor underlying the Western Balkans' cultural diffidence as to their 'European' prospects is a certain lack of strategic clarity about their reasons for wanting to 'become European'. First, they do not have that sense of an overwhelming external threat – such as the Soviet Union posed for Central Europe – from which they must at all costs escape through integration into the EU. Threat perceptions in the Western Balkans focus almost wholly on immediate neighbours within the region, and on rival ethnic groups within states. These tensions in fact weaken and divert efforts at political and economic reform, rather than strengthening and focusing consensus on EU integration. Second, political discourse in the former Yugoslav republics often betrays the legacy of 'Yugoslav exceptionalism' – proud memories of the post-Second World War period when this country went its own way independently of the Soviet bloc, developing a distinctively different model of communism and a 'non-aligned' foreign policy strategy that brought it considerable international prestige. And the Yugoslavs were rewarded for this with privileged treatment from Western powers. Thus some people today are resentful that the EU has already admitted countries like Romania and Bulgaria, which former Yugoslavs have been used to regarding as somehow more 'backward' and 'Balkan' than themselves. Yugoslav traditions of 'doing it their own way', as well as a certain nostalgia for an era that was certainly more comfortable than the post-Yugoslav era, still have an impact today in the form of a prickly reluctance to comply with the EU's often burdensome and intrusive conditionality. The idea that it might be *in their own interests* to implement most of the reforms demanded by the EU seems not always to be self-evident to political elites and societies. Instead, the EU itself can easily be construed in the familiar image of an unfriendly, even 'imperialistic' actor.

And third, there is widespread scepticism in the region about whether 'Europe' really wants them at all. From the perspective of the region, the EU failed them in the 1990s by its feeble and incoherent efforts to stop the outbreak of war. The EU's initial reluctance to 'take sides' in what was perceived as a civil war in Yugoslavia explains its hesitancy to intervene, but as a result the EU is still seen as a weak and unreliable guarantor of security by Croats, Bosniaks (Slavic Muslims) and Albanians. When finally more forceful measures were taken to end the conflict, the 'international community' (led by NATO but also including the EU) inescapably found itself taking sides. Economic sanctions were imposed on Serbia, which also had severe knock-on effects on the whole region. Then NATO bombed Serbian positions in Bosnia in 1995, and Serbia itself in 1999 in an intervention designed to prevent 'ethnic cleansing' of the Albanian population of Kosovo, which eventually paved the way for Kosovo's permanent severance from Serbia in 2008, winning recognition as an independent state by twenty-two EU member states. Hence the particular ambivalence of Serbs towards 'Europe'. But still five EU member states refused to recognize Kosovo, thus once again displaying the EU's political disunity, and, more importantly from Kosovo's perspective, not only insulting the new state but posing a very serious practical obstacle to its eventual EU membership, a perspective supposedly promised to the whole region.

Moreover, during the wars, the EU reimposed a visa regime on the whole region to stem to outflow of refugees. Hitherto, Yugoslav citizens, unlike their Central European counterparts, had been able to travel freely to, work and reside in EU countries. This restrictive policy remained in force for far too long, and still applies today to Kosovo, where it has been a major source of popular grievance. With considerable justification, people have asked how they were supposed to effect the 'return to Europe' when they could not even go there?

Many people in the region fear the EU could fail them again. Despite the EU's verbal 'Thessaloniki commitment', talk about 'enlargement fatigue' spread in the EU after the 2004 enlargement, the failure of the EU's Constitutional Treaty in the French and Dutch referendums in 2005, and the disappointing performance of the 2007 accession countries, Romania and Bulgaria. Most worrying has been the evident hardening of Germany's position on enlargement, by contrast with the period up to 2004 when it was the strongest supporter of the Central Europeans' accession. At the time of writing, with the EU in deep crisis, the economies of Greece and several other member states on the verge of meltdown and the euro's future in doubt, the EU hardly inspires confidence. It is not surprising that in the Western Balkans people frequently ask, 'Why should we do all these painful reforms if the EU isn't going to let us in anyway, or isn't going to be able to offer us the rewards we expected?' Yet it is an illusion that the reforms the EU demands are optional – most of them would be required even if EU membership were not on the agenda, and the EU has and will continue to provide considerable financial and technical support. The harsh reality is that a more sceptical, enlargement-weary and economically straitened EU public nowadays will only be ready to accept as members states that they fully trust to play by the rules and deliver on their commitments to reform.

'Enlargement fatigue' is not a new phenomenon. Aspirant member states in their approaches to the EU have always encountered ambivalence, lack of interest and indecision on the part of certain member states when confronted with enlargement, and this was certainly apparent to the Central Europeans in the early 1990s. But the Central Europeans did not waver in their resolve, they simply got on with reform and thus presented the EU's enlargement sceptics with a new reality – a 'New Europe' – that simply could not be rejected. The Western Balkans have, by contrast, needed constant reassurance, encouragement, pressure, and, too often, more than that – namely, a direct EU/international security presence on the ground to keep them on track. This brings us on to the second point.

Problematic statehood

The Bulgarian sociologist Ivan Krastev boldly asserts: 'one clear thread is visible in the post-communist puzzle of success and failure: only nation-states have succeeded in the European integration project' (Krastev, 2003). By that he meant not 'ethno-national' states, but unitary states founded on a basic national consensus, with functional institutions accountable to citizens and unchallenged jurisdiction within secure borders. It was only with the consolidation of Croatia's independent statehood in the late 1990s, after the dismantling of ethnic Serbian separatist 'autonomous republics' (which resulted in the physical expulsion of the vast majority of Croatia's minority Serbian population), and after the death of the wartime nationalist leader Franjo Tudjman in 1999, that the country felt able to redefine its national identity in terms compatible with 'European' values, and to direct its energies fully towards reform, which was then promptly rewarded by the EU (see Vlahutin in Batt, 2004). All the other states of the region remain, to various degrees, problematic – new, weak, some very small, most suffering deep internal political and/or ethnic divisions, mired in the unresolved conflicts of the past – 'unfinished' as states in vital respects.

Albania and Macedonia avoided direct involvement in the wars of the 1990s, but both have proved weak and vulnerable to sudden breakdown. For example, *Albania* virtually imploded as a state in 1997, as a result of the collapse of several pyramid investment scams into which a large proportion of the population had deposited all their savings in the desperate hope of a quick exit from dire poverty. The government collapsed and anarchic social disorder followed, including raids on the army and police stores of weapons (many of which then found their way into Kosovo, where they helped transform the Kosovo Albanian nationalist movement into a national liberation army). There followed an explosion of organized crime in Albania, involving smuggling of drugs, weapons, illegal migrants and trafficking in women for prostitution. With close international support and monitoring, the Albanian state has since been cobbled together again, but it still functions weakly, with deeply polarized politics and endemic corruption, both of which have proved to be serious obstacles to coherent reform, and little progress has been made on the road towards EU membership.

A key challenge for *Macedonia* has been to overcome deep ethnic division between an ethnic Macedonian (orthodox Slav) majority and a large (about 25 per cent) Albanian minority, concentrated in the west, bordering Albania. Macedonia held together through the 1990s, carefully avoiding involvement in the wars (although it was hard hit by the economic shocks delivered by the break-up of Yugoslavia and the imposition of international sanctions on Serbia, its main market). But in 2001, Macedonia came alarmingly close to ethnic civil war between the Macedonians and the Albanian minority. Timely international (EU and US) diplomatic engagement led to a peace agreement (the Ohrid Accords), followed up by NATO military and civilian police missions that were subsequently taken over by the EU. Only constant close support and pressure from the EU has secured implementation of the Ohrid Accords, and the start of a still unfinished process of consolidating the state. Macedonia remains vulnerable to developments beyond its borders, in particular to the political instability of its neighbour Kosovo, whose population is mainly ethnic Albanian. Shadowy extremist nationalist Albanian movements exist that aspire to redrawing borders to create a 'Greater Albania', which implies dismembering Macedonia. How influential these are should not be exaggerated, but neither should their existence be ignored (see Batt, 2008). Consolidation has not been helped by the 'name dispute' with Greece, which refuses to accept the state's title of 'Republic of Macedonia', on the grounds that this represents an implicit territorial claim on northern Greece, a major part of historical Macedonia. The Greek veto in the UN meant that Macedonia only won UN membership in 1993 under the contorted provisional title of 'Former Yugoslav Republic of Macedonia' (usually abbreviated to the obscure-sounding 'FYROM'), a title which Macedonia resents enormously and itself never uses.

Endless fruitless rounds of bilateral negotiations under UN auspices have so far failed to find a satisfactory compromise. Greek frustration has led it to block both NATO membership and further steps towards EU accession, even when the European Commission has deemed its reforms adequate to allow it to move forward. Macedonian frustration at this has led to a distinct turn to introverted nationalism on the part of the ethnic Macedonians, which inflames both Greek and local Albanian-minority sensibilities and exasperates Macedonia's international sympathizers.

Fighting ended in *Bosnia and Herzegovina* (BiH) in 1995 with the signature of the Dayton Peace Agreement, which secured recognition of the new state by its neighbours and at the same time established an international protectorate to oversee implementation of the agreement and post-war reconstruction. This is still in place. Although democratically elected parliaments and governments exist, they function under the supervision of an internationally mandated High Representative with powers to overrule parliamentary decisions and even to sack elected officials (although in recent years High Representatives have been much constrained in the use of these powers). For many years, the High Representative's role was backed by a substantial international security presence, and later the EU-led European Union Force 'Althea' military mission and an EU Police Mission. Although these missions are today much reduced in scale and scope, the fact that they remain in place signals that BiH is still not, in practice, a fully sovereign state, and that serious question marks hover over its viability and sustainability.

The price of compromise at Dayton was a constitution that unfortunately entrenched the ethnic divisions between Bosniaks (South Slav Muslims), Croats and Serbs by recognizing the two powerful 'entities' that emerged in BH during the war: Republika Srpska, a 'quasi-state' that Bosnian Serbs had envisaged (and some still envisage) eventually uniting with Serbia; and the Federation of BiH, arising from a wartime alliance formed under international pressure between Bosniaks and Croats (who had been at times fighting each other). The return of refugees to their former homes, particularly of minority communities driven out by 'ethnic cleansing' by forces of the ethnic majority in the given area, has only been partially successful. The complex and unwieldy structure of multi-level and highly decentralized government, set up to pacify the demands of the respective ethnic communities, has proved predictably dysfunctional in fostering consensus and implementing reform, the pace of which is slow and erratic.

Constitutional reforms – in particular, the strengthening of common state institutions at the expense of the ethnic entities and cantons – are required if BiH is going to be capable of concluding and implementing the Stabilization and Association Agreement (SAA). But reaching agreement between the three ethnic groups on constitutional reform – as well as on many other lower-level issues – is a bitterly contentious business. The Serbs vehemently resist any diminution of Republika Srpska's powers. The Croats contest the dismantling of the ten ethnic cantons into which the Federation itself is sub-divided – unless the two cantons in which they form the majority are allowed to break away and form a third, ethnic Croat entity (which some of them hankered after as the first step to uniting with Croatia). And the Bosniaks cherish the dream of centralized, unitary statehood for BiH. Although they often deploy the language of civic republican idealism to promote this option against the entrenched nationalisms of the other two, the argument is nevertheless by no means ethnically neutral, and certain Bosniaks see centralism as a means of more effectively asserting their interests as the largest ethnic group. Elections regularly reconfirm the overwhelming appeal of ethnic nationalism to BiH voters, and the intractability of the basic conflict over statehood. Although the ethnic parties that had their origins in the war have weakened their hold over time due to internal splits and scandals, newer post-war parties still feature wartime leaders in prominent positions who are ready in election campaigns to exploit ethnic insecurities as egregiously as ever. While the EU 'sticks' have withered, the EU's 'carrots' seem not to exert sufficient power in this context, and BiH has only moved forward on the EU track because of the EU's readiness to overlook shortcomings in BiH's fulfilment of the conditions in order that the country not fall too far behind the rest.

Unresolved statehood issues have also bedevilled the progress of *Serbia and Montenegro*. When the other Yugoslav republics seceded in the early 1990s, these two republics remained hitched together in the rump Federal Republic of Yugoslavia. But by 1997, *Montenegro* found the alliance with belligerent Serbia under Slobodan Milosevic too costly. It began to go its own way, cultivating Western support, building up its separate institutions, and even adopting the euro as its currency. After Milosevic was ousted from power in Serbia in October 2000, Montenegro launched a campaign for outright independence. This was not at the time welcomed by the EU, which wanted to avoid further destabilizing fragmentation in the region. Instead, Javier Solana, the EU's High Representative for the common foreign and security policy, brokered agreement on a reconstituted State Union of Serbia and Montenegro. However, the price of Montenegro's consent to this was that a referendum on independence would be allowed after the elapse of three years. As a result, neither republic had much interest in committing itself to the State Union as a long-term proposition. It finally became clear to the EU, and the majority of Montenegrin voters, that both republics were more likely to move faster to EU integration as separate states.

In May 2006, Montenegro held a referendum at which a majority (55 per cent) voted in favour of independence. Since then, Montenegro has made up for lost time, rapidly advancing to win EU candidate status by December 2010, and hoping to start accession negotiations in 2012. Thus after Croatia, post-independence Montenegro has made the most progress along the EU path. Its democratic maturation, however, has been held back by the dominance of a single party (whose leader, moreover, has occupied the top state and government posts without a break since the early 1990s), and the lack of an effective, united opposition. The independence and quality of the print media is, on the other hand, rather higher than elsewhere in the region, and there is a lively, active independent civil society. But the country is poor, and, like most other states in the region, riddled with corruption and weak in administrative capacity. The minorities of Albanians and Bosniaks/Muslims are quite well integrated, but the new state has to overcome the political alienation of the significant minority of voters who opposed independence. Many of these identify as Serbs by nationality (32 per cent of the total population), and regard Montenegrin identity as merely a variety of the larger Serbian one. Reconciling this group to the new reality of independent Montenegrin statehood is eased by accelerated EU integration, which all groups say they want. But – as is the case with the other communities of Serbs in the region – reconciliation also depends on how far Serb leaders, not least the leaders in Serbia's capital, Belgrade, continue to toy with traditional ethno-nationalist aspirations to unite 'all Serbs in one state'.

Serbia itself emerged from the wars a deeply troubled country (see Batt, 2005). Having launched three wars in the 1990s in the name of Serbian national unity, it finds it hard to accept that it lost all of them. Still smarting at its rejection in 2006 by Montenegro – the one neighbour it took for granted as a loyal ally – in 2008 it was confronted with the ultimate challenge of the internationally supported independence of *Kosovo*. The latter was a part of Serbia under virtual martial law until 1999. Albanians (estimated at 95 per cent of the population of Kosovo) were treated dreadfully by the Serbian regime under Milosevic. By 1998, an armed Albanian rebellion had begun. The response of Serbian security forces in 1998–99 was brutal in the extreme, culminating in a deliberate large-scale campaign to expel the entire Albanian population from the province, at which point, NATO intervened (for the background, see Independent International

Commission on Kosovo, 2000) Thereafter, Kosovo remained formally a province of Serbia but was governed as a quite separate entity under a UN-mandated interim international administration, and an international (NATO and EU-led) security presence. Politically unstable, with deep divisions among the Albanian parties, and economically impoverished, with very high levels of unemployment and large numbers of 'angry young men', Kosovo struggled along in limbo for several years. Now the Serbian minority population were vulnerable: almost wholly alienated from public life, a dwindling population of about 120,000 living in fear of regular attacks from vengeful Albanian neighbours and organized gangs. In March 2004, the Serbs faced a concerted series of mass pogrom-type assaults in which over 50,000 Albanians took part, and the international military and police forces lamentably failed to offer protection. That finally pushed Kosovo's international overseers to bring 'final status' onto the agenda, while at the same time giving top priority to the questions of minority security, mainly but not only focused on Kosovo's Serbs. The independence package finally implemented (with only ambiguous UN approval, due to Russia's veto) provided some of the most far-reaching guarantees of minority rights (including to self-government) to be found anywhere, but to no avail: the local Serbs have little or no confidence in their future in Kosovo and have boycotted the new political institutions, instead establishing a secessionist zone in the north-east under the control of militants over whom Belgrade has little control, while continuing to provide resources in support (for more detail see Judah, 2009). International supervisory institutions remain as part of the independence package, albeit less intrusive than those still in place in BiH, while Kosovo's international status remains abnormal and hardly 'final', as it has been blocked from joining the UN due to the vetoes of Serbia, Russia and many other states which have not recognized it (including five EU member states). The prospect of EU membership is equally unclear, despite EU reassurances that 'eventual' membership is still envisaged.

In Serbia, many still entertain the hope that Kosovo will someday return to Serbian jurisdiction, and the 2008 denouement was widely regarded as a national catastrophe. Although many are prepared to admit in private that this relieves Serbia of responsibility for a politically troublesome and economically burdensome province, public discourse is full of resentment against the Albanians and the international community, held responsible for Serbia's loss of the territory, which national mythology cherishes as the 'cradle' of Serbian identity. It is thus of no avail to try to persuade Serbia that in fact it would make much faster progress towards EU integration if it could only leave the 'Kosovo question' behind. No political leader in Belgrade has yet been willing, or felt able, to tell Serbian voters what most of them already know (as opinion polls show): that Kosovo was lost back in 1999 if not earlier, and will never be recovered. Since October 2000, when the ruthless and manipulative Slobodan Milosevic was removed from office in a 'democratic revolution' that recalled the mass popular uprisings of 1989 in Central Europe, expectations that Serbia would rapidly leave its past behind have proved illusory and, instead of leading the region's 'return to Europe' as by far its largest state, Serbia's relations with all its neighbours in the region are to a greater or lesser extent problematic. Democratic development has been held hostage to an unrequited nationalism, which Serbia's Democratic Party, holding the Presidency from 2004 to 2012 and dominant partner in the coalition governments 2008–12, has avoided confronting. The split in the Serbian Radical Party in 2008 (then the largest parliamentary party) has, however, allowed scope for more pragmatic and opportunist nationalists to ditch the hardliners (led by an indicted war criminal in custody in the Hague) intent on marching Serbia back into the international isolation of the Milosevic era.

Since then the Serbian Progressive Party has been following the route the Croatian nationalist Croatian Democratic Union (HDZ) took after the death of wartime leader Franjo Tudjman, moderating the previously strident nationalism with a commitment to continue Serbia's EU integration path, albeit with distinct 'eurosceptic' overtones. This won them the Presidency in 2012, and the largest share of parliamentary seats. At the same time the party is strongly pro-Russian, and professes the wish to 'balance' the EU against closer ties with Russia. Whatever its eventual composition, the new government will continue the previous policy on Kosovo, denying any inconsistency between maintaining that Kosovo is still part of Serbia while at the same time seeking to join the EU. How long Serbia can go on playing politics as a game of avoiding these fundamental choices depends upon how much it really wants to accelerate its integration with the EU. In practice, when the Kosovo issue has become an obvious obstacle to achieving some valued EU prize – notably, visa liberalization – Serbian governments have been ready to leave Kosovo out of the deal. Serbia reached EU candidate status in March 2012, and when this leads on to EU accession negotiations, many more such compromises will be demanded. Thus both internal evolution and gradual rapprochement with the EU can be seen acting to 'normalize' democratic politics in Serbia and consolidate statehood on the basis of the *de facto* borders, i.e. excluding Kosovo.

In conclusion to this section, we should note that questions of statehood and national identity were by no means absent from the transitions in Central Europe either: the Czechoslovak Federation broke apart, and the Baltic republics broke away from the Soviet Union to form new nation-states closely tied to the majority ethnic identity. Resurgent ethnic minority demands in the region – particularly the Hungarian minorities' demands for territorial autonomy – seemed to raise questions about the stability of state borders. But there was no appetite for violence, and armed conflict between states did not occur. Why not?

One explanation has to do with the centrality of the idea of 'returning to Europe' to the Central European revolutions of 1989, which tempered popular nationalism and focused elite energies on proving their nations' 'European' credentials and getting into the EU and NATO. They were thus receptive to the EU's message that no state could be accepted as a candidate for membership that had not first settled its relations with its neighbours and demonstrated respect for minorities. After unification in 1991, the new Germany moved swiftly to overcome the legacies of the Second World War in its relations with its eastern neighbours, and won their trust by its vigorous support for their EU integration. The break-up of Czechoslovakia could be peacefully negotiated after 1989, because the two nations had no history of fighting each other and no mutual recriminations over territory or minorities. It was mutual indifference, rather than mutual fear and mistrust, which undermined the common Czechoslovak state. The Baltic states' recovery of their independence was more fraught on account of the adverse reaction of their Russian-speaking minorities. Although Russia's rhetoric on their behalf often took on aggressive and threatening overtones, Russia refrained from armed intervention because of its concern to re-make its relationship with the West. And the Baltics' dependence on Western support (the United States and several other Western states had never recognized their annexation by the Soviet Union) at the same time constrained their anti-Russian nationalism *vis-à-vis* their minority populations.

By contrast, in the late 1980s and beginning of the 1990s, EU and other international players paid insufficient attention to developments in the former Yugoslavia, diverted by the overriding priority given to Central Europe and the crisis in the Soviet Union. It was simply taken for granted that Yugoslavia would follow the Central European pattern of peaceful democratization, and the danger of war was not taken seriously. The SFRY was seen as having a head start in transition, because its decentralized 'self-management' model was already quite market-oriented and had for decades been much more open to the West than communist-era Central Europe. Huge numbers of Yugoslavs freely travelled, worked and lived in Western Europe. The

Yugoslav communist authorities placed few restrictions on the publication and dissemination of Western media and culture. The Adriatic coast had been one of the most popular tourist destinations for West Europeans, and Yugoslav trade and economic cooperation with Western Europe was extensive.

But the complacent expectation that Yugoslavia could be left to manage its mounting internal problems by itself was fatefully misplaced. Although the SFRY had stood apart from the two Cold War power blocs in Europe, its survival in fact heavily depended on its position between the blocs. When that division between the blocs began to melt away, SFRY began to implode as Yugoslavia's national-communist leaders no longer felt constrained by their old fears of absorption into the Soviet bloc, and Western interest in the SFRY as an independent, Western-oriented communist regime declined. After 1989, Yugoslavia did not seem to matter any more. Only too late was it realized that the country needed much more, not less attention than before.

Stabilization of the new post-war order of states in the Western Balkans will continue to depend heavily on the EU's commitment to the region. In Central Europe in the 1990s, EU conditionality provided guidance and support to states, which often represented a deep intrusion into their internal domestic affairs by tightly constraining the range of policy choices for decision-makers. In the case of the Western Balkans today, EU involvement is even more far-reaching. The limited capacity of the regions' states to reform and take on the obligations of EU membership means that the EU's role is not just a matter of setting conditions and providing incentives, but helping to *build* the very states themselves so that they will be capable of responding to incentives and complying with conditions. This has worked so far in Macedonia, but the stability and functionality of BH and Kosovo will continue to depend for some time on the international, mainly EU, political supervision backed by military and police missions.

The case of Croatia shows clearly how the tempering of ethnic nationalism to make it compatible with a basic orientation towards European integration depends on first achieving basic security of the territory and its borders. This was achieved in Croatia in 1995, after the forcible dismantling of rebellious secessionist Serbian minority enclaves. For Serbia, however, the borders that it finds itself left with after the collapse of Yugoslavia leave large numbers of Serbs outside in neighbouring countries (chiefly BH, Croatia, Montenegro, and Kosovo) more or less dissatisfied with their lot and looking to Belgrade to support them. The reorientation of Serbian nationalism has begun, but the new Progressive Party President and the next governing coalition are as yet uncertain quantities. It is open to doubt, at least, whether their policies, rhetoric and behaviour will further support Serbia's coming to terms with its responsibilities for the wars of the 1990s, and with the reality of its statehood and borders. A further challenge remains to strengthen the readiness of Serbian communities outside Serbia to come to terms with the states in which they now live, to rebuild trust and reach mutually acceptable terms of coexistence with their fellow-citizens (see Batt, 2006). Here again, the EU's close attention will be demanded – experience shows that such profoundly sensitive and potentially explosive political processes cannot be left to the parties directly involved to manage by themselves, but needs strong external political support.

Breaking with the past: transition in war-torn societies

In the Western Balkans, 'leaving the past behind' and moving on to the new agenda of reform and EU integration is proving more difficult than in Central Europe, and not only due to the lingering problems of nationalism and statehood in the region. Making a clean break with the communist past is also complicated by the fact that the regions' previous communist regimes were to a large extent 'home-grown'. Communism was by no means the first choice of the majority of people, but the Yugoslav and Albanian communist regimes were independent of Soviet control and developed largely in opposition to it. Communism in Central Europe, on the other hand, was overwhelmingly imposed from outside by Soviet force, and so could more readily be rejected as an alien implant. Without Soviet backing, these regimes could not survive, so when the Soviet leader, Mikhail Gorbachev, decided in 1988–89 that Central Europe could 'go its own way', the communist regimes ceded without a fight and the former communist parties rapidly adjusted to the new conditions, re-inventing themselves as 'social democrats'.

The 'home-grown' character of Yugoslav and Albanian communist regimes – to this extent comparable with communism in Russia, Ukraine, Belarus and Romania in the period of Ceausescu's dictatorship – meant that they penetrated, and became much more firmly embedded in, the respective societies, and developed powerful internal mechanisms to sustain their rule. The vested interests attached to these (in the state apparatus, the economy and, crucially, the military and security sectors) have been, correspondingly, much harder to dislodge. One cannot help noticing that the transition from communism in all these countries has been slower, more contested, chaotic and threatened by violence, than was the case in Central Europe. Social resistance to communism was weaker and alternative non-communist elites struggled to emerge. Intellectuals were heavily dependent on the regimes, and both communist and nationalist ideological currents were much more powerful than liberal democratic ideas.

War had a devastating impact on the economies and societies of the region: key professional and managerial elites fled abroad, Western countries imposed visa regimes to stem the tides of emigrants and asylum-seekers, and tourists stayed away. Self-centred, obsessive nationalism led to political introversion and estrangement from the rest of Europe. External economic ties were cut as economies geared up for war, and, in Serbia's case, an international economic embargo was imposed. Recovering from war is not just a matter of making good the damage to property and infrastructure – restoring the material *status quo ante* – but of tackling its deeper impact on patterns of political economy and social psychology.

The transition away from the peculiarly dysfunctional system of Yugoslav self-managed socialism towards a market economy had already begun by the time war erupted, and continued in erratic fits and starts alongside the reorientation of economies to a war footing. In this unpromising context (greatly compounded in Serbia by the impact of Western economic sanctions), economic transition was diverted into very damaging blind alleys. Economic dislocations and shortages vastly inflated the profits of black-marketeers, who turned into local 'warlords' with a vested interest in sustaining ethnic conflict and undermining formal peace agreements still today. Privatization was exploited by powerful individuals with close ties to the ruling elites and to the burgeoning security apparatus. War set the stage for a variety of 'crony capitalism', dominated by narrow self-serving coteries. This went much further than in Central Europe, where corrupt 'insider' privatization was constrained by more robust legal and institutional checks and competition from foreign investors.

The state itself in Western Balkan countries was distorted by the growth in power of the military and security forces during the wars. Corruption reached such dimensions that the state was 'captured' and thoroughly perverted by association with organized crime. The formidable challenges these forces could subsequently pose to new democratic elites seeking to undo the damage were tragically illustrated by the assassination of the pro-Western and reformist Serbian Prime Minister Zoran Djindjic in March 2003, in revenge for the arrest of Milosevic and his transfer to the International Criminal Tribunal for the former Yugoslavia in the Hague, where he was subsequently put on trial for war crimes. The Polish leader Lech Walesa once pithily explained to Western audiences that the transition from socialism back to democratic capitalism would be like trying to turn a fish soup back into a tank of live fish. For many Western Balkan economies, the fish-tank was smashed and the fish just rotted during the war years.

Wholly new spawning grounds are gradually emerging, but so far these are producing only small fry – small-scale private businesses, overwhelmingly in trade and services rather than productive industry. Much of this private sector is unregistered, so provides no revenue for the state. It has no chance of access to domestic capital for development, and provides little additional employment. In the absence of large inflows of foreign investment (deterred by the continued instability of the region), an unprecedented pattern of de-industrialization has taken hold in parts of the region, as large-scale industry collapses, and individual workers turn back to the countryside for survival, supplemented by ad hoc unregistered earnings in the 'grey' economy. More recently, the impact of the global and eurozone crises has only added to the challenges the region faces.

The impact on society has of course been devastating, most of all for the sizeable numbers of refugees and displaced persons whose fate still remains to be settled. There are thus serious questions to be asked about the social capacity to withstand and respond positively in future to the shocks that the restarted economic transition will bring. Polish, and even more so Romanian, workers and consumers had taken a battering in the last years of communism, but exhaustion and frustration in the post-war Balkans run much deeper. Most West Balkans economies are still only at the early stages of economic transition – restructuring and privatization of large public enterprises is only now beginning, yet unemployment levels are already at least 35 per cent, and in some countries may be as high as 60–70 per cent. Balkan societies have shown extraordinary resilience and resourcefulness in coping with the impact of war, but survival has entrenched some informal economic practices – resort to the black market, tax evasion, smuggling, conspicuous consumption instead of reinvesting profits in firms, etc. – that are hardly conducive to rapidly reaping the benefits of democratic and market reform.

The most salient political legacies are profound mistrust of politicians of all hues and systematic evasion of the state. These are quite rational responses where politics is still a dirty business and near-bankrupt states have little to offer citizens. But mass 'internal emigration' undermines the capacity of new democratic elites to build legitimacy, and deprives them of the self-confidence needed to implement the necessary reforms – hence the tendency to revert to ethno-nationalist prejudices in elections, instead of offering a 'vision of the future' that would have to include programmes of painful reform. Societies are fragmented into small informal 'networks' based on personal trust, at the expense of the formation of robust social movements and parties capable of calling leaders to account. 'Civil society', where it exists, is mainly confined to cities and almost wholly dependent on foreign 'democracy-promotion' financial assistance, which may alienate it from wide swathes of 'real' society. Thus would-be democratic elites find it hard to muster the courage – let alone the resources – to present a credible programme of reform to voters struggling in conditions of acute poverty and economic stringency.

This context offers ample opportunities for populist demagogues to keep ethno-nationalism on the boil, which suits the interests of shadowy, criminalized interests whose roots are still in the past. A key part of breaking with the past is bringing those involved in war crimes in the 1990s to justice. Serbia's new democratic Prime Minister Zoran Djindjic took a first bold step in this direction by arresting Slobodan Milosevic and delivering him to the International Criminal Tribunal for the former Yugoslavia (ICTY) in the Hague in 2001. But after Djindjic's assassination in 2003, his successors have either lacked the political courage or the will to continue. Key ICTY-indicted wartime leaders – notably, the Bosnian Serb leaders Radovan Karadjic and General Ratko Mladic – remain at large, sheltered by supporters linked to the old military and security apparatus, financially backed by organized criminal interests. Serbia's unsatisfactory compliance with the ICTY then led to the EU suspending SAA negotiations in 2006, and may also hold up the SAA process in BH, where Republika Srpska is still sheltering war criminals. Cooperation with the ICTY is unpopular and deeply divisive: many people continue to revere these individuals as 'war heroes', while others see them as murderous criminals. Thus both reconciliation among the peoples of the region, and progress towards EU integration are held up, if not completely blocked, as long as the past is allowed to overshadow present needs and reorientation to the future in political life.

Conclusion

To return to our original question: how far are the challenges of transition that the countries of the Western Balkans face today comparable to those surmounted in Central Europe after 1989? In a broad sense, once the war is over, there is much in common – all the states of the region are now democracies, albeit fragile, and committed to EU integration. But they are starting out on this path after a delay of ten years of devastating war that has made the starting point of transition much less favourable in many respects, hence the weakness of the internal drivers of reform. Moreover, some major issues of statehood in the region that were at the heart of the wars of the 1990s are still not fully resolved: the viability of BiH, Kosovo's place in the region and in the wider world, and, last but not least, the reorientation of Serbian nationalism and the reconciliation of the Serbs to the new territorial dispensation in the region. At the same time, the EU, as the key external driver of reform, seems to be less wholeheartedly committed to the Western Balkans than it was to the Central Europeans in the 1990s, as several EU member states have lapsed into a bout of 'enlargement fatigue' since 2004. Yet it is widely recognized that the EU cannot abandon the Western Balkans, which, with the accession of Romania and Bulgaria in January 2007, has become a region wholly surrounded by EU member states. Neither the EU, nor the states of the region, really have much choice but to work together – in their common interests – on the long haul towards the promised land of democratic stability, economic prosperity and EU integration.

Chapter 5

The East Europeans: Ukraine, Belarus and Moldova

Andrew Wilson

'Eastern Europe' is a shrinking concept. The EU has an 'Eastern Partnership' of six states, but Armenia, Georgia and Azerbaijan are normally classed as the 'South Caucasus', leaving a motley crew of three. Ukraine was convulsed by the 'Orange Revolution' in 2004, but the period of 'orange' government from 2005 to 2010 proved a big disappointment. In the next election in 2010 the 'orange' President Viktor Yushchenko lost to none other than Viktor Yanukovych, the man whose supporters had tried to fix the vote in 2004. Despite an image makeover helping him to win a free vote, Yanukovych then moved quickly to dismantle Ukraine's democratic gains and imprison his opponents. In Belarus, Alyaksandr Lukashenka, the 'last dictator in Europe', has been in power since 1994. His re-election in 2001 and 2006 was widely claimed to be rigged and the harsh crackdown on the opposition after the 2010 election led to the EU and USA imposing sanctions, leaving Belarus dependent on Russian subsidy for survival. In Moldova, Vladimir Voronin was President from 2001 to 2009, as head of the only post-Soviet ruling party to still proudly call itself 'Communist'. But in 2009 it lost power to the 'Alliance for European Integration', which has gained high marks from the EU, despite parliamentary gridlock rendering Moldova unable to elect a head of state until 2012. Do three such apparently dissimilar countries therefore really have anything in common? What similar dilemmas do they face?

Background

Ukraine and Belarus, alongside Russia, are East Slavic nations, with all three being descended from the medieval state of (Kievan) Rus'. The Mongol invasions in the thirteenth century divided Rus', but affected Belarus least – which is one possible origin of the name Belarus, or 'white Rus'. Some Belarusian historians claim that subsequent Lithuanian rule over their territory involved only nominal pre-eminence over an extant Slavic culture, even after a union with Poland under the Treaty of Lublin in 1569 that led to most locals adopting the Greek Catholic faith, until this was suppressed by the Tsars in 1839, though many remained loyal to the idea of a multi-ethnic 'Lithuania' (Litva). A powerful 'west-Russian' movement also developed in the nineteenth century amongst the newly dominant Orthodox; while a specifically national Belarusian movement only really began to appear after 1905. Soviet Belarus was initially very small, until territories were redistributed from the Russian Republic in 1924 and 1926 and gained from Poland in the 1940s. Post-war Belarus was an ironic beneficiary of Soviet development policy, after devastation in the Second World War.

Ukraine, on the other hand, developed a vigorous alternative Orthodox culture, independent of Moscow, in the seventeenth century. After the Cossack Rebellion of 1648, a 'Hetmanate' was established in east-central Ukraine, which, despite a loose alliance with Moscow established by the Treaty of Pereyaslav in 1654, survived as a quasi-state until 1785. Moreover, unlike Belarus, almost all of whose modern territory was absorbed by Russia in the late eighteenth century, west Ukraine fell under Habsburg rule in 1772, where a powerful nationalist movement had developed by 1914. Ukraine therefore witnessed rival political convulsions in 1917–20, one in central and one in western Ukraine, while the east and south, where urbanization and industrialization were largely a product of late Tsarist and Soviet rule, either supported the Bolsheviks or Whites, or went their own way. The western territories became part of inter-war Poland, Czechoslovakia and Romania: so, like Belarus, Ukraine was only territorially united as a result of Soviet military power in the 1940s.

Moldova was an independent medieval principality from 1359, at its strongest under Stefan the Great (1457–1504), before becoming an Ottoman vassal in 1538. Eastern Moldova or Bessarabia, the land between the rivers Prut and Dnestr (Nistru in Romanian), was annexed by Russia in 1812. Moldovan territory west of the Prut united with Wallachia as Romania in 1859. Both territories were part of Greater Romania after 1918; but the Soviets established a rival 'Moldavian Autonomous Republic' in 1924 east of the Dnestr as part of Soviet Ukraine. The Moldavian Republic was then expanded to swallow most of Bessarabia in 1945, but, with Romania also in the socialist camp, less emphasis was now placed on the cultural distinctiveness of the region (the theory that the Moldovans were descended from a mixture of Dacians and Slavs, Romanians also from the Vlachs, hence their languages are supposedly different). Nevertheless, the leaders of the Soviet Republic always came from the Dnestr territory rather than Right Bank Moldova proper, or were outsiders, until 1989 (King, 2000).

All three Soviet Republics developed opposition movements in the late Soviet period, but also a mixture of centrifugal and Russophile forces. The Belarusian People's Front was by far the weakest of the three, and could only win 8 per cent of the seats in the 1990 elections. The People's Front of Moldova originally won just over a quarter of the seats, but the previously powerless communist officialdom or *nomenklatura* on the Right Bank joined forces, and flirted with the idea of reunion with Romania, prompting a rebellion in the Left Bank territories now calling themselves 'Transnistria' (King, 2000).

The Ukrainian movement 'Rukh' also won a quarter of the seats, almost all in western and in urban central Ukraine, but the local communist elite was split between 'national communist' and conservative wings. All three states only declared their independence after the abortive hard-line coup in Moscow in August 1991.

Minorities and regions

All three countries are ethnically diverse. Ukraine and Moldova are also marked by strong regional identities (Katchanovski, 2006). Both states have therefore found it hard to build strong governments with coherent reform programmes, though in the Moldovan case this is because of divisions between voters on the Right Bank, as much between the two banks of the Nistru – the 'Transnistrian' region established its *de facto* autonomy after a brief but bloody war in 1992. The 152,000 Gagauz (ethnically Turkish, Orthodox in religion) in the south have also claimed self-determination – rather more peaceably – and Gagauz Yeri has been a 'national-territorial autonomous unit' since 1995. According to the 2004 census, boycotted in Transnistria (where the population is supposedly 32.1 per cent Moldovan, 30.3 per cent Russian and 28.8 per cent Ukrainian), Moldovans make up 75.8 per cent of the population. Ukrainians are the largest minority with 8.4 per cent, Russians 5.9 per cent, Gagauz 4.4 per cent and Romanians 2.2 per cent. The Transnistrian problem is therefore more regional than ethnic. Almost as many Russians (108,000) live in the Moldovan capital Chisinau as in Transnistria. As a further complication, many Moldovans are Russian-speaking. In Right Bank Moldova, Communist support is stronger in rural areas and in the north and amongst the Gagauz, the Alliance for European Integration in the centre and south-west.

The Transnistria problem is supposed to be resolved by the '5+2' group (Transnistria, Moldova, Ukraine, Russia and the OSCE, plus the US and EU as observers); but Russia proposed an alternative 'Kozak Memorandum' in 2003 that would have turned Moldova into a federal, arguably even confederal, state, with Transnistria, which only has 12 per cent of the population of Moldova as a whole, having equal veto powers over state policy. Chisinau therefore endorsed a rival plan drawn up by Ukraine's President Yushchenko in 2005, which argued that the 'three Ds' – democratization, demilitarization and decriminalization – should precede federalization in the region. After years of rampant smuggling, an EU Border Assistance Mission (EUBAM) was set up in 2005 to try and impose a proper customs regime. Russia meanwhile preferred to pressurize Chisinau, imposing punitive trade barriers on Moldovan wine.

The authorities in Transnistria held an unrecognized referendum in September 2006, when 97 per cent backed independence and the option of eventual union with Russia, and 95 per cent rejected the alternative of reunification with Moldova. The long-serving self-styled 'President' Igor Smirnov was surprisingly ousted in elections in December 2011, but his successor Yevgeniy Shevchuk continued to base his policies on the 'mandate' of 2006.

Ukraine is a resolutely unitary state, with the exception since 1991 of the Republic of Crimea. Ukraine's historic ethnic minorities (Poles, Jews and Germans) had all shrunk to less than 1 per cent by 2001, although around 250,000 Crimean Tatars have returned from forced exile in 1944, mainly since 1989. The Russian population stood at 17.3 per cent in 2001, down from 22.1 per cent in 1989, and the Ukrainian majority at 77.8 per cent. Linguistically, however, Ukraine is more equally divided between Ukrainian-speakers and Russian-speakers, although language competences and preferences overlap.

Regional differences, however, are more profound than ethnic ones. In elections in the 1990s, the most salient divide was between the west and the rest, with the nationalist former Habsburg territories in a distinct minority, although in the highly polarized 1994 election the divide was on the river Dnipro. Voters in the west and some in central Ukraine (45 per cent of the total) bought the argument that independence should trump economic difficulties; further to the east (52 per cent) they considered salvation lay in restoring ties with Russia. New President Kuchma's highly eclectic approach to the national question bought stability for a time, while the opposition under Viktor Yushchenko de-emphasized cultural nationalism and consolidated their appeal in central Ukraine.

In elections since 2004, the main divide has mirrored the border of the old Polish Commonwealth, between the historical west Ukrainian and Cossack heartland and the Russian-speaking territories of the south and east that were largely developed under late Tsarist and Soviet rule. The 'orange' forces won the 2004 election decisively, and were given a second and third chances by voters in 2006 and 2007 (see below), but lost in 2010.

The most acute region of conflict remains Crimea. Ukraine's worst moment was in 1994, when local elections brought pro-Russian forces to power. Boris Yeltsin had just prevailed over his nationalist-communist opponents in the October 1993 crisis, however, and refused the Crimeans an audience. Russia was then distracted by the Chechen War beginning in December 1994, allowing Kiev to reduce Crimea's autonomy. Local politicians remain a law onto themselves and the peninsula is highly corrupt. The Crimean Tatars have yet to be integrated into local society.

In theory, Belarus is more united, ethnically, linguistically and regionally. The 2009 census reported 83.7 per cent of the population were Belarusians; the main minorities are Russians (8.3 per cent), Poles (3.1 per cent) and Ukrainians (1.7 per cent). Just over half (53 per cent) of the total population claimed Belarusian as their native language, and 23 per cent claimed to use it at home. Regionally, there is gradation rather than division: Lukashenka's support has always been lower in the north-west and in the capital Minsk. In practice, however, all the above figures mask a consensus assigning low status to Belarusian culture, and a dominant model of nested national identity, where Belarusian identity is assumed compatible with what President Lukashenka bizarrely but accurately terms 'Soviet-Orthodox' identity. His foreign policy trajectory since 1996 – closer to but not uniting with Russia – reflects the preferences of most Belarusians. On the whole, however, identity politics are less prominent in Belarus, which has given Lukashenka more freedom of manoeuvre.

Political systems

Both Belarus and Moldova adopted their constitutions in 1994; Ukraine was the last post-Soviet state to do so, in 1996. Moldova, however, changed tack to become a parliamentary republic in 2000. Belarus adopted key amendments to change state symbols in 1995; and a coup-by-referendum in 1996 established a much more presidential regime, which was further strengthened after a third referendum abolished presidential term limits in 2004. In Ukraine a package of constitutional reform negotiated at the height of the Orange Revolution in December 2004 temporarily turned Ukraine into a parliamentary-presidential republic after 2006, before President Yanukovych strong-armed the Constitutional Court into reversing the changes in October 2010. The authorities also restored the mixed election system for the parliamentary elections in 2012, bringing back majoritarian con-stituencies where the government's 'administrative resources' would be decisive. The barrier for representation was raised to 5 per cent.

All three states have suffered from over-mighty presidents abusing their powers: as with Lukashenka after 1996, Kuchma in his second term and Yanukovych since 2010 in Ukraine, and Moldovan presidents Lucinschi in 2000 and Voronin after 2005. Politics in Moldova has been more 'balanced' since 2000, but the key provision that 61 out of 101 MPs are needed to elect a president proved difficult to meet after 2009. Ukraine's new system after 2006 helped diffuse power but also promoted gridlock, and the country has swung back strongly in an authoritarian direction since 2010.

Economy

All three states suffered severe depression and inflation in the 1990s. Belarus's post-Soviet output collapse was shorter and shallower, with positive growth returning in 1996. Ukraine and Moldova only resumed GDP growth in 2000.

Belarus claims its relative success is based on a unique 'Belarusian model' that has maintained state ownership and subsidy, restored trade interdependency with Russia and prevented the emergence of 'oli-garchs' by avoiding corrupt privatizations. But Belarus has also free-ridden on Russian assistance, especially cheap energy and trade credits, equivalent to a claimed 30 per cent of GDP, and on unusually high investment levels in the late Soviet period. Recovery was particularly impressive in Lukashenka's second and third terms (2001–10), with average GDP growth topping 7 per cent per annum (on official figures), and the average monthly wage rising from $70 to $500. However, Russia signalled a much tougher stance immediately after Lukashenka's re-election in 2006 (see below). By 2011 it was clear the Belarusian 'model' was only sustainable with Russian support, as the balance of payments deficit approached 15 per cent of GDP and annual inflation topped 100 per cent.

Ukraine failed to begin proper economic reform in the early 1990s. Complete economic collapse was averted when new President Kuchma launched an emergency stabilization plan in October 1994, but Ukraine then drifted into an unhealthy equilibrium of partial reform, 'state capture' by oligarchs and increasing corruption. As Prime Minister in 1999–2001, Yushchenko cleaned up corruption in the energy sector and kick-started economic growth, but Ukraine's powerful oligarchs were able to force his ouster in April 2001. GDP growth accelerated over the following three years, reaching a heady 12 per cent in 2004, but largely thanks to over-performing export sectors, especially in chemicals and steel – hence the severity of the downturn in 2009, with GDP falling by 15 per cent. The Ukrainian economy remained dominated by oligarchs, who endorsed the turn to Russia for support in 2010, but many of whom depend on open markets. The EU became Ukraine's biggest trading partner with the addition of the new members in 2004, but still only has around a quarter of Ukraine's total trade. Russia is still Ukraine's largest single state market, and the temptation to join the Single Economic Space first proposed in 2003 has been great. Russian economic pressure since the Orange Revolution has reinforced fears of dependence, even after a temporary cut in the gas price in 2010.

Moldova's equivalent of the Yushchenko government was the short-lived administration headed by Ion Sturza in 1999, which at least moved the issue of market reforms on to the agenda, but at a time when the region was badly hit by domino currency crises. Due to its lack of natural resources, Moldova has plenty of criminals but no real oligarchs, although President Voronin's son Oleg, head of FinComBank, is one of the country's most prominent businessmen. Transnistria is notoriously a transit territory for drugs, armaments and people smuggling – in both directions, as 're-export' to Ukraine avoids customs duties.

Moldova is the poorest of the three countries, with remittances from nationals working abroad making up almost 30 per cent of GNP, and agriculture remains strong. The biggest source of corruption is control of trade and money flows. The new Alliance for European Integration government oversaw economy recovery after 2009, but has also parcelled out the local economy among its constituent parties.

Foreign policy

All three states have had a 'pendular' foreign policy since 1991. All fall within the European Neighbourhood Policy since 2004, and the Eastern Partnership since 2009, rather than the zone of likely EU expansion. In all three, residual Russian influence is still strong. Nominally 'multi-vectoral' foreign policy sometimes swings closer to Russia, sometimes to the West. Belarus reoriented most decisively with the election of Lukashenka as President in 1994, but Russia has grown increasingly weary of his demand for subsidies. Moldova temporarily swung westward under Voronin after 2003, and more permanently with the Alliance for European Integration after 2009. Ukraine has been most inconsistent; even the Orange Revolution failed to establish a more single-minded pro-European approach.

The 'Community of Russia and Belarus' was established in 1996, and upgraded first to the 'Union of Russia and Belarus' in 1997–98 and then the 'United State of Russia and Belarus' in 1999. The last treaty, as yet unimplemented, envisages joint political institutions, a common currency and citizenship, and a common defence and foreign policy. However, to most politicians on both sides it mainly serves a declaratory purpose. Equal union between two states so unequal in size is a non-starter; Putin has disingenuously proposed that Belarus' six regions should simply be added to the Russian Federation's 83 administrative units. Lukashenka's personal relations with Putin are not as good as those he enjoyed with Yeltsin, and Russia under Putin has pursued its economic interests more aggressively. After supporting Lukashenka again in the 2006 election, the Kremlin was less willing to forgive the promises made to open up to Russian business that Lukashenka made, and broke, in 2001. Gazprom finally won control of BelTransGaz, which controls the main pipeline network across Belarusian territory to Central Europe, in 2011, but other targets remain elusive. Relations with the EU have remained frozen at the pre-PCA (Partnership and Cooperation Agreement) stage since the political crisis of 1996. The USA has taken a more aggressively anti-Lukashenka approach, with Congress passing the Belarus Democracy Act in 2004.

In Moldova, the issue of independence was decisively settled by the referendum in March 1994, when 95.4 per cent rejected union with Romania. The Transnistrian problem has acted as a brake on any putative Western orientation, however. Moldova was the first former Soviet state admitted to the Council of Europe, in 1995, but it also signed the CIS Customs Union in 1994. Voronin skilfully played the Soviet nostalgia card at the 2001 elections, but his prioritization of domestic problems was apparent after his rejection of the Kozak Memorandum in 2003. The Alliance for European Integration has proved the 'star pupil' of the Eastern Partnership, leap-frogging Ukraine in terms of visa liberalization.

Ukraine's explicitly 'multi-vectored' foreign policy was most successful in the mid-1990s. The de-nuclearization agreement signed with Russia and the USA in January 1994 removed Soviet nuclear weapons stationed on Ukrainian territory, and helped Ukraine temporarily become the third largest recipient of US aid, with $228 million in 1996. Ukraine signed a Charter on Distinctive Partnership with NATO in 1997 and a Partnership and Cooperation Agreement with the EU in

1994, which came into operation in 1998. Russia recognized Ukraine's independence and borders in a Treaty on Friendship, Cooperation and Partnership in 1997. Agreement on joint ownership of the Soviet Black Sea Fleet and basing the Russian share in Crimea was also reached in 1997, and in 2010 controversially renewed until 2042.

The Gongadze affair, however, (see below) left Ukraine cold-shouldered by the West and more dependent on Russia. A window of opportunity to improve relations after the Orange Revolution was missed by the time the EU's constitution was rejected by French and Dutch voters in May–June 2005, with a new Action Plan signed at the height of post-Orange euphoria in February 2005 little different from the document negotiated under Kuchma. The orange period did at least produce the beginnings of negotiations on a new Association Agreement in 2008, concluded in 2011, but not ratified due to Yanukovych's persecution of the opposition.

Recent political developments in Ukraine: early steps

Ukraine's first President Leonid Kravchuk (1991–94) led the 'national communist' group that had embraced the idea of sovereignty in 1990 and, belatedly, independence in 1991, but his term was beset by economic difficulties. His successor Leonid Kuchma at least achieved a semblance of economic order on taking office, and a new currency and constitution by 1996. But his second term (1999–2005) was marked by political drift, a reversion to semi-authoritarianism and corruption at the highest levels. Former Prime Minister Pavlo Lazarenko (1996–97) fled the country in 1999, accused of embezzling at least $114 million. Other 'oligarchs' became super-rich on the back of corrupt privatizations and rake-offs from energy deals.

Kuchma's second term was also notorious for the murder of the editor of a campaigning internet site, Hryhoriy Gongadze, whose headless body was discovered in a forest outside the capital Kyiv in November 2000. Secret tapes were released on which Kuchma was heard ordering Gongadze's beating or kidnapping – if not apparently his actual murder. The protest campaign to force Kuchma's removal was initially unsuccessful in 2000–01, but it empowered a new opposition. A sort of 'pluralism by default' (Way, 2006) has existed in Ukraine since 1991 due to its weaker state, divided elites and stronger regional identities, at least in comparison to Russia. Paradoxically, a reform government was attempting to clean up the economy at the same time as the Gongadze affair, and its leaders, Viktor Yushchenko, Prime Minister until April 2001, and his deputy Yuliya Tymoshenko were the main beneficiaries of the protest vote at the parliamentary elections in March 2002.

The Orange Revolution

The authorities toyed with various options in the run-up to the next presidential election in 2004. In December 2003, the Constitutional Court was persuaded to rule that Kuchma could stand for a third term, but he was too unpopular. In April 2004, the authorities tried to change the constitution, so that any incoming president would have much less power. The attempt fell only six votes short of the two-thirds majority required, with 294 rather than 300 votes out of 450. Option three for the regime was to impose a single candidate on its disunited supporters – Prime Minister Viktor Yanukovych, who represented the strongest regional clan from Donetsk. However, Yanukovych also represented the region's considerable financial resources and often thuggish political culture, which alienated many in the ruling elite.

Yanukovych also won the backing of Russia, which endorsed a populist campaign: a doubling of pensions, promises to upgrade the status of the Russian language and attacks on the USA and NATO, all designed to appeal to voters in east Ukraine. The Yanukovych campaign also used 'political technology', particularly the covert sponsorship of extreme nationalists to campaign in unwanted support of Yushchenko. The opposition was harassed, and most notoriously, in September 2004 Yushchenko was poisoned at a secret meeting with the heads of the Ukrainian Security Service.

The authorities expected one or more tactics to deliver a knockout blow, but had not reckoned with the growth in opposition sentiment and civic organization since 2000. Their attempts to divide the opposition were also unsuccessful: even the highly ambitious Tymoshenko stood aside to back Yushchenko. The Socialists also joined his coalition after the first round of voting in October, although at the price of forcing Yushchenko to commit to their pet project of constitutional reform. The centrist leader of the Industrialists' Party, Anatoliy Kinakh, also backed Yushchenko. The Communists, both the 'official' party led by Petro Symonenko and the more radical version backed by the Party of Regions and led by Oleksandr Yakovenko, backed Yanukovych, as did another left-wing firebrand paid to demonize Yushchenko, Nataliya Vitrenko.

The authorities had expected to win with minimal fraud in round one, but, despite manipulation of the vote count for ten days, Yushchenko still ended up officially ahead. They therefore resorted to fraud that was exceptionally crude, even by Ukrainian standards, in the second round three weeks later, when over a million extra votes were added to the count overnight, mainly in Donetsk, where turnout supposedly soared from 78 to 97 per cent. The corrupted Election Commission attempted to declare that Yanukovych had won by 49.5 to 46.6 per cent. However, a massive exit poll, with 15,000 interviewees, indicated that Yushchenko had won by 53.7 to 43.3 per cent (see Table 5.1).

But even the opposition did not expect the torrent of protest unleashed by the fraud, with over 100,000 on the streets of Kyiv by the end of the first day and over 500,000 by day three. Repressive measures were apparently not considered until a week into the protests, but many of the oligarchs were already hedging their bets, so the divided regime was soon tempted to compromise. More surprisingly in retrospect, so was the opposition. Tymoshenko urged more radical measures, like the occupation of government buildings, but others were mindful of the mistakes made during the failed protest campaign of 2000–01: so the crowds both stayed put and stayed peaceful.

A compromise package adopted by parliament on 8 December opened the way to a repeat election on 26 December, but only in return for constitutional reforms, similar to those that had failed in April, that shifted power to the oligarch-dominated parliament after a year's delay in January 2006. A Kuchma loyalist, Svyatoslav Piskun, was reappointed as Chief Prosecutor on 9 December, amid rumours that a private deal had been reached guaranteeing the ruling elite safety from prosecutions.

Table 5.1 *Ukrainian presidential election, 2004 (percentages)*

Candidate	First round, 31 October 2004	Second round, 29 November 2004	Third round, 26 December 2004
Viktor Yushchenko	39.9	46.6	51.2
Viktor Yanokovych	39.3	49.5	44.2
Oleksandr Moroz	5.8		
Petro Symonenko	5.0		
Nataliya Vitrenko	1.5		
Anatoliy Kinakh	0.9		
Oleksandr Yakovenko	0.8		
Others	1.7		
Against all	2.0	2.3	2.3
Invalid votes	3.0	1.6	1.5

The aftermath

The 'third round' vote was remarkably similar to pollsters' estimate of the real vote in the second round, with Yushchenko beating Yanukovych by 51.2 to 44.2 per cent. Tymoshenko became Prime Minister, but Yushchenko sought to balance her power by installing one of his business allies, Petro Poroshenko, as head of an expanded National Security Council. The two were soon at loggerheads, as Poroshenko represented the Our Ukraine financiers who now expected a payback from the new government. Arguments also raged over Tymoshenko's populist economic policy, including misguided attempts to control the prices of meat and energy and right some of the wrongs of the Kuchma era by 'reprivatization' – meaning first the nationalization and then the resale of industries that had been corruptly privatized. As the list was open-ended, business confidence and domestic investment collapsed, although in the end only one reprivatization was conducted, that of the Kryvorizhstal steel mill, sold to two of Ukraine's biggest oligarchs (Viktor Pinchuk, close to Kuchma, and Rinat Akhmetov, close to Yanukovych) for $800 million in 2004, but now reaching a price of $4.8 billion from Mittal Steel.

Each side accused the other of corruption. Poroshenko was said to be running a shadow government to pursue his business interests, and Tymoshenko to be skewing the reprivatization process to favour 'her' oligarchs. Most damagingly, circles close to Yushchenko were accused of maintaining and profiting from the corrupt RosUkrEnergo scheme, set up by Ukrainian and Russian oligarchs in 2004 to siphon off profits from the gas trade.

In September 2005, Yushchenko took the radical step of sacking all those involved, Tymoshenko included. However, his first attempt to appoint a more 'business-friendly' government headed by the centrist Yuriy Yekhanurov on 20 September fell three votes short. Yushchenko then signed a hugely controversial 'memorandum' with none other than Viktor Yanukovych to secure the extra votes, declaring 'the impermissibility of political repressions against the opposition', in other words making public the immunity promise for the old regime. The memorandum even included an amnesty for election fraud. Yekhanurov won 289 votes at the second attempt, but Tymoshenko now moved into vocal opposition.

The fragile unity of the new arrangement was broken in January 2006. Russia temporarily reduced gas supplies to Ukraine to undermine the orange government, but just as European consumers downstream were complaining loudly enough to force Moscow to back down, Ukraine signed a curious deal which both accepted higher prices and increased the role of RosUkrEnergo. The Yekhanurov government was formally censured but limped on. Disillusioned orange voters switched to the Tymoshenko camp.

The 2006 elections

The parliamentary elections in March 2006 were doubly important because the constitutional changes that took effect in January transferred so many powers to parliament. They would also be the first elections to be decided wholly on the basis of proportional representation and with the new 'imperative mandate' rule (deputies would lose their mandate if they left the party they were elected to serve). Parliament would now sit for five years rather than four; dissolution would only be possible if it failed to fulfil its functions, for example by failing to assemble. The elected party groups would form a formal 'majority', which would now select the Prime Minister and government, though the President still directly appointed the ministers of defence and foreign affairs and the heads of the National Bank and Security Service. Balance and stability were the aims of the reforms, but in the long run they exacerbated the problem of a divided executive and transferred the political gridlock in parliament into the other institutions of state.

The political crisis since September 2005 allowed Yanukovych's Party of the Regions to make a strong comeback. However, voters in central and western Ukraine were prepared to give the orange parties a second chance. Yushchenko's Our Ukraine came a poor third, but Tymoshenko's surprisingly strong second place meant that a new orange coalition was likely, as together Tymoshenko's Block, Our Ukraine and the Socialists held 243 out of 450 seats (see Table 5.2).

Nevertheless, negotiations dragged on for over three months. Our Ukraine's business wing was reluctant to see the return of Tymoshenko

Table 5.2   *Ukrainian parliamentary election, 2006*

Party	Vote (%)	Seats
Party of the Regions	32.1	186
Tymoshenko Block	22.3	129
Our Ukraine	13.9	81
Socialists	5.7	33
Communists	3.7	21

Note: 3 per cent was the barrier for representation.

as Prime Minister, and began to contemplate a shock deal with Regions instead, despite the message from their voters. Yushchenko's insistence on pushing Poroshenko as Chair of Parliament provoked a crisis in July, when the Socialists sensationally defected to form an alternative 'anti-crisis coalition' with Regions and the Communists instead. Socialist leader Oleksandr Moroz would be Chair of Parliament, but Yanukovych would be Prime Minister. Hopelessly outmanoeuvred, Yushchenko's only crumbs of comfort were the 'Universal of National Unity' signed in August, which nominally committed the new government to maintaining Ukraine's post-2004 course towards democracy and European integration, and the six Our Ukraine ministers who temporarily joined the new coalition, although only 30 out of 81 of its deputies could bear to vote for Yanukovych.

The 2007 crisis

The fig leaves were soon discarded. Finance Minister Mykola Azarov abused tax powers to reward business supporters and punish opponents. The Our Ukraine ministers were forced out within months. Yanukovych then turned on Yushchenko with a relentless campaign to usurp presidential power, questioning his rights over decrees and the appointment of local governors, and even encroaching on the 'reserved' foreign policy sphere. Yushchenko appointed the equally thuggish Viktor Baloha in a misguided attempt to fight fire with fire from an alternative centre of power in his Presidential Administration.

But Yanukovych overstepped the mark with a brazen campaign of bribery and intimidation to try and build a constitutional majority in parliament. The defection of eleven deputies in April 2007 allowed Yushchenko to claim a clear breach of the 'imperative mandate' and issue a decree to dissolve parliament. As he lacked the power to do so, both sides were now in clear breach of the constitution; but both sides also corrupted the Constitutional Court, which proved unable to adjudicate. Various judges and the Chief Prosecutor were fired, the Tymoshenko Block withdrew from parliament to render it inquorate, and troops moved on government buildings. The final compromise on early elections in September was only reached because of Yushchenko's private reassurance that Our Ukraine would form a coalition with Regions.

But that was not how it turned out. Voters gave the orange parties a third chance, Tymoshenko's Block surged ahead and the Socialists failed to cross the 3 per cent barrier. Yushchenko was forced to accept the return of Tymoshenko as Prime Minister in December 2007, though she controversially chose to pad her majority via an alliance

Table 5.3   *Ukrainian parliamentary elections, 2007*

Party	Vote (%)	Seats
Party of the Regions	34.3	175
Tymoshenko Block	30.7	156
Our Ukraine – People's Self-Defence	14.1	72
Communists	5.4	27
Lytvyn Block	4.0	20

with the small party led by former parliamentary chair Volodymyr Lytvyn, a motley collection of old Kuchma loyalists. Lytvyn got his old job back (see Table 5.3).

Tymoshenko's second premiership was dogged by more bitter personal struggle with Yushchenko, who increasingly sought to balance her with Regions' support. Yet another set of new elections were narrowly avoided in autumn 2008. Arguably, however, Tymoshenko held on too long as PM, as her popularity was severely dented when the global economic crisis led to Ukrainian GDP shrinking by a massive 15 per cent in 2009 (the second economic downturn while she was Prime Minister). Yet another gas crisis in January 2009 resulted in an even longer seventeen day cut-off of supply. Tymoshenko conceded a move to market prices, but managed to squeeze RosUkrEnergo out of the market. The IMF helped the economy survive, but Tymoshenko ruptured relations in late 2009 by refusing to raise domestic gas prices.

Bitter divisions also emerged over a hasty application to join NATO made in January 2008 and whether to support Georgia in its war with Russia in August 2008 – which promptly scuppered Ukraine's NATO bid. Tymoshenko's main achievement was joining the WTO in February 2008.

Incumbency was therefore a problem for both Yushchenko and Tymoshenko at the next elections in 2010. Yushchenko could only manage a humiliating 5.5 per cent, but urged his diehard supporters not to vote for Tymoshenko; who also suffered from low turnout in west and central Ukraine and a massive 4.4 per cent vote 'against all' in the second round. Two fresh faces, former Foreign Minister Arseniy Yatseniuk and Serhiy Tihipko, Yanukovych's campaign manager from 2004 and now an independent banker, also polled well, particularly among the nascent middle classes; Tihipko at least would ultimately throw in his lot with Yanukovych, along with most of the oligarchs. But Yanukovych's vote held steady enough to win by default. Incredibly, the man who had tried to fix the election in 2004 was now

Table 5.4   *The Ukrainian presidential election, 2010 (percentages)*

Candidate	First round	Second round
Viktor Yanokovych	35.3	48.95
Yuliya Tymoshenko	25.0	45.50
Serhiy Tihipko	13.0	
Arseniy Yatseniuk	7.0	
Viktor Yushchenko	5.5	
Petro Symonenko	3.5	
Volodymyr Lytvyn	2.3	
Oleh Tyahnybok	1.4	
Anatoliy Hrytsenko	1.2	

president – and vehemently denied any wrongdoing in 2004 (see Table 5.4).

Yanukovych as President

Yanukovych had hired expensive US consultants and campaigned as a changed man, but did not govern as one. Tymoshenko's tragedy was that she was unable to convince voters that Yanukovych posed a threat to democracy, but so it proved. The 'imperative mandate' was ignored once again, as was the principle that only parties can make up the formal Rada 'majority' that elects the Prime Minister, not individual deputies, in order to replace Tymoshenko as Prime Minister with Azarov in March 2010. In June, a highly centralizing judicial reform was passed. In September, the Constitutional Court was purged, leading to its controversial verdict in October completely reversing all the constitutional changes adopted in 2006. The media and security services were increasingly politicized. Corruption accelerated. In January 2011, Freedom House downgraded Ukraine to only 'partly free', even before the government began a series of prosecutions of its opponents, including former Interior Minister Yuriy Lutsenko and Tymoshenko herself, who in October 2011 was sentenced to seven years in prison for supposed 'abuse of office' in signing the January 2009 gas deal.

Yanukovych engineered a rapprochement with Russia, and formally abandoned the goal of NATO membership; but even with Russia, Ukraine was truculently independent. The Tymoshenko trial scuppered an Association Agreement with the EU, but the government only upped the ante, announcing more charges against her in 2012. Yanukovych seemed bent on aggrandizing his personal power, with a series of appointments of literal and metaphorical 'family' members in the winter of 2011–12 suggesting he sought to become an oligarch in his own right.

Politics in Belarus

From 1991 to 1993, Belarus was run by former Communists who had made their peace with the opposition Popular Front; but the Popular Front was not strong enough to provide the *nomenklatura* with a cover story to justify their retention of power. The introduction of a presidential system in 1994 therefore opened the door to the populist Alyaksandr Lukashenka, whose attacks on both *nomenklatura* corruption and 'nationalists' struck a chord with voters. Zyanon Paznyak won 12.9 per cent for the Popular Front; but the elite split between the more Russophile Prime Minister Vyacheslav Kebich, with 17.3 per cent, and 9.9 per cent for the more national communist Stanislaw Shushkevich, whom Kebich had forced out as Chair of Parliament. Lukashenka won 44.8 per cent, and triumphed over Kebich in the second round with 80.1 to 19.9 per cent.

Lukashenka quickly moved to consolidate his power. In May 1995 he called a referendum to restore Soviet symbols and establish 'equal status' for the Russian language with the Belarusian. Elections for a new parliament in 1995 went less well for Lukashenka. The Popular Front was wiped out, but 28 seats out of 198 went to centrist parties, and 95 were independent, with 42 for the Communists and 33 for the Agrarians, Lukashenka's rivals as Russophile populists. A bitter struggle between president and parliament ensued, until a second allegedly fixed referendum in November 1996. Seven questions in all tested both parliament's and the president's plans for a new constitution; but Lukashenka used the 70.5 per cent approval for his constitution on question two (turnout was supposedly 84 per cent) to ignore the rival proposals, circumvent a negotiated solution and replaced parliament with a docile 'Palace of Representatives', to which he shifted loyalist MPs. He then declared a new republic, and started his five-year term again from scratch.

Opposition to Lukashenka was demoralized and divided. Some chose exile or boycott. In 1999–2000, several prominent opponents of the regime 'disappeared', presumed dead. Attempts to hold a presidential election on schedule in 1999 were frustrated. Only 'official' parties, most notably new pro-Lukashenka versions of the Communists and

Agrarians, and a Belarusian version of Vladimir Zhirinovsky's 'Liberal Democrats', were allowed into the new Palace of Representatives elected in 2000, 2004 and 2008.

In 2001 Lukashenka stage-managed his re-election with 75.7 per cent against 15.7 per cent for Uladzimir Hancharyk, a trade union leader, the 'united candidate' of the remaining opposition, and 2.5 per cent for Syarhei Haydukevich, leader of the loyalist Liberal-Democratic Party. In his second term (2001–06), Lukashenka moved towards a stricter authoritarianism, particularly after Ukraine's Orange Revolution in 2004 (Silitski, 2005). In October 2004, he orchestrated another referendum allowing him to stand for more than two successive terms.

The 2006 election then became something of a test-case in 'counter-revolutionary technology'. The opposition was kept off elections committees, foreign observation was kept to a minimum, and real exit polls were replaced by fake polls that echoed the official result. The mainstream opposition again chose a 'united candidate', Alyaksandr Milinkevich, a quiet technocrat; but Alyaksandr Kazulin also stood for the Social Democratic Party, and was backed by exiled businessmen. Haydukevich stood again, his real function being to demonize Lukashenka's opponents as a supposed 'neutral'. After four days of unsupervised early voting (31.3 per cent of the vote) leading to a supposed turnout of 92.6 per cent, Lukashenka claimed 82.6 per cent support (see Table 5.5). After six days of protests, the authorities violently dispersed a final demonstration on 25 March, with scores arrested, including even Kazulin (Marples, 2006).

Lukashenka's third term was marked by declining Russian support, internal elite conflict and growing economic problems. Lukashenka announced some minimal reforms and was able to win support from the IMF when the global economic crisis hit in 2008 – just enough to keep the economy above water until he ended the programme in April 2010, once the IMF began to demand real reforms. But that was enough to carry the economy through to the election in December 2010 (see Table 5.6). After an initial Potemkin 'liberalization' allowing a pro-

Table 5.5   *Belarusian presidential election, 2006*

Candidate	Vote (%)
Alyaksandr Lukashenka	82.6
Alyaksandr Milinkevich	6.0
Syarhei Haydukevich	3.5
Alyaksandr Kazulin	2.3

Table 5.6 *Belarusian presidential election, 2010*

Candidate	Vote (%)
Alyaksandr Lukashenka	79.7
Andrei Sannikaw	2.6
Yaroslaw Ramanchuk (United Civic Party)	2.0
Ryhar Kastusiow (Party Popular Front)	2.0
Uladzimir Niakliaew (Tell the Truth!)	1.8
Vital Rymashewski (Christian Democrats)	1.1
Viktar Tsiareshchanka	1.1
Mikalai Statkevich (Social Democrats)	1.0
Ales Mikhalevich	1.0
Dzmitry Us	0.5
Against all	6.5
Turnout	90.7

liferation of opposition candidates, including new largely Russian-speaking movements like Tell the Truth!, the regime cracked down harshly, making 700 arrests, including seven of Lukashenka's opponents. Sannikaw and Niakliaew were particularly badly treated, with Niakliaew beaten on arrest and Sannikaw allegedly tortured in prison.

The EU and USA agreed sanctions in January 2011, which were then progressively expanded, leading to a major row and the withdrawal of all EU ambassadors in February 2012 (the US has had no ambassador in post since 2008). Belarus was left with only Russia for an ally, but the price looked likely to be high with the economy under severe strain as three devaluations of the Belarusian rouble in 2011 halved living standards. Russia agreed to a short-term bailout in November 2011, but took over full control of BelTransGaz and had a long list of other assets to buy.

Politics in Moldova

Until the Communists took power in 2001, Moldovan politics was characterized by extreme instability. The pan-Romanian Popular Front took power in 1990, followed by the *nomenklatura*-dominated Agrarian-Democratic Party in 1994 and the three-party 'Alliance of

Democracy and Reform' in 1998. However, none of the three saw out a full four-year term, suffering various splits and recombinations instead. Moldova's first two presidents also had unstable single terms: Mircea Snegur (1991–06) abandoned his original allies in the Popular Front, and Petru Lucinschi (1996–2001) was initially more pro-Russian, but foundered when he attempted to fix the constitution and increase his powers as President. All governments have been beset by the *de facto* secession of Transnistria, which has become a hotbed of corruption (Lynch, 2003).

Moldova became a parliamentary republic in 2000, but the parliament originally elected in 1998 was unable to choose a president. Lucinschi miscalculated by calling early elections in February 2001, at which the Communist Party of the Republic of Moldova (PCRM), led by Vladimir Voronin, triumphed with 50.1 per cent and 71 out of 101 seats. Voronin proved pragmatic in office (March, 2005), continuing with privatization in some areas, notably wine and tobacco, home to some of his more commercially minded supporters. Initially, Voronin also tried to appease Russophile voters, but proposals to make Russian the second state language and the introduction of more 'Moldovan' (rather than pro-Romanian) history text books provoked demonstrations in 2002, and Voronin accepted a Council of Europe compromise that placed a moratorium on the first proposal.   A serious break with Moscow came with Voronin's rejection of the Kozak Memorandum in 2003, and his flirtation with a pro-European course thereafter.

Relations with Moscow were back on track by 2007, but at the time of the 2005 elections, with Voronin also trying to co-opt some of the energy from Ukraine's Orange Revolution, Russia tried to clip his wings by supporting a pincer movement involving the far left and the motley centrists regrouped in Democratic Moldova. But the PCRM still won 46 per cent and 56 seats, and Voronin was again elected President after Democratic Moldova quickly collapsed into its constituent parts: Our Moldova with 22 seats, the Democratic Party with eight and the Social-Liberal Party with four (March, 2005; March and Herd, 2006).

The PCRM co-opted the Christian Democrats into a type of loyal opposition, allowing them control of EU TV. Voronin's second term saw an increase in corruption and increasingly heavy-handed rule. His son Oleg developed a close relationship with nascent business groups. Rivals were harassed, including the imprisonment of former Defence Minister Valeriu Passat in 2005–07, the brief arrest of Social Democratic Party leader Eduard Musuc in 2006 and the attempt to take over Pro TV in 2008. But Moldova remained pluralistic: there was no single asset or company, control of which allowed politicians to

Table 5.7 *Moldovan parliamentary elections, April 2009*

Party	Vote (%)	Seats
PCRM	49.5	60 (+4)
Liberal Party	13.1	15 (+15)
Liberal Democrats	12.4	15 (+15)
Our Moldova	9.8	11 (−11)

take over the country (Popescu and Wilson, 2009). In the 2007 local elections two thirds of local councils were won by the opposition, including the Liberal Party's Dorin Chirtoaca in Chisinau.

In the original April 2009 elections, the Communists claimed a majority of 60, but were one deputy short of the 61 needed to elect one of their own, either Voronin or Prime Minister Zinaida Greceanii, as President (see Table 5.7). Protest demonstrations organized by social networks initially caught the authorities off-guard. However, unlike the Orange Revolution in Ukraine where the youth group Pora had clear rules of engagement, the youthful Moldovan crowd seems to be led astray by *agents provocateurs*. Parliament was burnt, the police made 295 arrests, many were beaten and four deaths were reported. Voronin blamed foreign plotters, mainly the Romanians, whose ambassador was declared *persona non grata*, and businessman Anatol Stati, supposedly the financial backer of the opposition. But the authorities were unnerved and could not get the extra vote they needed in parliament, leading to new elections in July 2009 (see Table 5.8).

Marian Lupu, the ambitious Chair of Parliament, backed by another local businessman, Vlad Plahotniuc, defected to the Democratic Party in June; the Communists lost 4.8 per cent of the vote and twelve seats. The other opposition parties were the more ideological and pan-

Table 5.8 *Moldovan parliamentary elections, July 2009*

Party	Vote (%)	Seats
PCRM	44.7	48
Liberal Democrats	16.6	18
Liberal Party	14.7	15
Democratic Party	12.5	13
Our Moldova	7.3	7

Table 5.9   *Moldovan parliamentary elections, November 2010*

Party	Vote (%)	Seats
PCRM	39.3	42
Liberal Democrats	29.4	32
Democratic Party	12.7	15
Liberal Party	10.0	12
Our Moldova	2.1	–

Romanian Liberals and the more pragmatic Liberal Democrats, who included business interests close to leader Vlad Filat and Chiril Lucinschi, son of the former President. Together with the declining remnants of Our Moldova, the four parties formed an 'Alliance for European Integration' government (AEI) with 53 seats. The AEI stabilized the budget and introduced well-timed reforms to improve relations with the EU, which had just launched its Eastern Partnership in May 2009: liberalizing the domestic media market, passing a new election law that, inter alia, lowered the threshold for representation from 6 to 4 per cent, and drafting an incipient judicial reform.

The AEI gambled with a referendum on a new constitution in September 2010 that aimed to restore the direct popular election of presidents and make the state language Romanian. A superficially impressive 87.8 per cent voted yes, but only because the Communists called for a boycott, so turnout was only 30.3 per cent, just short of the necessary third. The failure led to yet more parliamentary elections in November 2010 (see Table 5.9).

The Communists dropped another six seats. The Liberal Democrats emerged as the strongest partner in the AEI, but the fourth member of the coalition, Our Moldova, left parliament altogether. So overall the AEI only advanced from 53 seats to 59, still two short of the magic number of 61. However, despite the head of the Russian Presidential Administration Sergei Naryshkin's flying to Chisinau to try and set up an alternative coalition involving the Communists and Democrats, the AEI was reconstituted.

Visa liberalization and DCFTA (Deep and Comprehensive Free Trade Agreement) dialogues with the EU began in 2011. After 900 days without a head of state, the jurist Nicolae Timofti was finally elected President in March 2012, with the votes of three Socialists led by Igor Dodon, who split from the Communists in November 2011, and one independent. This removed the threat of early elections, which the resurgent Communists might have won.

Conclusion

The foreign and domestic policies of all three states are shaped by the same factors in differing combinations: the legacy of Russian and Soviet rule, historical regional, ethnic and linguistic divisions, and authoritarian legacies. All three also have historical European traditions, but geopolitically are balanced between a recrudescent Russia and an EU still digesting the expansions of 2004 and 2007. Belarus is clearly the outlier of the three, given President Lukashenka's increasing tendency towards autocracy and autarky. The underlying factors Belarus shares with its southerly neighbours may reassert themselves in time, but only once the regime's carapace begins to crack. Moldova and Ukraine have more in common than one might expect, with both making muddled progress towards markets, democracy and Europe; but Moldova has pulled ahead since 2009, while Ukraine has dramatically regressed since 2010, despite the high expectations raised by the Orange Revolution. After 2007 Moldova gained the advantage of Romanian sponsorship inside the EU, while Ukraine has been busy losing friends since 2010.

Chapter 6

The EU and Central and East European Politics

Nathaniel Copsey

European integration was at the heart of the Central and East European countries' plans for modernization and democratization after 1989. Joining the European Union, or 'returning to Europe' in the slogan of the day, also had a deeply symbolic value, drawing a line under the communist past and marking a return to normality. Negotiating the terms of membership actually took far longer than anticipated, but Poland, Hungary, the Czech Republic, Slovakia, Slovenia and the three Baltic countries finally secured accession fifteen years after the revolutions of 1989 in 2004, with Romania and Bulgaria joining in 2007. Much of the EU's impact on Central Europe actually came in the long period of preparation for membership, through the process known as 'conditionality' (Schimmelfennig and Sedelmeier, 2005), although the positive effects have continued since accession and the new member states have even begun to have an impact on policy-making with the EU.

This chapter has two main aims. First, it looks at how the Central Europeans went about integration with the European Union and their pattern of membership since then. Second, it looks at the impact of the European Union on domestic politics, public opinion, institutions and public policy. It achieves these aims as follows. First, it looks at how the states came to join the EU between 1989 and 2009, including the negotiations and the fallout from the way in which they were carried out. Second, it looks at the impact of the EU on institutions, politics and public policy. Third, it looks at the impact the new member states have had on the EU as a whole.

Before proceeding any further, at the outset of this chapter it is essential to acknowledge the limitations of labelling ten highly diverse European countries as one single group. What they share in common – pre-communist historical legacies, the communist past and a transformational path from one-party rule and the planned economy to liberal democracy and the free market – is as important as their many and varied differences. A continuing shared experience that provides the logic for this chapter, however, is that of being relative newcomers to the European Union. Even here, some states are more integrated than others – Slovenia, Slovakia and Estonia all use the euro, for example; the others do not yet do so – but what is important is that some objective differences between these states and the old West European EU-15 remain. These singularities may be found in, for example, per capita income data or the degree to which democratic practices are embedded in their societies. Above all else, however, the difference is most readily spotted in snatches of conversations along the corridors of the European institutions, where the Central Europeans remain to their mild irritation 'the new member states'. Yet the argument of this chapter is that the objective reasons for drawing this distinction between 'old' and 'new' member states will persist for some time to come, and that there remains therefore considerable value in studying the Central European countries' relations with the EU collectively.

'Returning to Europe': European integration in the 1990s and 2000s

For most of the Central European countries, the decision to choose European integration was taken promptly after the democratic revolutions of 1989, with Poland, for example, signing a Trade and Cooperation Agreement with the then European Communities in September of that year. What came next were drawn out and highly complicated negotiations with the European Union for Association or 'Europe' Agreements, followed by full membership talks. The process was completed by the 12–13 December meeting of the European Council in 2002, which was followed by the signing of the Accession Treaties in Athens on 16 April 2003.

In the late 1990s, the applicant countries were divided into two groups. The first, known as the Luxembourg group after the European Council where they had been invited to join, consisted of Poland, Hungary, Estonia, Czech Republic and Slovenia plus Cyprus. The second, known for the same reason as the Helsinki group, consisted of the laggards Bulgaria, Romania, Slovakia, Latvia and Lithuania plus Malta. Various possibilities for enlargement were considered, including taking the whole of each group in two stages, or the racetrack approach, where the candidate countries concluding negotiations and reaching the finish line would enter one by one. Given the scale of the shock to the EU institutions that such an enormous enlargement would surely entail, the EU in the end opted for a 'big bang' approach of taking all the countries at once – although Bulgaria and Romania were to join two-and-a-half years later to allow them more time to prepare themselves for the demands of membership.

Negotiations between the EU and the Central Europeans were complicated by a number of factors. In the first place, the volume of the *acquis communautaire* (the EU's body of regulations and directives – in other words EU law) had increased sharply since the 1980s as a result of the introduction of the single market, and continued to increase. This meant the Central Europeans were chasing a moving target. It is also sometimes forgotten that the member states did not make it clear until relatively late in the game (the European Council of 2002) that they were *definitely* going to enlarge the Union at all! This point most of all demonstrates the one-sided nature of the negotiations. Moreover, in contrast to previous enlargements in the 1980s and 1990s applicants were required not only to transpose (add the laws to their national statute books) the *acquis* prior to accession, but their adequate implementation of EU rules was also to be verified by the European Commission in painstaking detail. This 'screening' of the *acquis* was in fact just one small part of a much greater process referred to as *conditionality* (for a useful review of differing opinions on this see Haughton, 2007). Conditionality – as the name suggests – boiled down to the EU insisting that states wanting to join the Union would have to meet a number of conditions in order to do so. In exchange for meeting the terms of membership, they received various incentives from the EU, such as development assistance (money and technical expertise) or access to parts of the single market in the short term, with full membership to be awarded at the end of the process (sometimes called 'the golden carrot').

The elementary political, economic, legal and administrative requirements for a state to be eligible for consideration for EU membership were set out in the 1993 Copenhagen criteria (named after the Copenhagen meeting of the European Council), with the detail to be filled in at a later stage by the Commission:

> Membership requires that candidate country has achieved stability of institutions guaranteeing democracy, the rule of law, human rights, respect for and protection of minorities, the existence of a functioning market economy as well as the capacity to cope with competitive pressure and market forces within the Union. Membership presupposes the candidate's ability to take on the obligations of membership including adherence to the aims of political, economic and monetary union. (European Council, 1993)

There is a wide and excellent literature on pre-accession conditionality (see most notably Schimmelfennig and Sedelmeier, 2005; Grabbe, 2006; Hughes *et al.*, 2004; Jacoby, 2004; Pridham, 2005; Vachudova, 2005), which argues that the process was driven by a rational cost-benefit analysis of the merits of EU membership on the part of elites, in which the potentially enormous gains after membership hugely outweighed the price of compliance with EU norms and rules.

To summarize, the Central Europeans often found themselves unwillingly cast in their dealings with Brussels as supplicants – or *demandeurs* in EU terms. Having said that, there is no doubt that the support of the EU was a powerful anchor for the Central and East European states, which at that time were engaged in the tricky business of creating free market economies and liberal democracies governed by the rule of law. In essence, the EU provided a blueprint for reform, although implementing a system of governance designed for the richest countries in the world was a heroic task. During the tough membership negotiations, the Central European teams inevitably found themselves having to make most of the concessions. For some, this cast a shadow over their first years of membership of the European Union. It is worth taking a brief detour in the chapter to look again at the substance of those negotiations between the EU and the Central Europeans to understand what was at stake.

The negotiations

During accession negotiations, the EU always begins from the stance that would-be members should implement all of the *acquis* in full before joining. This position was set out both in the Copenhagen criteria and in the negotiating directives given by the Council to the EU's team of negotiators. The EU negotiators' room for manoeuvre was further restricted by the requirement that there must be unanimous consent of all the member states for the ratification of an accession treaty. Some elements (known as 'chapters') of the negotiations were particularly difficult to close, including matters relating to energy, agriculture, environment, free movement of persons, Justice and Home Affairs, financial questions, institutional questions, and much else besides. Despite the inflexible opening position of the member states, there was clearly some room for trade-offs to be made in negotiations. Crudely, this boiled down to less money from the Common Agricultural Policy and European funds for the new member states in exchange for concessions such as temporary restrictions on the sale of farm land to foreigners and extra time to implement the *acquis* in a number of areas where the functioning of the internal market would not be too gravely impaired.

An interesting general observation about the negotiations between the EU and the Central Europeans in the late 1990s and early 2000s is that the underlying cause of the slow speed with which these negotiations were conducted could be put down to a lack of trust between both parties. Within the EU, there was deep concern in some quarters about the costs of bringing on board a large number of relatively poor countries, and their capacity to adapt to the demands of EU membership. On the part of the Central Europeans, there was resentment at being treated, in their minds, as second-class citizens, and a niggling suspicion that the EU might never let them in at all. It did not go unnoticed that the process of negotiating enlargement took much longer for them than it had done for wealthy Austria, Sweden and Finland in the 1990s. The enlargement process was also more drawn out than it had been for relatively poor Spain or Portugal in the 1980s – let alone Greece, which had been admitted in 1981 despite the Commission's recommendation to the Council that it was not at that time suited for EU membership. A further suspicion existed that the Commission was insisting that the then candidate countries become 'perfect member states' necessitating a higher level of compliance with EU regulations and directives than was the case in the old EU-15. This observation is all the more interesting in hindsight, particularly from the standpoint of the current crisis of European integration, symbolized by the euro area's troubles. All of the states that got into the deepest trouble – Greece, Ireland, Portugal, Spain and Italy – were 'old' member states, and in some cases, had probably been admitted into the euro before they were truly ready, for political reasons. Thus in a sense the Commission was right all along about the need to fulfil particular criteria before being able to join the club – but the lesson appears that conditionality and bureaucratic controls only work (Gallagher, 2009) or work best (Schimmelfennig and Sedelmeier, 2005) when the state in question has not yet joined the EU.

In the end, the negotiations with the Central Europeans were successful, and they made it into the EU with derogations (the right to a temporary exemption from EU rules) from the norm on both sides (for the detail on this see Vassiliou, 2007). These included, on the EU side, an insistence that direct income payments to farmers in the new member states begin at only 25 per cent of the EU-15 level, rising slowly to the full level thereafter. Some member states closed their labour markets to citizens of the new member states for an extended period. Germany and Austria, for example, did this for a full seven-year period until May 2011. Towards the end of the difficult and hard-fought negotiations, there were concerns that the electorates of the then candidate countries would reject the bargains that were eventually struck. As the following section shows, this did not materialize.

The impact of EU membership on public opinion and political parties

Despite some variation across the region, support for EU membership and a sense of EU identity is more or less the same as the European average of around 54 per cent (see Eurobarometer, no. 72, Autumn 2009). Most Central Europeans believe their country has benefited from EU membership. This statistic implies that the new member states are not radically different in their experiences of, and attitudes towards, the EU than the old EU-15. This section examines the degree to which this is true in two areas: public opinion and political parties. In doing so, it touches on an ever-more salient issue in EU politics: the question of legitimacy, in other words the widespread acceptance of the European political system's democratic credibility. A few words on the importance of this topic are essential here.

Ever since the Maastricht era of the early 1990s and the transformation from a European Community to a European Union, questions about the legitimacy of the EU have grown in direct proportion to the increase in its competences and powers. In certain segments of the public across the whole EU – often but not always the poor, the less well-educated, the disenfranchised and the elderly – a widening gap, a eurosceptic chasm even, has opened up between them on the one hand, and the European political elite on the other. This is what McCormick refers to as 'a damaging psychological barrier between Europeans and the EU, preventing the development of ties that must exist between leaders and citizens in order for a system of government to work' (McCormick, 2002: 147). Legitimacy is therefore a hugely salient issue in European politics. It is all the more important in the new member states for at least three reasons.

In the first place, as noted above, they are all countries that emerged in the 1990s from authoritarian, non-democratic rule within an international system that seriously compromised their sovereignty through the Brezhnev doctrine. Exchanging one externally imposed regime for another, also perceived as illegitimate, would have been disastrous. In the second place, as detailed in the section on negotiations and conditionality, the EU asked all the new member states to undertake far-reaching reforms, nearly all of which were non-negotiable. If the EU were not seen as legitimate, it would greatly damage its ability to make these kinds of requests. In the third place, the support of the EU for

democratic consolidation in the 1990s greatly aided their transformation (Vachudova, 2005). In one case, that of Slovakia, the EU's actions
in excluding Slovakia from membership negotiations in 1998 can be
said directly to have contributed to the fall of the populist and at times
anti-democratic government of Vladimir Meciar (Pridham, 2008). It is
not an exaggeration to say that the present-day prosperity and success
of Central Europe is, to a considerable extent, a creation of the
European Union. And if the EU cannot claim legitimacy here, then its
odds of doing so elsewhere would be slim indeed.

Public opinion on the European Union in the new member states is
varied, but appears to point towards a positive consensus that is tempered by passivity or even apathy on the part of voters. On the face of
things, this is not radically different from the rest of the European
Union. The evidence for the positive consensus is to be found first and
foremost in the accession referendum results across the Central
European countries, which ranged from 92.5 per cent approval in
Slovakia to a still clear 67 per cent in favour in Latvia (the other results
were: Slovenia, 89.9 per cent; Hungary 83.7 per cent; Lithuania, 89.9
per cent; Poland, 77.5 per cent; Czech Republic, 77.3 per cent; and
Estonia, 66.8 per cent – neither Bulgaria nor Romania held a referendum; see Taggart and Szczerbiak, 2009). There were no marginal
results (although turnout was disappointing, again a hallmark of post-
communist politics across the region), and these results actually compared rather well with the 1995 accession countries, where the results
ranged from 52.8 per cent approval (Sweden) to 66.6 per cent approval
(Austria) – with Norway of course voting against by 52.2 per cent.

Although voters could (just about) be persuaded to turn out in reasonable numbers to vote for the historic decision to enter the European
Union, the same could not be said when it came down to taking part in
the more humdrum European Parliament elections of 2004 and 2009,
as Table 6.1 shows. Here turnout in 2004 was below the EU average in
all but one country, Latvia, and below the EU average in all but two,
Latvia and Estonia, in 2009. Voter apathy in Central and Eastern
Europe is even more notable when one considers that the average was
of course brought down by the Central Europeans.

Enthusiasm for the European project across the region has always
been rooted in the notion of EU membership as a part of a wider long-
term plan (trouncing de Tocqueville's idea that democracy must always
be about the present since voters are unconcerned by the vagaries of
the future), which in turn also helps to explain why older Central
Europeans voted 'yes' to something they did not feel would be of use
to them in the national referendums on accession – they felt that they
were approving something that would benefit their children and grand-

Table 6.1 *Turnout in European parliament elections in the Central European countries, 2004 and 2009 (percentages)*

Member state	Turnout (2004 election)	Turnout (2009 election)
Bulgaria	–	37.5
Czech Republic	28.3	28.2
Estonia	26.8	43.9
Hungary	38.5	36.3
Latvia	41.3	52.6
Lithuania	48.4	20.5
Poland	20.9	24.5
Romania	–	27.7
Slovakia	17.0	19.6
Slovenia	28.3	28.0
EU Average	45.6	43.2

Source: adapted from Taggart and Szczerbiak (2009).

children. But it was also rooted in a strong emotional sense of a break with the miserable communist past – and also showing Moscow and others that a profound change had taken place. Interestingly, the most tangible benefit of EU membership, in the opinion of most in the region, is the freedom to travel and work freely in other member states – this sentiment is particularly supported by the 25–39 age bracket, which is logical since it was of course this group which took advantage of this freedom in such large numbers after 2004.

The EU in domestic politics

Membership of the European Union appears to have had relatively little impact on political parties or domestic politics to date. No new parties have been formed to oppose the EU integration project nor have election campaigns in most states been fought on 'European' issues *per se* (although governments have fallen after losing credibility on European issues). There is little evidence of the downward Europeanization of domestic politics after 2004, as demonstrated in the case of Poland by Szczerbiak and Bil (2008). Haughton (2009) has characterized the influence of the EU on party politics across the Central European countries in three ways: as constraint, a spillover and a point of reference. These are worth exploring in turn.

Constraints on domestic politics were primarily limited to those areas where the EU retained conditionality. Membership of both Schengen (the borderless travel zone between 26 European countries, with a common external frontier) and the euro area were the two major policy challenges that remained after accession. In a more loose, but still very important fashion, EU membership served to draw the boundaries of what was politically possible. This boundary might at times appear elastic, but it was nonetheless present. Good examples of the constraints imposed by the EU might be found in policy towards national minorities (usually more controlled) or in the room to voice illiberal preferences on social policy (limited). Political parties of all colours, from the centre-right Law and Justice in Poland to the centre-left Smer-SD in Slovakia, might flout European norms in the immediate post-accession period, as, more recently, has the national conservative government of Viktor Orban in Hungary (who compared the EU with the Soviet Union; see *Financial Times*, 15 March 2012), but in doing so they subjected themselves to a barrage of criticism domestically and internationally.

Spillovers from EU accession could be found in the way in which some political debates in the new member states became increasingly framed in an EU context. Energy, the use of structural funds, migration policy or agreements between political parties to 'suspend hostilities' (as was the case in Slovenia: see Kajnc, 2009, on this) whilst their country held the EU's rotating presidency are all good examples of this. The very fact of EU membership as a reference point for domestic politics could be identified in two ways. First, by the entry into the domestic political lexicon of the notion of 'European standards' as a stick with which to beat political opponents allegedly in violation of these. This is perhaps one of the few unique features of the Europeanization of Central European politics. It is hard to imagine a political party in, say, France or the Netherlands, let alone the UK, berating another for perceived slights to European standards. More importantly, the reference point of the European Union is best located in its role as a valence issue (an issue on which politicians and voters share the same opinion, be it positive or negative) in domestic politics. In other words, if a state is to participate in the European Union, it should do so competently. Incompetent managers of European affairs may be punished by voters, as happened in the Polish parliamentary election of 2007 (although European policy was just one of several areas of perceived incompetence). Emphatically, this does not mean that European policy may determine an electoral outcome, rather it is one factor of many in making a judgement on the abilities and credibility of the political parties.

The impact of EU membership on political institutions and governance

The European Union is a technocratic political system, which means that the ability of a Member State's civil service to coordinate their national policy position between sectoral ministries, is of vital importance. The representatives of a Member State need to 'speak with one voice' during negotiations in Brussels and not contradict each other if they are to be effective. The quality of the diplomatic service, and staff seconded from other ministries, that are tasked with these negotiations is of equal importance. Both for policy-making and for the implementation of EU laws at national level (environmental protection being a good example), the participation of non-state actors is also vital. These two elements will be reviewed in turn.

In the first few years of membership, the administrative capacity of the Central European states was considerably below what was needed, and it is this factor perhaps best explains the gaffes attributed to the new member states in their early years of membership (on the, at times, chaotic Czech Presidency of the EU, see Benes and Karlas, 2010; on Poland's early years of membership see Copsey and Pomorska, 2010) although their performance did improve considerably over time as, for example, the highly effective Polish Presidency demonstrated (Pomorska and Vanhoonacker, 2012). Those early new Member State presidencies that managed to lead the EU effectively for six months did so precisely because they delegated so many powers to the Council of the European Union and the other institutions, as was the case for Slovenia (Kajnc, 2009). A second area that has attracted attention is the ability of the new member states to work with what Börzel (2009) refers to as 'new modes of governance', that is, the participation of non-state actors in a less hierarchical policy-making and implementing system. In this area, the new member states again did not perform particularly well. What all of this underlines, perhaps, is that for all of the enormous efforts of the new member states in adapting to the demands of EU membership, developing deep or consolidated democracy (Linz and Stepan, 1996) and effective multi-level governance simply takes a very long time, as Spain, Portugal or Greece demonstrated after previous enlargements. The academic debate on the lasting effect of EU conditionality beyond enlargement is divided, with some scholars (Epstein and Sedelmeier, 2009; Sedelemeier, 2012) arguing that pre-accession institutional changes persist 'even after the EU's sanctioning power weakens' (Sedelemeier, 2012: 20), whilst others argue that EU norms, rule and values were absorbed in a 'superficial or declaratory' manner (Gallagher, 2009: 3).

Two further effects of EU enlargement need a brief mention here. In the first place, national parliaments have the right to scrutinize EU legislation under the Lisbon treaty. This creates a considerable burden for European Union affairs committees across Central Europe and in practice (in common with the old member states) there is neither the time, resources nor the interest to do so in a thorough way. In the second place, post-accession, the coordination of the different aspects of European policy remained very important, but lost the pre-eminence it had enjoyed whilst membership was contingent on maintaining the pace of a rapid programme of reforms. In some member states, such as Poland, the Foreign Affairs Ministry took the opportunity to win back responsibility for the coordination of European policy. In retrospect this may appear odd, since European policy post-accession is largely domestic in nature, albeit with a sprinkling of elements of what appears to be foreign policy, such as preparing for summits.

Impact of EU membership on public policy

The issue of the uneven implementation of EU regulations and directives across the Union has long been of interest both to the European Commission and to academics. Prior to the 2004 accession, there were concerns that new member states, such as Poland, would reduce the speed and effectiveness with which rules were enforced as soon as the strict conditionality applied by the Commission was withdrawn. Preliminary evidence (Falkner *et al.*, 2008) shows that although transposition of EU directives is better than their implementation, this is not radically better or worse than in other member states of the Union. Thus to a certain extent, although the new member states are not necessarily as perfect as the Commission's screening of the *acquis* was supposed to produce, they are by no means worse than the average of the old EU-15 when it comes to implementation of regulations and directives.

Accession brought full participation in nearly all aspects of EU policy for the Central Europeans. Two of these brought massive material advantage: the Common Agricultural Policy and access to the Structural and Regional development funds. In the first instance, despite only benefiting at first from a lower level of support through the direct income payment, the Common Agricultural Policy proved to be veritable bonanza for Central European farmers as guaranteed prices for certain agricultural products brought great profits (and of course higher prices for consumers). Structural and development funds constituted a similarly rich vein to be mined by the Central Europeans. Poland alone received some €67 billion in EU funds for development assistance between 2007 and 2013. Resources on this scale were able to fund infrastructure development on an unprecedented scale.

Two major public policy challenges remained for the Central Europeans after accession: full participation in the Schengen zone of free movement and joining the euro area. The former has now been achieved by all the Central and Eastern European members, except for Bulgaria and Romania. Indeed free movement between European countries is the most frequently cited benefit that the Central European public cites in opinion polls soliciting their views on EU enlargement. The latter challenge of joining the euro has proven much more complicated, and is worthy of investigation in more detail.

Economic and Monetary Union (EMU)

All the Central European new member states have a legal obligation to join the euro area as soon as they meet the Maastricht convergence criteria for membership (see Dyson, 2006). Their journeys towards membership were at varying speeds. Slovenia joined in 2007, followed by Slovakia in 2009 and Estonia in 2011. The dates at which the others will enter the single currency are not yet known: there is no fixed timetable and official government announcements are not always reliable. The best guide therefore as to when a Member State might join the euro area is its progress in meeting the five Maastricht convergence criteria (originally contained in the European Treaty of Maastricht of 1992), which are as follows:

- *Price stability.* In the year preceding assessment, inflation must be no higher than 1.5 percentage points above that of the three best-performing member states (i.e. those with the lowest inflation).
- *Budget deficit.* This must not exceed more than 3 per cent of GDP.
- *National debt.* This must not exceed 60 per cent of GDP.
- *Long-term interest rates.* These should not exceed by more than 2 per cent those of the average of the three member states with the lowest levels of inflation.
- *Participation in the Exchange Rate Mechanism.* The country in question must join this system of fixed exchange rates and stay in the narrowest band with no currency realignment for at least two years.

Joining the euro is not without controversy. In the first place – as the euro area crisis of the 2010s showed – it comes with a considerable amount of economic burden sharing between members. The bailouts to Greece (a much wealthier state in per capita and absolute terms) were hugely unpopular in Slovakia. Predictably (as the segment below on the influence of new member states shows), Slovak protests were ignored. Euro area membership in political terms also involves adjustment costs (Buiter and Grafe, 2004), touches upon state sovereignty (Jones, 2002: 23) and means giving up a 'symbolic marker in nation-building efforts' (Risse, 2003: 487). There were relatively few serious critical voices about joining the euro area in the new member states, although, for example, both President Klaus in the Czech Republic and the conservative Law and Justice party in Poland expressed fears about losing the sovereignty that had been so hard-won from Moscow to the bureaucrats of Brussels.

There can be little question that membership of the euro area would be hugely advantageous to the new member states in economic terms. First, they are expected to have declining levels of aggregate public debt in the medium term since their economies are likely to grow quite rapidly as they converge with their wealthier Western neighbours. Second, their economies are closely linked to the core euro area in their pattern of trade, and particularly to Germany, the euro area's anchor. Third, the worst stage of the Great Slump or financial and economic crisis of 2008–09 demonstrated beyond any question that small and open emerging economies benefit from the shelter that membership of a reserve currency brings in terms of economic and political credibility in the eyes of international investors. In other words, the risk of capital flight is greatly diminished. The currencies of the new EU member states with flexible exchange rates fell in value by between 17 per cent and 29 per cent between July 2008 and March 2009 (with the Polish złoty tumbling furthest) (Allam, 2009: 31). Unfortunately, the effects of the financial and economic crisis on interest rates, inflation, currency stability and government borrowing all served to push the non-euro area new member states further away from eligibility for membership of the single currency. In the medium to longer term, all the Central European countries will join the euro for precisely the same reasons that compelled them to join the European Union: it offers political and economic safety and security in a changing and dangerous world.

Impact of the new member states on the EU

Lastly, the chapter turns to the fascinating question of upward Europeanization, that is, the influence of the new member states on the EU. Apart from Poland, the Central European countries do not have, and will probably never have, the capacity to exercise influence in the EU in the way that we understood large, older member states such as France, Germany or the UK to have done in the past, through for example the setting of the Common Agricultural Policy in the 1960s or the Single Market in the 1980s. Although Poland is the only large new Member State, this emphatically does not mean that the Central European countries acknowledge any right to leadership of their regional group. Hungary is a former imperial power with a certain idea of itself and its place in the world. The Czechs and Slovaks, similarly, do not appreciate their northern neighbour, Poland, 'attempting to put on political weight'. The Baltic countries also do not look to Poland for guidance. Yet the new member states have exercised some influence on the European Union. This section of the chapter considers how.

The capacity of a state to exercise power and influence in the European Union is determined by fixed and variable factors (Copsey and Pomorska, 2010, 2012). The fixed factors are population and economic weight *vis-à-vis* the other member states. On this scale, only Poland scores relatively highly, but these are factors that lie usually beyond the control of a national government. Some (but not all) of the variable factors that determine influence do lie within the control of a national government and these are as follows.

Of primary importance is the intensity with which a state holds a given policy preference – in other words how important a policy area is to that state. Second, comes the skill of a state at building alliances with other member states in the Council of Ministers and within the European Parliament to push its ideas and preferences forward. Policy-making in Brussels to a great extent is about making trade-offs, putting together package deals and having a keen eye on the big picture. States that can play this game well tend to get what they want. A third factor is administrative capacity, that is the ability of its civil servants to play the Brussels game and guide an idea through the numerous committees and informal policy-making forums. A fourth component of influence is the persuasive advocacy of a state, which boils down to its skill at winning others over to its side of the argument. Member states tend to have greater persuasive skills in areas where they are judged to have a particular specialism or expertise. A fifth element is the receptiveness of other member states to the proposition being put forward. Part of this is therefore about making sure that what is being proposed is broadly in line with what may be considered acceptable. The sixth and final factor is the domestic political strength of the government putting the idea forward. Domestic political strength can be played both ways by a skilful politician. On the one hand, weak governments can push for concessions by arguing that they will not be able to sell a different package back home – and that this may put at risk the viability of what is being proposed. On the other hand, strong governments can push forward relatively radical measures safe in the knowledge that they are backed by powerful majorities in their Member State.

Learning how to play the 'Brussels game' that are the sum of these variable factors takes a long time. It also takes a considerable period for a new Member State to build a network of high-level officials in the Commission, Council or External Action Service. This is in part because promotion within the European institutions remains to a considerable extent based on seniority. The Central European countries with predominantly younger officials in post may take some time to build up a quota of senior officials who will be better placed to understand the domestic political context of their home member states. The small size of most new member states also implies that the pool of qualified candidates will in any case be rather small. Nonetheless, policy successes have been won by the new member states in key areas, such as the multi-annual financial framework from 2007–13, which provided considerable support for economic development in the form of structural, regional and development funds. A second important area of success in uploading policy preferences was the field of relations with the European Union's eastern neighbours. As a result of a joint Polish and Swedish initiative in 2008, the EU launched the so-called Eastern Partnership for its six eastern neighbours (Armenia, Azerbaijan, Belarus, Georgia, Moldova and Ukraine) in 2009. This was a policy area that was of vital national interest to the Central European countries for geographical and historical reasons as much as political or economic ones. What the Eastern Partnership demonstrated best was that the new member states had learnt a great deal about the political game in Brussels. Poland chose Sweden as a partner not only because of its ability to navigate the committees of the Council of Ministers, but also because it was perceived as a neutral, even altruistic, player in foreign affairs. Both the persuasive advocacy of Poland and the other Central European member states in calling for action in this area was boosted by the Russian intervention in Georgia in 2008, which crucially swung the view of France, the state at that time holding the rotating presidency.

Conclusions: have the Central European member states changed the EU?

At the outset of this chapter, it was argued that accession to the European Union, or rather preparation for membership, changed the Central European countries in a profound fashion: socially, institutionally, politically and economically. The reforming blueprint of European integration accompanied by the sticks and carrots of conditionality provided the stability that was essential for successful transformation in Central Europe in the 1990s and 2000s. Two general conclusions may be drawn from the substance of this chapter. First, that after accession, the effect of European Union membership on the Central European countries was limited. Second, that the new Central European states, for all of their specificities and shared experiences, are not so radically different to the old EU-15 in their pattern of relations with the European Union in terms of public opinion, the importance of the EU in domestic politics, and their early experiences of membership in comparison with countries that joined in earlier waves of enlargement. All new member states struggle to learn the rules of the Brussels game in the early years of membership. Moreover, the early evidence (Falkner *et al.*, 2008) appears to show that they are not much better or worse than the other member states at implementing EU regulations and directives. Many of the differences that remain between 'old' and 'new' member states will be eroded over time as the economic gap narrows and the political experience gained through membership increases. Some will remain, of course, since many communist and, particularly, pre-communist political legacies (such as nationalism) will persist perhaps indefinitely. An important question still remains to be examined in this concluding section: have the Central European states changed the EU?

The European Union of the 2010s is far larger and far more diverse – linguistically, historically or economically – than the pre-2004 EU-15. Yet studies of decision-making since enlargement show that it seems to function just as well as it did as a small West European club of wealthy countries (Hagemann and De Clerk-Sachsse, 2007). Falkner's (2008) study complemented this by demonstrating that the implementation of EU rules does not differ widely between older and newer member states. What has changed, however, are the rules under which the European Union functions. The significant changes brought in by the Lisbon treaty, which amongst other things reformed the rules on voting in the Council of Ministers, established the European Council as a permanent institution, increased the powers of the directly elected European Parliament and set up the European External Action Service, was introduced originally as the 'European Constitutional Treaty' to cope with the demands of accession. These were not small changes, and they were also a direct result of enlargement.

The degree of integration between the old West European and the new Pan-European EU is much more varied. Not all member states participate in the Schengen area or the single currency. Free movement of workers was also introduced by degrees. Yet as this chapter showed, the enthusiasm of the Central European member states for the euro and for Schengen means that within a few years, full participation in all areas of EU activity will have less to do with being an 'old' or 'new' Member State and more to do with political choice – as the non-participation of the UK, Sweden and Denmark in the euro shows.

When it comes to the question of 'more Europe' or deeper European integration, here again it could be argued that although enlargement increases the complexity of arriving at a consensus, there are no reasons for thinking that the Central Europeans (with the exception of the Czech Republic) need be a restraint. With the arguable exception of Poland, the Central European member states are small countries with a vested interest in multilateral decision-making and strong supranational institutions with the power to protect their interests from their larger and stronger neighbours. That said, the effect of 'digesting' the 2004 and 2007 enlargements will continue for quite some time to come, perhaps until a high degree of convergence with West European standards of living and governance have been achieved, which although the process is happening more quickly than anticipated, may take some time yet.

Looking back at the accession of the Central European countries from the gloomy standpoint of the euro crisis in the 2010s, it could be argued that the big-bang enlargement served to provide an overwhelming vote of confidence in the European integration project. Endorsements continue with the steady flow of new member states into the euro area – despite the crisis – and the Schengen zone. Enlargement has brought significant challenges in the shape of European identity or solidarity between Europeans, that is, determining who gets what from the common budget in a system where some member states are considerably poorer than others. What is interesting about the solidarity crisis of the 2010s was that it was primarily fought between the core euro area's northern member states (particularly Germany) and the southern or peripheral euro area countries (such as Greece, Spain, Ireland, Portugal or Italy). In other words, it is clear that the great test of the bonds of European solidarity was pre-ordained before the Central Europeans joined the EU and therefore had nothing to do with enlargement. Taking stock, it seems reasonable to conclude that EU enlargement has been an extraordinary success on a scale quite unimaginable in 1989 – for 'old' and 'new' member states alike as well as for the wider European integration project.

Chapter 7

The International Transformation and Re-regionalization of 'Eastern Europe'

Rick Fawn

How easy it was before 1989. 'Eastern Europe' meant eight European countries that existed on world maps and that were ruled by one-party socialist regimes: Albania, Bulgaria, Czechoslovakia, East Germany, Hungary, Poland, Romania and Yugoslavia. The overlay of inter-state institutions gave only minor complication: as socialist rule disintegrated in 1989, Albania and Yugoslavia were outside the Warsaw Treaty Organization (WTO) and the Council for Mutual Economic Assistance (CMEA); while some socialist countries outside Europe (Cuba, Mongolia and Vietnam) were members of the latter.

Beyond such conventional vocabulary of Cold War politics, however, the term 'Eastern Europe' was profoundly contested and rejected by a handful of brave, and often mercilessly persecuted intellectuals, and a few knowledgeable and sympathetic Westerners. Their alternative was 'Central Europe'. The difference was anything but semantic.

To make that point of the difference in the quality of the terms, and also to demonstrate the unrecognizability of pre-1989 'Eastern Europe' today, consider briefly how that so-called region has been transformed. First, before 1989 the region was bound to Moscow for military and economic planning through the CMEA and the WTO. Although a modicum of national initiative, or indeed evasion, was possible within the organizations (Romania had even achieved a somewhat distant position within the WTO, aided by the withdrawal of Soviet military forces in 1958), they were hardly consultative, let alone consensus-based bodies. Despite official rhetoric that declared each institution to be a counterpart, respectively, of the West's NATO and the Organisation for European Economic Cooperation (the precursor to the current Organisation for Economic Co-operation and

Development) and the European Economic Community, both structures served to allow Moscow to direct East European domestic policies, and to reinforce the USSR's superpower status as the leader of a bloc of countries.

If anything, however, the CMEA exported and regionalized elements of the Soviet Union's central planning system. Rather than establishing a common market for 450 million consumers, it created economic irrationality on an international scale and failed to alleviate shortages. The WTO was ostensibly to protect militarily the vulnerable populations of Eastern Europe from the apparently still 'fascist' (West) Germans and their 'imperialist', 'warmongering' capitalist Western allies. Instead, the WTO not only subordinated national armed forces to Moscow's control but also became, in 1968, the only multilateral military alliance in history to attack itself. The new governments that came to power in the wake of the negotiated revolutions of 1989 sought to terminate these two institutions; within two years both were gone. Soviet military forces were completely withdrawn from Czechoslovakia and Hungary in 1991, and from Poland in 1994. The three Baltic republics, whose annexation by the Soviet Union was not recognized by many Western governments in any case, regained their sovereignty by 1991; and by 1993 occupying Soviet military personnel had left Lithuania, and the year after the last forces departed from Estonia and Latvia.

But removing one regional sets of structures, controls and imposed regional allegiance and identity did not in itself make for another. Our current perspective may be of the 'old East Europeans' (if one is even old enough to think in those terms) now as part of the EU and NATO. Even better, cheap flights whisk visitors to Prague and Warsaw and Ljubljana and Tallinn, and the Schengen visa-free, borderless travel area that now includes post-communist countries means not even a cursory passport check upon arrival. If this happy situation is viewed as natural, even an unconscious historical fact (as it might now be to younger generations) that achievement is due heavily also to the geopolitical transformations initiated and pursued by the post-revolution governments in the region. Many, though not all, of the CEEC (Central and East European countries) are in the Organisation for Economic Cooperation and Development, a group of countries dedicated to sharing solutions for maximizing economic growth (see Table 7.1 for comparison). While successor states to the former Soviet Union seek to emulate OECD practices, and Russia has sought membership, none has been admitted to the Organisation.

Being part now of a Euro-Atlantic or a 'Western' identity is not to be taken as inevitable. The acceptance of these countries into NATO and the EU was not a foregone conclusion – indeed it was initially quite the opposite. Neither of these institutions greeted the 1989 revolutions with immediate offers of membership. Instead, although some in the West were keen for advancing relations with new former Soviet bloc states, the governments in those states worked to convince their new Western interlocutors to think differently about their countries, populations and region. By transforming Western conceptions about old 'Eastern Europe' the region could eventually pry open the doors to Euro-Atlantic institutions. That some of the countries covered by this volume – several in the West Balkans and Belarus, Ukraine and Moldova – currently remain outside membership of NATO and the EU demonstrates that the so-called 'Europeanization' process has geographic limitations. Many of the former are closer to the EU through Stabilization and Association Agreements, which might eventually produce EU membership; even with the EU's Eastern Partnership (EaP), the latter, however, are likely to remain far removed from the prospect of accession. Indeed, while far-ranging, the EaP nevertheless specifically excludes EU membership as a goal for the six post-Soviet European countries partaking in it.

This chapter first provides an assessment of regional cooperation initiatives that have involved post-communist states since the regime changes of 1989. It concentrates on multilateral inter-state formations, although some sub-state, cross-border cooperation has also occurred. The chapter categorizes the inter-state formations on the basis of first, those that are chiefly functional – that is, they take as their organizational and membership basis countries that share seemingly objective common interests, ones that arise from sharing a geographic space: these are, the Central European Initiative (CEI), the Council of the Baltic Sea States (CBSS), and the Conference on the Black Sea Economic Cooperation (BSEC). Consideration is given after that to a distinctive formation – the 46-member Regional Cooperation Council (RGG), which was established as part of wider efforts to stabilize and rebuild the Balkans. Consideration is then given to Visegrad cooperation. That initiative remains by far the smallest in membership of all these regional groupings, consisting of (only) the Czech Republic, Hungary, Poland and Slovakia, and the only one composed exclusively of former socialist bloc states, it nevertheless demonstrates how constructing, maintaining and then projecting a new regional identity has influenced the development of post-communist Central and East Europe. A final section considers the current regional institutional relations of the West Balkans and the post-Soviet European states of Belarus, Moldova and Ukraine.

Table 7.1 *Regional organizational memberships in Central and East Europe*

Country/grouping (total membership numbers as of 2012, including non CEES)	NATO (28)	EU (27)	OECD (34)	Visegrad (4)	CEI (18)	CBSS (12)
Broad geocultural orientation and time formation of grouping	*Western, pre-1989 organizations*			*Post-1989 regional initiativ for or involving Central an*		
Albania	X	*			X	
Belarus					X	
Bosnia and Herzegovina		*			X	
Bulgaria	X				X	
Croatia	X	3			X	
Czech Republic	X	X	X	X	X	
Estonia	X	X	X			X
Hungary	X	X			X	
Kosova[4]		*				
Latvia	X	X				X
Lithuania	X	X				X
Macedonia, Republic of[6]		^			X	
Moldova					X	
Montenegro		^			X	
Poland	X	X				X
Romania	X	X			X	
Serbia		^			X	
Slovakia	X	X	X	X	X	
Slovenia	X	X	X		X	
Ukraine					X	
Other post-Soviet countries						
Armenia						
Azerbaijan						
Georgia						
Kazakhstan						
Kyrgyzstan						
Russian Federation						
Tajikistan						
Turkmenistan						
Uzbekistan						

1 *Key*: In alphabetical order by abbreviation: BSEC – Organization of Black Sea Economic Cooperat CBSS – Council of the Baltic Seas States; CEI – Central European Initiative; CIS – Commonwealth Independent States; CSTO – Collective Security Treaty Organization; CU – Customs Union; EU – European Union; EurAsEC – Eurasian Economic Community; NATO – North Atlantic Treaty Organization; RCC – Regional Cooperation Council; SES – Single Economic Space.

Notes: * Albania, Bosnia and Herzegovina, and Kosova are officially considered 'potential candidate EU accession. ^ Macedonia, Montenegro, and Serbia (and, outside the Central and East European re Iceland and Turkey) are EU candidate countries. GUAM admitted Uzbekistan in 1999 at which poin group became GUUAM. Uzbekistan left in 2005 and the group reverted to GUAM.
2 Eurasian Economic Community.

RCC (46)	BSEC	GUAM-OECD[1]	CIS (9)	CSTO (8)	EurAsEC[2] (6)	SES (4)	CU (3)
d principally st European states		Post-1991 formations involving only Soviet successor states					
X	X						
			X	X	X	X	X
X	X						
X	X						
X							
X							
X							
X							
X							
X	X	X	X				
X							
X							
X							
X	X						
X							
X							
	X	X	7			X	X
	X		X	X			
	X		X				
	X		8				
			X		X		X
			X		X	X	9
	X		X		X	X	X
			X		X		
			X		X		

atia was officially in 2012 an acceding country to the EU, and expected to enter the EU on 1 July 3.

lling as used, in the Albanian language, by the government of Kosova.

UN Interim Administration Mission in Kosovo (UNMIK), on behalf of Kosovo.

e constitutional name, although Macedonia was recognized in the UN by the name 'Former Yugoslav ublic of Macedonia).

raine never ratified the agreement creating the CIS, and therefore is not a former member, but partici-es in CIS meetings.

rgia left the CIS in August 2009 following war with Russia in August 2008.

2011 the government of Kyrgyzstan had declared its intentions to join the Customs Union and in 2 the Russian government had given its support.

Regional state formations in Central and Eastern European after the Cold War

If there was a point at which the superpowers and their allies agreed an end to the Cold War and began formulating a new set of state relations, it would have been the meeting in Paris in November 1990 of the Conference on Security and Cooperation in Europe. Even before that, however, new inter-state formations were being created, and by actors other than the USA or even major West European states, to accommodate the seismic changes brought by the end of socialist rule and of expiring Soviet control in Eastern Europe. Chronologically, the first was what is the now 18-member Central European Initiative (CEI). This was launched by Italy in November 1989. It also has particular relevance to this volume, including as members almost all of the countries that fall within its purview.

Like the CBSS and BSEC, the CEI maintains a predominantly functionalist agenda, working on low-political issues of (ideally) mutual benefit, such as transportation, technology and tourism, as well as, more recently, some security issues such as coordination on combating transnational crime and on developing minority rights protection. The CEI, which started among its ranks with only a single member-state of the EU, Italy (Austria only joining the Union in 1995), now has 12 of its members in that supranational entity, developed as its principal aim to bring its members 'closer together' and to assist their accession to the EU ('1.1 Objectives', available at: http://www.ceinet.org).

EU accession for all of its members is an ambitious aim, and the CEI's importance and functionality remain questionable. Even the survivability of the outfit may be in doubt. Its greatest accomplishment might be its existence, having overcome one death and serious challenges since. The forerunner of the CEI was founded in 1978 among not the national governments but provinces, Lander or republics in Austria, Germany, Italy, Hungary and Yugoslavia. In 1989 as revolutions swept Eastern Europe, the government of Italy proposed convening this grouping at the national level. Reflecting one interpretation of those changes, this new grouping became not only the first postcommunist regional cooperation initiative, but also the only one to be established with an explicit reference to traditional power politics. The group was formed on 11 November 1989, two days after the fall of the Berlin Wall, which, while powerfully symbolic, was still but one of East Germany's closed border crossing points.

As auspicious and innovative as this initiative was, its main architect Italian Foreign Minister Gianni di Michelis intimated that it was a measure to 'contribute to a more even balance of power' in view of the consequences of German unification (Di Michelis, 1990). In 1991 the *Pentagonale* was seen 'to serve as a vehicle for Italian influence as well as a barrier to German expansion into post-communist Central Europe' (*The Economist*, 1991). Germany was excluded from the national-level successor to Alpen-Adria, while additional post-communist countries were invited to partake.

Thus, membership was expanded in March 1990 to Czechoslovakia, where some of Central Europe's most prominent communist-era dissidents had come to power in 1989, particularly Vaclav Havel and Jiri Dienstbier, and who were actively engaged in foreign policy experimentation and entrepreneurship. Even though that landlocked country was removed from the Adriatic, its leadership was keen for varied and new diplomatic formations. It also advocated thereafter for the inclusion of its neighbour, Poland, which joined in 1991. Expanded membership and the absence of the original geographic markers meant that the group was named more descriptively regarding the number of countries, with Czechoslovakia as the *Pentagonale* and then Poland as *Hexagonale*. The Italian terms were taken in recognition in deference to the national pedigree. But just as the group seemed to gather greater membership and better prospects for influence, its momentum ceased with the outbreak of war in Yugoslavia.

The grouping was relaunched at a summit in Vienna in July 1992, at which the Yugoslav successor states of Slovenia, Bosnia and Herzegovina and Croatia gained membership. The group adopted the new name (in English, and with English as the working language) of the Central European Initiative. Considering that it had not used such a name before and that its membership was still predominantly Balkan/south-east European and/or Adriatic, the selection may well have indicated a desire for geocultural relocation. Indeed, as will also be mentioned regarding Visegrad, several south-east European countries were keen to change the outward perceptions of their geocultural location by shedding reference to themselves as 'Balkan', much as the former 'East Europeans' were intent on banishing that term. In 1993, the CEI continued to expand, admitting Macedonia (and using that name rather than by the cumbersome qualifier of 'Former Yugoslav Republic', which was required by Greece for its entry into the United Nations). The CEI developed, at its Trieste Summit of 1994, an 'Association Council' for Belarus, Bulgaria, Romania and Ukraine, and included Albania a few months later. The Initiative's Warsaw Summit elevated all associates into members; Moldova sought and received membership in 1996, raising participation to 16. Yugoslavia (by then only Serbia and Montenegro), nevertheless was excluded from the CEI until its leader Slobodan Milosevic fled the country in October 2000, being quickly accepted a month later. Once Montenegro separated peacefully in 2006 from Serbia, it became the eighteenth and final member-state. Not that there are obvious additional neighbouring candidate countries, but some officials have said, partly because of the difficulties that CEI faces, that no plans exist to expand the CEI's membership.

The CEI presents itself as 'regional cooperation for European integration and bridge between macro-regions'. To that end, its summits include participation from major international financial institutions and other regional cooperation forums, including the European Bank for Reconstruction and Development, the European Investment Bank (EIB), the World Bank, the Adriatic and Ionian Initiative, BSEC and the RCC (Regional Cooperation Council), and the European Commission (CEI website, last accessed 28 June 2012).

The diversity of its membership – from the pariah dictatorship of Belarus to new member states of the EU and NATO – seems to disadvantage the workings of the grouping, rather than providing for a means of increased mutual understanding. Some of the diplomats attending its meetings have said that not all member states bother even to send delegations to all meetings. The 2011 summit was attended by only four of the 18 prime ministers, with two countries sending deputy prime ministers, and others their ministers of the economy. The capacity of the CEI to function, despite important and noble aims, has been increasingly called into question. One Central European diplomat familiar with both the CEI and Visegrad called the former, with 18 member countries, 'small cooperation' while the latter, with only four, was 'big cooperation' (interview, 2012). In addition, although the CEI has signed working agreements with similar and overlapping regional initiatives, it risks being overtaken by them. One such instance is the Adriatic-Ionian Initiative, advanced strongly by Italy, which again uses geographic references points to define its identity and purpose. By choosing 'Adriatic-Ionian' the formation specifically refers to the 'basin around which it revolves is almost a "closed area" and, in the future perspective, an "inland sea" of the EU. A circumscribed sea, which connects (now) member states and other countries and, at same time, represent the natural access to the sea of the Danube Macroregion' (website, last accessed 28 June 2012).

Diplomats from neighbouring countries note how the Adriatic-Ionian Initiative both challenges the role of the CEI and also highlights Italy's position in this region, and at the expense of Germany and Austria. Alternative geographic conception for south-east Europe, such as using 'the Danube', naturally and necessarily include Austria and Germany (or at least Bavaria), but not Italy; by contrast, use of the

Adriatic excludes Austria and Germany and retains and highlights Italy (interviews, 2012). Purporting to share major common aims, such as EU accession and a common geocultural space, does not ensure cooperation. The CEI's capacity remains limited. The success of a similar formation – the CBSS and the BSEC – are somewhat better as they have, at least in principle, greater coherence from the common interests that arise in dealing with objectively defined geographic entities. However, deeply divergent types of member states continue to provide them with challenges.

A joint Swedish–Polish proposal in September 1990 resulted in a Conference which eventually saw the participation of all countries bordering the Baltic: Lithuania, Latvia, Estonia, Denmark, Germany, Sweden, Norway, Finland, Russia and Poland. Another Conference, proposed by Denmark and Sweden, again, was held in March 1992, which resulted in the Council of the Baltic Sea States. The CBSS includes all ten littoral states of the Baltic Sea, the European Commission, and the (officially called) 'exception' of far-removed Iceland, which was admitted in March 1995. A second is the Organization for Black Sea Economic Cooperation (BSEC), a Turkish initiative launched formally in 1992, following Turkish interest for involvement in the south of the former Soviet Union as well as into South-eastern Europe. Unlike the CBSS, BSEC extends far beyond the littoral states of the Black Sea to include both Balkan and Caucasian states, such as Albania and Armenia, that do not lie on that body of water.

Initiatives such as the CBSS and BSEC are limited by two related factors. One, they are each very functionally based, that is, concentrating not on high security but low-political issues that are meant to be win–win, such as transportation, energy and the environment. Indeed, the CBSS even specifically excluded security from its mandate, presumably realizing that trying to address any such issues with such a diverse membership, including the Russian Federation, could paralyse any other initiatives. Of course even low-political functional issues can and do become politicized and even influence national security. It is therefore not surprising that the second consideration – membership – has also limited these groupings, both regarding their stipulated (and limited) mandates and also in elevating them to higher objectives that might fundamentally change the geopolitical and geocultural orientation of their region. The CBSS and the BSEC initiatives have homogenous memberships – NATO and EU members, former communist regimes and former Soviet republics, and the Russian Federation. Officials and analysts in some national ministries say that Russia particularly obfuscates working relations in these bodies, although the

Secretariat (perhaps unsurprisingly because of the requirement of a neutral status) maintains that the Russian government maintains a positive, constructive and often proactive stance within the Council (various interviews). In contrast to the CEI, CBSS summits are regularly attended by member states and with appropriate level of representation. The Secretariat notes also that Russian foreign ministers always make a point of attending.

Among the achievements from BSEC's concentration on functional activities is that it has succeeded in establishing a regional bank to facilitate investments, although lending been provided to individual countries rather than for multilateral initiatives. BSEC remains important for providing forums and institutional cooperation among countries with either strained relations or those even in a state of war. Thus for the former (though outside the remit of post-communist states), Greek–Turkish relations have been aided by duality in the running of major BSEC activities: the Secretariat is in Turkey while finance and research activities are headquartered in Greece. BSEC officials point to the Organization's ability (otherwise unrecognized) to improve relations between Georgia and Russia before the war of August 2008, and to the membership of Armenia and Azerbaijan, who lack bilateral relations due to the conflict over Nagorno-Karabakh. The twentieth anniversary summit of BSEC, held in June 2012, was not attended by the president of Armenia but other senior Armenian officials did participate.

Another set of regional formations confront both legacies of war in the Balkans and the region's relative lack of development. A first initiative, convened by Bulgaria in 1996, was the South-East European Cooperation Process (SEECP). The SEECP launched the RCC in Sofia in February 2008. The Regional Cooperation Council consists of 46 countries and international institutions; in this way the RCC is the most atypical of all regional formation by having its composition made up of a majority of extra-regional actors. The RCC engages in a range of activities to develop the region, from economic and energy to societal and security. It claims 'genuine regional ownership' but also the support of its European and international partners (see for example, RCC Annual Report 2011–12: 14). The RCC signals the importance of the Balkans to Euro-Atlantic interests and seeks to provide a unique functional forum in which divergent national Balkan-state interests can be reconciled on a regional basis and the practical aspects of regional development can be overseen and, indeed, financed, by other countries and international institutions. Groupings such as the CEI, CBSS, BSEC and the RCC, despite some weaknesses, have nevertheless helped to transform regional relations by creating new sets of relations across what was the socialist bloc. These different groupings should also demonstrate that the choice of geographic names has been important in jettisoning associations with 'old' and often pejorative terms. Although any name could have been used for such formations, 'Eastern Europe' is not among them. Neutral ones, based on objective geography, are, such as the Baltic and the Black Seas. The 'Balkans' tends also to be replaced either by 'South-eastern Europe' or by the functionally descriptive, like the Regional Cooperation Council.

The one grouping that has had a profound impact on the geopolitical reorientation of its members, and to a significant but under-appreciated extent also on the transformation of European security, is Visegrad. This is a group, among other attributes, that chose a different appellation for itself, although the geocultural significance of 'Central Europe' was then tied directly to it, ,and then was successfully projected within and beyond that region. It deserves careful attention for the role it has played in achieving the leading foreign policy aims of its members and in changing the overall dynamics of post-communist regional relations and security.

Visegrad

The geocultural repositioning of the core of the 'old' Eastern Europe – the Czech Republic, Hungary, Slovakia and Poland – was by far the most successful. How that was achieved rested not only on domestic changes but also on a particular regional transformation, and the successful projection of that regional transformation on Western policy audiences. Yet the importance of Visegrad cooperation to the geopolitical transformation of the old Eastern Europe into Central Europe is often unknown or ignored. To go 'back to Europe' and change 'Eastern Europe' into 'Central Europe' was a central tenet of Central European societal and foreign policy thinking after the 1989 revolutions.

This section first outlines how Visegrad helped to project a new image of a Central European region onto the West and thereby help to facilitate the region to come 'back to Europe'. Having established its importance, Visegrad's origins are briefly assessed. Then, by drawing on some of successive failures of Visegrad and of observer comments of its demise, the section demonstrates, counter intuitively, the vitality of Visegrad. A final part shows Visegrad's contemporary importance, including its – and the EU's – engagement with the West Balkans and European parts of the former Soviet Union.

Visegrad and getting 'back to Europe'

Going 'back to Europe' ultimately meant entry into the EC/EU and NATO. But neither of those institutions (despite what might retrospectively be claimed) initially contemplated extending membership to the newly liberated countries of the Soviet bloc. True, some forms of engagement were offered; but both had to be convinced of even the idea of membership. To underline this divide between Central European aspirations and Euro-Atlantic institutional lethargy or fear, consider the views of some of those confronting the situation from the former's perspective. Magda Vasaryova, a post-communist Czechoslovak ambassador and then Slovak ambassador and Slovak Secretary of State for Foreign Affairs, stated that from the vantage of 1991 the Central European goals of NATO and EU membership 'seemed virtually impossible to achieve' (Vasaryova, 2006: 77) Czech president Vaclav Havel, who commanded unparalleled moral respect in the West, could still find it necessary to write in 1994 in the US journal *Foreign Affairs* about the moral duty of NATO to accept like-minded countries in order to sway the Alliance to open its ranks (Havel, 1994).

Central European personalities who led the efforts to win entry into NATO and EU attest that Visegrad was central to attaining that outcome. When Czechoslovakia, Hungary and Poland became the first post-communist countries to secure Association Agreements with the EC in December 1991, which were also signed at a joint ceremony, Czechoslovakia's Foreign Minister credited that prompt achievement to the coordination provided by Visegrad, while his Hungarian counterpart called the Agreements 'a very visible endorsement of the Visegrad model' (Jeszenszky, 2006: 62). Poland's first post-communist president, the Solidarity leader Lech Wałesa, considered the 'tangible fruits' of Visegrad cooperation to be Central Europe's membership of NATO and the EU (Wałesa, 2006: 81). Hungarian diplomat Andras Simonyi called Visegrad a 'historic success' which won 'the trans-Atlantic community's embrace' (Simonyi, 2006: 96). Principal foreign policy advisers in post-communist Czechoslovakia call Visegrad 'a powerful negotiating tool' for achieving NATO membership and add that Visegrad's 'close and coordinated work ... compelled American and Western European politicians to open the doors of the Atlantic alliance to us' (Vondra, 2006: 80; Zantovsky, 2006: 84). While Visegrad cooperation was meant to ensure that the Central European countries did not work against each other in trying to seek Western institutional membership (such nationalist competition nevertheless still did occur), one diplomat involved in Central European cooperation since 1990 asserted that Visegrad was also important in securing accession precisely *because* it made each country more aware of national preparations for accession, and the closeness of cooperation created a positive cooperation that spurred each other on to meet EU accession requirements (interview, Budapest, February 2012).

Certainly, Visegrad by itself could not win NATO or EU membership for its countries. Sympathizers and supporters were needed in the West. But cooperation through Visegrad helped to dispel the negative connotations of the region and to create some forms of practical cooperation that could then contribute to the accession process, including by giving evidence of Central European commitment to the Euro-Atlantic integration process. Within that process Visegrad cooperation signalled to the West that not only would the region's old historical animosities not reignite but that the countries and peoples of the region were placing themselves on a new and positive footing. That footing was intended to be one that the EU itself would recognize as mirroring its aspirations on burying national rivalries and antagonisms in supranational cooperation. Rudolf Chmel, once a post-communist Czechoslovak ambassador and more recently a Slovak Deputy Prime Minister, recounted in 2012 that back in the early 1990s 'in the mind of the West' Slovak–Hungarian relations posed the real threat of an ethnic explosion' (*Visegrad Insight*, 2012: 44). Visegrad's founding Declaration pledged to respect every form of coexistence and to bury the region's hostilities in new-found positive cooperation.

Having suggested that Visegrad contributed to the accession of Central Europe to Western institutions, the chapter now can give some space to its origins.

Visegrad's origins

Visegrad was unquestionably strongly rooted in both communist-era dissident values and in the limited but important physical cooperation among those dissidents. Such a heritage was absent from the other forms of regional cooperation described above.

With the backdrop of NATO and the EC hardly embracing Central Europe, and with the crushing of peaceful protestors in the Baltic in January 1991 (some of whom lost their lives), the three leaders of Czechoslovakia, Hungary and Poland met at the Hungarian town of Visegrad, used previously to crown Hungarian kings, and announced their cooperation with the Visegrad Declaration of 15 February 1991. The Declaration made positive, if very selective use of common history, to signal that the three countries were abandoning the region's history of inter-ethnic tension and mistrust. Better still, they were thereby reasserting values that were fundamentally European and would thereby not only contribute to, but be an essential part of, the ongoing integration of 'Europe' (http://www.visegradgroup.eu).

Tangible Visegrad cooperation pushed forward, often prompted by external events. The August 1991 coup attempt by the Soviet military and security services against Gorbachev was the atmosphere in which joint meetings of Visegrad defence ministers were convened and then contributed to the holding of Visegrad's second presidential summit, in Krakow. There the Three declared their common intention to seek NATO membership. Visegrad also demonstrated to the EC that the three countries could cooperate. They confirmed trade liberalization among themselves, and while that never exceeded what was required of them in the Association Agreements with the EC, the resulting Central European Free Trade Agreement uniquely showed the willingness of a group of post-communist countries to organize themselves economically. And this not easy to do; the countries were direct competitor in several major fields. By using 'Central Europe' in its name CEFTA again helped to promote a new image of the region. Neighbouring post-socialist countries sought to join it, seeing it as a marker of their own transformation and a means of approaching the EU. Several countries were eventually admitted before CEFTA had to dissolve when its members acceded to the EU (the Union not permitting prior free trade agreements to stand). Nevertheless, the EU itself chose the name CEFTA for the free trade region it launched in 2006 for the Balkans. Central Europe had become a viable name used by other actors for other regions.

A further mark of Visegrad's transformative effect was that countries around Visegrad, particularly in the Balkans, wanted membership of Visegrad, and made clear, in what could be called self-effacing comments, that such membership and its connotation of 'moving' to Central Europe would have signalled their own successful transformation (see Fawn, 2001 and 2010). Despite all of these successes, however, Visegrad had had many near-death experiences. Its many resurrections attest to its importance.

The break-up of Czechoslovakia was a particular blow; its central geography and its Visegrad-inspiring leadership were lost at the end of 1992. (Havel would become president of the Czech Republic but Dienstbier remained out of foreign policy.) More importantly, the hypermarketizing strategies of the new Czech prime minister, Vaclav Klaus, led him to denigrate Visegrad cooperation. In Slovakia, the overtly nationalistic policies of Vladimir Meciar antagonized the Hungarian minority and inter-state relations with Hungary. Meciar's coolness towards Euro-Atlantic integration and flirtation with Russia (especially consideration of the purchase of a Russian air defence system) put a block on the prospect of accession. Slovakia was excluded from the first round of EU and NATO negotiations. This called into further question the rationale of Visegrad. With the electoral defeats of Klaus in 1997 and Meciar in 1997 and 1998, all four countries were keen to renew cooperation and a Visegrad II was launched in 1999.

Because Visegrad's primary aims of EU and NATO accession were achieved, we might therefore reasonably expect that Visegrad's importance in each member's foreign policy to disappear. To kill doubts, Visegrad leaders specifically agreed on the group's continuation beyond EU membership. In May 2004, Visegrad leaders therefore deliberately issued a sequel Declaration, at Kromeriz in the Czech Republic: from inside the EU the group would continue and would contribute to the development of European values. That was reiterated two years later, on the fifteenth anniversary of Visegrad's 1991 foundation, by Visegrad ambassadors abroad who jointly wrote of the success and continuation of the group. Then on the twentieth anniversary of Visegrad cooperation, in February 2011, a major summit was convened in Bratislava. Another declaration reaffirmed Visegrad's continuation. The heads of state of Austria, Germany and Ukraine, as 'major partners of Visegrad', were also invited and attended. The event was significant and eye-catching enough that, according to V4 representatives, the British and French governments asked to know why they had not been included (interviews, February 2012).

Declarations are one thing; actions another. Further evidence of Visegrad's longevity comes from its integration into regular governmental activity. Visegrad National Coordinators are located in the respective national foreign ministries. But in successive years of asking about the formulation of Visegrad activities, Visegrad really has gained an independent life in many ministries, that is, other ministries across the four Visegrad countries proactively initiate and pursue policies together (interviews). The successive national V4 presidencies also indicate a range of initiative among all V4 ministries. Slovakia's Vasaryova, who also served as State Secretary in the Slovak Ministry of Foreign Affairs, attests: 'Visegrad cooperation is a daily reality in the work of all government and state institutions' (2006: 78). But perhaps the best indicator of Visegrad's success after EU accession and within in the EU came in November 2009 when French president Nicolas Sarkozy publicly questioned the need for a group meeting to coordinate their positions before European Council meetings. Now the group meets before all major summits, including for NATO, and issues statements, such as it did in advance of the NATO Chicago summit in May 2012. As one Visegrad diplomat put it, such pre-summit group coordination 'is completely normal' (interview, July 2012).

In addition, according to regional diplomats, Visegrad has become a brand name and a trademark with recognition overseas and in international business activity, particularly in east Asia, helping to make its members appear as a coherent investment area. National V4 diplomatic representatives talk openly of the near-impossibility of their (small) countries having name recognition globally and, practically, of attracting trade and investment. They clearly recognize the benefits – and cost-effectiveness – of acting as one region globally. Added activities include 'Visegrad Houses' overseas, the first being in Cape Town, South Africa, and a second planned for Crimea, Ukraine, which not only provide information on the region, but also provide consular services for Visegrad citizens.

A final area for evidence of Visegrad's continued vitality and the creation of its own niche of influence concerns neighbouring areas of the EU. Visegrad cooperation has been called by its sponsors an 'engine of a more dynamic EU policy towards Eastern and South-Eastern Europe', one able to export democracy and freedom throughout this region (Simonyi, 2006: 97). As Wałesa commented after accession: 'Cooperation between the Visegrad Group and other countries, especially those of Eastern Europe, has become an important assignment.... We can play an essential role as a bridge' between the EU and NATO with those post-communist states still outside of those institutions (Wałesa, 2006: 82).

Visegrad has aimed to push the EU to increase its involvement in the West Balkans and Eastern Partnership (EaP) countries. The Hungarian presidency noted, rightly, that success would depend on the willingness of EaP countries to engage. The presidency programme called for the V4 to

> seek to support political and social-economic reforms of the Eastern Partner States, facilitating approximation towards the European Union and the best possible compliance with EU values and standards. Support should be maintained in order to create the necessary conditions to accelerate political association and further economic integration between the European Union and interested Eastern Partners. (*2009/10 Hungarian Presidency*, 2010)

A sympathetic but independent assessment wrote, 'During the Hungarian V4 presidency the [Visegrad] member countries coordinated their activities concerning the Western Balkans and presented a united policy towards the region in the EU bodies, which was a major achievement' (Koles, 2011: 89).

V4 diplomats routinely comment on how their region, through previous membership of the Soviet bloc, knows the rest of the former communist world better than their Western partners, as well as having experience of political-economic transformation and of the Russian language. Tangible features of specific Visegrad cooperation with other post-socialist countries come through the International Visegrad Fund (IVF). The Fund declares itself to be single largest provider of scholarships for foreign study to and in Ukraine. These were 'a gift to Ukraine after the Orange Revolution' (interview, February 2012). Even if the government of Viktor Yanukovych downgraded the Euro-Atlantic ambitions of the preceding, pro-Western Viktor Yushchenko administration, he accorded importance to Visegrad. Within that was both practical cooperation and also Visegrad's European values. Ukrainian leaders regularly express strong interest in participation in V4 activities, including military cooperation. Visegrad representatives emphasize the group's intentions to continue to work with Ukraine and to bring it closer to Europe. Yanukovych stated in May 2011: 'I would like us to spread the Visegrad spirit of unity and partnership across the entire region of Central and Eastern Europe. Today, through our region passes the line that divides European countries into "members" and "non-members" of the EU. We cannot allow this barrier to become firmly established and turn into a new artificial "Berlin Wall" of Europe' (cited in *States News Service*, 2011). Perhaps most striking is the success the IVF has with Belarus. While Belarus–EU relations are very strained, including the imposition of travel restrictions on Belarusian officials, the IVF maintains an extensive scholarship and exchange programme with the country. IVF officials explain that none of these relations has ever been affected and that the Belarusian government maintains a positive outlook on the cooperation. Visegrad's outreach to the West Balkan and EaP countries is a microcosm of remaining dilemmas of post-1989 European geopolitics – where and how those countries 'fit' in Europe constitute the final section.

The future orientation of the West Balkans and post-Soviet European states

The West Balkans are clearly drawing closer to the EU. While accession for the whole region may be a long process (as we discuss in the previous chapter), all countries have been offered Stabilization and Association Agreements; and between 56 and 73 per cent of individual West Balkan state trade is with the EU, and with often much of the remainder being with fellow CEFTA states. Albania and Croatia entered NATO in 2009; most others want Alliance membership. Because of the status of Kosovo, Serbia might be an outlier in Euro-

Atlantic integration. Serbia's president-elect Tomislav Nikolic said in May 2012 that Serbia was on the road to the EU; that it would continue building relations with Russia meanwhile, and he discounted membership of NATO.

Atypical of all CEEC (Central and East European countries), Belarus remains strongly tied to Russia. In the 1990s, bilateral agreements established a 'Community', then a 'Union', then a 'Union State' of Russia and Belarus (see Wilson, 2007: 107), although Russian enthusiasm for integration dissipated under Vladimir Putin. Belarus's trade remains dominated by Russia (46.5 per cent, versus 31.6 per cent for Ukraine and 18.4 per cent for Moldova). Belarus has joined regional economic formations that place it with non-European post-Soviet states. It participates in the Single Economic Space (with Ukraine, Russia and Kazakhstan), and in the Eurasian Economic Community, in which it is the only one of the CEEC, and whose membership is predominantly Central Asian. Belarus also formed the Customs Union with Russia and Kazakhstan, which entered into force on 1 January 2010 (with expectations that Kyrgyzstan will be admitted). Regional political and security state formations further indicate Belarus's eastward foreign policy priority. Belarus is, again, alone among CEEC in its membership of the Collective Security Treaty Organization, which commits it to the collective defence of Russia, Armenia and four Central Asian states.

By contrast, Ukraine seeks membership of both the EU and NATO, and NATO has reiterated that it (and Georgia) will enter the Alliance, although the specifics and timetable of accession remain unstated. As discussed above, Ukrainian governments have sought close working relations with Central Europe. Ukraine's total trade remains slightly more with Russia than with the EU (31.6 compared with 28.6 per cent) but the former is dominated by energy. Moldova has been reorienting itself also – unlike Belarus or Ukraine, it has membership of CEFTA, which facilitates inter-Balkan trade and trade with EU. Moldova's trade within CEFTA is negligible, but 45.3 per cent of all of its trade is with the EU, in contrast to 18.4 per cent with Russia. Although Ukraine and Moldova participate in the structures of the Commonwealth of Independent States – the principal inter-state formation that succeeded the Soviet Union – Ukraine has never ratified its charter. More importantly, in 1997 Ukraine and Moldova formed, with Georgia and Azerbaijan, a group that took the names of its members (between 1999 and 2005 Uzbekistan also joined, during which time the group was GUUAM). This formation was seen as an expression of geopolitical repluralization in the CIS (see Kuzio, 2000) and while the group formally denies such, it has been viewed as a counterbalance to

Russian influence in post-Soviet space (including with American support) and to limit CIS structures to economic, rather than political or military, cooperation. At its 2006 summit, GUAM added the suffix of the Organization for Democratic and Economic Development.

However much the governments and people of Belarus, Moldova and Ukraine might choose their foreign policy orientation (regime change in Belarus could bring a sharp reorientation towards the West), it is clear that these three countries, along with Armenia, Azerbaijan and Georgia, have become at least an ideational battleground between the EU (and to an extent NATO) and Russia. The EU's 'Eastern Partnership', launched in 2009, was intended to enhance relations with those six countries, including preparations for comprehensive free trade and visa liberalization, leading to what the EU calls 'gradual integration in the EU economy' (European Union External Action Service, 2012), as well as developing good governance in each of those countries. To that end, EaP summits have provided an added opportunity for the EU to criticize undemocratic and human rights-abusing behaviour directly to governments responsible, particularly in Belarus.

Despite reassurances, the Russian government has viewed the EaP as part of a zero-sum contest for control over the lands between it and the EU. Russian president Dmitri Medvedev said 'We do not want the Eastern Partnership to turn into a partnership against Russia.... We tried to convince ourselves but in the end we couldn't'. Russian Foreign Minister Sergei Lavrov warned that the EaP summit seemed like a 'choice' to the states invited to the EaP summit: 'either you are with Russia, or with the European Union' (quotations from Benes, 2009).

The principal – and vexing – dilemma in the reconfiguration of Eastern Europe is how each of those countries can exercise their own interests; how Euro-Atlantic institutions and Russia can each accommodate those interests, and then reconcile their difference between them.

Conclusion

On the one hand, post-communist regional cooperation initiatives have generally been meant as intermediary measures, particularly for accession to EU and NATO. On the other hand, more than two decades of history – and the fact of EU and NATO accession – demonstrate that some of these groupings not only retain purpose but advance robust, dynamic agendas. Some are withering; some are overgrown by overlapping, competing formations; still others, despite doubts, have blossomed. What they have all done is to give a level of interaction within the 'old' Eastern Europe – that is between those states, and in some cases even between those societies – as well as providing an added mechanism for external involvement. Still further, these groupings have helped to change the Western conception of a backward, grey 'Eastern Europe' by providing both alternative names and also, to varying degrees, tangible evidence of regional stability, even of regional harmony. These changes, often ignored in the considerable library on 'transition', do constitute part of the post-1989 transformation. Visegrad certainly helped to convince NATO and the EU of these countries' viability as partners. And in the case of some regional formations, perhaps foremost again that of Visegrad, they have also gained a life and purpose in their own right. While EU influence over the rest of the West Balkans will continue, probably culminating in accession, the relationship of Belarus, Ukraine and Moldova (not to mention the Caucasus) between Brussels and Moscow is likely to remain in flux, if not aggravating relations between. That large issue notwithstanding, Central and Eastern Europe has undergone a revolutionary geopolitical transformation since 1989 and now also features regional suprastate actors and identities that are part of their own – and of Europe's – new institutional architecture.

Chapter 8

Executive Leadership

Ray Taras

A litmus test for establishing the similarity of post-communist political systems with their Western European counterparts is to look at the structure of executive leadership. Even though 'the institutional models of democracy are very few' (Przeworski, 1992: 99), the majority of Central and Eastern European states have chosen a model that is a mix of parliamentary and presidential government.

National constitutions specify which offices are executive and how much power is vested in them. Generally, some combination of the office of president, prime minister and cabinet ministers (or government) makes up the political executive. However constituted, executive leadership is checked by the legislative and judicial branches of government. It would appear, then, that examining executive leadership can parse the distribution of political power in a country. But there is a caveat.

Not all shifts of political power show up when the focus is on the political executive. For example, the case of Hungary under the Fidesz government after 2010 has entailed constitutional change and transfers of power that conceal the shift back to authoritarianism. Significant political changes have taken place without overt enhancement of the powers of the executive office held by the prime minister, Viktor Orban. Instead political power has been shifted to the governing party, Fidesz, by giving party deputies in the legislature greater law-making authority. Quasi-governmental institutions with considerable political autonomy were set up that were stacked with Fidesz appointees serving long terms, like boards overseeing television and radio broadcasting. This chapter considers what we do learn about political power by focusing on executive leadership.

What is the political executive?

The core of any political system is its executive branch of government. Before countries had parliaments, judiciaries and bureaucracies, they had executive leadership, whether in the form of absolute monarchs, emperors, strongmen, sultans or caudillos. In a modern political system, the political executive is expected to share power with other government branches and be checked by them. Nevertheless, it is the political executive that is ultimately responsible for exercising leadership and formulating policy, in short, for governing a country.

Significant differences in executive leadership exist across this region. There may be *intra-executive* conflicts, especially in recently constructed political systems (Figure 8.1). These have frequently involved 'a political struggle between the president and the prime minister over the control of the executive branch' (Sedelius, 2006: 19). Far more common are *executive–legislative* conflicts in both presidential (such as the US) and semi-presidential (the French Fifth Republic) systems. These are more likely when the executive office and the legislature are controlled by competing political parties. The parliamentary model (the UK) is not immune from conflict between cabinets (the executive) and legislatures, never more so than when no party commands a majority of parliamentary seats.

Political executives differ in terms of their social background and career paths, the process by which they arrive in office, the powers that they hold, and the policies that they pursue. The size, competence and ambitions of the state bureaucracy shape political executives as well.

Simple typologies of the political executive can be based on two dichotomies: effective (the president of Russia) versus ceremonial (the king of Spain); and individual (the German chancellor) versus collective (the British cabinet) (Almond and Powell, 1983: 106). Executive power evolves over time, as in the stronger American presidency we see today and the enhanced role of the prime minister in Britain.

Given such different evolutionary paths, it is no surprise that Central and East European countries have taken distinctive approaches to constructing executive power. Thus, though Poland and Belarus are neighbours, the constitutional, electoral and political checks on the Polish president and prime minister contrast starkly with the virtual unaccountability of the political executive – the presidency – in the former Soviet republic. The general trend across the region has been a linear process of limiting the powers of the presidency, whether in Hungary where they were never great, to the Czech Republic after Vaclav Havel's presidency, or most recently in such Balkan states as Croatia and Serbia where presidents have seen their powers eroded. Belarus has defied this evolutionary process.

Ukraine, exceptionally, has continued to swing between presidential and cabinet-legislative dominance. Constitutional changes enacted in 2004 changed the system from presidential to parliamentary–presiden-

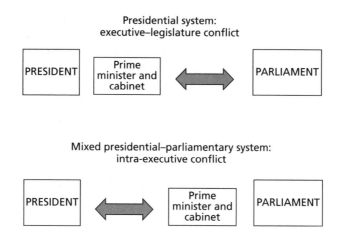

Figure 8.1 *Conflict in presidential versus conflict in mixed presidential-parliamentary systems*

tial; this occurred on the initiative of then prime minister Viktor Yanukovych's party which had captured control of parliament and wished to circumscribe presidential power. But in 2010, shortly after he had been elected president, the Ukraine Constitutional Court, now comprising justices appointed by Yanukovych himself, ruled that the 2004 changes were unconstitutional and reinstated the strongly presidential system envisaged in the original post-communist constitution of 1996. Similar to the case of Vladimir Putin in Russia, Yanukovych has empowered the office he occupies.

Three general types of executive government can be identified in modern democracies. The first is *cabinet government* in which political leadership is entrusted to a prime minister and those of her colleagues who head the important departments of government. A test of whether cabinet government exists is whether it accepts collective responsibility before parliament for the policies it pursues. The Czech Republic, Hungary, Poland, Slovakia and Slovenia are countries that early in their post-communist development opted for cabinet government. While there have been strong prime ministers in the new democracies – Vaclav Klaus in the Czech Republic (who is now president), Janez Drnovsek in Slovenia and, arguably the most powerful of all, Milo Dukanovic in Montenegro – so have there been in Britain, exemplified by Margaret Thatcher and Tony Blair.

The second kind of executive government is the *presidential system*. It is distinguished by the fact that there is a single head of the political executive who is elected to office directly by voters. In this model, the president usually combines the roles of head of government and head of state, that is, effective and ceremonial roles. In a cabinet or parliamentary system, on the other hand, the head of state largely performs a ceremonial role. The office holder in a presidential system appoints the top members of the cabinet and they become a part of the executive branch. Belarus under Alexander Lukashenka, Ukraine before the Orange Revolution and after 2010, Romania in the early 1990s and Yugoslavia under Slobodan Milosevic had presidential systems of government.

Sometimes these cases are considered to make up a super-presidential system:

> a huge apparatus of executive power that overshadows other state agencies and the national legislature in terms of its size and the resources it uses; a president who controls most or all of the levers of public expenditure; a president who enjoys the power to make laws by decree;...a legislature that enjoys little real oversight authority over the executive branch; and a judiciary that is appointed and controlled largely by the president and that cannot in practice check presidential prerogatives or even abuse of power. (Fish, 2000: 178–9)

Super-presidentialism is a system favoured by many of the non-European former Soviet republics in the Caucasus and Central Asia. Russia under Vladimir Putin has been called a super-presidential system. Its appeal is the ease with which quasi-democratic features can be blended with non-democratic practices. It can pass as a form of post-communist authoritarianism which masks the existence of a personal dictatorship and one-party system.

The third kind of executive system is *parliamentary government*. Here the elected legislature is dominant and, paradoxically, it wrests executive power from the executive branch. The classic example of such a system is the Third (1875–1940) and Fourth (1946–58) French Republics where the legislature was able to overthrow cabinets with ease. If we regard turnover of prime ministers and their cabinets triggered by parliamentary crises, rather than by electoral verdicts, as the marker of parliamentary government, then Poland qualified as a parliamentary-dominant system from 1989 to 2007. But since then its executive volatility sparked by an unruly legislature has vanished.

Does high executive turnover matter? One eight-country study of the region highlighted the dependent character of executive and parliamentary turnover: 'executive volatility takes on significance only after legislative volatility is also included' (Forestiere, 2010: 915). Thus Poland's revolving carousel of prime ministers in the 1990s and 2000s was a product of the volatile party system found in the legislature. By contrast, where there is 'increased executive stability, allowing governments to enact and implement reform..., the quality of governance can be very high (Forestiere, 2010: 924). Significantly, Poland's impressive economic performance at a time of economic crisis elsewhere in Europe took place when its executive volatility was ending. The first post-communist-era Polish government to be entrusted with a second term, the administration headed by prime minister Donald Tusk, occurred in the 2011 elections.

The appeal of mixed systems

Executive structures in the region have been characterized by fluidity and hybridity. A mix of presidential–parliamentary government has appeared the safest choice for democratic consolidation, for reasons that include the following.

A pure presidential system, first of all, generates a zero-sum game: the winning candidate takes all, as in Belarus under Lukashenka. A parliamentary system, by contrast, increases total payoffs, with many parties gaining influence even while losing elections. Losers in this system have an incentive to stay in the game because they are heartened by the prospect of expanding their representation or of obtaining positions of power next time around. Mixed presidential–parliamentary systems have produced greater rotation of leaders – presidents, prime ministers, and cabinets – than a presidential one ordinarily would.

The best example of a hybrid system is the semi-presidentialism of the French Fifth Republic, which has had wide appeal in post-communist Europe. In constitutional terms, the president holds wide executive powers. Thus, after his election in 2012 Francois Hollande appointed his own prime minister and cabinet even though the legislature was still controlled by a rival political bloc. The Fifth Republic weathered uneasy periods of 'cohabitation,' such as between a socialist president and conservative government (1986–88), and a conservative president and socialist prime minister (1997–2002). These episodes established the convention that under cohabitation the strong presidency envisaged by the constitution is set aside in favour of semi-presidentialism.

Cohabitation in the more volatile conditions of post-communist Europe has not always worked as smoothly. Various issues have triggered intra-executive conflicts, in particular when executive officeholders are attached to different parties. Thus the election of a liberal *president* in Bulgaria in 1996 precipitated a wave of anti-socialist demonstrations demanding the immediate resignation of the socialist *government* even though it had a mandate to rule for two years more. By contrast in Poland a former communist who was elected president, Alexander Kwasniewski, encountered few difficulties in working with a prime minister from the Solidarity camp between 1997 and 2001. In the Czech Republic right-wing president Klaus, elected by parliament in 2003, was at loggerheads with the Social Democratic prime minister in 2005–06. The virtual tie between leftist and conservative blocs in the 2006 parliamentary election provided Klaus with the opportunity to strengthen his position by nominating a prime minister from his own party.

Executive experimentation

Fifth Republic-type semi-presidentialism requires direct election of the president, which has not been the case in Albania, the Czech Republic, Estonia, Hungary, Latvia, and Moldova since 1996. In these countries, the president is selected indirectly, by parliament, and real executive power is likely to be exercised by the prime minister, usually the leader of parliament's largest party. The direct election of the president, for example in Poland, of itself does not guarantee that he will exercise real political, as opposed to formal, executive power. Like their French counterpart, Central and Eastern European presidents generally serve five-year terms (four in the case of Romania). Like France's National Assembly, their parliaments have a four-year mandate (the exception is Slovenia, where it is five). The extra year in most presidents' terms privileges the office and is suggestive of semi-presidentialism. But in practice it is the president's need to compromise when deadlock with parliament occurs that distinguishes this model.

When presidents in the new Europe have been forced to compromise, it has required them to concede some presidential powers. As across much of the region, the executive powers of Bulgaria's presidency began to dwindle in the mid-1990s at a time when its incumbent belonged to a political bloc different from that of the prime minister. Similarly, when Iliu Iliescu regained the presidency in Romania in 2000, the office was markedly weaker than the one he had been elected to in 1990 and 1992. Two of the most remarkable shifts from a presidential system to semi-presidentialism occurred in Croatia and Serbia. The end of the Tudjman and Milosevic eras led to the rise of legislatures that recast their political executives along the lines of Slovenia.

Croatia and Serbia began to recognize that efficient and adaptive institutions presuppose a society's willingness to abandon dysfunctional institutional arrangements. As Douglass North, Nobel laureate in economics, emphasized, 'the society that permits the maximum generation of trials will be most likely to solve problems through time' (North, 1992: 81).

A major dilemma facing constitutional framers after communism's end was resolving the tension between the imperatives of democracy and those of efficiency. The choice would affect the political executive in that a preference for deliberative democracy would favour the legislative branch; priority given to the virtues of efficiency and management, by contrast, would bolster the executive branch. In a handful of states, particularly former Soviet republics outside the Baltic region, the deck was stacked about equally against both democracy and efficiency. In general, the specific historical, economic, and social conditions of each country shaped the selection of institutional arrangements.

The distribution of both constitutional authority and political power has changed significantly since 1989. Petr Kopecky noted 'a trend towards a changing balance of power between executive leadership (and agencies) and their respective legislatures across the region'. But this trend has involved increased legislative assertion over the political executive, not the reverse as the author suggested. Kopecky's argument is that 'the partial stabilisation of political parties and party systems, together with the institutional reforms of the core executive and the enlargement of the EU, have eventually led to a marked increase in the control exercised by political executives over parliaments in the region' (2004: 142). Yet with the exception of Belarus, no all-powerful president or prime minister has emerged, and instead political power has typically been exercised by prime ministers holding office for short periods of time and kept in check by parties, parliaments, and presidents (Figure 8.2).

Factors shaping the political executive

Many factors have influenced the choice of model of political executive. Constitutions adopted in the 1990s reflected a backlash against communist authoritarianism and its centralized system of executive power, a new set of expectations about the role of civil society in governance, the different political traditions of the individual states, the individual preferences of actor–agents, and the international normative regime dominant at the time. Let us consider each of these factors in turn.

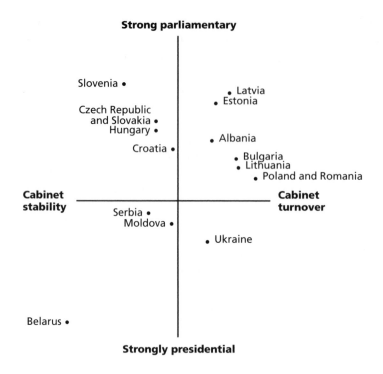

Figure 8.2   *Type of political system of cabinet turnover*

Backlash against communism and new public expectations

The constraining experience of communism served as a catalyst for putting greater trust in representative institutions rather than strong rulers, and this logic continues to be operative a quarter of a century after the region's democratic breakthrough. Even if we were to accept the contentious proposition that most Central and Eastern European societies historically preferred rule by strong leaders, the political environment was very different when these states enacted regime change beginning in 1989. Survey results from the 1990s onwards indicated that respondents increasingly prized a representative form of government over strong leadership. While some societies embraced representative democracy at the outset in 1989, in others democratic values and practices grew on citizens.

Democracy presupposes that citizens support the institutions that are created and consent to the leaders who emerge. Put another way, 'constitutional forms are lifeless or irrelevant if they do not have the support of the people. That is why even though elites propose, the masses dispose' (Rose, Mishler and Haerpfer, 1998: 8). If institutions are the hardware of democracy, what people think about them makes up democracy's software (Agh, 1996: 127). Democratic rule and efficient government are not irreconcilable, for 'The ideal democratic system is representative and has effective leaders. Logically, the two criteria can be mutually reinforcing, in so far as leaders may gain effectiveness by mobilizing popular support, and effective action increases a leader's popular support' (Rose and Mishler, 1996: 224). But there was danger of a contrary process developing. Robert Tucker, long-time analyst of Soviet politics, speculated about 'the possibility of an authoritarian personality serving as leader in the regime of a constitutional democracy, and, conversely, of a democratic personality serving as the leader in an authoritarian system of rule' (1981: 68).

While public opinion can act as a safeguard against a return to authoritarian practices, it can also be manipulated to serve those in power. On the basis of a case study of Bulgaria, one author concluded that a decade after communism's collapse, 'political elites use opinion polls not to extend political power to citizens, but to concentrate it in their own hands' (Henn, 2001: 67–8). Instead of populist government, which pollster George Gallup had thought would result from elites knowing voters' preferences well, Joseph Schumpeter's notion of competitive elitism, in which leaders acquire information about the electorate's views in order to obtain a competitive advantage over adversaries, has become more common practice (Schumpeter, 1976).

Differing political traditions

Another factor influencing the emergence of executive structures is a nation's prior experience with different forms of government. In this region, political structures of the inter-war period were particularly important in affecting thinking about new institutional designs. Baltic nations looked back on their pre-1940 independent states and sought to reconstruct them after 1989. Advocates of a presidential system in Czechoslovakia and Poland held up the examples of towering inter-war state-builders like Tomas Masaryk and Jozef Pilsudski.

In the case of Hungary, no inter-war leader was dominant for long enough to inspire nostalgia in the 1990s; the authoritarian inter-war leader Admiral Miklos Horthy had been a controversial figure, and one of the reasons given for torpedoing the idea of a directly elected president in 1990 was the danger of a strong executive as exemplified by Horthy. Hungarians' wariness of a strong executive was made apparent when the ambitious Viktor Orban was not re-elected to a second term in 2002 after he had stated his intention to redefine the office of the prime minister along the lines of the powerful German Chancellor. When he returned as prime minister in 2010, he crafted more indirect ways to accumulate power without overtly making the executive office stronger.

Both Bulgaria's and Romania's inter-war experience of illiberal politics and authoritarianism served as a model to be avoided for post-communist state-building. By 1997 both countries had shaken off the worst legacies of communism and, in the case of Bulgaria, had even catapulted the heir to the Bulgarian throne to the post of prime minister. In former Yugoslavia, south Slav nations took advantage of the end of communism to escape from a Serb-dominated state. Croatia, Macedonia and Bosnia-Herzegovina initially established strong presidencies to help accelerate the escape. Slovenia was exceptional in that its break from Yugoslavia was relatively peaceful and swift and it did not need a powerful executive who could take decisive action. Ironically its prime minister, Drnovsek, ended up holding executive power much longer than the autocratic rulers of the other Balkan states.

Actor–agent preferences

The legal experts who write a constitution and the political actors in executive and legislative branches who ratify it are the agents which determine what executive power will look like. Their interests count, therefore, especially since 'The decisive step toward democracy is the devolution of power from a group of people to a set of rules' (Przeworski, 1992: 14). Taking this step is not a mere technical affair for 'Each political force opts for the institutional framework that will best further its values, projects, or interests' (ibid.: 80). Especially during political transition, 'the chances of the particular political forces are very different under alternative institutional arrangements' (ibid.: 40).

The executive structures that emerged in the 1990s were products of bidding and bargaining among interested parties, not simply rational outcomes arrived at by disinterested state-builders. A few cases are illustrative. Those who favoured a strong presidency (like Lech Walesa in Poland) were often the politicians who were the strongest candidates for that office. Those who felt comfortable under cabinet government (like Klaus in the Czech Republic) were usually adept party leaders who performed best in a parliamentary system where technical and brokering skills counted most.

An instructive case of how quality of leadership resulted in different institutional outcomes was in the two constituent parts of former

Czechoslovakia. One study concluded that 'Rather than deep cultural differences between the two countries on the mass level, differences in economic performance, or a previous communist regime of different nature, it is the elite and political competition which function in a different way, and this is what accounts for the different political outcomes' (Kopecky and Mudde, 2000: 77). The Czech political elite united in support of fundamental democratic principles whereas their Slovak counterparts were deeply divided over how to promote national and regime identity. Leaders, their styles, and their personalities affect the character of a political system, then. Especially critical in a transition period is the emergence of 'leaders with the personality formation appropriate to democracy' (Lasswell, 1986: 196). This may help explain why Slovakia was a slow starter in transitioning to democracy when compared with the Czechs.

International norms

The global ascendance of political liberalism and economic neoliberalism in the 1990s was simultaneously a product of communism's defeat and a force promoting a normative shift towards democratic reforms. Political transition occurring in a period of unrivalled American power was bound to reflect the preferences of the then-dominant state. In retrospect it is surprising that the allure of the American presidential system and the stress on individual freedoms did not have a greater impact on constitutional framers in Central and Eastern Europe. Individual liberties were seamlessly inserted into new constitutional documents, but replicating the powerful US executive branch in the region appeared both an intimidating and incongruous task.

Constitutional framers looked to the political experience of Western Europe, which offered an apparently more salient and viable model of institutional architecture while still reflecting the norms of liberalism. A cabinet system of government was *de rigeur* in EU-15 states, exemplary in their political stability, social consensus, and prosperity. EU eastern enlargement would, it was thought, set off a process of 'executive Europeanization' that would help integrate both parts of Europe (Goetz, 2000).

Apart from ideal-type institutional designs and political values, Western Europe's leadership culture evoked envy among numerous politicians in the emergent democracies. In the early 1990s, the role of chief executive played by British prime minister Thatcher was fresh in the minds of emerging conservative groups in these states. The plodding but reassuring style of long-serving German Chancellor Helmut Kohl, who had presided over unprecedented prosperity and political unification, appealed to politicians who lacked charisma but possessed resilience. Another admired German Chancellor was Konrad Adenauer, who had consolidated the West German state and helped produce an economic miracle after the Second World War. For politicians with messianic aspirations – and there were many among those who had spearheaded the victory over communism – Charles de Gaulle of France, founder and centrepiece of the Fifth Republic, cut an especially imposing figure. For more authoritarian-spirited 'democrats', Spanish dictator Francisco Franco as well as Chilean dictator Augusto Pinochet, both of whom had crushed Marxism and set up virtual one-party states, became role models. The paternalism of US president Ronald Reagan also had widespread appeal in the early transition years.

The initial fascination with Western executive leadership faded rapidly as the difficult years of transition produced disillusionment with quick fixes. Almost everywhere in the region, leadership based on charisma took a back seat to one reflecting skilful management of executive–legislative relations and formulation of tried-and-true policy programmes.

The social background of Central and Eastern European leaders

Writers, movie directors, child film stars (and identical twins to boot), stunt pilots, electricians, economists, engineers, philosophers, sociologists, geologists and communist-era bureaucrats have all served as political executives in Central and Eastern Europe since 1989. While occupationally diverse, they have been overwhelmingly male and middle aged. The majority comes from a privileged intelligentsia background, that is, they are well educated, have professional and white-collar occupations, and are financially well off. Elite members have variously used free market, nationalistic, pro-Europe, social democratic and, more recently, anti-EU and xenophobic rhetoric to get elected. They have almost never used the threat of coercion or violence to stay in power. Most have learned to be expert in the art of coalition building, consistent with the finding that 'post-totalitarian leaders tend to be more bureaucratic and state technocratic than charismatic' (Linz and Stepan, 1996: 47).

An issue that might appear critical to the selection of democratic leaders in the region is what they were doing during the communist period. Surprisingly, a critical mass of the first generation of political leadership had ties to the old communist system:

In virtually all post-communist countries, including those which have abandoned old political habits, familiar faces from the communist past dominate the landscape.... Everywhere, individuals who have dropped out of the elite since the fall of communism are outnumbered by those who have maintained or improved their positions, by a ratio of almost nine to one in Russia and over two to one in Poland and Hungary. Until age attrition takes its toll, the best prospects for success under democracy will belong to those who were successful under communism. (Liebich, 1997: 68)

Age attrition has now taken its toll on the presence of communist-era officials in the executive branch of government. In the Baltic states the average cabinet minister is in his or her mid-40s – a reflection of the need to marginalize Soviet-era cadres. In Poland and most other states in the region, the average ministerial age is in the lower 50s. Age attrition has not caught up with two western former Soviet republics, however. Ukraine's president and twice prime minister, Yanukovych, was a Communist Party official entrusted with top management posts before the country became independent. Belarus president Lukashenka had been in charge of a Komsomol (Young Communist) organization and state farm in the Soviet period. By contrast, a shift in 2009 in the balance of power between communists and democrats in Moldova had the effect of removing communists from the political executive. In a systematic attempt to accelerate the removal of former communist cadres, Poland and Hungary launched energetic decommunization programmes around 2005 after earlier campaigns had stalled.

Three sitting presidents in the region have been removed from power by extraordinary means, but their association with communism was not the primary reason for their ouster. Milosevic, Serb leader of a Yugoslavia in its death throes, refused to accept his electoral defeat in 2000 and resigned only after protesters had stormed parliament. He was arrested soon thereafter and delivered to the International Criminal Tribunal for Yugoslavia to face charges of war crimes. In contrast, president Roland Paksas of Lithuania became the first leader in all of Europe to be impeached. In 2004 the Constitutional Court found that he had acted improperly in granting Lithuanian citizenship to a Russian arms dealer and parliament voted to remove him from office. Finally, Hungarian president Pal Schmitt was forced to resign in 2012 after his doctoral degree was revoked on grounds of plagiarism. An appointee of prime minister Orban, it appeared that Fidesz's withdrawal of support for Schmitt had proved decisive in his resignation. There are still cases where it is ex-communists that punish their democratic political opponents. Yulia Tymoshenko, who narrowly lost the

2010 Ukraine presidential election to Yanukovych, was shortly thereafter accused of abusing her power in 2009 while serving as prime minister by concluding a natural gas contract on favourable terms to Russia, and was sentenced to seven years' imprisonment and thrown in jail in 2011. In Belarus, there are no former democratic prime ministers for Lukashenko to jail.

Dissidents from the old communist regime have not been as successful in gaining power as former communists. Winning elections requires different political skills and resources than winning out over communism. The list of political executives who were formerly communist party members is long, while only a few post-1989 presidents and prime ministers can 'boast' of having been incarcerated by communists. The most prominent were Hungary's first democratically elected prime minister Jozsef Antall, Havel, and Wałesa. It may seem puzzling that relatively few 'old warriors', hardened by years of struggle against communism, held power for long in the emergent democracies. Some never could get away from their combative, ideological ways while others turned from politics to capitalism: the communist *nomenklatura* sought to enrich itself but so did many dissident intellectuals (see Eyal *et al.*, 1998).

The rise of a professional political class also took place in the transition years. Many young professionals whose formative experience was of 'goulash communism' in the 1970s, when communists promoted a more Western-oriented economic system, came to power after 1989. In general, executive power in the formative post-communist years was assumed by members of the baby-boom generation born in the early years of East European communism.

Regime change did not increase the representation of women in the political executive. On the contrary, in both executive and legislative branches of government the proportion fell. In 2007, for example, three of ten government ministers in Croatia – the region's leader at that time in female representation – were women, compared with about one-half in the Nordic states. The next highest-ranked countries in the region in 2007 included the three Baltic states with a ratio of about one in five female ministers (UNECE, 2012). At the end of 2010, Baltic leadership in entrusting high executive office to women had given way to Polish and Slovene pacesetting: five of nineteen cabinet posts were held by females in these countries. By contrast, the Czech Republic and Hungary had no women ministers at all in 2010 (Caramani *et al.*, 2011: 873).

The one woman in the region serving as a country's president or prime minister was Dalia Grybauskaite. Her diverse career included rank-and-file membership of the Communist Party of the Soviet Union, acting as Lithuanian finance minister and European Commissioner, standing successfully as an independent candidate for the Lithuanian presidency in 2009, and holding a black belt in karate – unlike Putin who has one in judo. A charitable interpretation of the under-representation of women in executive power is that they prefer to 'express their presence and political will in ways that are different from those of men – or of their sisters in long-established Western democracies' (Szalai, 1998: 200). Not everyone would however agree that women's absence from executive office-holding in the region is the product of women's preferences.

In the Baltic republics, and elsewhere too, a successful professional career in the West was an asset in gaining high office early in the transition. Returning émigrés were appointed as presidents (Latvia's Vaira Vike-Freiburga had lived most of her life in Montreal), prime ministers (Simeon, the claimant to Bulgaria's throne who changed his name to Simeon Borisov Sakskoburggotski when he served as prime minister from 2001 to 2005, had lived in exile in Madrid), and defence, foreign, and finance ministers. By the 2010s, however, returning expatriates were at no advantage in seeking to build a successful political career in their countries of origin.

The state machine and executive leadership

The real work of implementing executive decisions is carried out by bureaucracies, the operational appendages of the executive branch. In both democratic and undemocratic states the political executive appoints people to high administrative office who they expect will carry out policies consistent with their instructions. Public administration is hierarchical in nature, with the political executive at the top and various tiers of civil servants below. Bureaucracies are supposed to be rule-bound, impersonal and specialized, characterized by a division of labour, established routine, professionalism and merit. But another way that bureaucracies have been staffed – whether in communist or democratic systems – is through political patronage, nepotism, and social networks where merit is not a criterion.

In reforming the civil service, post-communist Europe confronted a dilemma: should communist-era bureaucrats, especially high-level ones, be allowed to keep their jobs or should they be replaced as part of a policy of decommunization? Two out-of-the-ordinary cases exemplify the dilemma.

The first post-communist government in Bulgaria was headed by Andrei Lukanov, a former communist who served as prime minister in

1989–90. He realized that his leadership prospects were linked to those of high-ranking bureaucrats: 'There was a natural coalition between remaining old administrative cadres and politicians from the renamed Communist Party, based on political loyalty and the need for both politicians and civil servants to "survive" under the new conditions' (Verheijen, 1999: 96). Inevitably, Bulgaria was slow to enact civil service reform.

By contrast, the most sweeping purge of communist-era civil servants was probably that undertaken in Slovakia in 1994 by the newly elected nationalist government of Vladimir Meciar. The first day of parliament was devoted almost exclusively to the dismissal of high-ranking civil servants and their replacement with political cronies. In addition, Slovakia, as well as Poland, expanded the size of the state machine in order to cast a wider patronage net: 'In a process of runaway state-building, these states grew without becoming more professional, effective, or autonomous' (O'Dwyer, 2006: 99). What Hungary's government under prime minister Orban did, after 2010 with large-scale cronyism in staffing a growing bureaucratic apparatus, appears likely to produce a similar outcome.

One of the conditions for EU membership identified by the EU in the late 1990s entailed 'administrative conditionality' – the requirement that candidate states implement civil service reform. Most did overhaul their state machines even if actual rule adoption differed from one country to another (Dimitrova, 2005: 85). But the temptation to stack the higher echelons of state administration with fellow travellers did not go away. A study of Hungary – one that seems typical of the region – concluded that even after repeated attempts at reform, 'governing parties have a deep reach into the ministries in that they can potentially exercise political control over the staffing of the entire ministerial civil service' (Meyer-Sahling, 2006: 294). Polarization of politics between ex-communist and anti-communist camps has allowed party patronage and politicization of the ministerial bureaucracy to continue notwithstanding the EU *acquis*. Thus governments of neither the left nor right have incentives to depolitize the civil service. Conversely, 'the senior bureaucracy has come to be dominated by officials whose tenure is bound to that of alternating government and whose career interest in commuting between public administration, politics and the private sector contradicts efforts to depoliticise post-communist civil services' (Meyer-Sahling, 2004: 98).

An index of senior civil service politicization suggested that its extent varied across the region's states. The Baltics showed low levels of politicization, even at the very top of the ministerial bureaucracy. At the other end of the spectrum were Slovakia and Poland where

'Politicisation reaches down three and four levels into the ministerial hierarchy and is more intense than in the other countries' (Meyer-Sahling and Veen, 2012: 9). Such political patronage is related to executive volatility: 'New, incoming governments tend to perceive major problems of control *vis-à-vis* bureaucrats who have served their predecessors in government. The consequence is a pressure to politicise the senior ranks of the ministerial bureaucracy' (ibid.: 18). But whether the decrease in executive volatility which we have noted will produce less patronage appears dubious. Some opportunistic political parties may limit their corrupt ways under certain conditions (Grzymala-Busse, 2007), but no iron laws of politics exist to reassure us of this.

Conclusion

The balancing act in governance is holding political executives accountable to representative bodies while giving them the space to show leadership and initiative. Our analysis indicates that the vast majority of the region's states have now reached an equilibrium in balancing these two requirements. The skilful construction and adaptation of executive power has much to do with this achievement. The quality of leadership in the region's states has varied and produced uneven outcomes, but the structures and parameters of executive power are today robust.

Chapter 9

Elections and Voters

Sarah Birch

Elections are widely recognized as the keystone of representative democracy. In the Central and Eastern European context, there are two key aspects of elections that are worthy of consideration: electoral systems (the rules and regulations associated with the casting of votes and the conversion of votes into seats), and voting behaviour (the decision whether or not to vote and the choice(s) made at the polls). Electoral systems allow citizens to express their political preferences; in addition, they influence the development of party systems and the composition of government. In this chapter we shall see that there was an initial shift towards list-based forms of proportional representation across the countries of the region, followed by a greater degree of institutional stability. The chapter will also consider the ways in which elections allow citizens to interact with government: whether they vote or not (turnout), and what election outcomes reveal about voter preferences. In other words, this will be the chapter in which we discuss 'conventional' participation.

With the exception of Belarus and Russia (lying outside the scope of this volume), all the Central and Eastern European states have generally managed to achieve levels of election quality that enable these states to be classified as democracies. Though the road to credible elections has been somewhat rocky in states such as Albania, Bulgaria, Macedonia, Moldova, Romania, Serbia and Ukraine, there is relatively little concern after two decades of competitive polls that elections in most of the region might be wracked by widespread fraud.

We start in the next section with consideration of how elections were conducted and what political role they played under communism. There follows a section on the principal developments in electoral system architecture in Central and Eastern Europe since the collapse of communism. The third section considers trends in rates of electoral participation, followed in the final substantive section by an analysis of patterns in vote choice in the region. And there is a brief conclusion to end.

Elections under communism

In order fully to understand elections in post-communist Central and Eastern Europe, it is necessary to make a brief diversion into the electoral institutions that were in force in this region during the communist period. The communist states of Europe used elections to maintain and legitimate their political systems, rather than to select the political direction a country was to take. The elections held during the communist period were universally held under absolute majority electoral systems that in theory required a second round of voting if no candidate achieved at least 50 per cent support in the first round. In practice, however, it was rare that run-off ballots were conducted, as pre-selected candidates almost always won the posts for which they were standing. Voting took place in multi-member constituencies in Poland and the German Democratic Republic; elsewhere single-member districts were employed.

During the communist period, elections were the object of various forms of subtle and not-so-subtle manipulation by the authorities. Though voting was nowhere formally compulsory, heavy pressure was exercised on voters to encourage them to take part, generating turnout figures of well over 90 per cent in most cases. And while there was in no case a direct ban on competitive candidacies, a variety of mechanisms were employed to ensure that the electoral options available to voters did not represent genuine political alternatives (see Furtak, 1990). In some cases (the USSR, Czechoslovakia) the communist party took charge of nomination procedures and ensured that there was but one name on the ballot. In the USSR, for example, voters had the 'choice' of either depositing the ballot in the box unmarked (thereby indicating a vote in favour of the single name thereon) or crossing out the name of the candidate to indicate a vote against that person. In order to indicate a 'negative' vote of this type, they had the option of using a screened-off polling booth, but given that the vast majority of voters deposited their ballots in the box unmarked, the very fact of resorting to use of the private polling booth was potentially seen as a sign of political disloyalty.

In other cases, such as Poland and Bulgaria, non-communist parties remained in existence throughout the communist period and won seats in parliament, though such 'satellite parties' formed part of communist-led 'fronts', and were allocated certain seats in advance of each election. In such cases, voters thus had no more real choice than they did in states where there was only one party. In Yugoslavia, voters did have real choice at election time, but this was restricted to a selection of individuals, rather than a political choice between competing policy platforms.

In the late 1980s, a number of communist states started to experiment with offering voters greater choice at elections. Hungary and the USSR began to use multiple candidacies along Yugoslav lines as a means of encouraging voters to select those with the most desirable personal qualities, though partisan competition was still not allowed. At the same time, a grassroots movement in Poland led to election boycotts which significantly reduced participation. All in all, however, there was remarkable uniformity in the form elections took and the ends to which they were used by communist regimes. Rather than being institutions for gauging popular preferences and selecting between policy options, elections were devices designed to mobilize the population and to make it complicit in the decisions of the communist parties that were in charge of making policy. They thus served as instruments of manipulation, popular control, and legitimation of communist rule.

Electoral systems

Electoral systems are a central feature of the institutional set-up of any democratic polity. Not only do electoral systems channel popular preferences, they also play an important role in shaping political party development and in structuring the style of politics in a country. Furthermore, comparative research has shown that electoral systems are one of the most important factors influencing the composition of governments. These general findings are highly relevant to the Central and East European context.

Electoral system design has played an important role in Central and East European politics since the transitions from communism in the late 1980s and early 1990s. Elections have been the terrain on which many of the most significant debates in the region have played themselves out, and the rules of the electoral game have been intimately associated with deliberations over the nature and role of political institutions in the post-communist setting. There has thus been considerable diversity in the choices made in the region's various states, as well as in the effects of these choices. There have, nevertheless, been a number of common trends in post-communist electoral institutional design that stem from the specific features of the communist system and perceptions about what needed to be done to dismantle it. The aim of this section is to provide an overview of the causes and consequences of electoral system design in post-communist Europe, and to assess the main features of the electoral systems in the region.

The overall story of recent electoral system development in Central and Eastern Europe has been initial moves toward proportional representation as a means of institutionalizing multi-party politics, followed by considerable tinkering with the details of systems. Some states, such as Ukraine and Macedonia, have experienced three different electoral system types during the post-communist period, but Central and Eastern Europe has been largely free of the frequent radical overhauls of electoral institutions that some had predicted in the early stages of the transition.

Before proceeding to more detailed analysis of electoral systems in post-communist Europe, a word is in order about what is meant by this term. Strictly speaking, the term 'electoral system' can be taken to refer to many elements of electoral legislation, from registration procedures and boundary delimitation methods, to electoral commission composition, campaign finance regulations and dispute adjudication mechanisms. In the academic literature, however, the term 'electoral system' is generally taken to refer to the aspects of electoral legislation relevant to the conversion of popular preferences into elected representatives – namely the options available on the ballot, constituency delineation, and the formula for converting votes into seats. It is mainly in this sense that the term will be used here, though reference will also be made to other aspects of electoral system design broadly understood.

This discussion will be concerned with the design of electoral systems for lower (or only) houses of parliament, as these are the institutions that are generally recognized as having the greatest impact on the political configuration of a state. The three main electoral system types that have been employed in Central and Eastern Europe are: (1) the single-member district (SMD) systems in which the territory of the state is divided into a number of constituencies, and one member of parliament is elected from each (either by plurality (as in the UK 'first-past-the-post' system) or by absolute majority, as in the French two-round system); (2) list proportional representation (PR), employed throughout most of Western Europe, in which voters vote for party lists, and members are elected to parliament from these lists in proportion to the votes cast for each; (3) mixed systems that combine SMD and PR.

The consequences of the collapse of communism were nowhere more evident than in electoral practices, whose role and meaning changed dramatically in the first genuinely competitive electoral events held in most cases shortly after the transition was initiated. It is therefore not surprising that reform of electoral institutions should have played a prominent role in the transition process. Electoral reform was a central topic of debate in the round table negotiations held in Poland,

Hungary, Czechoslovakia and Bulgaria, and such reforms were in each case among the most important outcomes of these events (see Elster, 1996). In most other cases, electoral reforms were decided through the normal parliamentary process shortly after the initial transitions. (The exceptions are Romania (1990) and Russia (1993), where electoral laws were issued by decree.) In all cases the most important actors were the emerging democratic elites, together with former communist power-holders. Ordinary citizens played very little part in electoral reform, and advice from established democracies of the West was hardly more influential (Birch *et al.*, 2002).

Following the electoral reforms that accompanied the initial transitions, electoral legislation continued to be a hot topic of debate in virtually all of the Central and East European states. Large-scale reforms have been relatively rare, and most of the changes in electoral legislation have been a matter of altering the details of the electoral process. Thresholds have been raised and lowered, constituencies have been redrawn and electoral administrative practices have been revised, but most of the Central and East European states have stuck with the electoral systems they adopted immediately following transition. This is not to say that the post-communist electoral systems are set in stone, however, as recent reforms in Albania (toward PR), Bulgaria and Romania (toward mixed systems) attest.

Since the collapse of communism, there has been a general trend to introduce more proportional elements to Central and East European electoral systems (see Birch *et al.*, 2002). Some countries made the move to proportional representation at the time of transition, while others initially adopted mixed electoral systems, most of which have subsequently been replaced by full-scale PR. A few states – Albania, Belarus, Macedonia, Ukraine – stayed with their single-member district absolute majority systems for the first post-communist elections, but with the exception of Belarus, these were all abandoned in favour of mixed systems (subsequently to be replaced by full PR in Albania, Macedonia and Ukraine). Belarus thus remains the only state in the region to have a SMD system, though Romania moved from PR to a mixed system prior to its 2008 election, and neighbouring Bulgaria also shifted (back) from PR to a mixed system in time for its 2009 election.

There are a variety of reasons for the general shift in the direction of more proportional electoral systems. The aim of reformers was in all cases to ensure, first, that elections would be conducted on a multi-party basis, and second, that they would be free of manipulation by the communist authorities (see Birch *et al.*, 2002). PR was associated by post-communist reformers with multi-party politics, as it institutionalizes competition between parties and strengthens partisan organization. Single-member districts, on the other hand, were associated with localised politics that focuses on individuals (often based on patronage networks established by well-known communist leaders under the *ancien régime*), and were for this reason widely viewed as being less democratic. List PR was seen as a means of embedding political competition on a multi-party basis and preventing backsliding into one-party politics. It was also perceived as a means of strengthening parties as institutions; when parties rather than people became the object of election, fledgling political organizations had an incentive to build strong party structures in order to attract the popular vote. Voters, for their part, have an incentive to investigate the policy platform that the party stands for, rather than thinking of it simply in terms of the individuals who make it up. PR was thus first and foremost a means of shifting political competition from personalized to programmatic competition, in other words, from competition between individuals to competition between ideas. Not surprisingly, this shift took place soonest in countries where anti-communist elites gained full political control early on.

In this sense it was the party list element of PR, rather than the proportional outcome it generated, that was most attractive to Central and East European reformers. It is perhaps for this reason that non-list forms of PR or semi-PR were hardly considered. The single transferable vote (STV) was employed briefly in Estonia in 1990 under the influence of Estonian émigré and electoral law specialist Rein Taagepera, but it was soon abandoned and has not been seriously considered elsewhere (Ishiyama, 1996). Other semi-proportional systems such as the single non-transferable vote have hardly been contemplated in any post-communist state.

The most striking feature of current electoral system design in Central and Eastern Europe is the general similarity in key elements of institutional design with those of the established democracies of Western Europe. There are, to be sure, more mixed electoral systems in the eastern portion of the continent than the western, but all in all, the fifteen years following the communist collapse has witnessed a considerable convergence between East and West in the area of electoral institutions. The dominant feature of electoral system design in both parts of the continent is list proportional representation. Table 9.1 provides an overview of key elements of electoral system design in 21 post-communist states.

Electoral systems have a variety of effects on both the style of politics in a state and on political outcomes. In the post-communist setting, electoral systems have been shown to have a number of the same

Table 9.1   *Electoral systems in Central and Eastern Europe (most recent lower house elections)*

Country	Year of most recent election	Electoral system	Single-party threshold (first tier PR seats) %	Preferences in PR list voting?	Success requirement in single-member seats
Albania	2009	PR	3–5	No	Abs. maj.
Belarus	2008	SMD	N/A	N/A	Abs. maj.
Bosnia & H.	2010	PR	3	Yes	N/A
Bulgaria	2009	Mixed	4	No	Simple maj.
Croatia	2011	PR²	5	No	N/A
Czech Rep.	2010	PR	5–15[1]	Yes	N/A
Estonia	2011	PR	None	Yes	N/A
Hungary	2010	Mixed	5	No	Abs. maj.
Kosovo	2010	PR²	None	Yes	N/A
Latvia	2011	PR	5	Yes	N/A
Lithuania	2008	Mixed	None	No	Abs. maj.
Macedonia	2011	PR²	None	No	N/A
Moldova	2011	PR	2–9[1]	No	N/A
Montenegro	2009	PR	3	No	N/A
Poland	2011	PR	5–8[1]	Yes	N/A
Romania	2008	Mixed²	5–10[1]	No	Abs. maj.
Russia	2011	PR	7[3]	No	N/A
Serbia	2012	PR	5	No	N/A
Slovakia	2012	PR	5	Yes	N/A
Slovenia	2011	PR²	4	Yes	N/A
Ukraine	2007	PR	3	No	N/A

Key: PR: proportional representation system; SMD: single-member district system; Mixed: mixed or hybrid system combining elements of proportional representation and single-member district systems; Abs. maj.: absolute majority decision rule; simple maj.: simple majority (plurality) decision rule.
Notes: 1. Graduated threshold structure; higher levels for coalitions; 2. In addition, a small number of seats are allocated to ethnic minority and/or out-of-country voter groups through separate mechanisms; 3. Due to fall to 5 per cent in 2013.
Sources: www.electionguide.org; www.ipu.org.

impacts as they have in established democracies (though with important exceptions). But the post-communist setting differs from that of established democracies in one crucial respect: party systems developed in their current form only following the introduction of competitive politics after 1989; the party systems of Central and Eastern Europe are therefore largely the products of transition. Electoral systems shaped party systems in important ways (as well as being shaped by them).

Given that there is only one SMD system in the region – Belarus – and given that this state is generally recognized as being less than democratic, it makes sense in the analysis of post-communist electoral systems to focus mainly on the distinction between mixed and fully proportional systems.

Research has found that Central and East European PR systems are generally associated with larger party systems (as is the case in established democracies), except where the party system is not nationalized. In this case, election in SMDs can lead to considerable party system fragmentation and weakening (Moser, 1999; Birch, 2003). We observe this phenomenon, for example, in Belarus and Russia where SMDs have led to the election of large numbers of independents. In Russia (and also in Ukraine prior to the adoption of a fully proportional system), SMD elections also spawned many small parties, whereas the PR component of the ballot in these mixed systems was a consolidating force.

Overall, however, PR electoral systems are associated with larger party systems than their mixed counterparts. This is evident in the data presented in the second column of Table 9.2, which show the seat share of the largest party in the most recent (lower-house) elections in Central and Eastern Europe. As can be seen here, the 'winners' gained on average just under 40 per cent of the seats in these elections, requiring them in most cases to form coalition governments; in only five cases did a single electoral contestant win an absolute majority of the seats.

Having surveyed the contours of electoral system architecture in Central and Eastern Europe, we turn in the next two sections to consideration of how ordinary electors navigate their way through the electoral process. The next section will begin this undertaking by examining the decision whether or not to vote, before turning our focus in the following section to the choices people make when they do go to the polls.

Electoral participation

One of the most notable features of electoral politics in the Central and East European region is the dramatic decline in turnout that has characterized the post-communist period. There are a variety of reasons for this decline, having to do with socio-economic conditions, election timing and other factors (Birch, 2003; Kostadinova, 2003, 2009; Pacek *et al.*, 2009), and there is little evidence that the decline is being reduced as the post-communist states 'consolidate' their political systems. Following the collapse of a political system that pressured people into taking part in elections, many took advantage of their new-found freedom to abstain from politics, and once in the habit of at staying at home on polling day, many electors appear to have permanently checked out of electoral politics.

The most recent round of parliamentary elections in the region demonstrate that the electorates of several states are quite reluctant to vote, with average electoral participation just under 60 per cent (see Table 9.2) as against an average just over 70 per cent in Western Europe during the same period (Norris, 2011: 221). Recent turnout figures fell under 50 per cent in parliamentary elections in three states (Kosovo – 47.38 per cent, Lithuania – 48.59 per cent and Romania – 39.20 per cent). And in elections to the European Parliament, participation has been lower still: only 28 per cent of Czech electors made it to the polls in both 2004 and 2009, as did 21 per cent of Poles in 2004 and 25 per cent five years later. The prize for low turnout goes to Slovakia, which managed to get only 17 per cent of its electorate to vote in the 2004 European Parliament elections and 20 per cent in 2009.

Moreover, the trend we observe is a downward one, with electoral participation falling considerably in most countries since the early 1990s, when average turnout in 'founding' elections was 77 per cent (Birch, 2003: 63). Electoral systems have in most cases remained relatively stable in recent years, and they can therefore not explain such election-on-election declines. But electoral systems have been found to be a significant predictor of rates of electoral participation as well as the overall propensity of these rates to decline over time in the Central and East European region; turnout has remained highest in those states that have made a rapid transition to PR, and it has fallen most in states that have used the greatest number of SMDs (Birch, 2003). It is noteworthy that following the move from proportional representation to a largely majoritarian electoral system in Romania, turnout fell from 59 to 39 per cent.

Various studies have sought to identify the other causes of the propensity to vote in Central and Eastern Europe. These studies have pointed to factors that operate both at the system and the individual levels. At the system level, in addition to electoral system architecture, factors that have found to affect turnout are the type of election (presidential elections generally attract more people to the polls than parliamentary contests), location in the former Soviet Union (linked to lower turnout), level of development (less developed states have higher turnout, everything else being equal), and short-term economic change (inflation, economic growth and unemployment have all been found to depress turnout (Birch, 2003; Kostadinova, 2003; Pacek *et al.*, 2009).

Table 9.2 *Electoral results in Central and Eastern Europe*
(most recent lower house elections)

Country	Year of most recent election	Turnout as a percentage of registered voters	Seat share of the largest party (%)	Percentage change in seat share of the largest party since the previous election
Albania	2009	50.77	46.43	+6.43
Belarus	2008	76.74	5.45	−1.82
Bosnia & H.	2010	56.49	19.05	+9.52
Bulgaria	2009	60.95	48.33	+48.33
Croatia	2011	54.32	52.98	+16.38
Czech Rep.	2010	62.60	28.00	−9.00
Estonia	2011	63.53	32.67	+1.98
Hungary	2010	64.38	67.88	+25.39
Kosovo	2010	47.38	34.00[1]	−3.00
Latvia	2011	59.49	31.00	+2.00
Lithuania	2008	48.59	31.19	+13.46
Macedonia	2011	63.48	45.53	−5.69
Moldova	2011	63.37	41.58	−5.94
Montenegro	2009	66.19	59.26	+8.64
Poland	2011	48.92	45.00	−0.44
Romania	2008	39.20	34.85	+34.85
Russia	2011	60.10	52.89	−17.77
Serbia	2012	57.80	29.20	+29.20
Slovakia	2012	59.11	55.33	+14.00
Slovenia	2011	65.60	31.11	31.11
Ukraine	2007	62.02	38.89	−2.44
Average		58.62	39.55	13.69[2]

Notes: 1. This is the proportion of the seats elected through open electoral competition; 2. This is the mean of the absolute values of the figures in this column.
Sources: www.electionguide.org; www.ipu.org; www.electionworld.org.

At the individual level, studies have found that willingness to go to the polls is conditioned by the same sets of demographic factors that operate in other developed democracies, as well as by orientations towards the democratic system. Particular attention has been paid to the role of 'democratic disaffection' in shaping the propensity to vote. In a recent study, Norris finds that levels of satisfaction with democratic performance are lower in Central and Eastern Europe than in any other region of the world (Norris, 2011: 113). One of the principal complaints East Europeans have about their leaders is their propensity to engage in corrupt and otherwise unethical behaviour, and corruption perceptions could well have a 'demobilizing' effect, as the disaf-

fected disengage. Yet it could also be that anger at the poor performance of leaders mobilizes people to go to the polls and vote incumbent
leaders out by opting for the established opposition or political newcomers. Despite the intuitive appeal of the 'demobilizing' hypothesis,
studies by several scholars have found little evidence that the disaf-
fected are less likely to vote (Pacek *et al.*, 2009; Kostadinova, 2009),
and it seems they are more likely to exercise their democratic right to
'throw the rascals out'. In the light of this, it makes sense to consider in
greater detail the choices that voters make when they do decide to go
to the polls. It is to this topic that the next section is devoted.

Vote choice

The choices voters make when they go to the polls is a topic that has
fascinated political scientists for generations. One of the most interesting aspects of vote choice in Central and Eastern Europe is the
extent to which the overall patterns observed over the past twenty
years correspond to those in established democracies (Evans, 2006;
Tavits, 2005, 2008a; van der Brug *et al.*, 2008). Most scholars agree
that by and large, post-communist voters approach the task of
selecting representatives in ways that are fairly similar to those
employed by voters in established democracies, even if it took a few
elections for them to 'learn' the art of voting (Tworzecki, 2002). The
left–right cleavage familiar to students of Western European party
systems is also the dominant political divide in most of the Central and
East European states, with cultural cleavages of various sorts (religious, ethnic, moral, geopolitical) as the main secondary cleavages in
both 'old' and 'new' Europe.

Given the extent of the social, political and economic change witnessed in post-communist Europe over the past two decades, the similarity in overall patterns of vote choice in this region with that in other
democracies is in some sense remarkable. In another sense, this is
perhaps what we might expect in countries that have adopted electoral
and parliamentary architectures modelled on those in the West, and the
gradual convergence between the two halves of Europe in social and
economic terms. Moreover, most of the Central and East European
states have now joined the European Union, or are set to do so in the
near future, which puts further pressure on political elites in those
states to adhere to patterns of electoral competition familiar in existing
EU member states.

That said, there are several noteworthy differences in electoral
behaviour between post-communist countries and Western Europe.

The first characteristic feature of Central and East European voting that jumps out from electoral results is the ability of new or obscure 'flash parties' suddenly to gain large amounts of support in some countries (Pop-Eleches, 2010). Examples are the New Era Party in Latvia in 2002, which won a plurality of seats in parliament only eight months after its formation. Not long before this, heir to the defunct Bulgaria throne Simeon Saxkoburggotski had returned to the country and entered politics, forming the Simeon II Movement in Bulgaria which swept to power at the 2001 elections, displacing the parties that had dominated Bulgarian politics since the transition to multi-party politics. The in 2009, Bulgaria witnessed flash party success for the second time, when the newly formed Citizens for the European Development of Bulgaria (GERB) won the election with 48 per cent of the seats. Meanwhile in the 2008 Romanian elections, the breakaway Democratic Liberal party won a plurality of seats. Likewise the three-month-old Positive Slovenia party of Ljubliana mayor Zoran Jankovic won the 2011 elections in that country, as did the 'Let's Get Serbia Moving' coalition formed around the breakaway Serbian Progressive Party in the Serbian elections of May 2012.

This tendency is in part indicative of the fact that overall, voters in Central and Eastern Europe are not as loyal to political parties as their counterparts in the West. This is because fewer voters in the east have been socialized into long-standing attachments to parties of the sort commonly dubbed 'party identification'. The reasons for this are complex and can be traced to the relative weakness of civil society in the region, to the top-down nature of many political parties and to twenty-first-century trends in communication technology and social organization that have weakened party attachment across the democratic world. The communist legacy can also be counted as one of the major factors depressing Western-style party identification; scepticism with politicians of all colours meant that during the first few electoral cycles, identification *against* particular parties was greater than identification with them (Rose and Mishler, 1998).

Suffice it to say that the weaker partisan alignment of the Central and East European electorates has resulted in a second characteristic feature of elections in this region: overall higher levels of volatility in election results, with parties' vote shares witnessing sometimes dramatic shifts from one election to the next. The flash party successes noted above exemplify this trend, as do the often substantial changes in electoral fortunes of established parties. As shown in the final column of Table 9.2, the average absolute change in vote share of the largest party in the most recent election in the region was just under 14 per cent. In the cases of Bulgaria, Hungary and Romania, these shake-ups might be attributed in part to electoral reforms which had taken place prior to the vote, but it is more likely that willingness to alter electoral rules and restlessness with existing parties are both the product of general disenchantment with established political institutions. One of the practical consequences of high volatility is that few parties have remained in power for more than one term (see Chapter 11).

This trend was exacerbated in the early years of the new century when the previously solid support bases of the communist successor parties began to show signs of erosion in many states. In the context of party systems with overall levels of loyalty, ex-communist stalwarts had long exhibited the strongest consistent attachment to the social democratic parties that emerged in the wake of the communist collapse in the early 1990s. Yet gradual generational replacement, combined with the failure of the social democratic parties to navigate successfully through the choppy waters of global financial troubles, took a heavy toll on the core base of supporters that had backed many of these parties for nearly twenty years. Corruption scandals precipitated the fall from grace of communist successor parties in Poland and Hungary in 2005 and 2010 respectively (see Chapter 2). This trend is less evident in some of the former Soviet states, such as Moldova, where the communist party is still a major political player, but communist successor parties have generally fared poorly in those states that have joined the EU.

A third distinctive pattern visible in the region is the role of corruption and corruption scandals in structuring both party competition and electoral behaviour. The transition from communism to capitalism involved the prising apart of the state and the economy. This task was complex and was from the start bound to be fraught with ethical quagmires. The way in which state assets were privatized and otherwise disposed of created tremendous opportunities for corrupt activities that enabled many former communist elites to reinvent themselves as business people and use their connections to benefit from the sell-off of state goods. The failure fully to disentangle state and economy has also provided many opportunities for corrupt activities, as state subsidies have been exploited and state protection has been used to benefit 'insiders'. It is not surprising in this context that corruption has been a major electoral campaign issue in virtually all the states in the region.

The advent of competitive elections have provided an additional opportunity to engage in unethical conduct, and concerns about the administration of elections have shaped electoral competition and outcomes in a number of states, including most notably Ukraine in 2004 and Bulgaria in 2009. Allegations of vote-buying, campaign finance abuse and outright fraud have not only conditioned vote choices, but threatened to delegitimize entire electoral processes and compromise the democratic character of states. In some cases, there have even been fears that electoral irregularities might jeopardise the chance of countries to join the European Union, though there is scant evidence in practice that this proved a decisive factor in accession negotiations (Birch, 2011).

Given the popularity of anti-corruption messages, many parties have sought to position themselves as 'clean', 'outsider' entities capable of offering a fresh and morally attractive approach to politics, only to be implicated themselves in corruption scandals upon taking office: one thinks of the Ukrainian Green Party in 1998, and the Czech Public Affairs (VV) party in 2010 (see Chapter 2). The use of anti-corruption rhetoric as a campaigning tactic is certainly familiar to students of West European politics; it is the prominence of this theme in Central and Eastern Europe and its ability to shift votes that makes it a distinctive element of the electoral culture of the region (Kostadinova, 2009; Pop-Eleches, 2010).

A fourth noteworthy feature of the choices made by voters in Central and Eastern Europe is the attraction of many to extreme or 'anti-system' parties, particularly those of the far-right or populist type. Thus we observe the Life and Justice Party (MIEP) and later the Movement for a Better Hungary (Jobbik) win substantial amounts of electoral support in Hungary, as has the Greater Romania Party in that country and in Poland the Self-Defence party and the League of Polish Families (Pop-Eleches, 2010). Radical nationalist parties were from the start prominent players in most of the ex-Yugoslav states following the violent conflict that wracked the sub-region in the early 1990s, but the more recent rise to prominence of far-right parties in Central Europe following EU accession has caused concern.

Overall, the evidence suggests that the way people vote in Central and Eastern Europe is remarkably similar to the way they vote in the more established democracies of the West. Nevertheless, electoral behaviour in the post-communist states displays several characteristic features that can be traced both to the communist past and to the trajectory of post-communist development, including weak attachment to political parties and a tendency on the part of many voters to favour radical and/or new political options at the polls, often as a reaction to political corruption.

Conclusion

Institutions are but one of the factors that influence political developments in transitional and post-transitional contexts, and elections are but one type of institution. A wide variety of other forces have played a large role in shaping political developments in the post-communist world since the momentous events of 1989, including economic change, cultural shifts and events specific to each individual state. Nevertheless, elections have played a central role in political developments in Central and Eastern Europe since the late 1980s. Not only have debates over electoral systems been a forum in which key elements of state identity have been thrashed out, the systems implemented have also played a significant role in shaping election results the course of political change. And if Central and Eastern European voters are often discouraged with those they elect, it is ultimately the choices they make when they go to the polls that set the stage for politics.

Chapter 10

Representation and Accountability: The Parliaments

David M. Olson

Parliaments of Central and East Europe have been developing very differently from one another since their beginnings at the end of communism in the 1989–92 period. This chapter examines their differences, and also their similarities, over a two-decade series of election and parliamentary term cycles.

Legislatures and transitions

Communist rule ended in different ways among the CEE countries, with their legislatures having very different places within those transitions. In the Central European countries of Poland, Czechoslovakia and Hungary, for example, reform movements and the Communist Party could negotiate a transfer of rule, with their respective parliaments adopting the agreed new arrangements including an election procedure (Olson, 1993; Chiva, 2007). In the post-Soviet states of Ukraine, Moldova and Belarus, however, the last legislatures elected as parts of the USSR were in office when the USSR collapsed, and thus had the responsibility of coping with unexpected changes. They were more 'continuist' legislatures than reformist (Crowther, 2012). In the post-Yugoslavian states, and also in the Baltic states (though part of the USSR), the republic-level legislatures had increasingly become both reformist within and separatist from their respective communist federations and parties.

Though constitutions and party systems are the logical initial steps to understanding a stable political system, they were not the first features to emerge at the end of authoritarian rule. Constitutions were written, debated, and adopted by elected decision-making bodies. Parliamentary elections and beginning political parties came first; constitutions followed.

Parliamentary profiles

CEE parliaments tend to be organized as are the Western European parliaments with prime ministers and systems of permanent committees. The organizational profiles of CEE parliaments in 2012 are shown in Table 10.1.

The number of members of unicameral parliaments, and of the main chambers of bicameral parliaments, varies from 42 in Bosnia-Herzegovina and 90 in Slovenia to 460 in the Polish Sejm. The unicameral Ukrainian and Hungarian parliaments are the other large bodies of 450 and 386 members, respectively.

The usual purpose served by a second chamber (sometimes designated 'upper') in federal systems is to represent states or provinces, while the main chamber (sometimes the 'lower' chamber) is elected on the basis of population. Of the CEE countries, only Bosnia-Herzegovina is a federal system. Though not federal in structure, the second chamber in other CEE countries, as in Western Europe, is often based on regional or local units.

In bicameral parliaments, the size of the second chamber is smaller than the main chamber. The Polish Sejm of 460 members is complemented by 100 in the senate, while the Czech Chamber of Deputies of 200 members has only 81 members in the senate. Romania has the largest senate (140), while its lower chamber is among the region's largest at 327. Bosnia-Herzegovina is the smallest in both chambers: 42 in the main chamber and 15 in the second. The usual term of office for parliaments is four years, though Albania has five-, and Kosovo three-year terms. Most of the second chambers also serve a four-year term.

The two most recent election years prior to mid-2012 listed in Table 10.1 indicate that the stipulated four-year term can be shortened, mainly through a collapse of parliamentary support for the prime minister and governing cabinet, as in Latvia in 2011 and Slovakia in 2012.

The senates in both Poland and the Czech Republic were designed to serve immediate transitional purposes. The Polish senate resulted from a compromise at the pre-transitional conference between the Communist Party and reform groups to create a chamber for an open electoral contest, to contrast with a 'contract' main chamber with allocated party seats (Olson, 1999). The Czech senate, though agreed to in principle at the time the Czech and Slovak states separated from one another in 1993 to end the Czechoslovakian federation, was brought into existence only in its initial 1996 election (Reschova and Syllova, 1996). The Assembly of Kosovo is an unusual parliament, for it, as well as its state, are in the beginning stages of independence and self-government under UN and EU guidance (Taylor, 2005).

The beginning years for CEE parliaments were tentative and subject to change. Many of the legislatures changed names (to abolish 'Soviet' or 'Peoples') to show their changed political systems, and often reduced the size of large communist assemblies, especially in the former Soviet republics. Republics of former Yugoslavia, with three chambers, both reduced their number and changed their basis of selection. Many of the first parliaments in the beginning years also had a short term of two years for constitution writing (e.g., Bulgaria, Estonia, Lithuania, and the former Czechoslovakia).

Representation, elections and parties

Parliament, as the national level representative body of the state, is both the highest source of law and the organ of accountability to approve and also to review actions of the executive. Representation of the electorate typically is achieved by political parties both through elections to parliament and by their actions in parliament.

Election systems

Most CEE parliaments, as in Western Europe, combine multi-party systems with multi-member districts and proportional electoral systems (see Chapter 9). Belarus, however, retains the Soviet-era election system of single member districts, in which most candidates do not run as party candidates (OSCE, 2008). Lithuania and Hungary have a 'mixed' election system on the German model (Kostadinova, 2002), while Romania has added, in 2008, a single member district component to a proportional and multi-member district system for both chambers (Coman, 2012: 204–7).

A supplemental device to assure representation for ethnic or national minorities is to reserve a small number of seats filled though elections among their own voters (Reynolds, 2011: 99). For example, one seat each is allocated to the Italian and Hungarian minorities in Slovenia's main chamber. As another example, eight seats in the Croatian parliament were allocated to minority groupings in the 2007 and 2011 elections while three were reserved for Croatian voters abroad (OSCE, 2012). Minorities can also be represented through political parties. Slovakia, Romania and Bulgaria, for example, have ethnic-based parties which typically win seats.

Second chambers are also a means of representation through different constituencies, terms and election systems than usually found in the main chambers. One of the most distinctive election systems is the

Table 10.1 Profile of Central and East European parliaments

Country	Chamber name / National name	Chamber Structure	Election years[a]	Size	Term length	Number of parliamentary party groups	Number of committees
Albania	People's Assembly / *Kuvendi i Shqipërisë*	Unicameral	2005, 2009	140	5	3	8
Belarus	Council of the Republic / *Savet Respubliki/ Sovet Respubliki*[b]	Bicameral	2004, 2008	64	4	N/A	5
	Chamber of Representatives / *Palata pradstaunikou/ Palata predstavitelei*		2004, 2008	110	4	N/A	14
Bosnia-Herzegovina	House of Peoples / *Dom Naroda*	Bicameral	N/A	15	4	3	7
	National House of Representatives / *Predstavnicki Dom*		2006, 2010	45	4	7	7
Bulgaria	National Assembly / *Narodno sabranie*	Unicameral	2005, 2009	240	4	6	17
Czech Republic	Senate / *Senát*	Bicameral	2008, 2010	81	6[c]	7	9
	Chamber of Deputies / *Poslanecká sněmovna*		2006, 2010	200	4	6	18
Croatia	House of Representatives / *Hrvatski sabor*	Unicameral	2007, 2011	127	4	8	29
Estonia	Parliament / *Riigikogu*	Unicameral	2007, 2011	101	4	4	11
Hungary	National Assembly / *Országgyűlés*	Unicameral	2006, 2010	386	4	5	18
Kosovo	Assembly / *Kuvendi i Kosovës*	Unicameral	2007, 2010	120	3	7	13
Latvia	Parliament / *Saeima*	Unicameral	2010, 2011	100	4	5	15

Seimas

Country	Chamber	Type	Recent elections				
Macedonia	Assembly / *Sobranie*	Unicameral	2008, 2011	120	4	3	21
Moldova	Parliament / *Parlamentului*	Unicameral	2009, 2010	101	4	4	10
Montenegro	Assembly / *Skupstina*	Unicameral	2006, 2009	81	4	7	12
Poland	Senate / *Senate*	Bicameral	2007, 2011	100	4	11	9
	National Assembly / *Sejm*		2007, 2011	460	4	11	9
Romania	Senate / *Senat*	Bicameral	2004, 2008	140	4	5	18
	Chamber of Deputies / *Camera Deputaților*		2004, 2008	327	4	6	19
Serbia	National Council / *Narodna Skupstina*	Unicameral	2008, 2012	250	4	4	30
Slovak Republic	National Council / *Národná rada*	Unicameral	2010, 2012	150	4	6	19
Slovenia	National Council / *Državni svet*	Bicameral	N/A	40	5	8	7
	National Assembly / *Državni zbor Republike Slovenije*		2008, 2011	90	4	8	15
Ukraine	Supreme Council / *Verkhovna Rada*	Unicameral	2007, 2011	450	4	6	26

Notes: a Most recent two elections prior to 1 June 2012; b National names are given in two official languages: Belarusian and Russian; c Staggered terms of six years.

Sources: adapted from Albanian Parliament Website (www.parlament.al); Bosnian Parliament Website (www.parlament.ba); Bulgarian Parliament Website (www.parliament.bg); Council of the Republic of the National Assembly of the Republic of Belarus (www.sovrep.gov.by/index_eng.php/home.html); Croatian Parliament Website (www.sabor.hr); Czech Republic Senate (www.senat.cz); Estonian Parliament Website (www.riigikogu.ee); Hungarian Parliament Website (www.mkogy.hu); International Foundation for Electoral Systems (www.electoralguide.org); Kosovo Parliament Website (www.assembly-kosova.org); Latvian Parliament Website (www.saeima.lv/en); Lithuanian Parliament Website (www3.lrs.lt); Macedonian Parliament Website (www.sobranie.mk); Moldavian Parliament Website (www.parlament.md); Montenegrin Parliament Website (www.skupstina.me); Poland Parliament Website (portal.rada.gov.ua); Romanian Parliament Website (www.cdep.ro); Serbian Parliament Website (www.parlament.rs); Slovakian Parliament Website (www.nrsr.sk); Ukrainian Czech Republic Chamber of Deputies (www.psp.cz); Ukrainian Parliament Website (static.rada.gov.ua).

single member district system for the Czech *Senat*, in which one-third of the members are elected every two years for overlapping six year terms, as does the US senate. The result of the 2010 election, for example, was to provide the Social Democrats, the main opposition party to the conservative government in the main chamber, with a majority in the second chamber. Another distinctive system for second chambers is the Slovenian functional representation of members elected from business and professional organizations and also local governments.

Political parties from elections to parliaments

To achieve both representation and to form a majority, two rules encourage the formation of a few large parties in parliament from many small parties in the electorate: the electoral threshold, and the minimum size requirement for party organization in parliament.

The 'electoral threshold' is the definition in the electoral law of the minimum proportion of the vote (usually 5 per cent) which is needed to elect candidate slates and political parties to parliament (Moraski and Loewenberg, 1999). In the early years, as high as 30 per cent of the vote would be cast for many small parties, in Poland for example, which did not succeed in entering parliament. Those voters were not directly represented; they had cast a 'wasted' or 'excluded' vote. This proportion has now declined to approximately 10 per cent of the vote in recent elections in most CEE countries (Birch, 2007b: 170–4).

The second device to concentrate the party system in parliament is the definition in the parliaments' rules of the minimum size required to form a parliamentary party group. The minimum number of deputies to form a parliamentary party group has gradually been raised, in the large Polish *Sejm* for example, from five to fifteen members, while the minimum size in the much smaller Slovenian main chamber is three. Over two decades, the fragmented post-communist parties in the early elections have tended to become concentrated in fewer and larger parties (Olson and Ilonszki, 2012b: 123–5). Yet, new and usually small, parties have been entering parliament in the second decade (Sikk, 2005). New parties have recently entered parliament in the Czech Republic and Slovenia, and have been included in multi-party coalitions

Both rules together form a multi-stage single process – electoral and parliamentary – to encourage aspiring candidates to form large parties in both elections and in parliament, and to encourage voters to reward them accordingly. Compared with Western Europe, post-Communist

Party systems are more dispersed, but there is an increasing fragmentation in Western party systems (Hopkin, 2011).

The members

Communist-era legislatures were a demographic mirror to society; the composition of the membership reflected the desired social structure of the state. Workers, youth, women, and ethnic minorities, for example, were proudly displayed as evidence of the democratic character of communist rule (Welsh, 1980).

In the new parliaments, political diversity has replaced social diversity. The quota members of 'descriptive representation' are gone, and thus the social composition more resembles Western Europe – higher education, older age, fewer women, and more organizational and economic leaders, than in the whole society (Olson, 1994: 21–5; Kopecky, 2007: 151–3; Ilonszki and Edinger, 2008).

The Central European 'turnover' parliaments, in their initial parliamentary terms, were composed of political newcomers involved in the anti-communist reform movements, together with a substantial number of members of the newly reformed successor parties to the former communist parties. By contrast, in the 'continuist' post-Soviet parliaments of Moldova, Belarus and Ukraine, members of the last elected Soviet legislatures remained in office in the midst of Soviet collapse.

Membership turnover was high in the first several terms of office. One reason was that the newly elected members in the first election found that parliamentary life, with debate, arguments, amendments, compromises, and endless committee meetings, was not attractive. The other reason for high member turnover was the constantly changing election results. Each election defeated the current government parties (Jasiewicz, 2007: 204–5).

In four democratic Central European parliaments, re-election rates have varied from 45 to 71 per cent per election during the second decade, reflecting continuing changing party election results. Over a series of elections, however, a set of experienced members developed during the initial decade who have since been replaced during the second, for reasons of age if not of electoral defeat. In four Central European parliaments, for example, the average age is mid- to late forties (Mansfeldova, 2012).

The continuing 'constitutional recalibration' in post-Soviet parliaments (Crowther, 2012) has led to high turnover rates for members. Members of post-Soviet parliaments tend to be associated with both the old Communist Party and with *nomenklatura*-based institutions and practices (Olson and Norton, 2008b: 161–2; Crowther and Matonyte, 2009; Khmelko, 2012).

Members of parliaments often have personal connections to industries and interest groups. The term 'clientelist networks' is often used to characterize political elites generally, including parliamentary members, in post-Soviet states (Fink-Hafner, 2012; Crowther, 2012). Following service in parliament, former members have many career opportunities, including local government in Romania (Stefan, 2004) or election to the European parliament (Guasti, 2010).

Internal organization of parliaments

Once elected, deputies in parliament are organized and function through three internal structures of parties, committees, and leadership councils. Parliamentary party groups organize power through votes for government formation, while committees are functional groups for a portion of the parliamentary workload. The parliamentary leadership councils decide the agenda, schedule and organization of parliament.

Parliamentary party groups

In post-communist parliaments, parliamentary party groups (PPGs) are the basic building block of parliamentary organization and activity, as in most of the world's legislative bodies (Heidar and Koole, 2000). They nominate candidates for parliamentary speaker and vice-speakers. They are represented on the parliamentary leadership councils, they allocate their members to parliamentary committees, and individual deputies are usually granted floor time through their party groups.

The number of PPGs varied in 2012 from three in Albania and four in Estonia to ten in Serbia (Table 10.1). PPGs experience extensive changes in both leadership and internal structure, depending on election results. If they win, they suddenly become large, with many new and inexperienced members. If they lose, they suddenly lose many of their members. Their continuing members, however, thereby become the chamber's most experienced deputies and the most informed critics of the new government. Some PPGs disappear from parliament, illustrated in the 2010 election by the long-term Czech Christian Democratic Party. The impact upon parliament is the loss of a whole set of members and their leadership with their accumulated experience. New party groups, by contrast, with a set of new members, have to rapidly select their leaders and develop their own internal ways of acting and making decisions to function effectively in a complex institution.

There is constant interaction between PPGs and committees. The members hold a dual membership – of both PPGs and committees. The PPG members who sit on a committee become the party experts on the topics covered by those committees. They both advise their own party groups on policy options and negotiate with their counterparts from other PPGs to form committee decisions (Kopecky, 2000: 184–7).

Party unity is not constant; it is contingent (Linek and Rakusanova, 2004). At the extreme, dissident PPG members may leave their party group to form rival groups. The result of party disunity can be, as illustrated in the Czech Republic in 1997–98, a change in government in the middle of the parliamentary term (Mansfeldova *et al.*, 2002: 78). PPG members may be expelled as in Slovakia in 1996 (Malova and Deegan-Krause, 2000: 205).

Committees

Parliamentary committees are work-oriented; they are created to handle certain tasks on behalf of the whole body, and to report their advice on decisions to be made by the whole body. Committees existed in communist-era legislatures and have been adapted to new circumstances (Simon and Olson, 1980; Karpowicz and Wesolowski, 2002: 51–4).

CEE parliaments have about 20 committees in the main chamber, with a few less in the second chamber in bicameral systems (Table 10.1). The number of committees tends to vary with the size of parliaments and chambers. The Polish *Sejm*, with 460 members, has had 25 to 28 committees each term, while most of the small parliaments have 13 or fewer committees. Committee size varies from 4 to 40 members, depending on the size of parliament, the workload, and the members' evaluation of the importance and desirability of the committee (Crowther and Olson, 2002: 174–7, Khmelko and Beers, 2011: 505–6).

Committees have become an essential part of the legislatures' work on legislation, budgeting and oversight and are usually organized on the basis of the administrative structure of government. The general principle is that the jurisdiction of committees would roughly parallel the structure of administrative agencies as in most West European parliaments and the US Congress (Stroem, 1998). Both the Czech and Hungarian committees, however, are more structured on the basis of continuing policy problems, for the number and scope of ministries can change with every change in the composition of the government (Crowther and Olson, 2002). Other committees have a jurisdiction cutting across the administrative parallel committees, of which budgeting and justice are examples.

The general principle in the distribution of committee memberships is that each committee should be proportional to the chamber party composition. Committee chairmanships, by contrast, tend to be allocated to government parties. If, however, the chamber is closely divided between government and opposition parties, a proportional sharing of committee officer positions becomes more necessary. The allocation of committee officer positions, both chair and vice-chair, are often part of the agreement in the government formation process as one result of the last election (Crowther and Olson, 2002).

Committees are more stable than PPGs. Typically, the same committee structure is continued from one session to the next. One result of continuous committees is specialization in public policy in spite of the volatility of elections and political parties. Legislative committees can be more permanent than the government's ministries.

Chamber leadership

In the multi-party parliaments of CEE, a formal steering group among the party leaders is usually formed, a Parliamentary Leadership Council, or PLC, headed by the speaker (Khmelko, 2012).

Decisions about who shall be the presiding officer ('speaker') and perhaps vice-speakers, are typically made as part of the government formation process following each election. The speaker is usually a leader of one of the government parties. External presidents can attempt to install their chosen candidates as parliamentary speaker. In Ukraine, for example, two rival sets of parliamentary members held separate meetings in different locations to each select a speaker (Khmelko, 2012: 82–5).

The PLCs ('Convent of Seniors' in Poland) are themselves a product of the initial inter-party bargains for the distribution of seats and power within parliament. In parliaments with a clear majority, the opposition parties have been excluded from membership on the leadership councils. But when Moldova changed from a dominant majority in one election to a closely balanced multi-party system in the succeeding election, for example, the leadership council was changed from the majority to include the minority parties (Crowther, 2012: 50). Bill introduction and referral to committees, as well as the schedule of both committee meetings and floor sessions, are among their continuing topics. They also decide on the formation of special and temporary committees (perhaps for investigations of allegations of scandal or corruption). The Parliamentary Leadership Council is a replacement of the Soviet-era centralized presidium, dominated by the speaker and committee chairperson, as in Belarus. That system was unsuited to manage multi-party diversity and controversy (Kask, 1996; Linek and Mansfeldova, 2008). The formation of parliamentary leadership councils is an important step in the institutionalization of new parliaments (Olson and Ilonszki, 2012b: 128–30).

Activities of parliaments

CEE parliaments engage in three activities typical of legislatures around the world: legislation, budgeting and oversight. They also often select or remove the prime minister and cabinet, and can amend the constitution. In these activities, they simultaneously fulfil two basic functions, of interaction with the executive and of representation of the electorate.

Legislation

Revision of the legal order in the early years suitable for the post-communist economy and politics was an overwhelming task facing new and unprepared legislatures. In addition, they had the responsibility of preparing new constitutions.

As early as their second and third terms, the objective of many CEE countries to join both NATO and the European Union imposed upon the new legislatures the daunting task of debating and enacting, under considerable time pressure, the necessary legislation. NATO required the relevant committees and the armed services to develop ways of working with each other, while the multi-year EU negotiation process required constant legislative attention.

The EU task quickly led to the formation of a new special committee to meet with and advise government ministers in EU negotiations. For those countries which have joined the EU, that special committee has evolved into a new permanent committee concerned with EU legislation (Zajc, 2004; Chiva, 2007; Mansfeldova, 2012: 15–17, Fink-Hafner, 2012: 111–12).

Both parliaments and governments have been busy with legislation. In four parliaments over a two-term period (Czech Republic, Hungary, Poland, Slovenia, 1998–2008) approximately 2,000 bills were considered in each parliament, of which 50–86 per cent were government bills. About 90 per cent of government bills were enacted (Olson and

Ilonszki, 2012b: 121). The relative importance of government legislation in CEE parliaments resembles the practices of most parliaments in
liberal democracies around the world (Olson, 1994: 84).

This volume of legislation has led both parliaments and governments
to reorganize themselves to prepare suitable legislation. A constant
complaint by members of parliaments is about the carelessly written
bills from the government (Kopecky, 2007: 154–5). As in Western
Europe, CEE governments have been encouraged to equip a 'core executive' to coordinate their own internal activities to prepare legislation
which could, without delay, gain parliamentary approval (Goetz and
Wollmann, 2001).

Parliamentary rules and procedures have slowly changed to provide
faster deliberation for government bills, and also to discourage consideration of non-government bills (Zubeck, 2012). Legislatures, however,
also adopt rules to limit government' requests for expedited procedures, both in committee and on the floor (Olson and Norton, 2008b:
174).

Budgets

Budgeting is an annual task, in which a government's proposed budget
typically is submitted to parliament about three months in advance of
the beginning of the fiscal year. While the Finance Committee of
Parliament usually has jurisdiction, in several of the CEE parliaments
the Finance Committee sends portions of the budget to the other committees consonant with their legislative jurisdiction for their advice.

In the Czech experience, the departmentally related committees
usually recommend increases in their respective portions of the budget,
while the Finance Committee, in support of the government, is more
concerned with aggregate expenditures, tax receipts, and deficits
(Mansfeldova and Rakusanova, 2008).

Oversight

From motions of censure and impeachment to concern about adequacy
of education in any one municipality, parliaments raise questions about
the organization and conduct of government administration. In
Poland, for example, over the span of ten prime ministers in both
majority and minority governments, a total of 33 no-confidence votes
were presented in the Sejm; none passed (Millard, 2008: 386–7).

The bulk of detailed review of administrative action, however, occurs
in the permanent legislative committees. Committees of the Polish Sejm
review specific administrative agencies and actions. They frequently

recommend that the budget be increased in coming years, for the main problem has been a shortage of funds rather than a misdirection of effort or an inadequacy of personnel (Karpowicz and Wesolowski, 2002). The oversight activity and procedures now employed by the Sejm committees, originating in the communist period, have proven useful in the new era (White, 1982).

Though floor votes of no confidence can have a strong partisan and anti-government character, oversight through both committees and floor questions can occur without partisanship. In both Poland and in the Ukrainian *Verkhovna rada*, members seem to think and act more from reasons of constituency than concern for either party or government survival (Khmelko and Beers, 2011).

Legislative–executive relations

Legislators, as representatives, constantly interact with executive and administrative organs of the state, from chief executive, whether president or prime minister, to civil servants. They act on legislation, budgeting and the implementation of both legislation and budgets. Depending on the constitutional structure of the state, they may also participate in the selection and dismissal of government ministers.

In most CEE states, the prime minister and cabinet are selected by parliament following a parliamentary election. Since most elections result in a multi-party parliament, in which no single party has a majority (Slovakia is an exception following its 2012 election), the government typically is a multi-party coalition.

Several CEE parliaments select the president. For two years following the 2009 elections, for example, the Moldovan Parliament could not agree on the presidential selection. In the Czech Republic, the largest party's deputies did not vote for the party's official choice for president in 1993 (in secret votes), and thus a candidate from a different party was finally selected. The Czech response has been to amend the constitution for direct popular election, beginning in 2013.

Hungary illustrates the power of a prime minister as leader of the majority parliamentary party. Prime Minister Orban, whose party won a majority with enough seats in 2010, was able to amend the constitution. Powers of the judiciary and of financial bodies were altered through constitutional amendments by parliament, though the opposition parties (as we saw in Chapter 2) were strongly in disagreement and boycotted the final vote.

Executives, whether prime minister or president, normally introduce the bulk of legislation considered by parliament, most of which is ordinarily approved. The budget is also proposed by the executive, which as discussed in a previous section, is largely also adopted by parliament.

The approval rates of government legislation are often the result of negotiations among government, PPGs and legislative committees. Several bills to remedy defects in Polish health policy, for example, were initiated by the government. Other bills came from the *Sejm* Health Committee, most of which ultimately were adopted by unanimous votes (Millard, 2008).

CEE governments tend to change with every election and, not infrequently, during a parliamentary term. The result is a continual turnover in ministers with changes in their degree of experience and skill, and continual change in government policies. In these circumstances, parliaments often have a more stable internal structure and also more stable and experienced members, than do governments. The executive–legislative relationship is always an interactive experiment in progress (Kopecky, 2004; Zubek, 2008).

Institutionalization and conflict

Over two decades since the end of Soviet authoritarian rule, CEE parliaments have become increasingly diverse. They differ, not only in their current status, but also in their transitions and in their communist-era experiences.

Two contradictory trends in West European politics are not as pronounced in CEE: personalization, and a 'drift toward parliamentarism' (Webb, 2011: 78–9; Eising and Poguntke, 2011: 48). Personalization of party leaders and chief executives in CEE politics was more pronounced in the initial decade than in the second. Dominant leaders of dominant parties in Slovakia and Croatia, for example, have been replaced by competitive party systems. Belarus currently has a dominant president, and Hungary a dominant prime minister, while in countries with continued 'constitutional recalibration', rival sets of personalities contest one another, as in Ukraine and Moldova.

As dominant leaders and parties have been replaced by competitive party systems, the importance of parliaments has increased in relationship to the executive. But there has been, simultaneously, an effort to develop a centralized 'core executive' within the cabinet, countered by the development of parliamentary committees to equip parliament to think and act independently of the executive, whether president or prime minister. There has been considerable variation among CEE parliaments at any one time and over the two decades.

Though there has been a constant flux of both members and parties in CEE parliaments, internal parliamentary structures have developed over the two-decade period. PPGs have become more stable, and both leadership bodies and committee procedures have been defined and standardized through the adoption of new rules.

Continuity of organization and procedure seems more pronounced in Central European and Baltic parliaments than in post-Soviet parliaments, with the former Yugoslav and other Balkan parliaments in a somewhat intermediate position. In the post-Soviet republics, parliaments have been caught up in protracted conflict over both political power and constitutional authority.

Legislatures have been at the epicentre of conflict and decision-making in the post-communist countries. They have been the source of constitutions and of the formation of political parties and party systems. In many respects, there was more of a 'founding decade' than any single election or event which transformed some of the inert single-party communist legislatures into active, representative, and competitive decision-making bodies in the second decade.

Chapter 11

Political Parties

Paul G. Lewis

Political parties are an indispensable component of modern liberal democracy, and the outcome in Central and Eastern Europe in terms of democratization and party development since the end of communist rule has generally been a positive one (see Chapter 15). The region as whole thus provides extensive scope for competitive party activity, and its broadly democratic identity suggests that parties have successfully established themselves in the post-communist context. But that is not to say that political parties are well regarded, and they are even less trusted than they are in Western Europe. Levels of trust in the CEE countries belonging to the European Union averaged 12 per cent from 2001 to 2006, although the level rose slightly to 13.7 per cent over 2007–08 (European Commission *Eurobarometer*, various years). In elections held in 2006 and 2007, moreover, half the governing parties were returned to power, in sharp contrast to the early post-communist years when voters invariably took the opportunity to express their dissatisfaction with the incumbents and threw them out. This apparent trend came to an end during the further hard times that arrived in the wake of the ongoing global economic crisis. Weakened trust in parties was actually identified as the major generic problem of contemporary European democracy (Schmitter, 2011: 209), although whether they are less well regarded than politicians as a species is debatable. Parties of some kind nevertheless play a prominent part in the reasonably free elections that are held in nearly all the countries of the region.

Origins and evolution of CEE parties

General conditions for party development and institutional growth in the early post-communist period were not at all favourable. Little organized political opposition to communist rule in CEE was able to develop prior to its collapse, and even a powerful independent social movement like that organized by the Solidarity trade union in Poland during 1980–81 was effectively neutralized for much of the following decade. Only in Hungary was there a pattern of evolutionary regime change. Proto-parties came into being well before the end of communist rule, with the Hungarian Democratic Forum (MDF) being established in September 1987 and registered as a party the following year. As a rule, parties were established after or during the first democratic elections. They had not been prominent in the early stages of regime change, and they did not channel the pressures that helped bring about the end of communist rule. It was generally within a social movement or under an umbrella organization sheltering a number of diverse political groups and orientations that the newly formed opposition groups and infant democratic forces entered the newly liberated CEE political arena (see Chapter 12). This provided uncertain ground for party development. Even in the more rapidly democratizing countries of Central Europe, where the early anti-communist movements broke up quite rapidly, it took some time for the different political tendencies to become identified and for separate political parties to be formed. Patterns of party development were, therefore, quite complex and differed considerably both among the countries of the CEE region and between the contrasting sectors of the newly expanded political arena of each post-communist state (Lewis, 2000: 32–48).

Alongside socio-political movements like Solidarity in Poland and Civic Forum in Czechoslovakia that acted as birthplace and nursery for one group of new parties, there was also a major evolution of former ruling communist parties (Bozoki and Ishiyama, 2002; Grzymala-Busse, 2002). But not all on the left moved in the same direction. Those in Poland and Hungary transformed quite rapidly and with considerable success into a fair approximation of Western social democratic parties. These new socialists won several elections in the early years, although the Polish Socialists (SLD) suffered a dramatic loss of popular support in 2003–4 and the Hungarian MSZD had a similar fate after the 2006 election. The Communist Party of Bohemia and Moravia (KSCM) in the Czech Republic, on the other hand, has retained its traditional identity and remained a significant if marginal political force in successive elections. It may yet prove to be an acceptable government partner.

Parties of a 'historic' character trace their roots directly to parties of the pre-communist period. The Czech Social Democratic Party (CSSD) is the most striking example of such an organization while a Hungarian agrarian party, the Independent Party of Smallholders (FKgP), for some years built successfully on pre-war foundations. Ethnic minority parties have also emerged on the basis of durable social divisions and play a significant role in the party systems of several states. This has been the case with the Turkish minority in Bulgaria, Hungarians in Slovakia and Romania, Russians in Latvia and Albanians in Macedonia and the Kosovan portion of Serbia – before moves were taken to establish Kosovo as a separate state (which is now left with a significant Serbian minority). Some of these parties as well as nationalist/populist movements have gained momentum in recent years, the latter often gaining strength in opposition to those seeking to defend and promote the rights of minorities. Such sentiments fuelled the rise of Ataka in Bulgaria and sustained the momentum of Slovak Nationalists (SNS) and the Party of Greater Romania (PRM), as well as underpinning the electoral dominance of the Serbian Radicals (SRS), who gained the single largest share of the vote in the 2003 election and remained the second largest parliamentary group in 2011. This was a party formed during the hostilities of the early 1990s and was an extreme case even in the West Balkans. Its leader, Vojislav Seselj, was brought to trial at the War Crimes Tribunal at The Hague in 2006, but at the time of writing a verdict had not yet been delivered.

One problematic feature of the early post-communist period was the relatively large number of weak parties elected to the newly democratized parliaments, which then showed high levels of fragmentation. These have nevertheless declined over time as a number of major parties became established and electoral mechanisms refined (see Chapter 9). But electoral volatility has also been a prominent feature and remains at levels more than twice as high as those in the West. Electorates have often had volatility forced on them by the short lives and high rate of turnover of parties. While a high rate of party creation would have been expected to occur at the beginning of the post-communist period, signs of the intensification of the process some ten years into the democratic period were more surprising. The most meteoric rise was that of Tsar Simeon II, who returned to Bulgaria in 2001 and founded the National Movement (NDSV) that won 42.7 per cent of the vote in an election held little more than two months later. A less rapid, but nevertheless striking, ascent was that of Res Publica in Estonia, which carried a parliamentary election and supplied the prime minister for a coalition government fifteen months after it was founded in 2001.

These were not isolated cases. Similarly successful new parties emerged in Lithuania, Latvia and Poland around the turn of the century, and the propensity of elites to form new parties seemed to be a major factor sustaining the high levels of volatility. This tendency turned out to be a permanent feature of CEE party politics, and was later seen even in states that had developed more stable party systems.

New parties were successful in the 2010 elections in the Czech Republic as Public Affairs (VV) and TOP09 gained substantial representation and entered government, the far-right Jobbik and LMP (Politics Can Be Different, a green party) achieved parliamentary representation for the first time in Hungary, and Freedom and Solidarity (SaS) entered government in Slovakia. In 2011 former Latvian president Zatler's Reform Party (ZRP) gained 20.8 per cent of the vote and the recently established Movement of Janusz Palikot (RP) got 10 per cent in Poland. It has convincingly been argued that newness itself is a major political resource in CEE party politics.

Some countries have not evolved a viable form of democratic party politics at all. The case of Belarus, whose undemocratic characteristics have persisted since the early 1990s and remained a consolidated authoritarian regime in 2012, is a singular one. Conditions there provided few opportunities for the development and activity of effective parties, only partly because the political system is a presidential one (see Chapter 8). Parliamentary elections have been held since 1995 but were not deemed 'free and fair' by official international observers. Most deputies were elected as 'independents' and nearly all were loyal to President Lukashenka. But it is also questioned by informed observers whether the country has much of a constituency for democratic party politics at all, as parties were estimated to enjoy the support of less than 5 per cent of the electorate (Marples, 2009: 761). Opposition parties themselves remain critically divided and were unable to work out a common policy in the run-up to the 2010 presidential election.

The situation is rather different in the five states which are only partly free but classified as electoral democracies. In Ukraine – another former Soviet republic – new constitutional arrangements came into force in January 2006 and transferred many presidential powers to the parliament, creating a situation where all seats were won by representatives of parties in elections held the following March. But there is little sense in which the parties emerge as autonomous actors in Ukrainian politics, and the conditions of widespread corruption and patronage tie parties very closely to the interests of the business sector. The imprisonment of opposition leader Yulia Tymoshenko did not appear to improve the country's prospects of unfettered party competition (see Chapter 5). Moldova has had a chequered history since the dissolution of the Soviet Union, but the prospects for more effective party politics – despite a near-three year deadlock over the election of a president (only resolved in March 2012) and three elections held over 2009–10 – are now better following the electoral defeat in 2009 of previously well-entrenched communist authoritarian forces.

Albania, a similarly impoverished country, has experienced massive social dislocation since the demise of the communist regime that underpins a persistent crisis of democratic representation and the alienation of its citizens from the two parties that dominate the political space (see Chapter 4). The Socialist opposition continued to refuse to recognize the validity of elections held in 2009 while it in turn was charged by the government of mounting a coup attempt in 2011. Well over a decade after the war that tore the state apart in the 1990s, the party system of Bosnia and Herzegovina has other problems, being still largely based on ethnicity and – while its individual components may be well-consolidated and competitive – in this sense can be seen as a 'classic case of party politics gone wrong' (Hulsey, 2012: 68). Ethnic conflict has also produced problems in Macedonia, where an uprising of part of the Albanian minority in 2001 brought the country to the brink of civil war, with violence flaring up again in March 2012. The more proportional electoral system introduced as part of the solution to the 2001 conflict produced a more fragmented party system and the benefits have been limited. In most CEE countries, though, parties dominate the electoral process more effectively and act as the primary agents of parliamentary representation, with the democratic process being largely shaped by party politics.

Party organization

The problems involved in developing effective democratic parties in post-communist CEE have generally been associated with their thin membership base, weak organizational structure and the limited funds at their disposal. The resources available to CEE parties can be analysed under several headings.

Membership

In comparative terms, CEE party membership levels in the post-communist period have been, and remain, low. Parties were estimated to have enrolled between 1 and 4 per cent of the adult population by the mid-1990s in contrast to levels of 15 and 16 per cent in countries like Austria and Sweden. But at the same time, membership in UK and the Netherlands, at 2.5 and 2.1 per cent respectively, was in the same range and, while CEE levels have been relatively low, they were not markedly out of line with those of some countries of Western Europe. Later research presented another perspective on membership issues confirming not just the low – and generally declining – membership levels in CEE but also pointing to a more dramatic fall in party membership in Western Europe in the context of growing disengagement from established parties.

Further surveys painted a similar picture. In one sample of party membership in the democratic world, all CEE representatives included were located in the bottom half of the list. The fewest party members were found in Poland, and then Hungary and Latvia (Whiteley, 2011: 24). More recent data show yet lower membership/electorate ratios for Latvia, Poland, Hungary and the Czech Republic ranging from 0.74 to 1.99 per cent, with CEE countries scoring on average 3.0 per cent compared with 5.6 per cent in Western and Southern Europe (van Biezen *et al.*, 2012: 28–9). The main conclusion to be drawn from a range of sources is not so much that CEE parties have few members – which is indeed the case – but that this is not a surprising state of affairs in the light of broader European experience.

The highest levels of membership in CEE parties have generally been found in the old communist organizations of the region, their reformed successors and allied bodies. The KSCM still claimed 77,000 members in 2008/9 and the Polish Democratic Left Alliance 73,000. The original organizations had been far larger though and, in a survey conducted in 2004, the Czech Republic had one of the highest proportions of former party members while attempts to halt the continuing process of membership decline met with little success (van Biezen *et al.*, 2012). There have been signs recently, however, that the decline in overall party membership and persistence of low levels of party adherence has been reversed in some of the more dynamic and electorally successful parties of Estonia, Hungary and the Czech Republic. In the last two cases it was significant that membership was rising particularly in right-wing parties like Fidesz and the Civic Democratic Party – as much as threefold in the former case over the ten-year period up to 2005 (Linek and Pechacek, 2007: 262; Enyedi and Linek, 2008: 462).

Structure

The conditions of contemporary party activity, reluctance of much of the public to participate politically and elitist attitudes held by many CEE party leaders have all combined to give the members the parties did enrol a relatively marginal role in the organization as a whole. This has been reflected in the relative weakness of party structures. Questions of inner-party democracy have also often been ignored and rarely perceived to be much of an issue in party life. Post-communist politics and the contemporary practice of liberal democracy are thus generally understood to operate most effectively at national level and within the narrow confines of the political elite. This involves a limited conception of the political party, and provides few incentives for developing a party's organizational network or a sub-national structure. In this context, too, national party politics has also seemed to be quite disorganized and shown low levels of party unity. Once elected, parliamentary deputies have often joined another faction and party loyalty has been weak, particularly in Latvia, Lithuania, Slovakia and Poland. Recent research, however, has suggested that CEE and West European levels of party unity are not that different, although disunity has been prominent in Romania (Stefan *et al.*, 2012: 2).

There has, too, been little correlation between the development of organizational structure and party success at the polls. It was one of the paradoxes of the Polish election of 2001 that the party which had paid most attention to questions of institutional development and put most effort into organizing a national structure – the Freedom Union – failed to reach the electoral threshold and lost the parliamentary representation it had maintained since its formation in 1990. In Bulgaria, on the other hand, the NDSV of Simeon II won the 2001 election with virtually no members and minimal organization – a deficiency that made itself felt when the party performed dismally in the 2003 local elections. Detailed comparative CEE data on party organizational development is notable for its absence and, as LaPalombara (2007: 150) has pointed out, the extensive survey databases now available tell us remarkably little about internal organization and party dynamics in this context.

In line with patterns of party membership, however, it has been possible to identify some national differences in party structure. In Hungary, the resemblance of the new parties' structures to those of the former ruling communist party was remarked on at an early stage, the growth of professionalization and bureaucratization only leading to the emergence of a sharply restricted and elitist democracy. More recently, though, in line with its impressive membership figures, Fidesz showed 'even more spectacular growth in the number of local organizations' (Enyedi and Linek, 2008: 463). With more members on the ground, too, Czech parties have shown a greater capacity for development as autonomous units. They have had some power to manage their affairs, settle management and leadership issues on their own account and control their finances, but have been more successful in building party organizations at national level than in developing the local network.

The organizational assets inherited from the communist regime by successor parties have now diminished. As membership of the once all-powerful Czech KSCM dropped away – falling by over half between

1992 and 1999 – a decline also could be seen in the party's network of local organizations. Similar changes have occurred in parties that share some of the characteristics of this party model. The prominence of some leader-dominated parties like that of Meciar's Movement for Democratic Slovakia (HZDS) for much of the 1990s, a model replicated in several Balkan countries and former Soviet republics, was also partly based on the communist legacy and facilitated by control over state resources and the capacity for extensive patronage, conditions that were clearly more prevalent in the less democratized CEE countries. These features have diminished as pluralist democracy has consolidated, particularly in states more open to the influence of the EU, although particular problems remain in this area in Bulgaria and Romania.

The emergence of distinctive Western political entrepreneurs, typified by Silvio Berlusconi in Italy, has also found CEE parallels in business-firm organizations like Public Affairs (successful in the 2010 Czech election), Slovak media magnate Pavel Rusko's ANO, the Lithuanian Labour Party (DP) founded by Russian businessman Viktor Uspaskich, as well as several Latvian oligarch parties targeted by President Zatlers in his surprise 2011 call for 'purification' elections. Also prominent in CEE party politics has been another model first elaborated in the Western context, that of the cartel party. This also involves the idea of parties closely associated with the state, particularly dependent on it for funding, oriented to the maintenance of executive power and with limited local organization. But this model does not fully accord with specific features of CEE politics, particularly with respect to continuing party system instability and national forms of party organization (Krasovec and Haughton, 2011).

Funding

The weak base of many CEE parties and their leadership emphasis is also reflected in funding patterns. The distribution of state property and other assets at the end of the communist period gave parties associated with the former regime major advantages over their competitors. Membership dues also played a considerably larger role in the finances of communist and successor social democratic parties than in liberal and right-wing organizations. In the mid-1990s, the Czech communists as well as Hungarian and Polish Socialists drew from 20 to 43 per cent of their income from their members. In the 2000–5 period Czech communists still received 31 per cent of their income from this source, while a right-wing party like the Christian Democracy (KDU-CSL) was exceptional in deriving 11 per cent of its income from members during this period. Members did not provide more than 10 per cent of the income of any other major Czech or Hungarian party, and patterns of funding were little different for the leading Polish organizations. Precisely where the rest of the funds used to fund party activity have come from is not always clear, although national legislation generally provides for the publication of party accounts and full transparency of party finances.

Direct state funding for parties in Hungary and the Czech Republic was quite generous from the early years of post-communist rule, and the Hungarian Free Democrats (SZDSZ) obtained 91 per cent of their funds from this source in 1995. The situation in Poland was different, as there was no direct funding of party activity (apart from the reimbursement of election expenses) until 1997. But Polish parties soon followed the strong regional tendency to depend on the state for their income and, by 2003, three of the six parliamentary parties depended on this source for more than 90 per cent of their income. In the enlarged EU, nine of the ten CEE member states subsidise parties from the state budget, the exception being Latvia. Most of them, but not Slovakia, have also introduced regulation procedures to oversee party finances which help counter tendencies to corruption and the misuse of funds (Kopecky and Spirova, 2011: 28). Laws on the financing of political parties were also introduced in the Western Balkans after 2000, but there is little evidence to suggest that they have been applied very effectively. Party funding was identified as a problem area in Montenegro and one reason for the EU refusal to open negotiations for accession in 2010. Even in the better regulated states, however, a party's election prospects can still be affected by corruption and funding scandals and the Estonian Centre Party's (K) performance was thus weakened in the 2011 elections. Equally, in the Czech Republic, VV leader Barta – head of a new party standing on an anti-corruption ticket that went straight into government in 2010 – was himself convicted of corruption in April 2012.

The issue of how party activity should be best financed – as well as how party politicians' relations to financial resources should be regulated in general – remains a live and contentious issue in many countries. Three main problems have been identified in this area. The first is the lack of transparency and accurate reporting of party income. Second, the lack of a level playing field and the overall advantages enjoyed by government parties and, third, the deficiencies of representation as parties have few direct financial links with electors in contrast to those with the state or big corporations. But while finance is clearly an important condition of effective party activity, it is not particularly clear how important it is for the quite large numbers of new parties that continue to break through and gain entry to the parliamentary arena in a number of countries. A general impression is that finance is not a prime condition for political success, and that the continuing fluidity of the political constellation offers diverse opportunities and various points of access to the political arena. There are, however, some indications that the pattern of state funding in new CEE democracies is rather different from that in recently democratized southern European regimes – and that the tendency for funds to flow more strongly to the parties' central offices than to their parliamentary leadership may have major consequences for their patterns of development (van Biezen, 2003: 199–201).

Party systems

A major aspect of the development of parties in CEE and the way in which they operate as political actors is the nature of the party systems that evolve – or perhaps fail to – as a consequence of their interactions. The analysis of party systems is rather different from that of the parties themselves, as parties may emerge, survive and perform their political tasks quite adequately without developing much of a pattern of interaction or anything like a party system. The high level of electoral volatility seen in the region and its continuing capacity to generate new parties reflects the fact that the process of party system development has been a problematic one and that stability in this area has been limited.

Party system institutionalization

One approach to the topic is to focus on party system institutionalization, which is often linked to levels of democratic achievement. This has generally been associated with the work of Mainwaring (1999), who specified four conditions for the process. The first of these is stability in the rules and nature of inter-party competition, the second is the parties' ability to put down stable roots in society, a third is that major political actors regard parties and electoral processes as legitimate, and fourth, that party organizations should acquire an independent status and value of their own. The first condition is the easiest to find data for in the CEE context, as rates of electoral volatility can be readily calculated and the different states ranked on that basis. But this hardly provides a full picture of inter-party competition and features like parliamentary fragmentation, the role of political blocs and government closure in terms of party access should also be taken into account. A broader analysis of patterns of party competition has shown Hungary and the Czech Republic to be more institutionalized in this dimension (Enyedi and Bertoa, 2011: 138).

The success of parties in establishing social roots can partly be viewed in terms of membership levels, which are generally quite low although some exceptions have been detected. Survey data on degrees of partisan attachment throw further light on this aspect and, while attachment is generally found to be lower in new democracies, Poland started off with a relatively high level which then declined while Hungary and the Czech Republic had rising levels. Parties in the latter two countries have also been found to represent social cleavages more effectively. The low levels of trust in parties found in CEE suggest that the electorate does not see them as particularly legitimate, although the two perceptions are not quite the same. Survey data on the value attached to the democratic system and judgements on whether parties are necessary to make such a system work properly offer a further perspective on this factor, and value is attached again more readily to Hungarian and Czech parties as well as, more surprisingly, to Romanian ones. Information on party organization and how it is valued is particularly sparse, although it is clear that CEE party organization is relatively weak, with some significant exceptions being identified in this area.

From this brief overview it is evident that some countries are identified more frequently as having satisfied the conditions for institutionalization, and that the party systems of Hungary and the Czech Republic appeared to have stabilized more quickly than others. Similar conclusions were reached in other works, although signs were also detected that this stability might be subject to change. Parliamentary elections held in 2010 showed that such doubts were not unfounded. The Hungarian Socialist Party, having been in power since 2002, suffered a massive electoral collapse and two established parties, the Free Democrats and Democratic Forum, lost parliamentary representation altogether. Fidesz Hungarian Civic Union won an overwhelming victory (receiving 227 of the 386 parliamentary seats), and the extreme right-wing party Jobbik entered parliament with 16.7 per cent of the vote, as did the greenish LMP. In the Czech Republic an established parliamentary party, the Christian Democrats, failed to reach the threshold and for the first time since 1992 the two leading parties, Civic Democrats (ODS) and Social Democrats (CSSD), failed to capture 50 per cent of the vote between them. Two new parties, TOP09 and Public Affairs, entered parliament and also joined the government.

The two party systems generally regarded as the most institutionalized in the region thus turned out to be more open to change than pre-

viously thought, but these were not the only signs of growing instability. Governments fell in a number of countries and pre-term elections were later called in Slovakia, Slovenia and Latvia, at least partly
due to conflicts and problems of coalition maintenance caused by the
economic crisis and pressures of the international environment (see
Chapter 3). This was not so much of a surprise as the extensive
changes in Hungary and the Czech Republic, as the less institutionalized party systems were expected to be more susceptible to external
shocks. But the roots of the Hungarian and Czech changes could also
be traced back to more structural factors. The stabilization of the
Hungarian party system, for example, had involved a gradual reduction in the number of parties over two decades, which resulted in a situation of considerable polarization. The Socialists had achieved a
second term in government in 2006 that left them with a long list of
economic problems topped off with the consequences of the 2008 crisis
for which the electorate could readily hold them responsible.
Corruption issues had also become more prominent. Fidesz was, too, a
formidable political opponent which had transformed its identity over
the years and developed a highly effective electoral strategy. It was a
well-organized party with a sizeable membership, which made it an
exception in the CEE context, as did the country's electoral system,
which reinforced the Fidesz victory in terms of parliamentary seats.

The 2010 electoral shock in the Czech Republic had less obvious
roots, although it had been noted prior to the event that the larger
Czech parties seemed to be losing their grip on the electorate. The position of the ODS, which had with some difficulty formed a government
coalition after the 2006 elections, had steadily weakened and it lost its
parliamentary majority midway through the Czech EU presidency in
2009. Party leader Topolanek resigned as an MP after this, and then
stepped down from the party leadership just before the election. The
poor performance of the Social Democrats was more of a surprise. It
only gained three more parliamentary seats than ODS, having received
more votes than any other party, and was not in a position to form a
government coalition. Loss of support among young voters and attacks
from former colleagues weakened the party, but there also just seemed
to be a general disillusion among the electorate with existing parties.

The relatively high level of party system institutionalization in
Hungary and the Czech Republic was, therefore, no barrier to major
change in this area. Whether this has any implications in terms of the
broader political outcomes discussed in this context like democratic
accountability and openness to populist movements is another matter.
Suggestions that Central and Eastern Europe was backsliding politically once many states had become EU members and were no longer

subject to accession conditionality were generally exaggerated, and fears that the region as a whole was fertile ground for populist extremism have not generally been borne out (see Chapter 1). Extremist parties have more frequently emerged in the established democracies of Western Europe, and CEE populist tendencies have often tended to emerge in the centre of the party spectrum espousing values congruent with those of the democratic regime as a whole. In this context, though, the recent success of Jobbik in Hungary is a significant exception.

The impact of the EU

One distinctive influence on the development of CEE party systems was the requirement of democratic conditionality for the ten countries that joined the European Union between 2004 and 2007, as well as similar demands placed on current CEE candidates (all from the former Yugoslavia) and the continuing expectations of those with more distant prospects of EU membership. Confirmation of the democratic credentials and institutional identity of a post-1989 party by one of the major international groups or federations was often a major advantage in stabilizing its position and enhancing its status over competitors in the same area of the political spectrum – as well as rewarding it with financial and other advantages. In terms of its resemblance to the range of political families seen in Western Europe, the CEE party spectrum shows an increasing degree of development in terms of identity formation and ideological correspondence with European norms, but there are few signs of anything like a transnational party system developing at European level.

Several categories of party have also experienced problems in developing a European identity and affiliating with any of the European parties or groups in the European Parliament (EP). One group consisted of parties that derived directly from the ruling institutions of the communist period. This originally concerned quite prominent organizations like the Czech KSCM, but now only includes major parties in non-democracies like Kosovo and Belarus or countries with no prospect of EU membership in the foreseeable future like Ukraine (although the EP Alliance of Socialists signed a widely criticized cooperation agreement with Yanukovych's Party of the Regions in October 2010). Nationalist parties like Greater Romania, the Bulgarian Ataka, the Serbian Radical Party, nationalist Bosnian organizations and ethnic groups in Macedonia have also remained outside the EP party groups. Just two parties, from Estonia and Latvia, are members of the European Greens – European Free Alliance (EFA) group, and the two left-wing parties (Latvia Social Democrats and the Czech Communists) have joined the European United Left (GUE-NGL). Representatives from Lithuania, Poland and Slovakia have joined the radically Eurosceptic Freedom and Democracy group, while it is mostly Poles and Czechs who have linked with the British Conservatives in the European Conservatives and Reformists. The great majority of significant CEE parliamentary parties are thus linked with the leading European People's Party (EPP-ED), Socialist and Association of Liberals and Democrats (ALDE) groups. Increasing numbers of mainstream parties, particularly amongst the region's democratic leaders, are thus forging stronger links with the leading European party federations and becoming more 'European' in this sense.

A growing literature on Europeanization has focused on the impacts of the EU, and particularly the consequences of EU accession, on CEE parties and party systems (see Chapter 6). It was clear at a relatively early stage that any such process was neither uniform nor one-directional in its effects, and probably less than some analysts had anticipated (Lewis and Mansfeldova, 2006). Generally, though, it has been concluded that the less consolidated CEE party systems have been more susceptible to external influence and EU impacts than those in older member states (Sedelmeier, 2011: 20). Recent region-wide studies, on the other hand, have suggested that there has been little or no direct EU impact (Haughton, 2011b; Lewis and Markowski, 2011). A comprehensive analysis of Poland within the EU also finds little significant direct impact on the country's party politics, but rather the successful assimilation of 'Europe' into the logic of Polish domestic party politics (Szczerbiak, 2012: 183). An alternative view has nevertheless suggested that Poland's relationship to the EU has in fact been a factor affecting the birth of new parties (Markowski and Tucker, 2010: 538–41). Documented cases of the EU or its institutions exerting a direct influence on CEE party systems are indeed rare, although one recent case among the new member states was the action of the Party of European Socialists in suspending the Slovak SMER when it brought the national party (deemed to be intolerant and racist) into a government coalition in 2006. The suspension was lifted in 2008 after party leader Fico signed a letter committing the government to respect minority rights, with full membership of the EP group being granted the following year.

The EU has only once imposed sanctions on a member state. This occurred in 2000 in connection with a party-related issue in Austria when the far-right Freedom Party entered government. Developments following the massive victory of Viktor Orban's Fidesz in the 2010 Hungarian election put this possibility on the EU agenda for a second time, however, as the EP began to consider in 2012 whether Orban's government was respecting EU laws and values. In effect this raised the question of whether Fidesz was putting Europeanization into reverse in Hungary. Fidesz, in alliance with the Christian Democratic Party, gained 263 parliamentary seats, more than two-thirds of the total, and thus the power to amend the constitution and introduce certain 'cardinal laws' (see Chapter 2). Charges were made that Fidesz, as the main ruling party, was attempting to entrench its power by changing the rules of the political game through amendments to the electoral system, removing institutional checks and balances (in the judiciary and constitutional court) and enhancing its influence (particularly in the media) the better to secure future parliamentary majorities. The conflicts are unresolved at the time of writing and outcomes uncertain, but such developments at least raise the question of whether party system instability has contributed to potentially undemocratic and 'un-European' outcomes.

A related and equally relevant question is how far the pressures of European integration themselves contributed to the 'earthquake election' of 2010 and thus helped undermine party system stability. The growing polarization of the Hungarian party system was in fact preceded and initially conditioned by joint commitment to EU membership and a significant measure of collusion between the main parties (Mike, 2007). Later, strategies to mitigate the economic costs of regional and global economic integration and support Hungarian incomes could not be sustained once the country joined the EU and it became necessary to reduce the government deficit. It was just after re-election in 2006 that the Socialist government submitted its revised convergence programme to the European Council and the prime minister delivered his infamous speech on the need for austerity, which destroyed the party's credibility among the electorate when it was leaked by Fidesz and became the cue for massive opposition demonstrations (Bohle, 2010: 11). Such developments would not be understood as part of Europeanization in the normal sense, but they certainly reflect the consequences of European integration and the impact of international pressures on a national party system.

Further major EU anxieties arose over what was seen as an attempted *coup d'etat* in Romania, as the left-wing government took steps to impeach right-wing president Basescu. This led, in July 2012, to the Commission issuing the strongest warning yet to a member state that it was endangering democracy and the rule of law. Commission President Barroso stated that party political competition could not justify overriding core democratic values and Prime Minister Ponta moderated his actions, although the issue is far from resolved.

CEE party politics in comparative context

The trajectory of CEE party development has in some ways been more uncertain and diverse than many observers expected. Equally, the consequences of European integration have not been quite what was anticipated – but this has also proved to be the case in Western Europe, as recent developments have clearly shown. Party government throughout Europe has been difficult to maintain under conditions of economic crisis dominated by supranational forces, and CEE has hardly been immune from such tendencies in a situation where party systems and democratic government have only recently been introduced and hardly been consolidated. If the challenge to party government in Western Europe has been such that neither its effective functioning nor the maintenance of its legitimacy can realistically be envisaged in the future, it is difficult to see how the CEE situation can be any better (Mair, 2008).

Governments throughout Western Europe have fallen as a result of the pressures exerted by the post-2007 economic crisis, and tensions produced by the measures taken to manage the eurozone crisis created particular problems in some CEE countries as the established processes of party government failed to cope with the challenge. Early elections were held in Slovenia after the fall of the government when two coalition parties left over pension reform proposals put forward in September 2011 to deal with the debt crisis. The following month in Slovakia the government of Iveta Radicova, not long in office since elections held in 2010, was only able to secure parliamentary backing for the European Financial Stability Facility by agreeing to early elections (held in March 2012), which the SDKU-DS then lost. Both countries had been early CEE entrants to the eurozone. But the problems of party government in hard times did not just lead to pre-term elections. Often a government would fall, or just not be formed in the first place, and leadership exercised by a politically neutral technocrat or caretaker figure.

Equivalent examples can be found in Western Europe during the eurozone crisis, notably in Greece and Italy. They are often discussed in terms of a 'democratic deficit' but might more accurately seen as a variant of party government failure. Such cases have not been uncommon in CEE, and are not restricted to the very recent past. The Czech party system had experienced political deadlock on several occasions and problems were again apparent after the 2006 election, as the 200 parliamentary seats were split equally between right and left. A coalition government was finally installed, but it lost a vote of confidence little more than two years later and a caretaker government ran the country for nearly a year before new elections were held in 2010. More significant than the bare facts of weak party government, however, was the 72 per cent trust level accorded to caretaker prime minister Jan Fischer just before the election in contrast to the 20 per cent who had trusted Czech Democratic Party leader Topolanek exactly a year earlier.

The Hungarian government fell at just about the same time as the Czech and was replaced by a similar caretaker premier and 'government of experts', which proceeded to implement the fiscal stabilization measure for which the former Socialist government had to pay the electoral price. In a related series of developments, the Latvian government resigned followed massive riots during January 2009 in the context of the meltdown of the national economy. It was replaced by a relatively technocratic government under former Finance Minister and MEP Dombrovskis, who also maintained high approval ratings during a period of great economic stringency. Although there were major differences between these cases, they do show the growing failure of the form of CEE party government that had developed during the post-communist period. Established procedures of party politics were increasingly unable to provide effective democratic government or to meet the demands placed on the political sphere by a prolonged economic crisis. It may be argued that the electoral success of Fidesz in 2010 and its subsequent political dominance exemplifies a rather successful form of party government, but it remains to be seen how things develop and whether the new regime arrangements continue to sustain processes of party-based electoral competition.

A second major comparative theme concerns the overall trajectory of party development in new democracies and the different ways they might develop as political organizations. Broadly speaking, the different paths may be endogenous (relating to whether all parties follow a similar life-cycle), generational (whether the conditions under which a party first emerges shape its subsequent development), or whether a period effect is exercised and the external environment continues to have a significant effect on the emerging type of party (van Biezen, 2005: 150–2). One empirical study of parties in new democracies 'finds it tempting to conclude' that some kind of generational factor was shaping party development in new democracies and that there were few signs of convergence with party politics in established regimes, that is, they did not seem to follow a common life-cycle. There were also signs, however, that period effects might be growing in influence (Webb and White, 2007: 360–3). 1978 has been identified as a date after which new party systems tended to remain fluid and failed to stabilize (Mainwaring and Zoco, 2007). The perception of convergence, though, is strengthened by recent trends in party membership and structure, the attenuation of organizational capacity and growing failures of party government in a number of countries throughout Europe where democratic procedures were otherwise well established. This has generally been associated with the strong pressures exerted by the global and regional economic environment which, in the case of CEE, have become deeply embedded in the domestic economy and polity within a very short time-span. This, however, may also be interpreted as a 'period effect' which is clearly significant at the current juncture and has yet to make its full impact.

Chapter 12

Citizens and Politics

Krzysztof Jasiewicz

In September 2006, six weeks before the fiftieth anniversary of the tragic Hungarian Uprising, the people of Budapest took to the streets again. This time their goal was more limited than a half-century before: not the abolition of a hated Soviet-installed regime, but the resignation of a prime minister who only six months earlier had managed to win re-election (a rare feat in Central and Eastern Europe these days). A leaked tape revealed that Prime Minister Ferenc Gyurcsany, during the campaign, had misled the electorate about the real state of the Hungarian economy. Admitting this fact, Gyurcsany said 'We lied in the morning, night, and evening', which was a paraphrase of a 1956 admission and promise made by the Hungarian radio broadcasters 'We lied in the morning, and lied in the evening, we lied in daylight and lied at night. We shall lie no more'. The phrase that in 1956 was an honest act of remorse by people who had been but cogs in the Stalinist propaganda machine, in 2006 became a just cynical statement made by a political leader to his fellow comrades (and accomplices), not to the public. Gyurcsany, a Socialist, unwillingly confirmed here Karl Marx's famous quip, that history repeats itself 'the first time as tragedy, the second time as farce'.

The 2006 Hungarian protesters marched the streets of Budapest and fought the riot police to no avail. Gyurcsany's government rejected calls for resignation and his Hungarian Socialist Party (MSZP) stayed in power until the very end of the four-year term prescribed by the constitution (Gyurcsany himself resigned in 2009). But at election time, in 2010, the people of Hungary remembered who lied to them. The MSZP's share of votes fell from 43.2 per cent to 19.3 per cent and their number of seats in the parliament from 190 to a mere 59. An opposition party, Fidesz (whose members and sympathisers had been deeply engaged in the 2006 protests), swept the election, winning 263 of the 386 seats.

But the size of Fidesz's victory, as we saw in Chapter 2, spelled new troubles. By controlling over two-thirds of the seats, Fidesz gained a supermajority that allowed it to fill independent state bodies (such as the Constitutional Court or National Bank) with its loyalists and, above all, to make changes in the constitution without any regard for the voice of the opposition. In January 2011, thousands of Hungarians were back out on the streets again, this time to protest against a new constitution, which, in the opinion of domestic analysts and foreign observers, undermines the very foundations of Hungary's young democracy (see a cluster of articles by Jacques Rupnik and others in the *Journal of Democracy*, June 2012, vol. 23, no. 3).

Recent developments in Hungary illustrate well the shortcomings of an electoral democracy: important information may be withheld from the voters or manipulated by those in power; an unpopular, corrupt government can stay in power for years if the opposition lacks votes in the parliament to replace it; a free and fair election may give one party a supermajority, allowing it to bend the formal rules to its unfair advantage. These developments speak also of the limitations of mass protest actions: neither in 2006, nor in 2011 did Hungarian rulers yield to the pressure of street demonstrations.

Of course, not every government under any circumstances would be able to show such resolve. The current regimes of Central and Eastern Europe came into being as a result of popular revolutions against the communist rulers or their authoritarian successors that have swept through the region in 1989 and the following years. In almost every case, those revolutions involved a combination of two types of civic behaviour, one taking place on the streets, the other in the electoral booths. Sometimes, as in Poland or Czechoslovakia of the 1980s, mass street demonstrations and strikes initiated the change, to be followed by competitive elections – the real turning point in the process of political transition. In other cases, as in Yugoslavia in 2000 or Ukraine in 2004, spectacular street demonstrations followed fraudulent elections and were an expression of the will of the people who, unlike their rulers, were determined to treat democracy seriously.

Yet popular revolts and elections are but extreme forms of citizens' involvement in politics. People interact with the political system in a rich variety of ways. They join political parties or other organizations, come to meetings and rallies, collect – and make – monetary contributions, write letters of support to political leaders. They go on strike, occupy public buildings, boycott commercial organizations or political events (such as elections), sign petitions against political decisions. Forms of political participation are, virtually, countless. Consequently, scholars analyse political behaviour in many ways, looking at everything from individual motivations, to patterns of interaction (between individuals, groups, and/or institutions), to eventual outcomes (those desired and those unintended). For the purposes of this chapter, we will use a simple typology of political action, based on two criteria: (i) whether it engages its participants on a universal or particularistic basis, and (ii) whether it follows established conventions (cyclical or perpetual routines) or involves sporadic/transitory acts of mobilization (for more on these distinctions see Dalton, 1988). Of course, there are many other possible criteria to classify political action: it can be legal or illegal, overt or clandestine, peaceful or violent, successful or ineffective, and so forth. We believe, however, that the typology proposed here is helpful in exposing specific features of citizens' involvement in politics in post-communist Central and Eastern Europe.

In democracies, elections – presidential, parliamentary, local, supernational – take place with a certain regularity (every two, four or five years, or whatever is the constitutional requirement), and follow prescribed procedures; even exceptions to this cycle – such as early elections in parliamentary systems – are covered by established rules. Mass upheavals or rebellions, on the contrary, happen suddenly and seldom; no one can predict their occurrence with any accuracy and very few people can participate in such an event more than once in their lifetime.

Yet, dissimilar as they obviously are, national elections and revolutionary upheavals do have something in common: they tend to involve and engage all citizens of a nation-state – and to engage them as citizens, not as members of any particular group. Even if some people do not participate in elections (because they decided to boycott the act or because they are too apathetic to take part) or ignore the call to join a rebellion (because of fear or because they reject its goals), the outcomes of these universal (at the national level) events will in all likelihood be relevant for their lives.

By contrast, when people join political, economic, or cultural organizations (sometimes making a lifetime commitment), or when they decide to participate in an industrial strike, road blockade, or act of civil disobedience, they are usually motivated by some particular group interests. In any democracy, platforms of aggregation of particularistic interests (such as class, professional, ethnic, religious, regional, gender- or age-based) as well as forms of collective action are potentially countless. Just as universal ones, particularistic actions tend also to coalesce into two types, conventional (usually long-lasting) and protest (usually transitory and sporadic).

Schematically, the intersection of the two ways of looking at political behaviour may be presented as in Table 12.1. It should be emphasized that this scheme is a typology, not a classification of forms of political actions, which means that certain specific actions cannot be unequivo-

Table 12.1 *A typology of political action*

Types of political action	Universal	Particular
Convention	Elections	Organizational membership
Protest	Rebellions, revolutions, upheavals	Strikes, riots, demonstrations, petition drives, and so on

cally labelled as representing a given single type. For instance, an organization, such as a trade union or a political party, can be established one day and dissolved soon after, making it rather a sporadic phenomenon than a part of any routine (although the sporadic emergence and disappearance of political organizations has become a routine in many CEE states). Some actions launched to secure particular interests may over time develop into nationwide upheavals: such was the case of a strike in the Gdansk shipyard in 1980 that eventually gave birth to the Solidarity movement. Some upheavals last but a few days, other evolve into social movements active for months or even years and gaining, over time, resemblance to formal organizations (again, Solidarity is a striking example). Certain groups (such as intellectuals) can make a legitimate claim that protection of their particular interests (such as freedom of expression) has in fact a universal, and not just a particularistic value. Still, when discussing the involvement of citizens in politics in Central and Eastern Europe today, we can focus on the four types presented above, without ignoring important issues. Two forms of citizens' involvement, participation in elections and membership in political parties, are so critical for the functioning of any polity that they are given separate coverage in this volume (see Chapters 9 and 11). Here, we will focus on indirect and unconventional forms of this involvement. We will begin with mass upheavals, moving to the various forms of engagement in civil society, and then to protest politics motivated by particular interests. We will also look at the role of the media and conclude with a brief examination of mass political attitudes – the cognitive and affective foundations of political behaviour.

Mass upheaval

Why do people rebel? When do they rebel? Why are some rebellions successful and other are not? These and similar questions have been addressed in a vast political, historical, sociological, and psychological literature on revolutions, collective action, collective violence, and social movements (see for instance, Brinton, 1965; Davies, 1971; Eisenstadt, 1978; Gurr, 1971; Huntington, 1968; Kimmel, 1990; Moore, 1966; Sanderson, 2010; Skocpol, 1979; Smelser, 1962; Tilly, 1978, Tilly and Tarrow, 2007; Tilly and Wood, 2009). Occasionally, intense debates on these issues are prompted by the actual events of the day, as was the case of CEE twenty years ago, or the Arab Spring in most recent years. So far, scholars engaged in reflections on this subject are far away not only from any consensus on the causes and mechanisms of mass popular upheavals, but even from establishing a common terminology. We can agree here that the concept of revolution can be applied (albeit not always without reservations or qualifications) to the complex processes that entailed the collapse of communist regimes and the establishment of viable pluralist democracies and market economies in Central and Eastern Europe in the 1980s and 1990s.

Hence, we will without hesitation apply the term 'revolution' to events and processes as diverse as the Polish Solidarity movement of 1980–89, the Hungarian transition of 1989–90, the Velvet Revolution in Czechoslovakia (late 1989–winter 1990), the upheaval in the Baltic states (Lithuania, Latvia, Estonia) that lasted from 1988 to 1991, the violent events in Romania in December 1989 and January 1990, or the events in East Germany that culminated in the fall of the Berlin wall in November 1989. The term revolution seems also appropriate in relation to the less-spectacular and slower transformations that took place in Bulgaria (1989–91), Albania (1990–92), and Moldova (1991–92), as well as to the regime change in three (now former) Yugoslav republics: Slovenia, Croatia, and Macedonia. (For a more detailed analysis of these processes, see Jasiewicz, 1998.)

The term seems also adequate for the 'colour revolutions' that took place in some countries of the region in the first decade of the twenty-first century. These upheavals led to the collapse of authoritarian regimes that replaced the communist ones in several former Soviet and Yugoslav republics. (An extensive analysis of the 'colour revolutions' can be found in Bunce and Wolchik, 2011.)

In Serbia, post-Tito communist institutions evolved, not without the compliance of the population, into the authoritarian regime of Slobodan Milosevic; a (nameless) popular upheaval brought an end to his rule in 2000, after a decade of mismanagement and a series of lost wars. In Ukraine, the departure from the Soviet system in the early 1990s was, despite substantial popular involvement, hijacked at the elite level by former communist apparatchiks. The corrective came, over a decade later, with the Orange Revolution of 2004. Yet one still can pose a question as to what extent those events – undoubtedly one of the most spectacular and photogenic popular upheavals in the entire region – were in fact a true revolution and to what only a dramatic turnover within the political elite. The failure of Orange Revolution's leaders to implement successful reforms soon brought back to power the apparatchiks defeated in 2004.

Elsewhere in the region, one can hardly justify speaking of genuine revolutions. In Bosnia-Herzegovina, the new regime (whose democratic credentials still seem questionable) emerged as the result of a civil war, not a revolution. Similarly, Kosovo won its independence through a national liberation war and an intervention by the international community. Finally, Belarus has not seen a post-communist revolution to date; its authoritarian leader, Alexander Lukashenka, unabashedly emphasizes the continuity between his regime and the old Soviet days.

Despite local variations, the process of political change in all the Central and East European countries occurred according to the same general pattern, from polarization to fragmentation: a united opposition faced the old regime in a stand-off (at roundtable negotiations and/or during elections), but remained united only until the apparent defeat of the communists. But post-communist revolutions shared several other common features. In almost all cases, the upheavals were launched, or at least preceded, by a spectacular, massive display of national unity, in defiance of the formal rules and/or informal expectations of the communist system. In Poland, such a display came in June 1979 during John Paul II's first visit to his native land after becoming Pope, when millions attended open-air masses and services in an orderly fashion and a joyful mood, with the communist coercive apparatus nowhere to be seen. In the Baltics, the human chain of people holding hands joined the three capitals, Vilnius, Riga, and Tallinn, on 23 August 1989 – the fiftieth anniversary of the Molotov-Ribbentrop pact (the act that had sealed Soviet domination of the region). Only a decade earlier such a display of solidarity would have been unthinkable: very few people, if any, would have been ready to pass the threshold of fear, as the response of the Soviet regime would have been swift and ruthless. In Romania, the crowd that the regime assembled in Bucharest's central square on 21 December 1989 to cheer Nicolae Ceausescu delivering an address to the nation booed him instead, in front of TV cameras transmitting live the image of a falling dictator to all Romanian households and to the world. A similar function was fulfilled by the reburial of Imre Nagy and his associates (leaders of the failed 1956 revolution) in 1989 in Hungary, as well as by the massive demonstrations on Wenceslas Square in Prague in November 1989 and in several East German cities in late 1989, and also the ones in Belgrade (2000) and Kyiv (2004).

All these events played a dual function. First, they helped to clearly draw, in peoples' minds, the line separating us (the people) from them (the old regime). Second, they exposed the impotence of the old regime, unable or unwilling to 'restore order' and punish people for violating the prescribed routines of mass behaviour allowed in communist systems. In an apt metaphor, Kenney (2002) compares Central European revolutions with a carnival – a period of suspension, or even a reversal, of the usual rules in society. Consequently, the movements sparked by those events acquired a specific aura of charisma: a shared belief that the people acting in solidarity can accomplish goals that, until that moment, were at best only in the realm of political dreams (for the notion of a charismatic social movement see Jowitt, 1992 and Cirtautas, 1997). In most cases, this belief has become a self-fulfilling prophecy.

The 'charismatic moment' associated with spectacular events usually, if not always, had its impact not only locally, but across the region (and sometimes beyond). Solidarity's spectacular electoral victory in June 1989 and the subsequent creation, in defiance of the Brezhnev Doctrine, of a grand coalition government with only token communist representation, emboldened opposition leaders and the wider population in neighbouring countries. Then, the ensuing developments in East Germany, Czechoslovakia, and Hungary fuelled each other until the ultimate collapse of the old regimes. Bulgaria, Romania, Albania soon followed suit. Similarly, the 1989–91 events in Lithuania, Latvia, and Estonia gave inspiration to national liberation movements not only among the three Baltic states, but also in Ukraine, Georgia, and other Soviet republics. This quick diffusion of revolutionary ferment was undoubtedly facilitated by the modern media of mass communication, in particular television. Images such as of the fall of the Berlin Wall, of the trial and execution of Nicolae and Elena Ceausescu, or of Boris Yeltsin commanding resistance to the August 1991 coup transmitted a sense of defiance and victory across the region. (Patterns of emulation are sometimes strange. When in London in March 1990 youngsters opposing Margaret Thatcher's poll tax waved Union Jacks with a hole in the middle, they followed, without reflecting on the meaning of this gesture, the example of the December 1989 Bucharest demonstrators, who had cut off the disgraced communist insignia from the middle of the Romanian tricolour.)

In addition to the demonstration effect, in some instances popular upheavals were aided in more direct and tangible ways. The underground Solidarity in the 1980s received, covertly, significant financial and logistical support from abroad, mostly from Western trade unions. In the 1990s, pro-democracy movements in Yugoslavia or Ukraine were overtly aided by international NGOs, which supplied 'democratic know-how', in addition to printing presses, radio transmitters, and similar artefacts. Furthermore, as Bunce and Wolchik (2006; 2011) point out, 'graduates' of one 'electoral revolution' were often instrumental in facilitating another one in a neighbouring country (see for instance the Serb, Georgian, Polish, Czech, and Slovak contributions to the Orange Revolution in Ukraine). Since the onset of Arab Spring in 2011, journalists, pundits, and bloggers have made numerous comparisons between the revolutions in Arab states and the developments in CEE two decades ago. Obviously, one can see in these two sets of events striking similarities (in the patterns of emergence of 'charismatic moments', for instance), as well as profound differences (above all in the role of the international context). Hopefully, these comparisons will soon become the matter of serious scholarly endeavours.

Yet the access to information and the mobilizing force of the demonstration effect cannot alone account for the fact that it was not until 1989 that the success of a rebellion in one country (Poland) launched a domino effect across the region. An old saying, attributed to Vladimir Lenin, says that revolutions happen when 'the masses do not want the old ways anymore and the regime is unable to maintain the old ways anymore'. By the late 1980s, all mechanisms of legitimization for Central and East European communist regimes had exhausted their potential. In particular, the regimes could not any longer legitimize themselves as the creative force of a Utopian future. Two generations after the communist takeover, the promise of a better, more just political system and society remained utterly unfulfilled. But above all, the countries of Central and Eastern Europe experienced economic crisis, or at the very best, stagnation. The gap between their 'economies of shortage' (Kornai, 1980) and the affluent market economies of Western Europe and North America became wider than ever.

Hence, the course of Central–Eastern European revolutions seems to confirm the analyses of those theorists, who, following Alexis de Tocqueville (1955), point to the importance of relative deprivation (Gurr, 1970) or a widening gap between popular expectations and the actual fulfilment of needs (Davies, 1971) as factors leading to revolutionary ferment. Indeed, the 'masses' of the region did not want the old ways anymore.

On the other side of the equation, governments could not continue to act in the old ways either. Not only were they unable to keep up with the pace of economic growth in the West but, even more importantly, by the summer of 1989 they lost another tool of legitimization –

the Brezhnev doctrine (named so after Leonid Brezhnev, the Soviet leader who ordered the Warsaw Pact intervention in Czechoslovakia in 1968). The perestroika and glasnost campaigns in the Soviet Union made this instrument of Soviet regional domination obsolete, which became evident when the government of Mikhail Gorbachev accepted as legitimate Solidarity's victory in Polish elections. East European governments could no longer count on Soviet 'friendly assistance'; they could not even blackmail their own populace using the spectre of a Soviet intervention. Subsequently, they lost, gradually or suddenly, the allegiance of intellectuals, the unity within their own ranks, and the will and determination to use coercive means in protection of their rule (the mechanisms are outlined theoretically by Crane Brinton, 1965). Even where the top leader did not hesitate to resort to coercion (Ceausescu in Romania), the defection of his lieutenants made those efforts fruitless.

The gravity of the old regime's troubles had become apparent to some elements in its leadership even before the onset of popular unrest. Consequently, certain communist leaders, encouraged by the Gorbachev-led reforms in the Soviet Union, launched their own reformist actions. Those ranged from a genuine dialogue with the opposition in Poland or Hungary to a hasty retreat in Czechoslovakia (where Havel was elected president by a parliament that had been hand-picked by communists years before), to attempts at hijacking the process of change (such as a palace coup that ended the decades-long rule of Todor Zhivkov in Bulgaria). The attempts by liberal-minded communists to reform the economy and the political system in Hungary and Poland prompted Timothy Garton Ash to coin the term 'refolution' (Garton Ash, 1989b), which seems to reflect well the ambiguity of the situation in these countries on the eve of the first free (or in the Polish case semi-free) elections. This ambiguity was an outcome of two currents, the grassroots revolutionary movement on the one hand and the top-down institutional reforms on the other, seemingly flowing at the time in the same direction: toward a power-sharing agreement between the old regime and the opposition, or toward civil society gaining at least some influence over the state apparatus (for an account of the process in Poland see Hayden, 2006, for Hungary, Tökés 1996). But Garton Ash's essay was first published before the Polish (June 1989) and Hungarian (March–April 1990) elections brought an end to any ambiguity: the revolutionary current prevailed, the reform-minded communists could no longer have their cake and eat it. Still, the concept of 'refolution' grasps very well the nature of the processes of political change across the region, where the communist regimes more or less reluctantly helped to facilitate their own demise.

This leads us to another common feature of Central and Eastern European revolutions: their non-violent character. With the notable exception of Romania, these revolutions were remarkable in the commitment of their participants to use civil disobedience and peaceful demonstrations rather than any violent means in their quest for victory. Unlike in previous instances (GDR, Bulgaria, Czechoslovakia 1953; Hungary 1956, Poland 1956, 1970, 1976, 1981, Romania 1977 and 1987), the national communist authorities this time also refrained from using violence, even if only out of the above-mentioned impotence. Similarly, the non-violent ethos of protestors and the hesitation in use of coercive measures dominated the colour revolutions of the 2000s (in contrast to the developments in Syria in 2011–13).

While the revolutions in CEE seem to confirm some theoretical approaches (such as those of de Tocqueville and his followers, or Crane Brinton) and disconfirm other (Karl Marx, with his emphasis on absolute deprivation), they remain, almost two decades later, understudied within mainstream sociological and political theory. Sure enough, the literature covering particular cases is vast and contains important theoretical contributions (see for instance Touraine, 1983; Garton Ash, 1985 and 1993; Dahrendorf, 1990; Ost, 1990; Jowitt, 1992; Bernhard, 1993; Kubik, 1994; Ekiert, 1996; Tőkés, 1996; Cirtautas, 1997; Kenney, 2002, to name just a few), yet those scholars, whose substantive interest is not in the region but in theory, seldom utilize the available evidence from Central and Eastern Europe. Again, one can only hope that the interest in the Arab revolutions will stimulate re-examination of the CEE experience.

Civil society

Once the carnival of revolution is over, the focus of citizens' involvement in politics shifts away from the sporadic, unconventional, and universal, to the continuous, routine, and particularistic. As noted in Chapters 9 and 11 of this volume, this shift in the CEE polities has proven quite difficult. Turnout in elections has steadily declined; membership of political parties and other forms of political engagement remain low. The problem has not escaped even Poland, which might be surprising to anyone who has studied the history of civic resistance against communism in CEE. As noted by Padraic Kenney, 'As a result of the Solidarity experiment, there were far more people in Poland than elsewhere with experience in independent political activism – perhaps by a factor of 100' (2002: 15). Not much of this activism remains today.

Yet the low membership of political parties, when examined against the backdrop of more general patterns of participation in secondary organizations, becomes a symptom of another problem common to all post-communist polities, which is often referred to as 'the weakness of civil society'. Obviously, civil society – a complex, multi-dimensional phenomenon – cannot be equated with membership in formal organizations alone.

As noted by Cas Mudde in an earlier edition of this volume '(n)o concept has been so central to the discussions on Central and East European politics as that of civil society' (Mudde, 2007: 213). He adds that those discussions progressed from an early enthusiastic assessment to more recent lamentations over the state of civil society in CEE. Indeed, the revolutions of 1989–91 (and their colourful follow-ups after the turn of the century) have been often heralded as the triumph of civil society over a repressive, post-totalitarian state. This extraordinary display of civil society's might has been allegedly (and inexplicably) followed by its progressive weakening. But such demobilization after a 'popular upsurge' occurred also in post-authoritarian democracies of Latin America and Southern Europe, as noted by Guillermo O'Donnell and Philippe Schmitter (1986). Furthermore, as indicated above, revolutionary upheavals require a different kind of individual involvement than the routine daily actions for the sake of one's particular interests. Only in Poland was the collapse of the communist order preceded by long-lasting activities of a self-organized and self-governing underground society. Elsewhere, aside from the actions of a handful of dissidents, the burst of popular grass-roots activism was maybe intense, but usually short-lived. As a Czech (somehow self-congratulatory) saying goes: 'What took Poles ten years and Hungarians ten months, we accomplished in ten days.'

Mudde also points out the confusion stemming from the ways the concept of civil society is applied by various authors – scholars as much as pundits, politicians, and bureaucrats. Here, we will agree with Mudde and others (see in particular Linz and Stepan 1996) that, to maximize the concept's analytical potential, one has to distinguish civil society not only from the state (as had already the classics of the Scottish Enlightenment and the Hegelian-Marxist tradition who first introduced the term), but also from its political and economic counterparts. Hence, political parties, which in democracies typically have their roots in civil society, should be considered as parts of political society, because their role is to participate in the electoral competition for power within the state. Similarly, entrepreneurial activities of individuals, groups, and associations in the processes of production and distribution of goods and services are best understood as economic society, distinct from civil society, the non-economic sphere of human social activities. Furthermore, the concept of civil society does not cover certain forms of social relations, such as families or, more broadly, kinship groups, as it focuses on voluntary interactions and associations of individuals acting as citizens or members of a community (local, professional, etc.). Last but not least, since the revolutions in CEE were also a form of national liberation movement (against the imperial Soviet domination), the banner of 'civil society' has been also used (as noted by Mentzel, 2012) in relation to expressions of civic (and at times ethnic) nationalism, which only further confuses the issue.

On the other hand, the concept should not be defined too narrowly, which is often done by equating civil society with formal non-government organizations outside of the political system and the economy. One does not need to establish a formal organization to launch a collection of signatures under a petition or to build a playground for children in the neighbourhood, yet citizens' readiness to undertake such actions is no less indicative of the strength of the horizontal ties among them than the level of card-carrying membership in formally registered bodies.

Nevertheless, people's willingness to get engaged in voluntary associations remains a decent indicator of the strength and quality of social bonds in a given place at a given time. Marc Morjé Howard (2003: 69) in his analysis of 13 CEE polities (his sample includes East Germany, but excludes Poland, Moldova, and several post-Yugoslav states) compared with ten post-authoritarian polities (such as Spain or Brazil) and eight 'old' democracies (among them the United States and Scandinavian countries) points out that the average number of organizational memberships in post-communist CEE is, at 0.91, significantly lower than in two other groups (post-authoritarian 1.82, older democracies 2.39). Furthermore, his statistical analysis indicates that the communist past has a significantly stronger influence in determining this number than other factors, such as economic development, the current scope of civil liberties, or historical traditions associated with Western civilization (Howard, 2003: 83–84). More recent analyses confirm this picture, with some caveats. Bernhard and Karakoc (2007) demonstrate that the totalitarian past, regardless of its version (communist or Nazi), hampers the development of civil society more than a mere authoritarian experience. Wallace, Pichler, and Haerpfer (2012) point to negligible differences between post-communist nations that joined the EU and those that did not. Finally, Pop-Eleches and Tucker (2013) predict diminishing weight of communist legacies over time.

As well as scholars, international watchdog organizations also monitor the progress of democratization and development of civil society. Among the most respected for its objectivity and refined methodology is Freedom House, which, since 1995, publishes Nations in Transit, an annual report on 'Democratization from Central Europe to Eurasia'. In its assessment of civil society (one of seven dimensions in its rankings) Freedom House also focuses on formal organizations, but relies more on qualitative than quantitative measures. Its 2012 civil society rankings are presented in Table 12.2.

The best situation is in the countries that have already joined the EU, although some in this group have recorded a slight decline in recent years (Habdank-Kolaczkowska and Walker, 2011: 41). Lagging behind, but improving over the past decade, have been the Balkan states. By far the worst situation is among the non-Baltic former Soviet republics, although some (Ukraine, Moldova) have at the end of the previous decade recorded some progress.

As noted above, the membership in formal organizations, convenient as it may be as an empirical indicator, does not account for all forms of civic engagement. Citizens can also make other, singular or continued, contributions of time, effort, money, or other resources for the benefit of their local, professional, or other communities. Furthermore, the reservoirs of human energy suppressed in communist times have been, over the course of the past two decades, channelled mostly toward business and entrepreneurship, toward the 'economic' rather than 'civil' society. The participation in the transformation of the old command economy into a new market one took precedence over involvement in the development of civil society. The former might have indeed been a necessary condition of the latter. Voluntary civic associations, from chambers of commerce to charities to social clubs, tend to

Table 12.2   *Freedom House civil society rankings*

New EU members		The Balkans		Non-Baltic former Soviet states	
Bulgaria	2.50	Albania	3.00	Armenia	3.75
Czech Rep.	1.75	Bosnia	3.50	Azerbaijan	6.00
Estonia	1.75	Croatia	2.50	Belarus	6.25
Hungary	2.00	Kosovo	3.75	Georgia	3.75
Latvia	1.75	Macedonia	3.25	Moldova	3.25
Lithuania	1.75	Montenegro	2.75	Ukraine	2.75
Poland	1.50	Serbia	2.25		
Romania	2.50				
Slovakia	1.75				
Slovenia	2.00				

Note: 1 = highest, 7 = lowest.
Source: http://www.freedomhouse.org.

emerge to both facilitate and supplement the horizontal relationships among actors of the economic society.

Still, this process is likely to last not years, but generations. The enthusiasm of the times of upheaval has hardly been transformed into the commitments necessary to sustain routine, day-to-day activities. While at its pinnacle in 1981, Solidarity had almost ten million members, today the entire trade union membership in Poland is just a fraction of this number. Elsewhere in CEE the situation is not any better (see Crowley and Ost, 2001; Crowley, 2004). Weak trade unions find their match in underdeveloped business associations. The tripartite (labour–government–business) arrangements that have been instrumental in steering socio-economic development in many West European states have played no significant role in East Central Europe (ECE). The absence of strong formal organizations contributes to – and in turn results from – the growing role of informal ties and the blurring of lines separating politics from business. Consequently, corruption, cronyism and nepotism spread out and hamper the re-emergence of civil society. The Corruption Perception Index (CPI) published annually by Transparency International (2012) gives CEE much lower marks than those recorded by their West European counterparts. In 2011, among the CEE countries, the best results on a scale ranging from 0 (highly corrupt) to 10 (very clean) were recorded by Estonia (6.4), Slovenia (5.9), Poland (5.5), Lithuania (4.8), and Hungary (4.6), while Ukraine (2.3), Belarus (2.4), Moldova (2.9) and Kosovo (2.9) were the worst. (For comparison: the leader, New Zealand, scored 9.5, followed by two EU states, Denmark and Finland, both with 9.4; the UK recorded 7.8 and the US 7.1.)

Today, a generation after the collapse of communist rule, its legacy remains strong. The communists attempted to replace the natural horizontal ties of civil society with vertical ones, with party-state agencies playing at least an intermediary – if not leading – role in all public (and often also in private) social relations. As observed by Linz and Stepan in relation to Poland, the dissidents of the 1970s and 1980s attempted to create – with remarkable success – a civil society understood as 'the sphere of uncoerced activity not created by the state and virtually independent of the state' (1996: 270–2). This 'civil society against the state' dichotomy found its reflection in the theoretical writings of leading dissident intellectuals, from Adam Michnik (1985) and Jacek Kuron (1984) in Poland, to Vaclav Havel (1985) in Czechoslovakia and Gyorgy Konrad (1983) in Hungary. Their contributions caused, in fact, a revival of the somehow forgotten concept of civil society and sparked an intense debate among CEE and Western scholars (see in particular Cohen and Arrato, 1992; Keane, 1988; Ost, 1990; and Ekiert, 1996).

In the vision of the CEE dissidents, civil society must be based on strong ethical principles, in opposition to the immoral post-totalitarian state. Such principles are the source of the Havelian 'power of the powerless', but they also stimulate the rejection of political means, such as compromise, as a way to solve internal conflicts within a polity (the title of Konrad's book, *Antipolitics*, says it all). This attitude was instrumental in defeating communism, but also hampered the development of 'normal' democratic politics after the revolution (Havel and the leader of Solidarity, Lech Wałesa, both entered post-communist politics and became presidents of their respective nations, but neither ever fully understood the need to develop political parties as instruments of democratic politics). Furthermore, this attitude also undermined the transition from an 'ethical' to a 'normal' civil society: once the enemy, the communist state, was defeated, and moral victory achieved, there was no adequate basis for sustaining routine civic activities.

The mass upheavals of the late 1980s, early 1990s, and mid-2000s restored grass-roots-level social bonds, but only temporarily. East–Central Europeans, so apt at getting organized at times of crisis, seem indifferent, if not helpless, when it comes to managing their day-to-day affairs. Social atomization and anomie, induced along with the introduction of communist regimes decades ago, remain in place. Still, all these vicissitudes notwithstanding, we shall again agree with Cas Mudde that to properly assess the strength – or weakness – of civil society in CEE one should see the issue in its proper context. If the point of comparison is the recent past, the actual robustness of civil society at the time of the revolutions varied greatly from case to case and has been generally overestimated in collective memory. If one compares CEE states with their Western counterparts, it should not be forgotten that civic activism in the post-modern era also there takes different forms than in the (often idealized) past, and that Westerners also tend to 'bowl alone' (Putnam, 2000). Finally, as Freedom House data and other sources indicate, despite a few local setbacks, peoples of CEE have been consistently, if slowly, moving in the right direction: toward a civil society no longer engaged in a conflict with the state, but rather supplementing it in non-political and non-economic dimension of social life.

Protest politics

For several months in 2010, against the wishes of the Polish state authorities and their Warsaw city counterparts, a group of citizens prevented the removal of a cross placed in front of the presidential palace as a temporary memorial in honour of the late president Lech Kaczynski, who perished in a plane crash in Russia in April 2010. These self-appointed 'Defenders of the Cross' invoked Article 196 of the Polish penal code, which criminalizes the defiling of objects of worship. Their actions revived debates on freedom of speech, of worship, and of assembly, as well as on limitations a democratic state can legitimately place on those freedoms. The protesters refused to follow legally issued orders to disband and allow for the removal of the cross. Only after a tag-of-war that lasted several months was the cross moved to a nearby church.

Also in 2010, a group of organizations that included radical socialists, anarchists, feminists, and gay-rights activists called for the blockade of a march organized in Warsaw on 11 November (Poland's Independence Day) by radical right-wing nationalist associations. The organizers of the march requested and received proper authorization from the city authorities. Those calling for the blockade explicitly denied the right of the alleged 'neo-fascists' to hold a legal demonstration and refused to seek the city's permission for their counter-demonstration. The nationalists, despite police protection, were forced by the counter-demonstrators to alter the route of their march.

Both events may seem to be expressions of an 'uncivil society' in action: groups of extremists can ignore the rule of law and the will of the majority and achieve, at least temporarily, their radical goals. Of course, those 'uncivil' groups are also part of civil society (by definition, as social scientists use such terms in a descriptive-analytical rather than a normative way). But such actions illustrate, above all, the tension between the realization of particular, often legitimate, interests, and the formal requirements of a procedural democracy. In both cases the protesters invoked commonly accepted values (freedom of worship and a rejection of ethnic xenophobia) as the justification of their actions; in both cases, they dismissed the need to obey procedural regulations. 'We do not have to follow any rules, because we are right' was their credo. But who is right and who is wrong is a relative matter; claims to righteousness may contradict and offset one another. Only the application of formal, impersonal, 'objective' procedures allows us to sort out the merits of such claims. Of course, this tension, between the substantive ('whatever leads to the realization of my values is right') and formal ('whatever follows formal procedures is right') rationality, has been known, albeit not always effectively resolved, in any democracy. But in CEE, where the substantive rationality of the communist regime ('whatever served the party's interest was right') dominated for decades, this tension may sometimes become particularly acute. In extreme cases, it may lead to violence.

Yet, all these tensions and misunderstandings notwithstanding, the transition to democracy and a market economy in Central and Eastern Europe has been, by and large, surprisingly peaceful. In the early stages of systemic transformation it was expected that economic hardships might fuel class-based voting and promote electoral populism. For the same reasons, many expected high levels of industrial unrest: from work stoppages and strikes to street demonstrations and riots. Developments of this kind seemed likely because of the expected increase in the class consciousness of workers who had been deprived of the special position given to them by communist ideology and threatened by the rationalization of industrial production and employment. Indeed, as Branko Milanovic points out, the cuts in wages in CEE in the 1990s have been 'larger than those experienced by labor in major countries during the Great Depression' (1998: 30). Ost and Crowley compare economic contraction in Poland in the early 1990s and in Russia in the mid-1990s 'to that of Germany in the four years preceding Hitler's rise to power' (Crowley and Ost, 2001: 1). Yet, as noted by Ekiert and Kubik (1999), even in Poland, where instances of 'contentious collective action' have been in recent years (as in the past) more frequent than elsewhere in the region, at no time did they pose a serious challenge to the process of democratic consolidation.

Certainly, there have been many cases of industrial unrest across the region, from countries with a strong tradition of organized workers' movements and independent trade unions (Poland) to those where trade unions had been completely under communist party-state control (Ukraine). The 'economic anger' is not specific to workers alone, as evidenced by road blockades set up periodically by Polish farmers (but only until 2004, when they became eligible for EU agricultural subventions). Yet the overall frequency of economically motivated strikes and demonstrations in CEE does not deviate much from analogous instances in other democracies (see Welz and Kaupinnen, 2005). Even more importantly, nowhere in the region did industrial unrest so far rise to a point or assume forms that would significantly alter the nature of democratic politics.

Also the recession of 2008–10 and the austerity measures imposed by many European governments caused a much greater uproar within the 'old' EU members (such as Greece or Spain) than among the new ones, even if the scale of economic problems in, for instance, Latvia, Estonia, or Hungary was significantly greater than the EU average. One notable exception here is Latvia, where legal demonstrations turned into riots in January 2009, which prompted the resignation of PM Ivars Godmanis and his government a month later. More recently (January 2012) massive (and often violent) protests against health system reforms led in January 2012 to a change of government in Romania.

In ways parallel to the patterns of voting behaviour, sporadic political mobilization in CEE may be also instigated by non-economic (cultural) factors, such as ethnicity, religion, lifestyle, or simply the expression of certain values (for instance pro- or anti-democracy). Sporadic political actions of this sort are surely not uncommon across the region. Some have gained a certain level of fame – or notoriety. Suffice it to mention the controversies stirred by the wall raised in the Czech city Usti-nad-Labem to separate neighbourhoods inhabited by Romani (Gypsy) population from well-to-do middle class Czechs, or by the decisions of certain mayors in Poland to ban gay parades in their cities. Also the Budapest demonstrations mentioned at the beginning of this chapter seem to have been motivated more by outrage over violations of democratic principles than by any immediate economic hardships. But again, political actions stemming from cultural factors, while sometimes causing local disruptions of public order, have not so far undermined the fundaments of democracy.

More than by the grass-roots actions of citizens, democracy in CEE can be put in danger by politicians trying to manipulate popular discontent. Post-communist parties were among the first to use populism as a tool to enhance their chances in elections. Subsequently, various anti-establishment and even anti-system parties and movements began to score well in elections. Suffice it to mention the National Movement Simeon II in Bulgaria (the former tsar Simeon II of the House of Saxe-Coburg-Gotha became, for the 2001–05 period, Prime Minister as Simeon Saksecoburggotski); the extreme chauvinistic Jobbik party in Hungary that won 17 per cent of the popular vote in 2010; a Polish anti-system party, Self-Defence, which did well in the 2001 and 2005 elections, but has since collapsed; or the Smer-SD (Direction-Social Democracy) party in Slovakia, which under the charismatic leadership of Robert Fico won the 2006 and, after a setback in 2010, the 2012 general elections.

Political populism – understood here as a political discourse that calls for protection of the 'man in the street' from economic misfortunes (allegedly caused by reforms introduced for the benefit of narrow elites), usually coupled with ethnic or religious particularism or even xenophobia (again, in the name of protection of the in-group against alien forces and foreign schemes), has been present in East–Central European politics ever since the beginning of the transition (and before). Almost all East–Central European countries have aspired to join the European Union; eight (the Czech Republic, Estonia, Hungary, Latvia, Lithuania, Poland, Slovakia, and Slovenia) accomplished this goal in 2004, while two more (Bulgaria and Romania) joined in 2007, and one (Croatia) in 2013. Central European populists see in the European Union the epitome of their fears: free markets, open borders, supranational political institutions. The public debate on the EU membership has brought to the forefront the cleavage between particularistic and redistributive (and, in their extreme version, outright xenophobic–populist) attitudes and universalistic, liberal, pro-European ones. This cleavage typically combines the economic dimension (the losers versus the winners in the process of transition) with one stemming from a differences in values, and runs roughly along the lines predicted by some scholars at the onset of democratic transitions (Evans and Whitefield, 1993). The electoral resurgence of political populism has also recently taken place in several old member states of the EU (France, Austria, the Netherlands, Greece, Finland). This obviously opens up avenues for some rather odd political alliances and configurations. At the beginning of the new millennium, politics in Europe (not only Central or Eastern Europe) seem to have entered a new (but not quite unexplored) territory.

Yet, as of 2012, it is fair to say that the young democracies in Central and Eastern Europe have experienced the challenge of grassroots political activism at a moderate level, at most. They have managed to cope with this challenge remarkably well. They have been able to establish political mechanisms that help to diffuse and absorb political discontent and usually allow it to flow through the channels of electoral competition. In that respect, they are performing, on the average, no worse than typical old democracies or post-authoritarian polities.

Media

Grass-roots movements in this age of European integration and the internet may sometimes bring about surprising results. In January 2012, thousands of young Poles took to the streets – while others stayed in front of their computers. They were acting in concert: those on the streets protested in traditional forms, while their counterparts were busy hacking into government websites. Their aim was to prevent Poland from ratifying the ACTA (Anti-Counterfeiting Trade Agreement), an international accord establishing common standards for intellectual property rights enforcement. The protesters perceived ACTA as an attempt by the governments to limit freedom of expression and access to information by the millions of people who surf the web every day. Within days, and thanks to the utilization of social media, from Facebook to Twitter, the protest spread from Poland to other EU countries, in the East (the Baltic states, the Czech Republic, Bulgaria, Romania, Hungary) and the West (France, Germany, Austria, Sweden, UK). But the most astonishing was the reaction of the governments. First, the Polish Prime Minister agreed to reconsider the issue and halt the process of ratification, and soon other European governments followed suit. After several of its committees had re-examined ACTA and recommended against its implementation, it was rejected by the European Parliament in July 2012. Now, thanks to a protest movement that originated in CEE, it is certain that ACTA will never come to regulate our presence in cyberspace.

Above all, this story illustrates the change in the way the media contribute to the interaction between citizens and governments. In the traditional model, the media played a dual role. The printed press and the broadcast outlets functioned collectively as the 'fourth estate', acting as a watchdog (and hence providing checks and balances) over the three branches of government, the executive, the legislative, and the judiciary. But the press was also used by the governments (and sometimes the opposition as well) as a tool to manipulate the public opinion and mobilize citizens for political action – or discourage it. In democracies, the former function would typically dominate, although the latter has always been present as well. The authoritarian or post-totalitarian regimes, like those in the pre-1989 CEE, would perfect the latter and suppress the former. The rapid development of information technology, from a computer connected to the internet to a simple mobile phone, has changed the game. Now the lateral circulation of information among citizens is at least as important as the one-way vertical flow from media centres to the public. Talking back to a TV screen is pointless; sending a text message or posting on a blog do not have to be. People of CEE, in particular the young ones, seem to understand this truth very well.

But so do the governments. Freedom House in its annual multidimensional evaluation of democratization in the post-communist world includes an assessment of the independence of the media, from the traditional printed press to radio and television, to those present exclusively in cyberspace. Its 2012 rankings are presented in Table 12.3.

As in the case of civil society, the highest scores are recorded by the new EU members, although there is a significant variation from case to case here, from an impressive 1.50 in Estonia to a troubling 3.75 in Bulgaria or 4.00 in Romania. The situation is significantly worse in the Balkans (with Kosovo a negative outlier at 5.75), while in the non-Baltic former Soviet republics one can hardly speak of a free press

Table 12.3   *Freedom House independent media rankings*

New EU members		The Balkans		Non-Baltic former Soviet states	
Bulgaria	3.75	Slovenia	2.25	Azerbaijan	6.75
Czech Rep.	2.50	Albania	4.00	Belarus	6.75
Estonia	1.50	Bosnia	4.75	Georgia	4.75
Hungary	3.50	Croatia	4.00	Moldova	5.50
Latvia	1.75	Kosovo	5.75	Ukraine	3.75
Lithuania	2.00	Macedonia	4.75		
Poland	2.25	Montenegro	4.25		
Romania	4.00	Serbia	4.00		
Slovakia	2.75	Armenia	6.00		

Note: 1 = highest, 7 = lowest.
Source: http://www.freedomhouse.org.

(only Ukraine at 3.75 stands out as a positive outlier). Yet even in the countries with the best scores governments have attempted to exercise, via legislation and/or executive actions, undue control over media of all sorts, from newspapers to television to blogs and websites. Furthermore, as the fluctuation in Freedom House ratings demonstrates, the situation of the media has somehow deteriorated across the region over the course of the past decade (Habdank-Kolaczkowska and Walker, 2011: 42).

Yet sometimes the worst enemies of the free press are the media people themselves. While professional associations typically emphasize accepted standards of objectivity in reporting, journalists in both print and electronic media habitually blur the line between reporting facts and expressing opinions. The print media in CEE have a longstanding tradition of partisanship. In the past, major political parties were often owners and publishers of popular and influential newspapers, but this is no longer the case. In the worst instances, it is the authoritarian government that controls the press, either directly (through personnel policies and payroll) or indirectly (through intimidation and corruption). In the best examples, the press is partisan by choice and often free of any direct influence by political parties. It continues to play a watchdog role with respect to government policies and the actions of all political factions. Hence, while newspapers and magazines individually voice their various ideological preferences, they may collectively serve the public interest well. Similar partisanship can be found among privately owned broadcast media, not to mention the ideological patchwork of Internet-based wikis, blogs, and tweets. While the bias of the private outlets is commonly accepted, there is also an expectation that public media will maintain proper objectivity in reporting and editorializing.

Popular attitudes and democratic consolidation

Juan Linz and Alfred Stepan in their classic work on democratic transition and consolidation have this to say about the question of attitudes: 'Attitudinally, democracy becomes the only game in town when, even in the face of severe political and economic crises, the overwhelming majority of the people believe that any further political change must emerge from within the parameters of democratic formulas' (1996: 5). Indeed, if communism failed because it did not fulfil its promise of an efficient, prosperous economy and a fairer just society, the same supply-and-demand approach can be used to assess democratic regimes. Policies that alienate significant segments of population may not only bring down an unpopular government, but also undermine popular support for democracy itself. In the first half of the twentieth century, democracies across the region gave way to various authoritarian governments precisely because they failed to meet popular expectations. Will history repeat itself?

Opinions about governments' performance fluctuate greatly over time and from place to place. Yet, as Linz and Stepan point out, what really matters here is not the evaluation of particular governments, but the level of support for democratic procedures and institutions as the most appropriate way to organize collective life. If people who have personally (which was the fate of older and middle-aged Central and East Europeans) experienced the shortcomings of both democratic and undemocratic regimes opt in favour of the former, then one can be assured of the durability of democracy in the region. This issue has been addressed in several comparative and comprehensive research projects conducted in the mid-1990s (Rose, Mishler and Haerpfer, 1998; Plasser, Ulram and Waldrauch, 1998). The general conclusions stemming from these projects are moderately optimistic. Democracy seems to have taken root in Central and Eastern Europe, and to prove more attractive than its alternatives. Furthermore, while support for the current (democratic) regime is still tied to the assessment of economic performance (another attitudinal, hence volatile variable), rejection of non-democratic alternatives is more solidly rooted in structural factors, such as education, urbanization, and income (see Rose, Mishler and Haerpfer, 1998: 193). In Central Europe (the Czech Republic, Hungary, Poland, Slovakia) almost half of the population can be considered what Linz and Stepan (1996: 226–7) call 'confident democrats' – individuals who believe that democracy is both legitimate (preferable to other forms of government) and, by and large, effective in solving major social and economic problems. Still, this number is lower than the 70 per cent in neighbouring Austria (Plasser, Ulram and Waldrauch, 1998: 191); comparable estimates among post-authoritarian regimes are close to 80 per cent for Southern Europe (Spain, Portugal Greece), but for Latin America they are on the levels similar or lower than these in CEE (Linz and Stepan, 1996: 229). As Bernhard, Reenock, and Nordstrom (2003) demonstrate, new democracies experience a 'honeymoon' period, when the populace is willing to accept economic hardships. This period, however, ends at about the time of the third democratic election. After that, poor economic performance may undermine democratic stability.

The data cited above come from the middle 1990s. There are some indications that support for democracy in all Central European states has somehow eroded since then, but there has been a similar experience in several West European polities. Data collected by the European Election Studies (EES) project at the time of the most recent (2009) elections to the European Parliament in all 27 EU member states (available for download at www.gesis.org) suggest that, indeed, there may be a link between the performance of the economy and the assessment of democracy. In Poland, the only country in the entire EU that did not experienced recession in recent years, the fraction of those who say that they are very satisfied or fairly satisfied with democracy in their country was, at 68.2 per cent, not only by far the highest among the post-communist states, but also one of the best in Europe (only Denmark, Sweden, Finland, the Netherlands, and Luxembourg recorded higher marks). At the other end were countries deeply touched by the recession and economic turmoil: Latvia (15.8 per cent), Bulgaria (16.3 per cent), and Hungary (19.4 per cent); among the old EU members the lowest scores were recorded by Greece (27.8 per cent) and Portugal (30.4 per cent) (for comparison, the UK scored 56.3 per cent, France 60.6 per cent and Germany 65.7 per cent). The analysis of data from another project, the Comparative Study of Electoral Systems (CSES 3, available for download at www.cses.org), which includes non-European polities (among them a few post-authoritarian states) and covers elections that took place between 2005 and 2011, leads to similar conclusions. The status of being an old, post-authoritarian, or post-communist democracy matters less than recent economic performance. When the latter falters, then trust in democracy deteriorates, as the CSES data for Bulgaria, Iceland, or Spain indicate. When the economy improves, trust in democracy becomes more robust, as in Poland or Estonia. But the general trend remains the same: among post-communist nations quality of democracy is positively correlated with progress of pro-market economic reforms (Ekiert, Kubik and Vachudova, 2007).

Democracy is, by its nature, a tiring and unruly – often outright messy – enterprise. Arguably, Central European political elites do little to spare their people exposure to democracy's discontents. But, across the region, support for non-democratic alternatives does not approach threatening levels (if we set aside the genuinely undemocratic regime in Belarus). If anything, popular dissatisfaction with democracy is expressed by apathy and anomie, as discussed throughout this chapter. Democracy might be 'the only game in town', but many potential players prefer to stay home rather than join in.

Nonetheless, once again, Winston Churchill's famous *bon mot* finds its confirmation: 'democracy is the worst form of government except all the others'.

Chapter 13

Recovering from Transition in Eastern Europe: Neoliberal Reform in Retrospect

Mitchell A. Orenstein

Assessing the results of neoliberal reform remains controversial even twenty years after 1989. While neoliberal reform programmes appeared to have finally produced rapid economic growth in the 2000s after a long transitional recession, the 2008 global economic meltdown plunged Central and East European countries back into crisis. This chapter offers a mixed assessment of the results of neoliberal economic reforms and questions the easy compatibility of democracy and radical reform observed during the 1990s. Since the 2000s, both democratic and authoritarian countries in Eastern Europe have experienced rapid growth. Geopolitics, more than reform or democracy, seems to separate the winners from the losers. Successful countries are those that either joined the European Union or developed close political and economic relations with Russia. Those betwixt and between and those suffering internal strife (or both) still have not reached 1989 levels of economic production.

The background

In the past decade, one has increasingly heard the claim that the transition in Central and Eastern Europe (CEE) is over. With the onset of the international financial crisis, however, this boring if prosperous normality has been threatened. Further, the very nature of the transition which the post-Communist economies embarked on, in particular the effect and effectiveness of neoliberal reforms, is increasingly being called into question.

The EU-10, the ten post-communist countries which acceded to the European Union in the last decade, are often divided into four groups or varieties of capitalism, determined largely by the degree to which

Table 13.1 *Gross national income (PPP) per capita of EU-10 countries,
1990–2010 (US$)*

Country		1990	1995	2000	2005	2008	2009	2010
LMEs	Estonia	7300	6330	9530	15870	20710	19360	19810
	Latvia	7830	5420	8020	12880	17910	17210	16320
	Lithuania	9340	6200	8470	13860	18900	17230	17840
DMEs	Czech Republic		12800	14660	19450	23690	23380	22910
	Hungary	8560	8700	11290	16060	19120	19260	19550
	Poland		7320	10480	13520	17660	18250	19160
	Slovakia	7720	8360	10950	15720	22760	22260	22980
CME	Slovenia		13150	17570	23280	28260	26620	26530
Weak state	Bulgaria	4990	5360	6070	9840	13230	13250	13440
	Romania	5180	5340	5620	9280	14610	14630	14290

Source: adapted from World Databank (online at worldbank.org).

neoliberalism was embraced during transition. At one extreme, the
Baltic states, Latvia, Lithuania, and Estonia, were quite radical in their
neoliberal policies, and are classified as liberal market economies,
(LMEs), and marked by extreme international openness. Slovenia more
closely followed the corporatist policies of Western Europe, and is
referred to as a coordinated market economy (CME); the Visegrad
four, Hungary, Poland, the Czech Republic and Slovakia, fell some-
where in the middle and are classified as DMEs, or dependent market
economies. Finally, capitalism in Romania and Bulgaria has been characterized by the weak states in both countries.

The effects of the recent economic crisis on post-communist countries in the European Union have, with few exceptions, been tightly
linked to the variety of capitalism employed and therefore also to the
degree of neoliberal reform implemented (see Table 13.1). While the
Baltic states, which have become some of the most liberal economies in
the world, had shown great promise in the early 2000s, they were hit
very hard by the international crisis, likely due to their extreme
dependence on foreign credit; Estonia was one of the first countries to
show signs of an economic downturn. The year 2009 was the nadir,
with all three Baltic states experiencing double digit negative growth
rates: Estonia at −14.3 per cent, Lithuania at −14.8 per cent, and
Latvia with the sharpest decline, −17.7 per cent; for comparison, the
next highest rate of decline among CEE countries was Slovenia, at −8.0
per cent. The Visegrad countries performed much better on average,

with the glaring exception of Hungary, which continues to founder amidst a crisis which has spread into the political system. Slovenia, while experiencing a sharper decline than in the DMEs, has performed much better than the Baltic states. Furthermore, its unemployment rate has remained admirably low throughout the crisis, a marked contrast to the situation in the LMEs; Latvia was obliged to ask for IMF assistance due to large-scale civil unrest in the country. As this abysmal performance during the crisis appears to have offset some of the gains from growth in the most liberal economies, the ability of neoliberal policies to produce more robust, long-term economic development than less radical (and less painful) alternatives is increasingly unclear.

In the debate on neoliberal reforms, the stakes are high. In the balance lies not only the issue of how well the neoliberal economic project works in post-communist countries, but whether free market policies will continue to be adopted in other parts of the world, and whether such reforms are compatible with democracy. Central and East European countries have a unique place in these debates because they provided a testing ground of neoliberal economic policy in the heartland of communism. Moreover, many former communist countries simultaneously implemented free market economic policies and democratic political regimes, an approach that has invited duplication in developing countries around the world. The struggles of CEE thus have a unique and world-historic quality, and their success or failure remains a matter of importance to the future of democratic capitalism itself.

Sadly, an assessment of the results of neoliberal economic reforms in CEE must be mixed (see Table 13.2). While the communist heritage has been thoroughly transformed, the results have not been as positive as initially hoped. Neoliberal economic reforms brought on a tremendous transitional recession that most post-communist countries struggled to exit from even a decade after the initial shock. Just as free markets seemed to finally be delivering on their promise of high growth in the 2000s, the global economic crisis has shown the market economies of CEE to be especially vulnerable to economic downturn and capital flight. Moreover, the growth spurt of the 2000s and the crash that followed weakened the link between democratization and economic growth that seemed so obvious in the 1990s. All this could contribute to convincing people in developing nations that the project of building capitalism under democratic governance is beset with insuperable flaws and difficulties and could facilitate a return to a consensus on the benefits of authoritarian developmentalism. That would be a misfortune greater than the one that CEE has itself endured.

Table 13.2 *Gross national income (PPP) per capita of non-EU formerly communist countries, 1990–2010 (US$)*

Country	1990	1995	2000	2005	2008	2009	2010
Balkans							
Albania	2820	2980	4370	6220	8280	8500	8520
Bosnia and Herzegovina		1160	4920	6510	8970	8880	8910
Croatia	9500	7990	10720	14990	19620	19040	18680
FYR Macedonia	5540	4800	5830	7720	10600	11130	11070
Montenegro			6620	8320	13850	12870	12770
Serbia			5760	8410	11200	10890	11090
East Europe							
Belarus	4640	3400	5130	8540	12280	12530	13590
Moldova	3310	1480	1490	2650	3300	3040	3360
Russia	8000	5570	6660	11560	19850	18280	19240
Ukraine	5960	3120	3180	5520	7250	6240	6620
Caucasus							
Armenia	2040	1390	2090	4210	6340	5420	5660
Azerbaijan		1500	2090	3940	7770	8740	9270
Georgia	4430	1370	2300	3650	4840	4720	4990
Central Asia							
Kazakhstan		3630	4460	7830	9710	10140	10770
Kyrgyz Republic	1820	980	1260	1660	2120	2190	2070
Tajikistan	2140	810	820	1450	1910	2070	2140
Turkmenistan		1680	1930	4430	6700	7100	7490
Uzbekistan		1190	1420	2000	2630	2870	3110

Note: data for Kosovo unavailable.
Source: adapted from World Databank (online).

The communist heritage

Communism had a unique impact on CEE economies. A visitor to CEE in 1987 was struck by the many differences (and deficiencies) of the socialist economies in comparison to those of the West. CEE cities looked drab and dour. They were often dirty, bathed in coal soot, and lacked the vibrancy of commercial life one is used to in the West. Most businesses gave off a low-budget utilitarian feel compounded by a peculiar regimentation and sameness. All produce shops in Prague, for instance, were called 'Produce'. In the streets one could often see a line of parked cars that were all nearly identical, except for colour and model year, while the department stores were filled with poor-quality goods that few wanted to purchase. The only intrusion of quasi-

Western commercialism was in special hard-currency stores where entrance was restricted to card-holding members of the elite. Isolated from the general public, French perfumes and fine wines lived in these walled-off oases as a constant testimony to the better life lived abroad.

The organization of production in CEE economies was bizarre to behold. As a consumer of beer in 1990 Prague, I often wondered why beer bottles, though ostensibly from the same brewery, came in a variety of colours (often including brown and green in the same pack) and contained different volumes. I remained mystified until I visited a brewery, where I realized that these breweries collected used bottles on site, washed them, and sent them down the line in random order until they were filled by a 1950s-era machine that shot beer wildly into them. Beer would often overflow (this explained the frequent stickiness as well as the non-uniform level of beer in each bottle), bottles would break, and the production line would have to be shut down constantly to clear the slippage. Still, this beer cost five to ten US cents a pint, about one-twentieth of the price for a similar product in the West.

Stories of this type are endless. In one Polish car factory, workers on one level of the factory used sledgehammers to bend car frames produced on another level into shape to allow the installation of parts that would not fit otherwise. Janos Kornai's (1992) landmark description of the socialist economy, which develops academic concepts such as central planning and 'soft budget constraints', does not begin to describe the bizarre, Kafkaesque character of communist-era factory production. Communist enterprises were often run by capable people who struggled with serious structural problems. Their production levels and prices were dictated by the central planning office while the government ministry to which they belonged frequently took their profits and reallocated them to less efficient businesses. Moreover, finances were allocated by the state, production inputs often did not arrive on time or in sufficient quantity or quality, and most workers were not highly motivated. Accomplishing anything under these conditions meant that effective enterprise managers had to be politically connected, highly resourceful, forceful personalities and often had to bend the rules.

Communism ceased to be an effective economic system soon after the end of the Stalinist era and further decayed with the onset of Brezhnev's leadership. It had few defenders when it collapsed in 1989, even in the leading communist parties, where reform wings had long advocated the adoption of Western market methods. Indeed, mid-1980s marketization attempts in Hungary convinced many Hungarian socialist leaders that they needed to facilitate further commerce with Austria in order to develop their economy. In 1988, they took the fateful decision to open the border with Austria, which had the side-effect of enabling East Germans to flee in their thousands to the West via Czechoslovakia. This, and most importantly, the Soviet decision not to intervene in the domestic affairs of its former satellite states, set in train a series of events that led to the collapse of communist regimes across East-Central Europe.

Neoliberal economic reforms

When communism collapsed in 1989, a debate broke out over the best way to transform their economies. Battle lines were drawn between radicals, who believed in a sudden jump to a market economy, and gradualists, who believed that sudden transformation would cause too much social dislocation and that a more gradual change would bring better economic results. These debates were played out in economics institutes and universities across CEE, often with the direct participation of dozens of well-funded consultants from international financial institutions and Western universities. As the end of communism coincided with the rise of the market revolution set in train by US President Ronald Reagan and UK Prime Minister Margaret Thatcher, most Western economists and governments sided with the radicals and provided them enormous assistance from the Western international community. A so-called Marriott brigade of foreign consultants was deployed to help CEE governments set up laws, regulations, and strategies on nearly every matter of economic policy, while staying at the best four-star hotels in the country. The rest is history.

The winning idea behind the radical strategy was articulated by Adam Przeworski in his 1991 work, *Democracy and the Market*. A radical leap to the market risked a sharp economic decline as the old economy ceased to operate effectively in the absence of subsidies, government financing, and fixed prices. Unemployment would rise, perhaps to catastrophic levels, but the implementation of rapid privatization would result in the emergence of a new private sector. Assets would be transferred into private hands and free markets would work their magic, allocating assets into the hands of those firms that could use them most effectively. Only then would overall production increase. New technology and know-how would flow over newly opened national frontiers, and growth and consumption would resume. Radical reform would be painful but it would set CEE countries more quickly on a trajectory toward steeper growth. Gradual reforms might cause less pain at first, but also a slower and less decisive return to growth.

In most countries of CEE, radical reform was the order of the day. Radicals, such as Leszek Balcerowicz in Poland and Vaclav Klaus in the Czech Republic, rose to government economic posts as if by an unwritten law of gravity. They imposed shock programmes of economic reform, including tight monetary austerity, sudden removal of subsidies, rapid privatization, and liberalization of trade and investment. Sudden liberalization had an electric effect on former communist countries. It bankrupted thousands of companies that had been oriented toward the Soviet and Comecon (Council for Mutual Economic Assistance) markets and forced companies to compete with Western firms with much greater market experience and technology. As 90 per cent of trade shifted from East to West within two years, many enterprises shed jobs or were forced to shut for good. At the same time, liberalization and privatization created opportunities for whole new businesses, most visibly in the consumer sector, where demand had been depressed for many years. In Warsaw, Gdansk and Sopot, kiosks arose selling all manner of goods on main thoroughfares and in marketplaces. Shops began to transform themselves from dingy operations to glitzy Western palaces of consumption. CEE cities soon sprouted their first malls and big-box stores, such as Carrefour and Ikea, launching entirely new patterns of consumer behaviour and choice.

The problem was that new investment initially did not keep pace with the decline in production in the old state sector. Foreign capital was at first wary of investing in the post-communist economies. Economic relations with the CEE countries were new, and the rules were often unclear or changing. Few investors trusted that these countries would quickly join the European Union, although ten of them did in 2004 and 2007. While Jeffrey Sachs (1993) called heroically for a major Marshall Plan effort to support the CEE economies, this never occurred, and as a result, these economies lacked the investment to avoid what turned out to be a colossal post-communist recession, wiping out between 15 (Czech Republic) and 75 (Georgia) per cent of 1989 GDP.

Rapid reform produced many success stories, including entrepreneurs who made fortunes trading cars or consumer goods, or transforming state enterprises. However, the shock programme also caused massive dislocations among less resilient sectors and population groups. While neoliberal economists and politicians promised a quick recession, the transitional recession in CEE proved much more long-lived. According to the European Bank for Reconstruction and Development, in 2002, twelve years after the start of transition, most post-communist countries had not returned to their 1989 levels of economic output.

As a result of the transitional recession, poverty and mortality rates skyrocketed and fertility rates declined sharply. Increased inequality during the transition has led to an important if surprising result: despite all the economic improvements of recent years, most households in CEE surveyed in 2006 reported that they were economically better off under communism. Men, in particular, suffered from increased mortality rates. Losing their jobs and no longer being able to feed their children, many took refuge in drink and literally drank themselves to death. This was highly visible to anyone who took a train in CEE during the 1990s, as train stations had become colonies for the intoxicated. Women also suffered from the collapse of families, although many proved better able to adapt to the new market conditions. In some countries, such as Bulgaria, Romania and Ukraine, emigration became the norm as people sought refuge abroad from catastrophic economic conditions and human trafficking exploded. Anger began to be expressed in politics, as CEE voters began to elect populist politicians who gave voice to the workers who were laid off from their jobs in state enterprises and faced a bleak economic future. The success of Andrzej Lepper, the farmer-protester who blocked the roads with masses of meat or farm animals, and of politicians around Radio Maria, an openly anti-Semitic Catholic radio station, led the way in defining this new politics of reaction.

It is unclear how much suffering can be placed at the door of neoliberal economic policies. Liberal economists have pointed out, rightly, that CEE countries that went farthest with neoliberal policy reforms did better economically than their neighbours. Poland, one of the most radical reform countries, reached 127 per cent of its 1989 economic level by 2000, while non-reformist neighbouring Belarus was still at 63 per cent. During the 1990s and early 2000s, these data provided evidence for the view that neoliberal shock therapy had been 'inevitable' or 'necessary'. While reform clearly produced some unfortunate results, the alternatives were worse. Slower reforms would only empower communist-affiliated elites to feast off exceptional rents and keep these countries in a partial-reform equilibrium where the average person would suffer. Not engaging in neoliberal reforms also risked the return of communism, a risk too great for the West to accept.

Rapid growth that started in the region after 2000, however, began to unravel the relationship between neoliberal reforms and economic growth. Most CEE countries experienced rapid economic growth in the mid-2000s, whether or not they had imposed radical reforms. Russia and Ukraine were among the growth leaders, along with reform countries such as Slovakia and Latvia and even non-reformist laggard Belarus. By 2007, Poland was at 169 per cent of its 1989 level, while

Belarus was at 146 per cent. The EU-8 average was 151 per cent. Albania (which achieved 152 per cent of 1989 GDP in 2007), Armenia (143 per cent), Azerbaijan (160 per cent), Mongolia (153 per cent), Turkmenistan (204 per cent) and Uzbekistan (150 per cent) also posted rapid growth rates in the 2000s. The deciding factor for success was no longer tied to how radical reform had been; rather, the political system which had come to be put in place, the geopolitical alignment of the country, and the presence or absence of ongoing internal conflict were much more predictive of national economic success.

Following the 2008 financial crisis, the economic success of the post-communist space was again flipped on its head. EU countries, which adopted a litany of neoliberal reforms during the 1990s, did not fare well. Every EU-10 country entered recession in 2009, with Poland the only exception; those countries who reformed the most fared by far the worst. For countries that did not join the EU, among whom neoliberal reforms were far less prevalent, the situation was mixed. The Central Asian countries and Azerbaijan fared relatively well and came out of recession quickly; the Balkan countries experienced longer recessions, but ones that were relatively mild in most countries. Only two countries had sharp declines on a par with the Baltic States: Ukraine, which has not strongly allied itself to Russia or the EU; and Armenia, which has an ongoing conflict with Azerbaijan. In sum, such widely varying outcomes point to explanatory factors apart from the severity of neoliberal reforms for these countries.

Examining other factors

In considering the many differences between countries of the post-communist world which have influenced development, perhaps none has been more heavily debated than the presence and strength of democratic institutions. Democracy has been the wild card in CEE economic development. The 1989 revolutions were born in idealistic hope that new democracies could manage the transition to market capitalism even though the transition to a capitalist market economy had rarely been attempted under democratic governance before. Analysts expected a host of complications and thought that either democracy or reform would probably be jettisoned. We can hear the resonance of these worries in (probably exaggerated) contemporary newspaper reports that warned that mass protests might emerge from the economic troubles in the region. Scholars expected that efforts to create a capitalist economy would necessarily be painful and could therefore endanger the progress toward successful market economies. Joel

Hellmann (1998) argued that it was not workers but elites who were likely to overturn reform programmes to keep in place high 'transitional' rents from imperfect reform. Likewise, builders of capitalism were thought to be nervous about subjecting their economic reform programmes to democratic oversight. If the reforms were in danger, would they not seek to overturn democratic institutions to protect them? Scholars therefore considered the optimal sequencing of reform to avoid a mutual overturning of capitalism and democracy. Polish Finance Minister Leszek Balcerowicz and Western economist Jeffrey Sachs (1993) argued for rapid economic reforms to take place before a democratic electoral reaction made such reforms impossible.

Later, a host of scholars observing events in CEE reaffirmed the strong relations between democracy and growth by arguing that the dual transition 'tensions' had been a canard. Capitalism and democracy were not incompatible in post-communist countries. Rather, they were mutually supportive. The losers of economic reform did not turn against democratic institutions, and democracies did not reform to a lesser extent than authoritarian regimes. Correlations between democratization and EBRD (European Bank for Reconstruction and Development) Transition Report data showed that post-communist democracies reformed more than authoritarian regimes did and also returned to growth faster. Greskovits (1998) argued that 'it now seems justified to write in the past tense: the breakdown literature has failed'. These findings were bolstered by the strong correlation between economic growth and democracy in the 1990s. The new member states of the European Union seemed to have both.

The experience of neighbouring Russia, however, made this claim somewhat difficult to support. After mass privatization and the opening of the economy created a class of super-wealthy businessmen known as oligarchs, the degree of public voice in Russian elections dropped significantly. In the 1996 election, in which Yeltsin, supported by the oligarchs, was propelled back to the presidency on a wave of coordinated media support and well-financed campaigning, the massive economic power of the men behind Russian business interests led to an incredible influence over a government that was perpetually strapped for cash. By the time Putin ascended to the presidency, the value of a vote in Russia was already quite limited. The neoliberal reforms of the 1990s appeared to weaken what had been a broadly participatory democracy.

Furthermore, the boom in growth among post-communist countries in the first decade of the twenty-first century lifted nearly all boats: democracies and authoritarian regimes alike. The fastest-growing economies in CEE were Ukraine, Latvia and Slovakia (not to mention

Turkmenistan and Uzbekistan), hardly a testament to the greater growth performance of democracies. Indeed, the improvement in economic conditions in Russia (in contrast to CEE) seems to have taken place exactly because of that country's return to authoritarianism. According to opinion polls, most Russians believe that Putin's rule (as president and now prime minister) has promoted economic performance and prosperity.

The reality of the relationship between democracy and capitalism thus remains complex. Certainly, there is strong reason to believe that capitalism and democracy have been compatible in the new member states of the European Union. However, this is largely because of the external influence of the European Union. As is well known, the European Union demanded both democratic governance and market economics from prospective new member states. It aggressively imposed membership conditionalities and even brought into line several countries that initially seemed to waver on democracy or markets or both, such as Slovakia, Bulgaria and Romania. To become a member state meant to adhere to norms of democracy and market capitalism. Since the East-Central European countries needed EU membership in order to solve their geopolitical and economic dilemmas, they had to adhere to democratic governance. And when democratic governance is stable, it can help to support economic growth. Democracy creates a system of perpetual policy experimentation, in which each succeeding government has an opportunity to try policies that it thinks will work better to achieve growth. This institutionalization of policy innovation helps to explain why democracies on average outperform most authoritarian regimes in enabling economic growth.

Without supportive geopolitical conditions, however, democracy can have a negative impact on growth. When there are no international bounds on democratic competition, it can devolve into a free-for-all struggle between elites, as in Ukraine. Elites may not be satisfied with winning once and then letting the opposition take its turn in power. The concerned parties may have too much at stake to risk losing control and want to avoid losing rents from government-controlled businesses.

Under such conditions, authoritarian regimes may be better for growth, insofar as they place limits on elite behaviour and create a single set of rules of the game that enable participants to coordinate their expectations and behaviour. They create a Hobbesian world in which the Leviathan is empowered to pursue the common good. Of course, most authoritarian regimes fail at this. However, some do exceptionally well. While CEE countries experienced a roller-coaster ride after the end of communism, China managed to successfully transform its socialist economy without the deep transitional recession that cost CEE countries much of their pre-1989 economic output. It did this by keeping the hand of the state firmly in control while also maintaining a vast state sector that employs millions of workers in less than fully productive jobs. Such an approach is completely incompatible with democratic governance. Nevertheless, China has averaged 9 per cent growth for more than twenty years, causing a massive increase in living standards and a reduction in poverty from 53 per cent to 8 per cent in 2001. Unemployment stands at 3–4 per cent as compared with 10–15 per cent in CEE. Some will argue that the Chinese example is irrelevant to Central and Eastern Europe, as that path was precluded from the start. Nevertheless, the Chinese example, which has many followers in Asia, is an increasingly attractive development model and seems to have been influential in Putin's Russia.

The fate of democratic regimes in CEE highlights the impact of geopolitics on the success of transitioning economies. The importance of the European Union in the success of the EU-10 countries cannot be forgotten. EU membership gave these countries enormous growth prospects by making their markets, regulatory environments and trade relations much more secure. Countries which adopted the euro, such as Slovakia, benefited from greatly improved credit ratings; those which did not enjoyed the benefits of a low domestic currency and open access to the massive European market. One result of market harmonization has been a vast expansion of the East European car industry. An industry previous known for laughably substandard products, such as the Trabant, which fuelled the local equivalent of stand-up comedy, is now home (in Bratislava, Slovakia) to the Volkswagen Touareg. Yet the foreign direct investment that made these changes possible began to improve dramatically in 1998, the year that EU membership negotiations began and neoliberal reforms effectively ground to a halt.

Countries which allied more closely with Russia also fared well, buoyed in part by high commodity prices. In 2007, the worst-off countries were the ones that either had failed to advance to membership in the European Union or had not strongly allied with Russia, or had a history of civil strife, such as Moldova, Georgia and parts of the Western Balkans. According to the EBRD, those countries that had not returned to 1989 levels of GDP by 2007 included FYR Macedonia (96 per cent of 1989 GDP in 2007), Montenegro (85 per cent), Serbia (68 per cent), Ukraine (68 per cent), Georgia (60 per cent) and Moldova (51 per cent). Oil and other commodity price rises clearly played a role, but so too did internal conflict and geopolitical stability. The paths to growth have thus been varied – and not clearly connected to the extent of neoliberal economic reform.

Conclusion

The CEE experience since 1989 has been shaped by the shock therapy strategies of economic reform adopted in much of the region and the deep economic crisis they helped to induce. Twenty years later, it is still unclear whether these programmes were really the best path to reform and whether they (alone or in combination with other factors) were responsible for the upsurge in growth after 2003. In fact, countries have had different results from these policies. The new member states of the European Union experienced a U-shaped recession, eventually returning to growth after three to eight years. Countries further to the south and east took longer to embrace reforms and return to growth after the initial plunge. Some countries, such as Moldova, remain in serious economic difficulties. Others, such as Ukraine and Latvia, have proven vulnerable to crises in the international economy and are again on a trajectory of despair.

The jury is also still out on the relationship between democracy and development. In some respects, democracies have done better. Yet other important countries returned to growth only after they had eschewed democracy. Lurking in any assessment of the post-communist experience must be the comparison with China, which suggests that post-communist structural reform requires neither neoliberal radicalism nor democracy. China has grown dramatically and avoided the severe transitional recession that afflicted CEE by maintaining a large state sector, allowing a dynamic private sector to flourish alongside it, and using a single-party authoritarian political regime to direct policy and investment.

Geopolitics, meanwhile, has played an enormous role. For new member states of the European Union, democracy and advanced capitalism have indeed gone hand in hand. Those that failed to enter the European home have had a different experience. In the non-EU post-communist space, good political and economic relations with Russia and the absence of civil strife are the best determinants of well-being, not neoliberal reform or democratization.

In the wake of the financial crisis, the future of the European Union, and particularly the eurozone, looms more uneasily. As Russia becomes more dependent on eternally increasing prices for its natural resources, the long-term sustainability of its current growth kick, and that of its allies, also seems unclear. Ultimately, twenty years may simply be too early to tally the results of transition. The massive economic experiment launched in the heady days of 1989 will likely evade scholarly consensus for at least another twenty.

Chapter 14

Social Change and Social Policy

Terry Cox

With the end of communist rule and the dismantling of the distinctive economic and social institutions of the 'state socialist' system, the citizens of Central and Eastern Europe experienced profound changes to their ways of life and standards of living. In particular, patterns of social inequality and the institutional arrangements governing employment and social welfare underwent significant changes. In terms of inequalities, it was a case of the replacement of one pattern of social stratification that had been shaped by the policies and criteria of the state-managed and state-owned economy with a different pattern, shaped more by the pressures of a market economy. In terms of social welfare, the changes involved a move from a situation where communist governments had, in principle, provided a guarantee of employment and of a comprehensive range of welfare rights, albeit at a low level, to a system that sought to protect the most vulnerable, while the changes that were taking place in the economy allowed others the opportunity of significant gains in their incomes and standards of living.

Social structure of 'state socialism'

The period of communist rule in Central and Eastern Europe witnessed a rapid expansion of the industrial working class, an increase in the numbers of people in routine clerical and administrative positions to run the vast new bureaucracies of communist rule and its state-owned 'planned' economy, and the emergence of a new ruling elite of political and industrial managers and policy makers. Also typically (except in Poland) most peasants or individual family farmers were absorbed into collective or state farms. To begin with the 'socialist transformation' of East European societies involved rapid upward social mobility from peasant to worker and from both into managerial and professional positions, with increased levels of education leading to a growing intelligentsia.

As part of the state socialist system a centralized bureaucratic system for the provision of welfare services and the distribution of consumer goods and services was organized through governmental and often workplace institutions. Workplace organizations, including trades unions, were often responsible for providing canteens, shops, medical and welfare services, holidays and supervision for the children of their staff, and even entertainment. Trade unions took on the role of a transmission belt for the state, taking up individual complaints and problems, and dealing with welfare and even consumer issues on behalf of their members. In general, social policy was seen as the responsibility of government to a greater extent than in Western countries, and it was interpreted as aiming not only to provide social welfare and the satisfaction of social needs, but also to decrease social inequality and achieve social justice.

The official ideology of the communist regimes claimed that antagonistic class differences had been eradicated and that 'socialist society' was steadily reducing inequalities based on education, occupational skill, gender and ethnicity (nationality). However, as a consequence of communist policies of industrialization, there actually emerged a range of new social groups with different levels of qualification, status and income. Over time, as the new structures were consolidated, inequalities in income and standards of living persisted, upward social mobility slowed down and there was an increasing tendency for children to follow their parents into occupations of similar status (Lovenduski and Woodall, 1987: ch. 6).

There were two main bases for social inequalities in the state-managed system. First, official income policies set different levels of pay for different sectors of the economy, and within them, for occupations requiring different levels of education and skill. In most industries there were marked differences between a core of skilled workers, who tended to be male, and a periphery of unskilled workers, often containing a higher proportion of women. Second, there were inequalities in access to various goods and services that were not widely available for sale, but which were distributed through the workplace or on the basis of a person's professional or political position. For example, free or subsidized catering, health care, child care and holidays were allocated to workers by managers or the trade unions in their workplace. Various professions and elite groups also had further access to scarce goods and services through special closed shops and restaurants.

Social transformation and social policy

Following the fall of the communist regimes in the period 1989–91, major shifts in economic and social policy took place, aimed at dismantling the old system of centralized bureaucratic management of the economy and its accompanying social policies. The economic transformation, in turn, had consequences for social policy since it posed quite serious political dilemmas for governments in Eastern Europe. On the one hand economic policy created pressures for a reduction in employment and cuts in expenditure on social services, while on the other hand governments were afraid to cut too deeply for fear of losing electoral support. In general the trend was for governments 'to reform their system of social protection by shifting from the patchwork of universalistic, mainly employment-related schemes to greater reliance on social insurance geared to cover market-related "risks" or contingencies, and to means-tested social assistance' (Standing, 1996: 236). The provision of welfare services and the distribution of consumer goods and services, previously organized through governmental and workplace institutions, was dismantled and replaced by a variety of new mechanisms, provided by local government, private companies, new voluntary and not-for-profit organizations, and the churches.

In order to alleviate some of the consequences of unemployment, most countries in the region introduced income-related unemployment benefit schemes quite early in the transition period. In Hungary, this had begun under the reform communist government as early as 1988, followed by Poland in 1989, Czechoslovakia in 1990 and Slovenia in 1991. To begin with, the provisions of the schemes were relatively generous, reflecting concerns that unemployment could provoke serious discontent. Benefits were set at over 60 per cent of the previous wage in Hungary and Slovenia and began at 70 per cent in Poland, reducing by stages to 40 per cent after a year. After the break-up of Czechoslovakia, the rates were 60 per cent in Slovakia and 50 per cent in the Czech Republic. The time periods over which these benefits were available also varied. To begin with they were offered for an unlimited period in Hungary, for up to 24 months (depending on past employment record) in Slovenia and Poland, up to 12 months in Slovakia and six months in the Czech Republic. However, governments soon found these levels very difficult to sustain as unemployment rates rose and both the level and duration of benefits were cut back. For example, the maximum duration of unemployment benefits was cut to 12 months in Hungary, and also reduced by half in Slovakia and the Czech Republic towards the end of 1991, and Poland introduced a flat-rate benefit of 36 per cent of the average wage in 1992 (Kramer, 1997: 94).

Further measures to deal with unemployment included the establishment of employment offices to help people find work, to provide
training opportunities and to promote self-employment and small business development. In more informal ways, all governments in the
region also hoped to encourage a reduction in the size of the workforce
by encouraging women to stay at home or encouraging people to retire
early. To a significant extent, pensions policy was also used as a surro-
gate form of unemployment benefit: large numbers of workers, sometimes as young as fifty years old, were offered early retirement deals,
while others were awarded disability pensions, thus transferring the
costs to the pensions budget (World Bank, 2000: 293; Kramer, 1997:
82). The advantage of such moves for governments was that it produced lower figures for unemployment than would have been the case
otherwise, and softened the political impact of the decline in employment brought about by the transition. However, it had the disadvantage of further increasing the costs of welfare provision to the state on
top of the growing cost of providing unemployment benefit.

Alongside new policies to deal with unemployment, all governments
in the region also sought to expand social assistance payments to alleviate poverty during the initial years of the transition. In each case, the
new provisions set out a range of different grounds on which people
might be eligible for support, expanded the numbers of local offices to
administer the system, and gave local welfare workers quite large discre-
tion in deciding on whether applicants qualified for assistance. To begin
with, many liberal reformers had expected the large increase in social
assistance claims would be a short-lived episode in the early stages of
the transition and that the expansion of the market economy would
rapidly create new jobs and sources of income for those displaced by the
economic restructuring. They were soon to be disappointed as numbers
continued to rise. The situation became more serious as a consequence
of decisions to restrict the duration of the unemployment benefit entitle-
ments. For the growing numbers in long-term unemployment, there was
no alternative to applying instead for social assistance. Between 1990
and 1993, the numbers of applications for assistance doubled in
Hungary and trebled in Poland (Kramer, 1997: 100–1). The press
reported many cases of local offices becoming overwhelmed.

However, such initial measures did not remove the pressure for the
extension of market criteria deeper into the area of social welfare provision and social protection. During the 1990s, governments found it
increasingly difficult to meet the costs of the social welfare and healthcare systems they had inherited from the communist regimes. The
general trend was for the provision of healthcare to be devolved to
local governments and for some facilities, including some hospitals, to

be privatized. In the decade following the political transition, pension reform became an increasingly urgent issue. The increase in the numbers of people on pensions, or unemployed, or in unregistered employment where no pension and social insurance contributions are made, all contributed to making the existing pensions systems prohibitively expensive. While at the beginning of the 1990s most countries had a ratio of approximately one pensioner to three working contributors in their working population, by the late 1990s this had risen to two pensioners for every three workers in most countries, and to a ratio of around one to one, or worse, in Ukraine and Albania (World Bank, 2000: 292).

A variety of different solutions were proposed for creating more affordable pension systems, depending partly on the relative strength of different economies and the degree of sophistication of their financial systems. For the relatively stronger economies of Central Europe and the Baltic, arguments from liberal reformers and some international agencies (such as the World Bank) were in favour of adopting a 'multipillar' system. This combines a modified version of existing state 'pay as you go' systems (first pillar) with investment-based individual accounts (second and further pillars), thus spreading the costs between the state and the private financial sector. For poorer countries, especially in the CIS (Commonwealth of Independent States), the main debate concerned the degree to which the different pension rates currently paid to different occupations could be reduced to a flat rate, thus reducing costs to the state. Where this was attempted, for example in Macedonia, it prompted heated political debates and proposals for the reintroduction of greater differentiation of benefits (World Bank, 2000: 321–3).

Growing income inequalities

As a result of economic transformation, new inequalities emerged across the region, and were reflected in terms of income distribution, increased unemployment and poverty. Particular groups were affected more than others, including children, ethnic minorities, women and large families. The new emerging patterns of social exclusion and inclusion had significant implications and raise important questions for politics in Eastern Europe, with the emergence of new social cleavages and bases for political mobilization in relation to social class, ethnicity and gender.

Income inequality, as measured by the Gini coefficient, increased throughout Eastern Europe between the end of communist rule and the mid-to-late 1990s, and in most countries it continued to increase further, although usually at a slower rate, through the first decade of the new millennium. As shown in Table 14.1, across Eastern Europe as whole, in all countries for which data are available, inequality increased between the end of the 1980s and the late 1990s. The initial main reasons for the increase in inequality were the curtailing of 'state subsidies that distributed rewards and benefits and restrained inequality' and the emergence of 'a largely unregulated private labor market' (Heyns, 2005: 173). According to a study by Milanovic, 'the most important source of increase in the Gini is the "hollowing out of the middle", that is the movement of state-sector workers into either "rich" private sector activity or "poor" unemployment' (Milanovic 1999: 321).

Since the late 1990s the picture has been more uneven: while income inequality has decreased in most CIS countries, there have been further gradual increases in much of the rest of Eastern Europe. According to a World Bank study, 'by 2003, consumption inequality in the region as a whole looked broadly comparable to that in OECD countries and East Asia' (Dudwick *et al.*, 2005: 13). Thus, economic transformation would seem to have brought about similar patterns of inequality to those of more longstanding capitalist economies. However, what remains unclear, even from the most recent figures available, is what effect the global recession of recent years may have had on the distribution of incomes in the region.

There is a great deal of debate about the best methodology for measuring income inequality and the World Bank figures shown in Table 14.1 have attracted some criticisms (Heyns, 2005: 173–7), but they are used here because they offer a more comprehensive and up-to-date picture of all countries of the region than other available sources. The table uses the Gini coefficient to measure income distribution. This indicates the degree of income inequality, in this case between individuals, on a scale ranging from the hypothetical extremes of 0, representing perfect equality, to 100, representing the complete monopolization of all income by one person.

Poverty

As a result of growing income inequality there was increased pressure on the income levels of households at the lower levels of the scale of income distribution to fall below the poverty line. Milanovich has estimated that across the 'transition countries as a whole between the late 1980s and 1995 the numbers of the population in poverty rose from

Table 14.1 *Changes in income distribution (Gini coefficients) since the late 1980s*

Country	Gini coefficients		
	Late 1980s	*Late 1990s*	*Most recent*
Albania	n/a	29.12 (1996)	34.51 (2008)
Belarus	22.76 (1988)	30.28 (1998)	27.22 (2008)
Bosnia & Herzegovina	n/a	28.03 (2001)	36.21 (2007)
Bulgaria	23.43 (1989)	26.38 (1997)	28.19 (2007)
Croatia	22.78 (1988)	26.82 (1998)	41.34 (2008)
Czech Republic	19.40 (1988)	25.82 (1996)	n/a
Estonia	22.97 (1988)	37.64 (1998)	36.00 (2004)
Hungary	20.96 (1987)	24.93 (1998)	31.18 (2007)
Latvia	22.49 (1988)	33.52 (1998)	36.61 (2008)
Lithuania	22.48 (1988)	30.21 (1998)	37.57 (2008)
Macedonia	n/a	28.13 (1998)	43.17 (2009)
Moldova	24.14 (1988)	39.47 (1998)	33.03 (2010)
Montenegro	n/a	n/a	29.99 (2008)
Poland	25.53 (1987)	32.85 (1998)	34.07 (2009)
Romania	23.31 (1989)	29.44 (1998)	31.15 (2008)
Serbia	n/a	32.74 (2002)	27.80 (2009)
Slovakia	19.54 (1988)	25.81 (1996)	26.86 (2008)
Slovenia	23.60 (1987)	28.41 (1998)	31.15 (2004)
Ukraine	23.31 (1988)	28.96 (1998)	26.44 (2009)

Source: PovcalNet online tool for poverty measurement developed by the World Bank, http://iresearch.worldbank.org/PovcalNet/, last accessed 3 May 2012.

just under 14 million or 4 per cent of the population, to 168 million or 45 per cent of the population' (Milanovich, 1998: 69). Thereafter, according to a World Bank study, 'the resurgence of growth in the eastern half of the region, particularly in the CIS, resulted in a significant decline in poverty in the region during 1998–2003' (Dudwick *et al.*, 2005: 2). According to their estimates, whereas in 1998, 102 million people in Central and Eastern Europe (including Russia) were in poverty, and a further 160.7 million were vulnerable of falling into poverty, by 2003 the corresponding figures were 61.2 million and 153.3 million, meaning that over 40 million had moved out of poverty during that period.

Within this general picture, however, there is a significant amount of variation between countries. The World Bank study distinguished between four different sub-groups of countries in 2003: the 'EU-8' made up of the formerly communist countries that had been approved to join the EU in 2004, which had the lowest levels of poverty with the wider region; 'South-eastern Europe' which had experienced 'moderate' levels of poverty; as had the 'middle-income' CIS countries;

while the low-income CIS countries had high levels of poverty. As shown in Table 14.2, while the general trend was for poverty to increase at varying rates across Central and Eastern Europe between the end of the 1980s and the late 1990s, all countries then saw a decline in the incidence of poverty through the following years. (However, a note of caution should probably be introduced here in that the latest available figures may not reflect changes resulting from global recession since 2008.)

Table 14.2 shows the percentage of the population falling below two different poverty lines. An income equivalent to what $2.15 would buy reflects the absolute poverty line for European countries with cold winters, while the $4.30 line also takes minimal costs of clothing, housing and local transport into account. This latter rate approximates more closely to the official poverty lines adopted by several governments in the region and indicates those in a vulnerable situation that could become poor in an economic downturn. As with the measurement of inequality, there is much debate among researchers about the best way to measure poverty and to use a common standard so that international comparisons can be made. A common method is to estimate the absolute amount of money needed per day for subsistence in each country, including food and other necessary expenditure such as housing or clothing. A poverty line is determined in US dollars and then converted into national currency units using purchasing power parity (PPP) exchange rates in order to measure the relative purchasing power of different currencies for equivalent goods and services. This avoids the problem that goods have different prices in different countries, and takes into account different patterns of consumption between countries.

Behind these figures there was a more complex situation regarding which particular social groups were most vulnerable to poverty and what factors affected their situations. According to the World Bank, 'four characteristics stand out for raising poverty risk above average: being young, living in a rural area or (in some cases) a secondary city, being unemployed, and having low levels of education'. Of these four characteristics, being young has been noted as a major factor. In her review of research on poverty and inequality in the region, Heyns noted poverty among children was particularly worrying, and identified some of the changes in social policy discussed above as significant factors exacerbating the situation:

Throughout the region, social transfers and benefits that supported children have been cut back or dismantled. Child care programs, family support, and parental leave policies have been reduced, with funds redirected to cover unemployment; eligibility rules have been

Table 14.2 *Percentage of population below poverty lines*

Country	$2.15 per day			$4.30 per day		
	Late 1980s	Late 1990s	Most recent	Late 1980s	Late 1990s	Most recent
Albania	n/a	9.06 (1996)	5.87 (2008)	n/a	50.08 (1996)	46.88 (2008)
Belarus	n/a	5.07 (1998)	0.22 (2008)	6.63 (1988)	48.39 (1998)	2.98 (2008)
Bosnia & Herzegovina	n/a	n/a	0.25 (2007)	n/a	n/a	8.69 (2007)
Bulgaria	0.08 (1989)	3.43 (1997)	0.99 (2007)	0.58 (1989)	61.35 (1997)	18.16 (2007)
Croatia	0.07 (1988)	0.12 (1998)	0.10 (2008)	n/a	1.27 (1998)	0.55 (2008)
Czech Republic	n/a	0.2 (1996)	n/a	0.02 (1988)	1.04 (1996)	n/a
Estonia	0.10 (1988)	1.2 (1998)	1.93 (2004)	1.71 (1988)	27.71 (1998)	22.02 (2004)
Hungary	0.09 (1987)	0.58 (1998)	0.41 (2007)	0.54 (1987)	17.0 (1998)	5.96 (2007)
Latvia	0.05 (1988)	5.79 (1998)	0.44 (2008)	0.29 (1988)	38.70 (1998)	7.20 (2008)
Lithuania	0.17 (1988)	1.8 (1998)	0.55 (2008)	5.26 (1988)	28.39 (1998)	9.77 (2008)
Macedonia	n/a	4.96 (1998)	7.39 (2009)	n/a	39.49 (1998)	35.12 (2009)
Moldova	56.97 (1988)	56.47 (1998)	6.01 (2010)	98.1 (1988)	91.20 (1998)	49.31 (2010)
Montenegro	n/a	n/a	0.36 (2008)	n/a	n/a	8.46 (2008)
Poland	0.26 (1987)	0.57 (1998)	0.25 (2009)	5.82 (1987)	18.26 (1998)	10.81 (2009)
Romania	0.48 (1989)	13.09 (1998)	2.17 (2009)	4.98 (1989)	71.41 (1998)	31.31 (2009)
Serbia	n/a	n/a	0.91 (2009)	n/a	n/a	17.22 (2009)
Slovakia	n/a	1.61 (1996)	0.14 (2009)	0.18 (1988)	8.73 (1996)	2.87 (2009)
Slovenia	0.04 (1987)	0.04 (1998)	0.11 (2004)	0.41 (1987)	0.46 (1998)	0.76 (2004)
Ukraine	19.71 (1988)	10.42 (1996)	0.21 (2009)	88.39 (1988)	76.77 (1998)	10.30 (2009)

Source: PovcalNet online tool for poverty measurement developed by the World Bank, http://iresearch.worldbank.org/PovcalNet/, last accessed 3 May 2012.

tightened and periods of coverage shortened; family benefits are now means-tested and of limited duration ... Public spending on health care, medicine and educational materials have declined, with a larger share of costs being passed on to parents. (Heyns, 2005: 183–4)

Unemployment is also closely associated with the risk of poverty. According to World Bank data quoted in Dudwick *et al.* (2005), 'the unemployed face a higher-than-average incidence of poverty [and] there has been an ongoing deterioration in their position relative to the employed'. In particular in some CIS countries, including Belarus and Moldova, there was 'a sharp increase in relative poverty risk of the unemployed, basically reflecting the substantial improvements on the living standards of those in employment' since the late 1990s (ibid.: 57).

A further consequence of the economic transformation and the increase in poverty has been an increase in the incidence of certain ill-nesses, higher infant mortality and decreased life expectancy. To a significant extent, the legacy of the comprehensive state health care systems developed under communist rule were effective in maintaining much higher levels of welfare than exist in many countries with high rates of absolute poverty in other parts of the world. However, some serious problems began to emerge in the 1990s, especially in CIS countries. Male life expectancy declined by more than five years in Ukraine between 1989 and 1994, and by an average of over four years in the Baltic countries. High rates of infant mortality have also been recorded in some CIS countries and parts of South-eastern Europe. For example, infant mortality per one thousand live births was twenty-four in Albania, 19 in Romania and 18 in Moldova, compared with rates as low as 6 in the Czech Republic and Slovenia (World Bank, 2000: 41–3). In the following decade the situation remained uneven. While the decline in male life expectancy had generally been arrested, 'many of the proximate causes of high male mortality, notably the high incidence of cardiovascular and circulatory disease and death from accidents and acts of violence remain'. However, concerns remain about 'the very slow progress in achieving reductions in mortality and concerns about the delivery and quality of critical medical services' in CIS countries in the region (Dudwick *et al.*, 2005: 25).

The consequences of the global economic crisis

As yet the available statistical evidence does not provide a comprehensive picture of the consequences of the economic crisis across Eastern Europe and, as noted above in the discussions of inequality and poverty, a word of caution is appropriate about how the crisis may be affecting trends in these figures. However, the Life in Transition Survey (LiTS II) for the EBRD gives an early indication of the changes that are taking place, based on a combination of statistics on consumption and a survey of the subjective perceptions, beliefs and choices, of people in a broad range of twenty-nine 'transition countries' in Eastern Europe and Central Asia (EBRD, 2011). This shows that in 2009 this broader transition region was among the hardest hit by the global economic crisis, with GDP falling by 5.2 per cent and registered unemployment increasing. Three main consequences of the economic crisis were noted: in job losses, reductions in wages, and a decrease in remittances. 'On average, two-thirds of the population report being affected: 16 per cent of respondents declared that their household was affected "a great deal", 26 per cent "a fair amount", 23 per cent "just a little" and one-third "not at all". While this measure is subjective, it corresponds closely to shocks objectively experienced by households' (EBRD, 2011: 7). Over all, wage reductions affected more people than job losses but, while losing a job affected a smaller number of households, it resulted in higher losses for those households that were affected and increased the subjective effect of the crisis to a much larger extent than reduced wages.

In general the impact of the crisis was greater in South-eastern Europe than in other parts of the region covered by the survey, and the least affected were some EU member states such as Poland, the Czech Republic and Slovakia, where the perceived impact was closer to that reported for Western Europe. Across the wider transition region covered by the study, the poorest third of the population in each country was more likely to report that their household had been adversely affected by the crisis. This reflected the much greater likelihood that they had experienced job losses than was the case for richer households.

Households adopted a variety of different strategies to cope with lower incomes, the most common being reducing consumption, followed by using private resources as safety nets. About 70 per cent of the households that had reported they were affected 'a great deal' or 'a fair amount' by the crisis had to reduce their consumption of staple foods and health expenditure, and a similar proportion cut other types of spending.

A newly emerging social structure

What implications have the trends discussed above had for the emerging social structure and potential lines of political cleavage in the post-socialist societies of Central and Eastern Europe?

At one end of the social scale it is generally recognized that the market economy and privatization have created opportunities for a small number of people to become very wealthy. However, detailed statistics on the distribution of wealth are not available and have not been the subject of detailed research. This means discussion of the topic has to approach the question in more indirect ways. A debate has emerged on the key question of whether the societies of Eastern Europe are characterized by inequalities that give rise to elites defined in terms of political or managerial power, or whether economic power derived from wealth now provides the basis for political power; or in other words, is there a series of competing elites or is there an emerging capitalist class?

A widely held view in the early years of the transformation process was that the old political elites of socialism had converted their political capital into economic capital and become the new economic elite or capitalist class (Staniszkis, 1991; Hankiss, 1990). However, this was challenged by Eyal *et al.* (1998) on the basis of an analysis of the social backgrounds of the new economic elite in the Czech Republic, Hungary and Poland, who concluded that in post-socialist Central Europe at least, the new economic elites were not the owners of the resources they controlled, and a 'capitalism without capitalists' was emerging. Further studies of entrepreneurs in East Central Europe have provided insights into the family and social background factors behind the career paths of the new entrepreneurs, and that a significant group of business owners is emerging (Laki and Szalai, 2006; Johnson and Loveman, 2005) but no clear picture across the entire region can yet be discerned.

At the other end of the social scale, although more information is available, there are still many questions concerning what the trends might mean for a characterization of the emerging social structure. A key question concerns the impact of inequality and poverty on emerging patterns of social divisions in terms of class, ethnicity and gender. Research so far tends to suggest transformation is creating complex social divisions that are likely to undermine mobilization on the basis of social class. The complexity of overlapping class positions is further complicated by cross-cutting divisions based on ethnicity and gender.

The question of class formation

In relation to social class, a distinctive feature of poverty in Eastern Europe has been poverty in the working population rather than among the unemployed. Initially this emerged in categories of employment that were badly hit by the transition recession where wages fell well below price levels so that many people in employment were earning less than the average wage. The 2001 New Europe Barometer (NEB) survey found that only 34 per cent of employed people in the ten EU candidate countries reported that 'they earn enough to buy what they need'. This group ranged in size from 16 per cent in Slovakia to 58 per cent in Slovenia (the only country where a majority of the workforce had sufficient income from one job).

According to Smith *et al.* (2008: 306), the problem has continued and has been fed by 'a dual process of renewed labour market segmentation and the commodification and neoliberalisation of the labour market and its regulation'. In their detailed fieldwork research on 'two of the largest "socialist-era" housing districts in Central Europe', Nowa Huta in Krakow, Poland and Petrzalka in Bratislava, Slovakia, it was found that 'around one-third of members of households "at risk" of poverty were *in employment* ... suggesting the existence of high levels of "in work poverty"'. They tended to work in low-pay, low status and unskilled jobs in the service sector (Smith *et al.*, 2008: 292).

These findings reflect a situation throughout the region in which economic transformation has resulted in people achieving subsistence through a range of different kinds of work including growing their own food and various kinds of unregistered casual work in the 'grey economy'. The NEB survey found that 70 per cent of all respondents (employed, unemployed and pensioners) reported they could cope by drawing on a range of different resources. For individual countries this ranged from 59 per cent in Poland to 82 per cent in Slovenia (Rose, 2002: 13–15).

Smith *et al.* further note that 'the working poor are impelled to rely on more than capitalist labour processes, to engage in a diversity of income earning and livelihood activities with which to supplement earnings from primary employment'. In this they rely on 'a wide range of social and economic assets – social networks, land and property, and claims on the state – which are employed in attempts to develop alternatives or complements to formal employment and integrate not only commodified labour, but also domestic and reciprocal labour' (2008: 306).

To the extent that this pattern may be becoming general across the region as a whole, it has profound implications for the class structure of the societies of Central and Eastern Europe and on whether class will form a basis on which political mobilization may occur:

The fact that most working household members combine numerous forms of labour means that many also experience a shifting of their work identity, from employee, to contingent labourer, to self-employed, for example, and articulate these with their family and social roles in the exchange of domestic and reciprocal labour. These shifting identities connect to the performance of numerous class positions, making the identification of a singular post-socialist working class difficult. (Smith *et al.*, 2008: 306–7)

Ethnicity and inequality

In some countries ethnicity has been closely associated with poverty, especially in relation to the Roma throughout East Central Europe, the Turks in Bulgaria and Russians in Latvia (Dudwick *et al.*, 2005: 8, 11). As Emigh and Szelenyi have noted, the Roma moved from being under-privileged within the privileged heavy industrial sector of the socialist economy to becoming 'the poorest of the poor' with the collapse of this sector in the transition (2001: 8). Under state socialism, while the Roma in East Central Europe had suffered from segregation in terms of occupation, housing, educational opportunities, they had also been absorbed into formal employment to satisfy the centrally managed economy's chronic labour shortage. Although the jobs they held were mostly lower-grade, unskilled jobs, they lost these almost completely as a result of the economic transformation, leading to consequent high levels of unemployment and deprivation (Stewart, 2002; Ladany and Szelenyi, 2006). There has also been a spatial aspect to Roma poverty to the extent that the Roma are concentrated in villages and city ghettos, which tend to have higher levels of poverty among the majority of the population as well (Emigh and Szelenyi, 2001: 9). As Swain has also noted, 'Roma poverty was predominantly rural poverty', which has in some cases added geographical seclusion to social exclusion, exacerbated further by the 'political exploitation of open anti-Roma sentiment' by far-right parties such as Jobbik in Hungary, and even by some mainstream politicians (Swain, 2011: 1685).

The position of women in society

In somewhat different ways, the consequences of the economic transformation have also been serious for women's position in society. Most contemporary observers of the early years of the transformation felt that 'restructuring ... had dubious developmental consequences and adverse effects on women's role and status' (Moghadam, 1992: 22). However, as noted by Corrin (1998: 241), early attempts at any more precise assessment of women's situations as 'a balance sheet of gains and losses ha[d] little value' because 'the entire framework of the old times was different, and those apparent "advantages" that women had were deeply embedded into the oppressive logic of party-based control over their entire lives'.

An example of the complexity of the situation can be seen in relation to women's employment. On the one hand, women were under pressure to 'return to the home' as child care and education budgets were cut and jobs in the state sector declined. On the other hand, because women under state socialism had largely occupied jobs in services and finance, which were of low prestige but often required higher education, they were initially in a favourable position to take advantage of a growth in such jobs as the market economy expanded. By the early 2000s however, a new generation of young men was emerging to compete for such jobs and, at the same time, unemployment rates in most countries in the region were higher for women than for men (Fodor, 2005). A study by Pollert (2005: 222–5) has shown that by the early 2000s, the gap between men's and women's pay in East Central Europe had grown wider than the pre-accession EU norm when women's pay was around 80 per cent of men's. The main factors responsible for the deterioration of the position of women were 'the decline in social support for families, the drop in the real value of social benefits, the rising cost of childcare, and absence of work-family harmonisation policies – in sum, the reversal of those communist social policies which benefitted women workers (Pollert, 2005: 226).

As shown in Table 14.3, in the post-communist period since the mid-1990s, the most comprehensive data set, the UNDP's Gender Inequality Index, suggests that gender inequality remains a problem in

Table 14.3   *Gender inequality, 1995–2011*

Country	1995	2000	2005	2008	2011
Albania	0.61	–	0.33	0.31	0.27
Czech Republic	0.19	0.21	0.15	0.15	0.14
Estonia	0.36	0.24	0.24	0.19	0.19
Hungary	0.31	–	0.23	0.24	0.24
Latvia	0.37	0.30	0.22	0.20	0.22
Lithuania	0.28	–	0.20	0.21	0.19
Macedonia	–	–	–	–	0.15
Moldova	0.47	–	0.31	0.29	0.30
Poland	0.24	0.21	0.16	0.16	0.16
Romania	0.46	–	0.35	0.33	0.33
Slovakia	0.24	0.25	0.19	0.19	0.19
Slovenia	0.24	–	0.20	0.18	0.18
Ukraine	0.45	–	0.36	0.33	0.34

Note: '0' reflects complete equality and '1' reflects very high inequality.
Source: hdr.undp.org/UNDP Intranet, Gender Inequality Index Trends 1995–2011, last accessed 27 April 2012.

Central and Eastern Europe but that its extent overall has declined slightly. The index is based on a composite measure of inequality between women and men in reproductive health, empowerment and the labour market. A figure of '0' would reflect complete equality and '1' would reflect very high inequality.

Conclusion

A combination of overlapping class positions cross-cutting divisions based on ethnicity and gender make it difficult to discern how clear political cleavages are likely to form on the basis of social structural characteristics in the near future. In addition, as Swain has commented, 'when considering the social structures created by post-socialist capitalism, socialism's social and cultural legacy played a more significant role' (Swain, 2011: 1677). Clearly a distinctive kind of capitalist society is taking shape but whether its current characteristics should still be understood as 'transitional' or whether they are becoming embedded as part of a new variant of capitalist society is a question for further enquiry.

Chapter 15

The Quality of Post-Communist Democracy

Andrew Roberts

In the years before 1989, citizens of Central and East Europe eagerly looked forward to the arrival of democracy as a solution to their region's problems. Communist dictatorships limited fundamental human rights, produced stagnant economies unresponsive to people's needs, and destroyed the lives of millions. It was believed that the coming of democracy would change all this, leading to a new golden age.

But when the fall of communism actually did come in 1989, it was not at all clear that these expectations were being fulfilled. Some countries barely seemed to democratize (for example, Belarus), while others that seemed to democratize quickly after the transition soon backtracked into less free elections (for example, Serbia). Perhaps not as disturbing, but more surprising, is that even in the supposedly 'consolidated' or stable democracies in the region like the Czech Republic, Hungary and Poland, democracy may not be working well. Some have called these systems low quality democracies – yes, democratic at least in some basic sense, but not functioning the way democracy should. Indeed, post-communist citizens themselves have been some of the most vocal advocates of the view that they are living in low quality democracies.

But this conclusion is controversial, in part because it is hard to say what a high quality democracy looks like. If a country has free elections – as most in the region do – can we say that democracy is not working there? What then do we hope for from democracy? Does it have something to do with the way that citizens rule – whether their opinions are taken seriously – which is what the word democracy means? Or is a high quality democracy equivalent to an array of good outcomes – economic growth, lack of poverty, good healthcare, low levels of corruption? In other words, all the good things a people could want?

In this concluding chapter, I look at a variety of conceptions of democratic quality and how Central and East European countries fare under them. The overall question is: Are these countries low quality democracies or have they managed to throw aside their communist heritage and become fully functional modern democracies? The answer, as with most answers in politics, is that it depends: on the conception of quality and the specific country and issue you look at.

A paradox

I begin though with something of a paradox. Most of the countries in the region meet typical standards for a democracy. If we go by the ratings of international organizations like Freedom House or Polity (described in more detail in the next section), we see that relatively soon after the fall of communism, several countries had achieved high levels. As early as 1991, Bulgaria, the Czech Republic, Estonia, Hungary, Latvia, Lithuania, Poland, and Slovenia were all classified as 'fully free' by Freedom House or as 'democratic' by Polity and remained that way throughout the transition. Several other countries – Croatia, Romania, Serbia, and Slovakia – were scored as only partially democratic early in the transition, but by the year 2000 or so, they had reached nearly the same level as the early achievers.

So in this respect, objective and impartial observers from outside of the region believed that many of these countries were fully democratic. They received nearly the same ratings on Freedom House's rating of political rights as the US, Great Britain, France, and other countries widely regarded as democratic.

But if we then ask citizens of these very same countries what they thought of democracy in their own land, we see something very different. Most citizens in even the most democratic countries believed that democracy was not working very well in their own country. Consider the Central and East European Barometer, which regularly asked citizens in the region: 'Are you satisfied with the development of democracy in your country?' Over the first decade of the transition, on average dissatisfaction exceeded satisfaction by 28 percentage points. And these results were remarkably consistent across countries and across time – negative opinions dominated in virtually every country and year. Other poll questions show similar results. This is not to say that citizens want to turn away from democracy and return to communism. Not at all. They just as consistently approve of democracy as the best form of government. They simply think that their countries fall short on this standard. They see their own democracies as low quality democracies.

How can we reconcile these two trends – that international organizations say that democracy is strong and progressing in the region, but that citizens are not very sanguine about how democracy is functioning? There are a number of possible resolutions. Maybe one of the sides is wrong. But this seems improbable. Though measurement of democracy is not simple, the fact that various organizations come up with similar results suggests that there has been real progress in the region. Similarly, the consistency of public opinion also indicates that citizens are genuinely feeling dissatisfaction and see something wrong with their democracies.

One resolution to this paradox may be in the distinction between democracy and the quality or functioning of democracy. There may be a difference between having a democracy and having a democracy that works well. There may even be differences in the way that people define the quality of a democracy. Citizens and scholars may be looking at very different things. Before reading on you may want to consider what you think a high quality or well-functioning democracy looks like. What characteristics does it have?

Quality as procedures: do institutions allow for democracy?

The paradox suggests we should think harder about what the quality of democracy is. There are at least four different ways that one could conceive the quality of democracy which I describe in each of the next four sections. Figure 15.1 portrays these conceptions graphically.

A first cut, in the centre of the figure, would equate democracy with democratic procedures. This conception begins with the standard definition of democracy as a political system in which the 'most powerful

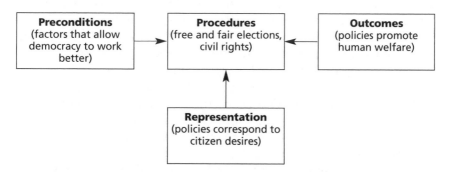

Figure 15.1   *Four conceptions of democratic quality*

collective decision makers are elected through fair, honest, and periodic elections in which candidates freely compete for votes and in which virtually all the adult population is eligible to vote' (Huntington, 1991: 7).

This definition is focused on rules or procedures. It looks for the presence of free elections, competition between parties for the people's vote, and the eligibility of all citizens to vote. Most scholars would add a number of additional conditions, like the maintenance of fundamental rights of speech, press, and assembly. For elections to matter, citizens have to be able to obtain information about politics and be able to persuade and organize their fellow citizens. The main point is that democracy is typically defined in terms of the existence and enforcement of rules that allow a people to rule themselves. Elections and rights are at the centre of these rules.

Though one might be tempted to say that a country is either democratic or not democratic according to this definition, there are gradations in the degree to which these conditions are met. A first conception of democratic quality would say that a country has a higher quality democracy when elections are freer, when more citizens are eligible to vote, and when citizens have a wider range of enforceable rights. An advantage of this conception is that it is possible to measure in a somewhat objective way. One can consider whether citizens are prevented from voting, whether there is fraud in vote counting, whether opposition candidates are persecuted or jailed, and whether the media give equal time to all sides.

In fact, as noted above, a number of organisations do attempt to measure democracy in this way. Thus, Freedom House (2012b) ranks countries based on a checklist including such elements as the presence of free and fair elections, whether those who are elected rule, whether there are competitive parties, and whether the opposition plays an important role and has actual power. These factors together produce a measure of what it calls political rights. Freedom House also measures the extent of civil liberties that includes freedom of expression and belief, associational and organizational rights, rule of law, and personal autonomy. This produces two scores on a 1 to 7 scale where 1 indicates the most free countries and 7 the least free.

Polity (Polity IV Project, 2012) uses a different set of indicators that includes the competitiveness of political participation, the openness and competitiveness of executive recruitment, and constraints on the chief executive. It ranges from +10 (most democratic) to −10 (most autocratic). The focus here is more on the specifically political aspects of democracy.

On both of these measures, Central and East Europe performs very well. Figure 15.2 shows the average of Freedom House's political rights

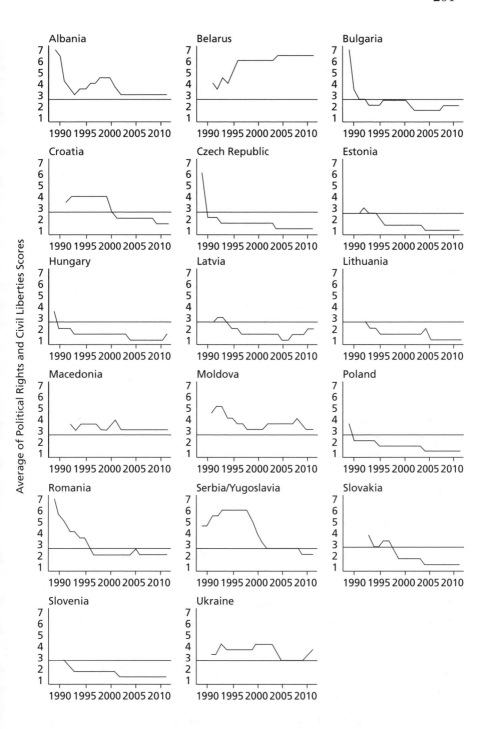

Figure 15.2 *Freedom House scores in Central and East Europe, 1990–2010*

and civil liberties scores for most of the countries in the region. As early as 1991, just two years after the fall of communism, Freedom House rated eight countries in the region as 'free' – a score of 2.5 or lower on their seven-point scale (the cut-off is indicated by the horizontal line). These countries were Bulgaria, Czechoslovakia (about to split into the Czech Republic and Slovakia), Estonia, Hungary, Latvia, Lithuania, Poland, and Slovenia. Polity gave out similar scores – those same countries received scores of between 7 and 10, among the highest.

What is also clear from the figure is the bifurcation between the countries that were consistently democratic and those that were not. The latter category includes Albania, Belarus, Macedonia, Moldova and Ukraine. A handful of countries moved from authoritarian politics to democratic politics. This includes Romania and Slovakia, which moved to the free category gradually over the 1990s, and Croatia and Serbia, which did the same in the 2000s. A final noteworthy trend is that there has been relatively little backsliding in the region. Democratic gains are typically consolidated rather than reversed – the lines move down or remain straight rather than going up.

This is not to say that things are perfect even in the higher-rated states. The issue of human rights still arises in these countries, typically with respect to minorities like the Roma throughout the region, Russians in the Baltics, Turks in Bulgaria, or Hungarians outside of Hungary. Indeed, the European Court of Human Rights receives proportionately far more cases from post-communist countries than from West Europe. Another sore spot is the press, which is frequently criticized for falling short on standards of objectivity and investigation of public officials.

Nevertheless, if one equates these measures with democratic quality, the quality of democracy in the region is relatively high. But should we stop there? While it appears that democracy exists in the region in the sense that elections are free and fair, can we say that democracy is the same as democratic quality? Maybe the existence of democracy is one thing and the quality of democracy is another. We might care as much what people do with these institutions as that they simply exist. Many would thus argue that we should go further than these democratic procedures and that is what the following conceptions do. Not surprisingly, on these alternative conceptions, post-communist countries usually rate less well.

Quality as preconditions: are citizens in a position to make democracy work?

While it might seem enough that countries hold free and fair elections while guaranteeing freedom of speech, press, and assembly, it is easy to see that even with these safeguards things might go wrong. Imagine a society where a small percentage of individuals control most of the wealth and the mass of citizens are living hand to mouth. Will elections in these circumstances produce real democracy or will elites be likely to exercise disproportionate influence not only over elections but over whichever party wins the elections? Indeed, such worries are rife in post-communist Europe. This leads some scholars to argue that procedural safeguards on democracy are not enough; they are in the words of the critics too minimalist. A number of other preconditions may be necessary for democracy to work as we wish. For elections to truly serve the common good, citizens must be in a position for them to matter.

In a sense the civil liberties mentioned in the previous section are one such precondition. How can democracy function without freedoms of speech, press, and all the rest? These freedoms are so fundamental to free elections that many scholars fold them into their definitions and assessments of democracy, but it is worth remembering that being free and participating in self-rule are two separate things. There are countries where elections are free but citizens have limited rights. The Baltic states have sometimes been called illiberal democracies because they have denied some rights to their Russian minorities. Conversely, one can imagine a liberalized autocracy where people do as they wish but have little choice of their rulers.

A more distinctive precondition might be a certain level of economic development. It is hard to imagine that citizens who are struggling to survive can make good use of elections. They may be too preoccupied to devote themselves to politics. And even when they do become interested, they may be susceptible to having their votes bought or influenced.

As far as post-communist Europe is concerned, there is a bright and a dark side on this score. On the one hand, these countries are not desperately poor. Most scholars would refer to them as 'middle income' – some on the high end of this category and others on the lower end. They have experienced considerable hardship since the transition especially in the early 1990s and today in the wake of the financial crisis (more about this at the end), but except among particular groups like the Roma, these countries have been able to maintain a reasonable standard of living for most citizens.

One can see this not just in incomes, but in what the World Bank calls human development (World Bank, 2012a). This concept combines income with health and education to see whether citizens have the capabilities to shape their own lives and participate in civic life, which is easier when education and basic healthcare are guaranteed. This inclusion of health and education actually helps the post-communist countries – they give their citizens more capabilities than one would expect given their incomes, though of course there is a range from countries that do very well on this measure, like Slovenia to those in South-east Europe, which have a substantial underclass.

A parallel worry is not just about dire poverty or lack of capabilities, but about a growing gap between rich and poor. As I noted at the start of the section, inequalities in wealth could be expected to translate into inequalities in political influence through both corrupt and legal means. Communist societies, as we noted in the previous chapter, were among the most equal in the world – everyone had nearly the same salary – but the transition to markets changed this. The emergence of millionaires and homeless have been some of the most eye-catching developments of the transition but, fortunately, these increases in inequality have not reached the extremes of Latin America. The standard measure of inequality, the Gini index, places them closer to the relatively equal countries of Western Europe and makes them more equal than the US (UNU-WIDER, 2008). But these trends do bear watching and worries that money buys influence are certainly prevalent in the region. For example, a recent corruption scandal in Slovakia revealed that high government officials were secretly meeting with prominent business people and campaign financing scandals in several countries have shown the same thing. While in Western Europe and the US one typically gets rich and then enters politics, in Central and East Europe one often enters politics in order to get rich.

Economics is not the only reason why democratic elections might not deliver their promise. Influence in politics depends not just on security, but on organization. It is hard for an individual by him or herself to have much effect on politics. Both learning about community problems as well as conveying this information to politicians depends on groups (Putnam, 1993). Indeed, the communists maintained power precisely by preventing citizens from forming independent groups that are referred to as civil society. Under communism, all groups from PTAs to birdwatchers had to be sponsored by the state.

One might expect civil society to revive after citizens were given the freedom to associate. In fact, post-communist citizens remain quite reluctant to join groups – not just those with explicit political aims like parties or labour unions, but also community groups, religious groups, and even sports and recreational clubs. The average citizen in the region joins far fewer voluntary organizations than their counterparts, not just in Western Europe, but in other new democracies as well (Howard, 2003). Without these organizational ties, citizens are less likely to get to know their fellow citizens much less work with them to solve public problems.

The problem extends into the political arena where citizens tend not to participate by signing petitions or even showing up at elections (Hafner-Fink *et al.*, 2011). Only about one in five citizens has signed a petition (compared with more than a majority in older democracies). Turnout in elections varies across the region – from a low of 39 per cent in Romania in 2008 to a high of over 85 per cent in the same country in 1990 – but on average citizens are not eager voters. On average, about 67 per cent of voters show up to vote and it appears that turnout has been gradually dropping over time by about 1.5 per cent per year (Czesnik, 2011). The reasons for the lack of participation are noteworthy too. One reason why citizens do not join groups is because they do not trust their fellow citizens and because they do not join groups, they never learn to trust, leading to a downward spiral. Whatever its cause, the upshot is that without a strong civil society citizens will be at the mercy of the rich and powerful and democracy will likely suffer.

A final precondition is the rule of law. The rule of law means that laws are enforced equally for all citizens. Without the rule of law there is little assurance that politicians will listen to citizens or that citizens will be protected from the state. This precondition is somewhat difficult to assess since violators will try to hide their violations, but one indicator that the rule of law is weak in a region is the very considerable immunity that government officials receive. While it is standard practice around the world to give officeholders some immunity for actions they commit in the line of duty, post-communist states have often granted lifetime immunity for all manner of infractions with predictable effects on the ethics of politicians.

To sum up, the claim in this conception is that without certain preconditions like reasonable standards of living, relative equality of wealth, civic engagement, and the rule of law, democratic elections will not produce true democracy. These claims are certainly plausible and in some cases are backed up by research. On the other hand, we see many of the same trends towards inequality and declining participation even the West. Similarly, we may not wish to give up on citizens simply because they are poor or lack other traits we associate with good citizenship. As the revolutions of 1989 showed, politics is not so deterministic. Citizens can effect change even under the least auspicious circumstances.

Quality as representation: are citizens actually ruling?

So far, we have considered democratic quality as the existence of democratic procedures or preconditions for democracy to work well. But

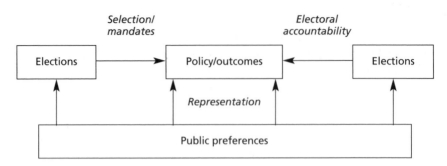

Figure 15.3   *Means of citizen control*

while these conceptions provide the scaffolding for democracy, they do not get at its inner mechanisms – the way that power is actually exercised. Democracy at its core means that the people rule and while elections give people the opportunity to rule by choosing the representatives they wish, this does not mean that those representatives listen to voters or even that voters put much thought into their choice.

A third conception of democratic quality thus asks whether citizens are getting what they want. Are citizens, considered as political equals, actually ruling? Citizens have two main tools to rule. One is elections, which they can use to both punish rulers and choose new ones. The other is their civil rights, which they can use to make their opinions heard both at elections and between elections. This section looks separately at whether citizens are ruling through these two means. Figure 15.3 provides a graphic representation of how citizens can rule.

Ruling through elections: accountability and selection

Elections are the most basic means of citizen rule, which is why they are so closely associated with democracy. What is less widely recognized is how elections give citizens two separate powers: the power to render a verdict on their current governors and policy and the power to select a set of possibly new governors and policies.

The first option is called electoral accountability. In a high quality democracy we would expect citizens to vote against incumbents who are performing badly and vote for those who are performing well. This not only rids the polity of bad politicians, it gives all politicians the incentive to do the best they can lest they lose office. We can say that citizens are ruling if they hold politicians accountable in this way.

Citizens in post-communist states do exceedingly well on this score. In fact, perhaps too well. Among the democratic countries, almost every parliamentary election in the region has led to the defeat of the incumbent government, sometimes in part, but often in whole. In the first place, consider how citizens rejected the ruling communists (or their successors) the first chance they had. In most countries, the old communists lost the first free elections, typically earning only about 10–15 per cent of the vote (exceptions include Bulgaria, Romania, and Yugoslavia). This came as something of a surprise given the organizational and publicity advantages of the communists, but it becomes more explicable when we remember their vast policy failings.

Even when we move to later elections, however, the trend of punishing incumbents continues. While incumbency is typically thought to carry benefits, in post-communist Europe it is mainly a cost unless backed up by authoritarian tactics. The average democratic government in the region came to power with 43 per cent of the vote and at the next election earned only 28 per cent, a drop of 15 per cent. Some of these defeats were truly dramatic, as when the ruling Democratic Left Alliance in Poland went from 47 per cent of the vote in 2001 to only 11 per cent in 2005. Some ruling parties in fact did not rise above the threshold for entering parliament at all. Of the parties that sat in government at election time, only about a third returned to government after elections and many of these were relatively small coalition partners.

This punishment of governing parties could be a good thing if voters were punishing them for their poor performance. And there is some evidence this is the case. Many studies have found that poor economic performance – whether high unemployment, low growth, or increasing inequality – have led voters to punish incumbents (Roberts, 2010; Tucker, 2006; Tworzecki, 2003). There is increasingly evidence that perceptions of corruption redound negatively on governments (Slomczynski and Shabad, 2012). In short, post-communist citizens have become adept at attributing blame to their governments and punishing them. This is all to the good for democratic quality.

But there are two negative sides to this story. One is that punishment may be too consistent. If governments have no chance of returning to office – if they know they are going to lose – then they have no incentive to perform well. Why do your best, if voters will still take revenge? The other is that this punishment does not always translate into support for the existing opposition. Rather voters often reject both the incumbent and the opposition and turn rather towards brand-new parties. While this novelty could be good, these new parties often lack strong ties with the electorate and have little experience in the nuts and bolts of governing and legislating.

Punishment and reward are not the only functions of elections or the only way that voters can use them to rule. In fact, there is a better case that voters should use elections not just to retroactively assess the past, but to proactively choose the future. This means that voters should look at the policy slates on offer and choose the one that is closest to their preferences with the expectation that those parties will follow through on their campaign promises. This conception is referred to as mandates or selection.

How well do post-communist countries fare on this conception? Perhaps not as well as on accountability. In the first place, the party platforms on offer are often vague or confusing. Most parties have not been around for long – both because the transition is so short and because of the high level of party turnover – so they have not developed strong reputations. Parties have also been hesitant to make definite promises and often distinguish themselves mainly by criticizing incumbents or emphasizing symbolic issues. While a study described later found that citizens can connect to parties, their task is not easy and becomes particularly difficult in countries with a lot of turnover and new parties. The Baltic republics and Poland have fared particularly poorly in this respect.

Voters also cannot count on parties to follow through on their promises or ideologies. It is easy to single out particular examples of this. Left-wing parties in some countries like Hungary and Poland have actually been stronger advocates of free markets than their right-wing counterparts. In one particularly notorious case, quoted in several different chapters of this book, the Hungarian Prime Minister was secretly taped telling fellow party members, 'We lied morning, noon, and night' (above, p. 204). There are even reversals in the opposite direction as right-wing parties discover that they are not ready to reduce the size of government or the welfare state, as in the Czech Republic.

This failure to follow through may not be entirely the fault of these governments. As small countries at the mercy of the global economy not to mention the World Bank, the IMF and now the European Union, they cannot simply do as they wish. A global recession puts even the best laid plans to rest. Nevertheless, the selection conception may not give voters as much control as we would hope.

Ruling over policy: correspondence and responsiveness

Elections are not the only means of ruling. Citizens can also have a direct impact on policy whether simply by holding views that politicians know are popular or by actually advocating, lobbying, and protesting. It is thus worth looking at the direct links between citizen preferences and policy. Is public opinion reflected in policy?

There are a number of ways to assess whether citizens are getting what they want. One is to compare the policy preferences of citizens with the preferences of the parties they vote for. This is termed called party representation. If parties hold the same beliefs as their voters, this gives us some assurance that they are representing those voters.

Do voters actually hold the same positions as their representatives on the major issues of post-communist politics like privatization, social welfare or church–state relations? One large study to look at this issue found that in fact voters and their preferred parties do share similar positions on these issues (Kitschelt *et al.*, 1999). For example, right-wing, nationalist and religiously inclined voters in Poland tend to support parties that feel the same way. This correspondence is not perfect – it is strongest on the left–right divide and on the most salient issues in politics. Parties also tend to be more polarized than their voters – they place themselves more to the extremes of the spectrum than their more centrist supporters. Nevertheless, the fact that voters largely share positions with their parties tells us that at least some representation is going on.

One could go further and look not just at whether parties represent their own voters, but at whether policy as a whole represents the public as a whole. This moves beyond looking at just policy positions to consider actual policy. Here the situation is trickier and the evidence more equivocal. At fairly broad levels, we can see a degree of correspondence. Voters in all of these countries largely favoured a move to a market economy and to joining the EU, to mention just two relatively prominent issues. And the speed with which countries moved towards a market economy and towards Europe is more or less related to public desires to do so (Roberts, 2010).

Consider the fact that over the 1990s, many more citizens in the region said that they supported the free market than opposed it. The Central and Eastern Eurobarometer, that asked this question in ten countries from 1991 to 1998, found that 63 per cent were in favour of a market economy, while 37 per cent were against, a difference of 25 per cent. In this respect, post-communist Europe differed from other democratizing regions like Latin America where the necessity of market reforms ran head on into major public opposition with the result that Latin America was wracked by massive protest and riots (Bunce, 2001). Post-communist countries have been fortunate to avoid this unrest, among other reasons, because the public and elites are more in accord on the direction of the country (Greskovits, 1998).

At a finer-grain level, however, the evidence is not in. It is easy to find issues where the public opposed government policy. Social welfare may be the best example. Most countries have engaged in some cuts in social programmes – whether raising the retirement age, introducing co-payments for healthcare, or ending rent controls. Such austerity is typically opposed by voters, though politicians frequently complain that they had no choice but to cut the budget in some way in order to avoid the wrath of international markets. Many market reforms like privatization of state-owned firms or price increases have met similar opposition. Though citizens do not want to return to the centrally planned economy of communism and have supported the general project of adopting Western economic institutions, many specific changes have been unpopular.

The amount of representation, however, is still very much uncertain. We do not really know the extent to which the majority gets its way. One prominent area of research is of inequalities in representation – whether certain groups get their way more than others – an issue that has come to the fore in all democracies. A recent study has found that the poor in particular are disadvantaged in representation (Enyedi and Markowski, 2011). Politicians appear to be listening, but we are not sure how much and to whom. Overall, there is reasonable evidence that voters have some degree of control in the region. On a number of policies, voters get what they want, though not when austerity takes centre stage. They are also adept at holding politicians accountable for the economy, but not so much at choosing the governments they want in advance.

Whether citizen control is what we want from democracy is another question. Yes, democracy means that the people can rule, but citizens can be as flawed as politicians. What happens if citizens do not know the costs and benefits of particular policies, like pension reforms or enterprise privatization? Or if they are uninformed about the policies that parties are offering for the future? Politics is just a small part of people's lives and it is a lot to expect them to devote much attention to it. While lack of public control means that politicians can do as they wish, the presence of public control means that unconsidered views focused on the short term may carry the day. For this reason, the technocratic (and undemocratic) conception of politics – that is, rule by non-partisan experts like economists – has been relatively popular in the region.

Quality as outcomes: do citizens benefit from democracy?

If the focus on preconditions starts at one end of politics and representation looks at the middle, then another way of evaluating democracy is to consider the results it delivers. For many citizens, this is the ultimate test of democratic quality. A good democracy is one that delivers the goods. And in fact this is the way that voters typically judge their governments. If a government has done well – produced jobs and economic growth, reduced crime, avoided war and civil unrest – then they will vote to re-elect it; if it has performed badly, they will vote to throw the bums out.

This standard of judging politics is sometimes called substantive representation. It asks not whether citizens get what they want as in the previous conception, but, to paraphrase the Rolling Stones, if they get what they need. Does government produce policies in the best interests of citizens? Because citizens often lack knowledge of policy and politics, what they want and what is best for them may differ. For example, it is sometimes the case that a country needs to tighten its belt to prevent it from going bankrupt, but belt-tightening polices are rarely popular.

The rub is in deciding what outcomes are in the best interests of citizens. Some are relatively uncontroversial. Prosperity is undoubtedly good, though there will be debates on how that growth is distributed and whether it is environmentally sustainable. Similarly important would be that governments manage to keep citizens out of poverty – especially the most vulnerable, such as, children and seniors – and provide them (whether through the state or markets) with universally available healthcare, affordable and available housing, and a high quality educational system.

It is not easy to judge how well Central and East European countries meet these standards. Prosperity differs across countries. Every country in the region suffered a massive recession at the start of the transition period with GDP falling by a fifth or more. The fact that every country met such a recession indicates that governments may not be at fault here. This may be the consequence of moving from central planning to markets, though there are arguments that some governments (for example, Poland) overshot the mark and that others hurt citizens by not undertaking necessary reforms (much of South-east Europe).

Later in the transition, most countries experienced a period of strong economic growth (though often with hiccups due to bad policy choices or the international economy). The recent financial crisis (on which more below) has shown some of this growth to have been unsustainable. Nevertheless, from a global perspective, these countries achieved a lot in turning their economies around under adverse conditions, at least until the recent crisis.

On social policies, results are a mixed bag. Communist regimes guaranteed jobs for all as well as healthcare, pensions, and housing though all of this with an asterisk – jobs were poorly paid (and the goods that could be bought with salaries were in short supply), while the universal social benefits were often of poor quality or subject to rationing. Post-communist governments maintained some of these guarantees – particularly in healthcare but to an extent in pensions and housing as well. Quality also saw improvements in places like healthcare with the importation of Western medicines, technology, and know-how.

These numbers, however, do not do justice to the controversy behind many of these policies which have been criticized as being bought and paid for by influential groups. Corruption is probably the outcome where these countries have encountered the most intractable problems and even suffered backsliding. Transparency International, which performs surveys of businessmen to assess levels of corruption, puts several countries like Romania (75 in the world), Bulgaria and Serbia (86), Albania (95), Moldova (112), Belarus (143), and Ukraine (152) close to the bottom of the list (Transparency International, 2012). The typical corrupt practice in these countries is probably the bribe paid by a businessman to receive a state contract or by a citizen to a state employee to receive benefits they are entitled to.

A more comprehensive way of evaluating policies can be found in a series of ratings of good governance carried out by the World Bank. The World Bank has surveyed a large number of citizens, firms, business information providers, public sector and non-government organizations to get a sense of how well different countries perform on measures like government effectiveness (how well the bureaucracy works) and regulatory quality (how efficient policy is). Surveys are not a perfect way of assessing how well government works, but many of those surveyed are experts and the large number of respondents probably does capture important tendencies.

Comparing scores on these indicators across the region and with West Europe, we find a degree of variation in the region (Berg-Schlosser, 2004). As one might expect, the richer and more democratic Central and East European countries fall slightly below the West, though at similar levels to Greece or Italy. The less developed members of the region move to the bottom of this pack and stack up toward the middle of the table worldwide. In fact, there is a strong correlation between these measures of governance and measures of democracy by Freedom House.

All of these policies also have measurable consequences for human welfare. In many countries life expectancy dropped after the transition, which may be connected with the transitional recessions. Recently these numbers have recovered, a product both of economic growth, healthier lifestyles, and improved healthcare (Safaei, 2012). Though pensioners have complained about their declining quality of life, in fact poverty rates among the elderly are relatively low as the old make up an increasingly large portion of the population not to mention voters (Ashgar, 2006). Poverty has certainly risen since the transition, though all the countries do provide a safety net, albeit one with significant holes.

In a sense, substantive representation is what democracy, not to mention politics, is all about. What we care about is the welfare of citizens and policy is what determines this. This is probably the explanation for the paradox discussed in the first section: that citizens in the region see themselves as living in low quality democracies. What they perceive is corrupt politicians who enrich themselves and fight with each other rather than choosing the best policies for the country.

On the other hand, these outcomes get better at something that might be called the quality of governance. Good governance is not exactly democracy and we might prefer to focus more strictly on politics when we talk about the quality of democracy, especially since there are disagreements on what counts as good governance. We should also not pretend that democracy and good policy always go together. There are certainly reasons why they should – politicians detached from the public may simply pursue their own personal interests. But there are also reasons why they may not – in particular, voters may not know what is good for them. While many studies of the region have found that democracy and good outcomes do go together and perhaps even support each other in the region, this is not inevitable (Commander and Frye, 1999).

The past and the future of democratic quality

Though it is clear that democracy in the region does suffer from flaws – low levels of participation and considerable corruption stand out most of all – it is also worth noting how much has been achieved and against considerable odds. Most countries in the region are stable democracies and became so relatively quickly after exiting brutal dictatorships. It also seems that citizens have the tools to discipline their elected officials and that those officials do keep an ear to the public, albeit imperfectly and perhaps only to certain segments of society.

These achievements, moreover, come against the background of a communist legacy that left them without any political parties (except for the Communist Party), or any tradition of bargaining or compromise, and had decimated civil society. One might note that communism did bequeath relatively equal societies and an educated and mostly middle-class citizenry, but most observers at the start of the transition were nevertheless sceptical that democracy could quickly flourish in this situation.

These countries were further handicapped by the nature of the transition. Most of them installed their democratic institutions in the midst of severe recessions. Meanwhile, the process of privatizing almost the entire economy created enormous potential for corrupt deals. As small, middle-income states surrounded by larger and richer neighbours, they had relatively little freedom to choose the policy paths they desired. They had to stick to the straight and narrow or be battered by global markets and rejected by the European Union. And there was no Marshall Plan to help these countries construct their democracies as there was for Western Europe after the Second World War. That so much was achieved under such adverse circumstances is worthy of admiration.

What does the future hold for democracy in these countries? Until a few years ago, the prognosis for the region was good. The fast starters had maintained democracy and even consolidated it, while the slow starters seemed to have picked up the pace and most joined the EU with only minor delays. At least outside of the former Soviet Union there was only forward progress and little backsliding.

But with the current financial crisis, this may be changing. The crisis has hit the European periphery as hard as anywhere. The Baltics have had to make enormous cuts in salaries and state services to avoid bankruptcy, while Hungary, Bulgaria and others have needed help from the IMF. This has led to a backlash against the ruling parties in many countries. This is to be expected when the economy turns bad, but there are some indications that this backlash is more than just a replacement of incumbents with the opposition.

The Hungarian case is the most disturbing. The elections in 2010 wiped out the ruling Socialists and gave the conservative-nationalist Fidesz more than a two-thirds majority, with which they had carte blanche to pass whatever legislation they wished. The election also gave significant votes to a far-right party with a penchant for anti-Semitic rhetoric who often teamed up with the government.

Fidesz went on to use this power to write a new constitution while barely consulting other parties. This constitution changed the electoral system to almost guarantee them a majority in the future. It also gave them enormous authority over the judicial system and the media among other areas (see Chapter 2). Hungary has not yet become a dictatorship, but the warning signs are there. While there are reasons peculiar to Hungary for why it is happening there – in particular, a tradition of nationalist politics and a suspicion of the Europe which deprived it of territory – the same dissatisfaction and the same turn to populists and nationalist is occurring elsewhere. It is yet to be seen whether the democratic gains in the region survive the economic buffeting they have recently received and the buffeting that may still be to come.

Guide to Further Reading

An excellent *general history* of the whole region is Janos (2000). Crampton and Crampton (1996) provide a useful historical atlas that illustrates the shifting nature of state borders in the twentieth century. Norman Davies' magisterial survey of Europe (1996) redresses the tendency of Western historians of 'Europe' to ignore the whole region, and Mazower (1998) sets out the wider pan-European context in the twentieth century. Mazower's history of the Balkans (2000) challenges Western prejudices about that region, as does Todorova (1997). Kundera's deliberately provocative essay (1984) sparked off a wide-ranging debate about the identity of 'Central Europe', and outstanding responses to this essay are gathered in Schopflin and Wood (1989). An illuminating perspective on national and ethnic issues by a leading historian of the region is Ingrao (1999). Inter-war history is well covered in Rothschild (1974), as is the communist period by Rothschild and Wingfield (2000). The meaning of the 1989 Revolutions is discussed in a most engaging way by Kumar (2001), and in a wider perspective by Lawson, Armbruster and Cox (2010). A systematic analysis of the 'return to Europe' is provided in Vachudova (2005).

There are still rather few *single-country monographs* that cover post-communist developments in Poland, Hungary, and the Czech Republic, but a good place to start is the Postcommunist States and Nations Series. Cox (2005), Dimitrov (2001), Henderson (2002), Roper (2000), and Smith *et al.* (2002) are all helpful in placing developments into a broader historical perspective, although they are now a little dated. The country chapters in Wolchik and Curry (2011) and Ramet (2010) help to bring the story up to date, as do the annual contributions to the Political Year Databook published as a special issue of the *European Journal of Political Research*. Given the time-lags of academic publishing, the best sources on more recent developments tend to be journalistic. The *Financial Times* remains the best daily newspaper for the region as a whole, but web-based sources such www.euroobserver.com, www.euractiv.com and the Economist's *Eastern Approaches* (http://www.economist.com/blogs/easternapproaches) are generally reliable. Many of the countries in the region also have their own English-language publications: the *Baltic Times*, for example, is a good source of information. In addition, election reports written by well-informed scholars are periodically posted on the European Parties and Referendums Network page (http://www.sussex.ac.uk/sei/1-4-2-8.html).

Mazower (2000) provides a brief historical overview of the *Western Balkans*; for Yugoslavia as a whole, see Lampe (2000). Outstanding accounts of the wars by journalists are Little and Silber (1996) and Sudetic (1998). Among the best academic accounts of the crisis of communist Yugoslavia are Cohen (1993) and Pavkovic (2000). Individual country studies are Tanner (1998) on Croatia, and Judah (2009) on the Serbs. On Kosovo, see the Independent International Commission on Kosovo (2000) and Judah (2008). On Bosnia, see Bieber (2005) and Bose (2002). On Albania, see Batt (2008), Vickers and Pettifer (2009) and Poulton (1995). More policy-oriented reports on the state of the region include International Commission on the Balkans (2005), and Batt (2004 and 2005). Essential for current political and economic analysis are the reports on the region of the International Crisis Group (www.crisisgroup.org) and the European Stability Initiative (www.esiweb.org).

The two standard histories of *Ukraine* are Magocsi (2nd edn, 2010) and Subtelny (4th edn, 2009). Wilson (2009) covers both history and the period since independence. Yekelchyk (2007) mainly covers the twentieth century. On politics since independence, the most analytical is D'Anieri (2006). See also Aslund (2009a), while on the Orange Revolution there is Wilson (2005a) and McFaul and Aslund (2006). On the Ukrainian economy, there is Aslund (2009), and on foreign policy Moroney *et al.* (2002) and Wolczuk (2002). Good works on *Moldova* are harder to find, but the standard work is King (2000). On *Belarus* the main book is Wilson (2011), but also try Garnett and Legvold (1999), Balmaceda (2003), Korosteleva, Lawson and Marsh (2003) and White, Korosteleva and Löwenhardt (2005).

For a comprehensive study of how *EU enlargement* took place and the process of conditionality, see Vassiliou (2007), Schimmelfennig and Sedelmeier (2005), Grabbe (2006), Jacoby (2004), Pridham (2005), and Vachudova (2005). On post-accession conditionality, see Sedelmeier (2012) as well as Epstein and Sedelmeier (2009); for an opposing view on pre-accession conditionality, see Hughes *et al.* (2004), and on post-accession conditionality Gallagher (2009). Those who are pressed can find a précis in Haughton (2007 and 2011a). On the question of the influence of the newer member states on the European Union, see Copsey and Pomorska (2010 and 2013). On the performance of the new member states within the EU see Copsey (2012) for the case of Poland. On the impact of the EU on political parties, see Haughton (2009) or Bil and Szczerbiak (2008).

On the *international politics of the post-communist region* more generally, see the websites of the regional initiatives discussed in this chapter. Those that concern Central and Eastern Europe include the

Central European Initiative (http://www.ceinet.org/home.php); the Council of the Baltic Sea States (http://www.cbss.st); the Organisation for Black Sea Economic Cooperation (http://www.bsec.organization. org); the Regional Cooperation Council (http://www.rcc.int); and Visegrad (http://visegradgroup.eu). The EU's External Action Service provides official information on the Eastern Partnership at http:// eeas.europa.eu/eastern/index_en.htm. Academic coverage of these groups in their formative periods is given in Cottey (1999). Book-length treatment of the original CEFTA is provided by Dangerfield (2000). A beautifully produced official account of Visegrad cooperation is given in Jagodzinski (2006), which also provides unique participant and external assessments of its achievements.

Political leadership after the 1989 revolutions is theoretically addressed in Przeworski (1991) and Colton and Tucker (1995). Higley *et al.* (1996; 1997) describe the formation of post-communist elites while Hanley *et al.* (1996) and Eyal *et al.* (2000) provide data on elite recruitment. Blondel and Müller-Rommel (2001) provide case studies of cabinet government while Baylis (1996), Protsyk (2005) and Sedelius (2006) examine intra-executive conflicts. Rose, Mishler and Haerpfer (1998) focus on popular attitudes to leadership, while Rose (2009) connects economic transformation to public opinion and electoral shifts. Baylis (1996) and Taras (1998) examine early post-communist presidents, and Bunce and Wolchik (2011) examine post-communist authoritarian leaders. Elgie and Moestrup (2009) compare the effects of semi-presidential systems on democratization across the region.

Electoral institution design in Central and Eastern Europe has received extensive coverage from scholars, especially in the years immediately following democratic transition. Since the early surge in interest in this topic, the study of Central and Eastern European electoral system change has tended to be integrated into global comparative analyses. Detailed discussions can be found in Elster (1996) as well as in Elster *et al.* (1998). Kitschelt *et al.* (1999) provides a slightly different angle on similar material, while Birch *et al.* (2002) includes case studies of electoral institution choice in eight states. There are also a number of studies of electoral system design in individual countries, including those found in Colomer (2004) as well as in Shugart and Wattenberg (2001).

Electoral system effects in Central and Eastern Europe have been studied mainly in journal articles and book chapters, including most notably Ishiyama (1996); Shvetsova (1999); Pettai and Kreuzer (2001); Kostadinova (2002); Bielasiak (2002 and 2005), and several of the chapters in the Colomer and Shugart and Wattenberg volumes mentioned above. Birch (2003) is a book-length treatment of the topic. In addition, the series of volumes entitled 'Founding Elections in Eastern Europe' edited by Hans-Dieter Klingemann and Charles Lewis Taylor and published by Sigma Press in Germany provides very useful material on individual countries.

Electoral behaviour (turnout and vote choice) in the region has been studied in numerous country-specific studies as well as a wide range of comparative analyses. Literature on this topic can be divided into early studies that sought to understand how voters in the merging democratic states in the Central and Eastern European region were reacting to the new democratic institutions in which they were embedded (e.g. Bielesiak (2002); Kitschelt *et al.* (1999); Millard (2004); Rose and Mishler (1998); Tucker (2001); Tworzecki (2002), Evans and Whitefield (1993)). Since then, scholars have mainly focused on changes in electoral behaviour in the region in response to developments such as democratic change, EU accession and the post-2008 economic downturn (e.g. Pacek *et al.* (2009); Pop-Eleches (2010); Tavits (2005; 2008a); van der Brug, Franklin and Toka (2008)). Studies that look specifically at electoral participation (turnout) include Birch, (2003, chap. 3), Kostadinova (2003; 2009), and Pacek *et al.* (2009).

For the early stages of *legislative developments* in Central and Eastern Europe, see Agh (1994), and Olson and Norton (1996). Committees are examined in Longley and Davidson (1998) and Olson and Crowther (2002), and parliamentary deputies in Ilonszki and Edinger (2008). Specific legislatures are compared in Kopecky (2001) and Olson and Norton (2008b), and seven CEE parliaments are compared over two decades in Olson and Ilonszki (2012b). Whitmore (2004) provides a detailed recent study of the Ukrainian legislature.

A survey of the first phase of *party development* in the region is contained in Lewis (2000) and more recent details of parties in the first eight countries to join the EU can be found in Jungerstam-Mulders (2006). Millard (2004) offers a useful analysis of party development in selected countries and the context in which they work. Valuable studies of major party families are found in Bozoki and Ishiyama (2002), Grzymala-Busse (2002), Szczerbiak and Hanley (2006) and Hanley (2007). Comparative studies of particular areas of party development are given in van Biezen (2003), Lewis and Webb (2003) and Webb and White (2007), while studies of parties in the context of European integration can be found in Lewis and Mansfeldova (2006), Haughton (2011b) and Lewis and Markowski (2011).

On *revolutions and mass upheavals* in CEE, see, among others, Bernhard (1993), Bunce and Wolchik (2011), Cirtautas (1997), Dahrendorf (1990), Ekiert (1996), Garton Ash (1985 and 1993),

Hayden (2006), Jowitt (1992), Kenney (2002), Kubik (1994), Ost (1990), and Touraine (1983). On the pre- and post-revolutionary *civil society*, as well as protest actions, see in particular Cohen and Arato (1992), Crowley and Ost (2001), Ekiert and Kubik (1999), Havel (1985), Howard (2003), Keane (1988), Konrad (1983), Michnik (1985), and Mudde (2007). Freedom House publishes in-depth analyses and current rankings of developments in the areas of *civil society and independent media* (as well as other fields, such as governance, elections and corruption) in its annual Nations in Transit volume (see Habdank-Kolaczkowska and Walker (2011) and http://www.freedomhouse.org).

Theoretical and empirical analyses of *popular attitudes* have been offered by Linz and Stepan (1996), Rose, Mischler and Haerpfer (1998), and Plasser, Ulram and Waldrauch (1998), among others.

For those interested in *varieties of capitalism*, Bohle and Greskovits (2009) or Myant and Drahokoupil (2012) provide excellent starting points. Concerning the political economy of transition in Eastern Europe and the post-communist bloc as a whole, Orenstein (2001), Balcerowicz (1994), and Gowan (1995) provide a good background. Cameron (2007) and Vachudova (2005) provide important analyses of the effects of EU accession on the political economy of Eastern European countries. Atoyan (2010) provides an excellent in-depth analysis of the financial crisis, its effects on the countries of Central and Eastern Europe, and the resulting effects on pre-crisis growth models in post-communist countries. Aslund (2009b) provides a strictly economic view of the crisis in these countries.

On *post-socialist capitalism* in Eastern Europe, see Martin (2012). For a detailed study focusing on one country in particular, including details on questions of poverty and inequality, see Hardy (2009). For the pioneering study of managerial capitalism see Eyal *et al.* (1998), and for a detailed study of entrepreneurs, see Laki and Szalai (2006). For detailed analysis and information on poverty and inequality, see the publications of the World Bank and especially Dudwick *et al.* (2005). For initial indications of the effects of the current economic crisis on living standards and poverty in Eastern Europe and the 'transition countries' more widely, see EBRD (2011).

Munck and Verkuilen (2002) discuss ways to measure *democracy*, while Freedom House (2012b) provides information about democratic changes in the post-communist region across a variety of indicators. Howard (2003) is best on matters of participation and civil society. On voting patterns, see Tworzecki (2003) and Tucker (2006), as well as the literature cited above. Kitschelt *et al.* (1999) look at the relation between voters and parties. A survey of many of the main indicators of democratic and governance quality in Central and East Europe can be found in Berg-Schlosser (2004). Roberts (2010) discusses conceptual-isztions of democratic quality and looks at representation in the region.

Given the time-lags of academic publishing, the best sources on more *recent developments* tend to be journalistic and electronic. The *Financial Times* provides the best daily coverage of the region as a whole; more comprehensive reports on current developments are provided by Radio Free Europe/Radio Liberty, available online at http://www.rferl.org/section/eastern_europe/173.html. The large and rapidly changing world of internet sources is perhaps best approached through the portals that are maintained by larger academic institutions, such as British Library in London (http://www.bl.uk/reshelp/findhelprestype/webres/slavonicinternetresources/slavoniclinks.html), the University of Pittsburgh (www.ucis.pitt.edu/reesweb/), the Bodleian Library at Oxford (www.bodley.ox.ac.uk/dept/slavonic/guide.htm), and the School of Slavonic and East European Studies in London (http://www.ssees.ucl.ac.uk/dirctory.htm). Several academic periodicals deal specifically with the politics of the Central and East European region, including *Communist and Post-Communist Studies* (quarterly), *East European Politics* (formerly the *Journal of Communist Studies and Transition Politics*, quarterly), *East European Politics and Societies* (quarterly), *Europe-Asia Studies* (ten issues annually), and *Problems of Post-Communism* (six issues annually).

Bibliography

Agh, Attila (ed.) (1994) *Emergence of East Central European Parliaments: The First Steps*. Budapest: Hungarian Center of Democracy Studies Foundation.

Agh, Attila (1995) 'Partial Consolidation of the East-Central European Parties: The Case of the Hungarian Socialist Party', *Party Politics*, 1(4): 491–514.

Agh, Attila (1996) 'Political Culture and System Change in Hungary,' in Fritz Plasser and Andreas Pribersky (eds), *Political Culture in East Central Europe*. Aldershot: Avebury: 127–48.

Allam, M. (2009) 'The Adoption of the Euro in New Member States: Repercussions of the Financial Crisis', EIPASCOPE, no. 1: 27–34.

Almond, Gabriel, and G. Bingham Powell (eds) (1983) *Comparative Politics Today*. Boston, MA: Little, Brown.

Appel, Hilary and Orenstein, Mitchell (2013) 'Ideas Versus Resources: Explaining the Flat Tax and Pension Privatization Revolutions in Eastern Europe and the Former Soviet Union', *Comparative Political Studies*, 46(2), (February): 123–52.

Ashgar, Zaidi (2006) 'Poverty of Elderly People in EU25'. Policy Brief. Vienna: European Centre for Social Welfare Policy and Research.

Aslund, Anders (2009a) *How Ukraine Became a Market Economy and Democracy*. Washington, DC: Peterson Institute.

Aslund, Anders (2009b) 'The East European Financial Crisis'. CASE Network Studies and Analyses, CASE – Center for Social and Economic Research.

Atoyan, Ruben (2010) 'Beyond the Crisis: Revisiting Eastern Europe's Growth Model'. IMF Working Paper, European Department, International Monetary Fund.

Auers, Daunis (2012) 'Election Briefing No.66: Europe and the Early Latvian Election of September 17 2011', EPERN Election Briefings.

Bakke, Elisabeth (2012) 'The Czech Party System 20 Years after the Velvet Revolution' in Elisabeth Bakke and Ingo Peters (eds), *20 Years since the Fall of the Berlin Wall. Transitions, State Break-Up and Democratic Politics in Central Europe and Germany*. Berlin: Berliner Wissenschafts-Verlag: 221–47.

Balcerowicz, Leszek (1994) 'Understanding Postcommunist Transitions,' *Journal of Democracy*, 5(4): 75–89.

Balmaceda, Margarita (ed.) (2003) *Independent Belarus: Domestic Developments, Regional Dynamics and Implications for the West*. Cambridge, MA: Harvard University Press.

Batt, Judy (ed.) (2004) *The Western Balkans: Moving On*. Chaillot Paper no. 70, October. Paris: EU Institute for Security Studies.

Batt, Judy (2005) *The Question of Serbia*. Chaillot Paper no. 81, August. Paris: EU Institute for Security Studies.

Batt, Judy (2006) 'Cross-border Minorities and European Integration in South East Europe: the Hungarians and Serbs compared' in John McGarry and

282

Michael Keating (eds), *European Integration and the Nationalities Question*. London: Routledge.

Batt, Judy (ed.) (2008) *Is There an Albanian Question?* Chaillot Paper no. 107, Paris: EU Institute for Security Studies.

Baylis, Thomas A. (1996) 'Presidents Versus Prime Ministers: Shaping Executive Authority in Eastern Europe,' *World Politics*, 48(3) (April): 297–323.

Benes, Karoly (2009) 'Whose "Sphere of Influence"? Eastern Partnership Summit in Prague', Central Asia and Caucasus Analyst, 3 June, available at: www.cacianalyst.org/newsite/newsite/?q=node/5122

Benes, V. and Karlas, J. (2010) 'The Czech Presidency', in N. Copsey and T. Haughton, (eds) *JCMS Annual Review of the European Union*, vol. 49.

Berg-Schlosser, Dirk (2004) 'The Quality of Democracies in Europe as Measured by Current Indicators of Democratization and Good Governance,' *Journal of Communist Studies and Transition Politics*, 20(1): 28–55.

Bernhard, Michael (1993) *The Origins of Democratization in Poland*. New York: Columbia University Press.

Bernhard, Michael, and Ekrem Karakoc (2007) 'Civil Society and the Legacies of Dictatorship,' *World Politics*, 59(4) (July): 539–67.

Bernhard, Michael, Christopher Reenock, and Timothy Nordstrom (2003) 'Economic Performance and Survival in New Democracies: Is There a Honeymoon Effect?', *Comparative Political Studies*, 36(4) (May): 404–31.

Bieber, Florian (2005) *Post-War Bosnia: Ethnicity, Inequality and Public Sector Governance*. Basingstoke: Palgrave Macmillan.

Bielesiak, Jack (2002) 'The Institutionalization of Electoral and Party Systems in Post-communist Europe', *Comparative Politics*, 34(2): 189–210.

Bielasiak, Jack (2005) 'Party Competition in Emerging Democracies: Representation and Effectiveness in Post-Communism and Beyond', *Democratization*, 12 (3): 331–56.

Bil, M. and Szczerbiak, A. (2008) 'When in doubt, (re-)turn to domestic politics? The (non-) impact of the EU on party politics in Poland.' EPERN Working Paper, no. 20, May.

Birch, Sarah (2003) *Electoral Systems and Political Transformation in Post-communist Europe*. Basingstoke: Palgrave Macmillan.

Birch, Sarah (2007a) 'Electoral Systems and Electoral Misconduct', *Comparative Political Studies*, 40(12) (December): 1533–56.

Birch, Sarah (2007b) 'Electoral Systems,' in Stephen White, Judy Batt and Paul G. Lewis (eds), *Developments in Central and East European Politics 4*. Basingstoke: Palgrave Macmillan: 161–73.

Birch, Sarah (2011) *Electoral Malpractice*. Oxford: Oxford University Press.

Birch, Sarah, Frances Millard, Kieran Williams and Marina Popescu (2002) *Embodying Democracy: Electoral System Design in Post-communist Europe*. Basingstoke: Palgrave Macmillan.

Blondel, Jean, and Ferdinand Müller-Rommel (eds) (2001), *Cabinets in Eastern Europe*. Basingstoke: Palgrave Macmillan.

Bochsler, Daniel (2010) *Territory and Electoral Rules in Post-Communist Democracies*. Basingstoke: Palgrave Macmillan.

Bohle, Dorothee (2010) *East European Transformations and the Paradoxes of Transnationalization*. European University Institute Working Paper. Florence.

Bohle, Dorothee and Bela Greskovits (2009) 'Varieties of Capitalism and Capitalism,' *European Journal of Sociology*, 50(3): 355–86.

Börzel, T. (2009) (ed.) *Coping with Accession to the European Union: New Modes of Environmental Governance*. Basingstoke: Palgrave Macmillan.

Bose, Sumantra (2002) *Bosnia After Dayton: Nationalist Partition and International Intervention*. Oxford: Oxford University Press.

Boulhol, Hervé, Sowa, Agnieszka, Golinowska, Stanislawa and Sicari, Patrizio (2012) 'Improving the Health Care system in Poland', *OECD Economics Department Working Papers*, no. 957, Paris: OECD, May, at http://www. oecd-ilibrary.org/docserver/download/fulltext/5k9b7bn5qzvd.pdf?expires= 1350300042&id=id&accname=guest&checksum=D2715CF56F59318C3B 0E22B27F94CE5A.

Bozoki, Andras and John T. Ishiyama (eds) (2002) *The Communist Successor Parties of Central and Eastern Europe*. Armonk, NY: Sharpe.

Brinton, Crane (1965) *The Anatomy of Revolution*. New York: Harper & Row.

Brubaker, Rogers (1996) *Nationalism Reframed: Nationhood and the National Question in the New Europe*. Cambridge and New York: Cambridge University Press.

Buiter, W. and Grafe, C. (2004) 'Anchor, Float or Abandon Ship – Exchange Rate Regimes in Selected Advanced Transition Economies'. Discussion Paper 3184, January. London: Centre for Economic Policy Research.

Bunce, Valerie (2001) 'Democratization and Economic Reform,' *Annual Review of Political Science*, 4: 43–65.

Bunce, Valerie J. and Sharon L. Wolchik (2006) 'Favorable Conditions and Electoral Revolutions,' *Journal of Democracy*, 17(4).

Bunce, Valerie J. and Sharon L. Wolchik (2011) *Defeating Authoritarian Leaders in Postcommunist Countries*. Cambridge and New York: Cambridge University Press.

Cameron, David R. (2007) 'Postcommunist Democracy: The Impact of the European Union,' *Post-Soviet Affairs* 23(3): 185–217.

Caramani, Daniele, Kevin Deegan-Krause and Rainbow Murray (2011) 'Political data in 2010', *European Journal of Political Research*, 50: 869–87.

CBOS (2011) 'Opinie o działalnosci partii politycznych', November, BS/140/2011, downloaded from http://www.cbos.pl/SPISKOM.POL/2011/ K_140_11.PD.F

Centrum pro vyzkum verejneho mineni (2012), 'Stranicke preference a volebni model v dubnu 2012', available online at http://www.cvvm.cas.cz/upl/ zpravy/101274s_pv120418.pdf.

Chiva, Cristina (2007) 'The Institutionalization of Post-Communist

Parliaments: Hungary and Romania in Comparative Perspective,' *Parliamentary Affairs*, 60(2) (March): 187–211.

Cirtautas, Arista Maria (1997) *The Polish Solidarity Movement*. London and New York: Routledge.

Cohen, Jean P. and Andrew Arato (1992) *Civil Society and Political Theory*. Cambridge, MA: MIT Press.

Cohen, Lenard J. (1993) *Broken Bonds: The Rise and Fall of Yugoslavia*. Boulder, CO: Westview Press.

Colomer, Josep M. (ed.) (2004) *Handbook of Electoral System Choice*, Basingstoke: Palgrave Macmillan.

Colton, Timothy J. and Robert C. Tucker (eds)(1995), *Patterns in Post-Soviet Leadership*. Boulder, CO: Westview Press.

Coman, Emanuel Emil (2012) 'Legislative Behavior in Romania: The Effect of the 2008 Romanian Electoral Reform,' *Legislative Studies Quarterly*, 37(2) (May): 199–224.

Commander, Simon and Timothy Frye (1999) 'The Politics of Postcommunist Economic Reform,' Transition Report 1999. London: EBRD.

Connolly, Richard (2011) 'Developments in the Economies of Member States Outside the Eurozone', *Journal of Common Market Studies*, 49(1): 251–73.

Connolly, Richard (2012) 'Developments in the Economies of Member States Outside the Eurozone', *Journal of Common Market Studies*, 50(2): 196–210.

Copsey, N. (2012) 'Poland', in Bulmer, S. and Lequesne, C. (eds) *The Member States of the European Union*. Oxford: Oxford University Press.

Copsey, N. and Pomorska, K. (2010) 'Poland's Power and Influence in the European Union: the Case of its Eastern Policy,' *Comparative European Politics*, 8 (3): 281–303.

Copsey, N. and Pomorska, K. (2013) 'The Influence of Newer Member States in the European Union: the Case of Poland and the Eastern Partnership,' forthcoming in *Europe-Asia Studies*.

Corrin, C. (1998) 'The Politics of Gender in Central and Eastern Europe', in Stephen White, Judy Batt and Paul G. Lewis (eds) *Developments in Central and East European Politics 2*. London: Macmillan.

Cottey, Andrew (ed.)(1999) *Subregional Cooperation in the New Europe: Building Security, Prosperity and Solidarity from the Barents to the Black Sea*. Basingstoke: Palgrave Macmillan in Association with the East-West Center.

Cox, John (2005) *Slovenia: Evolving Loyalties*. London and New York: Routledge.

Crampton, Richard and Ben Crampton (1996) *Atlas of East European History in the Twentieth Century*. London: Routledge.

Crowley, Stephen (2004) 'Explaining Labor Weakness in Post-Communist Europe: Historical Legacies and Comparative Perspective', *East European Politics and Societies*, 18(3) (August): 394–429.

Crowley, Stephen and David Ost (eds) (2001) *Workers After Workers' States*. Lanham, MD, and Oxford: Rowman & Littlefield.

Crowther, William E. (2012) 'Second Decade Second Chance? Parliaments, Politics and Democratic Aspirations in Russia, Ukraine and Moldova,' in David M. Olson and Gabriella Ilonszki (eds), *Post-Communist Parliaments: Change and Stability in the Second Decade.* London: Routledge: 32–56.

Crowther, William E. and Irmina Matonyte (2009) 'Parliamentary Elites as a Democratic Thermometer: Estonia, Lithuania and Moldova Compared,' *Communist and Post-Communist Studies,* 40(3): 281–99.

Crowther, William E. and David M. Olson (2002) 'Committee Systems in New Democratic Parliaments: Comparative Institutionalization,' in David M. Olson and William E. Crowther (eds), *Committees in Post-Communist Democratic Parliaments: Comparative Institutionalization.* Columbus, OH: Ohio State University Press: 171–206.

Czesnik, Mikołaj (2011) 'Voter Turnout and Electoral Success of Pro-European Parties in Post-Communist Europe,' in Paul G. Lewis and Radoslaw Markowski (eds), *Europeanising Party Politics? Comparative Perspectives on Central and Eastern Europe.* Manchester: Manchester University Press.

Dahrendorf, Ralf (1990) *Reflections on the Revolution in Europe.* New York: Random House

Dalton, Russell J. (1988) *Citizen Politics in Western Democracies.* Chatham, NJ: Chatham House Publishers.

Dangerfield, Martin (2000) *Subregional Economic Cooperation in Central and Eastern Europe: The Political Economy of CEFTA.* Aldershot: Edward Elgar.

D'Anieri, Paul (2006) *Understanding Ukrainian Politics: Power, Politics and Institutional Design.* New York: M. E. Sharpe.

Davies, James C. (1971) *When Men Rebel and Why.* New York: Free Press.

Davies, Norman (1996) *Europe: A History.* Oxford: Oxford University Press.

Deegan-Krause, Kevin (2006) *Elected Affinities: Democracy and Party Competition in Slovakia and the Czech Republic,* Palo Alto, CA: Stanford University Press.

Deegan-Krause, Kevin and Haughton, Tim (2012) 'In with the New (Again): "Annuals", "Perennials" and the Patterns of Party Politics in Central and Eastern Europe'. Paper prepared for the 70th Annual MPSA Conference, Chicago, 12–15 April.

Di Michelis, Gianni (1990) 'Europe: A Golden Opportunity not to be Missed', *International Herald Tribune,* 26 March.

Dimitrov, Vesselin (2001) *Bulgaria: The Uneven Transition.* London and New York: Routledge.

Dimitrova, Antoaneta (2005) 'Europeanisation and Civil Service Reform in Central and Eastern Europe,' in Frank Schimmelfennig and Ulrich Sedelmeier (eds), *The Europeanisation of Central and Eastern Europe.* Ithaca, NY: Cornell University Press: 71–90.

Dudwick, N., Yemtsov, R., Hamilton, E., Alam, A., Murthi, M., Murrugarra, E. and Tiongson, E. (2005) *Growth, Poverty and Inequality: Eastern Europe and the Former Soviet Union.* Washington, DC: World Bank.

Dyson, K. (2006) *Enlarging the Euro: External Empowerment and Domestic Transformation in East Central Europe.* Oxford: Oxford University Press.

Economist, The (1991) 'Hello, Neighbours', 13 July.

Eisenstadt, S. N. (1978) *Revolution and the Transformation of Societies.* New York: Free Press.

Eising, Rainer and Thomas Poguntke (2011) 'Government and Governance in Europe,' in Eric Jones, Paul Heywood, Martin Rhodes and Ulrich Sedelmeier (eds), *Developments in European Politics,* 2nd edn, Basingstoke: Palgrave Macmillan: 45–64.

Elgie, Robert, and Sophie Moestrup (eds) (2009) *Semi-Presidentialism in Central and Eastern Europe.* Manchester: Manchester University Press.

Elster, Jon (ed.) (1996) *The Roundtable Talks and the Breakdown of Communism,* Chicago and London: University of Chicago Press.

Elster, Jon, Claus Offe, and Ulrich K. Preuss (1998) *Institutional Design in Post-Communist Societies: Rebuilding the Ship at Sea.* Cambridge and New York: Cambridge University Press.

Ekiert, Grzegorz (1996) *The State Against Society.* Princeton, NJ: Princeton University Press.

Ekiert, Grzegorz and Jan Kubik (1999) *Rebellious Civil Society: Popular Protest and Democratic Consolidation in Poland.* Ann Arbor: University of Michigan Press.

Ekiert, Grzegorz, Jan Kubik, and Milada Anna Vachudova (2007) 'Democracy in the Post-Communist World: An Unending Quest?', *East European Politics and Societies,* 21(1) (February): 7–30.

Emigh, R. and Szelenyi, I. (eds.) (2001) Poverty, Ethnicity and Gender in Eastern Europe During the Market Transition. Westport, CT: Greenwood Press.

Enyedi, Zsolt and Fernando Casal Bertoa (2011), 'Patterns of Party Competition (1990–2009)', in Lewis, Paul and Markowski, Radoslaw (eds), *Europeanising Party Politics? Comparative Perspectives on Central and Eastern Europe.* Manchester: Manchester University Press.

Enyedi, Zsolt and Lukas Linek (2008) 'Searching for the Right Organization: Ideology and Party Structure in East-Central Europe,' *Party Politics,* 14(4) (July): 455–77.

Enyedi, Zsolt and Toka, Gabor (2007) 'The Only Game in Town: Party Politics in Hungary,' in Stephen White and Paul Webb (eds) *Party Politics in New Democracies.* Oxford: Oxford University Press: 149–78.

Epstein, R. and Sedelmeier, U. (2009) (eds) *International Influence Beyond Conditionality: Postcommunist Europe after EU Enlargement.* London: Routledge.

Eris, M. (2012) 'Improving Health Outcomes and System in Hungary', *OECD Economics Department Working Papers,* No. 961, OECD, http://dx.doi.org/10.1787/5k98rwqj3zmp-en.

European Bank for Reconstruction and Development (EBRD) (2007) *Transition Report 2007: People in Transition.* London: EBRD.

EBRD (2011) *Life in Transition: After the Crisis.* London: EBRD.

European Commission (various years), *Standard Eurobarometer Report*, at http://ec.europa.eu/public_opinion/archives/eb/eb76/eb76_en.htm.

European Commission (2002) *Candidate Countries Eurobarometer 2001*. Brussels: European Commission.

European Council (1993) Copenhagen European Council Presidency Conclusions, available at: http://europa.eu/rapid/press-release_DOC-93-3_en.htm.

European Social Survey (2010), Data downloaded from http://nesstar.ess.nsd.uib.no/webview/.

European Union External Action Service (2012), http://eeas.europa.eu/eastern/index_en.htm.

Eurostat (2012) *Real GDP Growth Rate*.

Evans, Geoffrey (2006) 'The Social Bases of Political Divisions in Post-Communist Eastern Europe,' *Annual Review of Sociology*, 32: 245–70.

Evans, Geoffrey and Stephen Whitefield (1993) 'Identifying the Bases of Party Competition in Eastern Europe', *British Journal of Political Science*, 23(4) (October): 521–48.

Eyal, G., Szelenyi, I. and Townsley, E. (1998) *Making Capitalism Without Capitalists: The New Ruling Elites in Eastern Europe*. London: Verso.

Falkner, G., Trieb, O. and Holzleither, E. (2008) *Compliance in the Enlarged European Union: Living Rights or Dead Letters?* Aldershot: Ashgate.

Fawn, Rick (2001) 'The Elusive Defined? Visegrad Cooperation as the Contemporary Contours of Central Europe', *Geopolitics*, 6(1): 47–68.

Fawn, Rick, (2010) 'Regional Relations and Security', in Sabrina Ramet (ed.), *Central and Southeastern Europe since 1989*. Cambridge and New York: Cambridge University Press: 495–518.

Fidrmuc, Jan (2003) 'Economic Reform, Democracy and Growth during Post-Communist Transition,' *European Journal of Political Economy*, 19: 583–604.

Fink-Hafner, Danica (2006) 'Slovenia', *European Journal of Political Research*, 45 (7–8): 1260–5.

Fink-Hafner, Danica (2012) 'Interest Representation and Post-Communist Parliaments Over Two Decades,' in David M. Olson and Gabriella Ilonszki (eds) *Post-Communist Parliaments: Change and Stability in the Second Decade*. London: Routledge: 100–18.

Fish, M. Stephen (1998) 'The Determinants of Economic Reform in the Post-Communist World,' *East European Politics and Society*, 12(1): 31–78.

Fish, M. Steven (2000) 'The Executive Deception: Superpresidentialism and the Degradation of Russian Politics,' in Valerie Sperling (ed.), *Building the Russian State: Institutional Crisis and the Quest for Democratic Governance*. Boulder, CO: Westview Press: 177–92.

Fisher, Sharon (2006) *Political Change in Post-Communist Slovakia and Croatia: From Nationalist to Europeanist*. New York: Palgrave Macmillan.

Fisher, Sharon, Gould, John and Haughton, Tim (2007) 'Slovakia's Neoliberal Turn', *Europe-Asia Studies*, 59(6): 977–98.

Fodor, Eva (2005) 'Women at Work: The Status of Women in the Labour Markets of the Czech Republic, Hungary and Poland', *Occasional Paper 3*. Geneva: United Nations Research Institute for Social Development.

Forbrig, Joerg, David Marples and Pavol Demes (eds) (2006) *Prospects for Democracy in Belarus*. Washington, DC: German Marshall Fund, available online at www.gmfus.org/doc/Belarus%20book%20final.pdf.

Forestiere, Carolyn (2010) 'Political Volatility and Governance in East Central Europe', *Slavic Review*, 69(4) (Winter): 903–24.

Fowler, Brigid (2002) 'Hungary's 2002 Parliamentary Election', ESRC 'One Europe or Several?' Programme, Briefing Note 2/02, May.

Fowler, Brigid (2004) 'Concentrated Orange: Fidesz and the Remaking of the Hungarian Centre-Right, 1994–2002', *Journal of Communist Studies and Transition Politics*, 20(3) (September): 80–114.

Freedom House (2012a) *Freedom in the World*. New York: Freedom House.

Freedom House (2012b) *Nations in Transit. Fragile Frontier: Democracy's Growing Vulnerability in Central and Southeastern Europe*. www.freedomhouse.org.

Frye, Timothy (2010) *Building States and Markets After Communism: the Perils of Polarized Democracy*. New York: Cambridge University Press.

Furtak, Robert K. (ed.) (1990) *Elections in Socialist States*. New York and London: Harvester Wheatsheaf.

Gallagher, Tom (2009) *Romania and the European Union: How the Weak Vanquished the Strong*. Manchester: Manchester University Press.

Garnett, Sherman W. and Robert Legvold, (eds) (1999) *Belarus at the Crossroads*. Washington, DC: Carnegie Endowment.

Garton Ash, Timothy (1985) *The Polish Revolution: Solidarity*. New York: Vintage Books.

Garton Ash, Timothy (1989a) 'Does Central Europe Exist?', in George Schopflin and Nancy Wood (eds), *In Search of Central Europe*. Oxford: Polity: 191–215.

Garton Ash, Timothy (1989b) *The Uses of Adversity*. New York: Random House.

Garton Ash, Timothy (1993) *The Magic Lantern*. New York: Vintage Books.

Goetz, Klaus H. (2000) 'European Integration and National Executives: A Cause in Search of an Effect?' *West European Politics*, 23(4) (October): 211–31.

Goetz, K. H. and H. Wollmann (2001) 'Governmentalizing Central Executives in Post-Communist Europe: a Four-Country Comparison,' *Journal of European Public Policy*, 8(6): 864–87.

Goetz, Klaus H. and Radislaw Zubek (2007) 'Government and Law-making in Poland,' *Journal of Legislative Studies,* 13(4) (December): 517–38.

Gould, John (2009) *Slovakia's Neoliberal Churn: the Political Economy of the Fico Government, 2006-8*, Bratislava: Comenius University's Institute of European Studies and International Relations working paper series.

Gowan, Peter (1995) 'Neoliberal Theory and Practice for Eastern Europe,' *New Left Review*, no. 213 (September–October): 3–60.

Grabbe, Heather (2006) *The EU's Transformative Power: Europeanisation through Conditionality in Central and Eastern Europe*. Basingstoke: Palgrave Macmillan.

Grabbe, Heather (2007) 'Central and Eastern Europe and the EU,' in Stephen White, Judy Batt and Paul G. Lewis (eds), *Central and East European Politics 4*. Basingstoke: Palgrave Macmillan: 110–26.

Greskovits, Bela (1998) *The Political Economy of Protest and Patience: East European and Latin American Transformations Compared*. Budapest: CEU Press

Grzymala-Busse, Anna (2002) *Redeeming the Communist Past: The Regeneration of Communist Parties in East Central Europe*, Cambridge and New York: Cambridge University Press.

Grzymala-Busse, Anna (2007) Rebuilding Leviathan: Party Competition and State Exploitation in Post-Communist Democracies. *Cambridge and New York: Cambridge University Press.*

Guasti, Petra R. (2010) 'The Parliaments of Central and Eastern Europe: Relationships among the Parliamentary Chambers in the Czech Republic, Poland, Romania and Slovenia and the Effects of Europeanization,' Paper presented to the 60th Political Studies Association, Edinburgh, UK, 29 March–1 April.

Gurr, Ted Robert (1970) *Why Men Rebel*. Princeton, NJ: Princeton University Press.

Habdank-Kolaczkowska, Sylvana and Christopher Walker (eds) (2011) *Nations in Transit. Democratization from Central Europe to Eurasia*. New York and Washington, DC: Freedom House.

Hafner-Fink, Mitja, Danica Fink-Hafner, and Alenka Krasovec (2011) 'Changing Patterns of Political Representation,' in Paul G. Lewis and Radoslaw Markowski (eds), *Europeanising Party Politics? Comparative Perspectives on Central and Eastern Europe*. Manchester: Manchester University Press.

Hagemann, S. and De Clerk-Sachsse, J. (2007) 'Decision-Making in the Enlarged Council of Ministers: Evaluating the Facts,' CEPS Policy Brief, No. 119, available at: http://www.ceps.eu/files/book/1430.pdf.

Hanley, Eric et al. (1996) *The Making of Post-Communist Elites in Eastern Europe: A Comparison of Political and Economic Elites in the Czech Republic, Hungary and Poland*. Prague: Sociologicky ustav CR.

Hanley, Sean (2001) 'Towards Breakthrough or Breakdown? The Consolidation of KSCM as a Neo-Communist Successor Party in the Czech Republic,' *Journal of Communist Studies and Transition Politics*, 17(3) (September): 96–116.

Hanley, Sean (2007) *The New Right in the New Europe: Czech Transformation and Right-wing Politics, 1989–2006*. London: Routledge.

Hankiss, Elemer (1990) *East European Alternatives*. Oxford: Clarendon Press.

Hardy, Jane (2009) *Poland's New Capitalism*. London: Pluto Press.

Harris, Erika (2002) *Nationalism and Democratisation: Politics of Slovakia and Slovenia*. Aldershot: Ashgate.

Havel, Vaclav (1985) *The Power of the Powerless: Citizens against the State in Central-Eastern Europe*. Armonk, NY: M. E. Sharpe.

Havrylyshyn, Oleh (2006) *Divergent Paths in Post-Communist Transitions. Capitalism for All or Capitalism for the Few?* Basingstoke: Palgrave Macmillan.

Haughton, Tim (2007), 'When Does the EU Make a Difference? Conditionality and the Accession Process in Central and Eastern Europe', *Political Studies Review*, 5(2): 233–46.

Haughton, T. (2009) 'Driver, Conductor or Fellow Passenger? EU Membership and Party Politics in Central and Eastern Europe', *Journal of Communist Studies and Transition Politics*, 25(4): 413–26.

Haughton, Tim (2011a) 'Half Full but also Half Empty: Conditionality, Compliance and the Quality of Democracy in Central and Eastern Europe', *Political Studies Review*, 9(3): 323–33.

Haughton, Tim (ed.) (2011b) *Party Politics in Central and Eastern Europe: Does EU Membership Matter?* London: Routledge.

Haughton, Tim and Deegan-Krause, Kevin (2012) '2012 Parliamentary Elections in Slovakia: The Building Blocs of Success', posted at http://www.pozorblog.com/2012/03/2012-parliamentary-elections-in-slovakia-the-building-blocs-of-success/.

Haughton, Tim, Novotna, Tereza, and Deegan-Krause, Kevin (2011) 'The 2010 Czech and Slovak Parliamentary Elections: Red Cards to the "Winners", *West European Politics*, 34(2): 394–402.

Havel, Vaclav (1994) 'A Time for Sacrifice: The Co-responsibility of the West', *Foreign Affairs*, 73(2) (March–April): 2–7.

Hayden, Jacqueline (2006) *The Collapse of Communist Power in Poland.* London and New York: Routledge.

Heidar, Knut and Ruud Koole (eds) (2000) *Parliamentary Party Groups in European Democracies.* London: Routledge.

Hellman, Joel S. (1998) 'Winners Take All: The Politics of Partial Reform in Postcommunist Transitions', *World Politics*, 50(2) (January): 203–34.

Henderson, Karen (1999) 'Slovakia and the Democratic Criteria for EU Accession', in K. Henderson (ed.), *Back to Europe: Central and Eastern Europe and the European Union.* London and Philadelphia: UCL Press: 221–40.

Henderson, Karen (2002) *Slovakia: the Escape from Invisibility.* London and New York: Routledge.

Henn, Matt (2001) 'Opinion Polls, Political Elites and Party Competition in Post-Communist Bulgaria,' *Journal of Communist Studies and Transition Politics*, 17(3) (September): 52–70.

Heyns, B. (2005) 'Emerging Inequalities in Central and Eastern Europe', *Annual Review of Sociology*, 31(1): 163–97.

Higley, John, Judith Kullberg, Jan Pakulski (1996) 'The Persistence of Postcommunist Elites,' *Journal of Democracy*, 7(2) (April): 133–47.

Higley, John and Michael G. Burton (1997) 'Types of Political Elites in Postcommunist Eastern Europe,' *International Politics*, 34(2) (June): 153–68.

Hodson, Dermot (2012) 'The Eurozone in 2011', *Journal of Common Market Studies*, 50(2): 179–96.

Hoen, Herman W. (2011) 'Crisis in Eastern Europe: The Downside of a Market Economy Revealed?' *European Review*, 19(1): 38.

Hopkin, Jonathan (2011) 'Elections and Electoral Systems', in Erik Jones, Paul Heywood, Martin Rhodes and Ulrich Sedelmeier (eds), *Developments in European Politics*, 2nd edn, Basingstoke: Palgrave Macmillan: 81–99.

Howard, Marc Morjé (2003) *The Weakness of Civil Society in Post-Communist Europe*. Cambridge and New York: Cambridge University Press.

Hudson, Michael and Sommers, Jeffrey (2012) 'Latvia is No Model for a European Austerity Drive', *Financial Times*, 22 June.

Hughes, J., Saase, G. and Gordon, C. (2004) *Europeanisation and Regionalisation in the EU's Enlargement to Central and Eastern Europe: The Myth of Conditionality*. Basingstoke: Palgrave Macmillan.

Hulsey, John W. (2012), '"Why Did They Vote for Those Guys Again?" Challenges and Contradictions in the Promotion of Political Moderation in Post-War Bosnia and Herzegovina', in Peter Burnell and Andre W. M. Gerrits (eds) *Promoting Party Politics in Emerging Democracies*. London: Routledge.

Huntington, Samuel (1968) *Political Order in Changing Societies*. New Haven, CT: Yale University Press.

Huntington, Samuel P. (1991) *The Third Wave: Democratization in the Late Twentieth Century*. Norman, OK: University of Oklahoma Press.

Huntington, Samuel (1996) *The Clash of Civilizations and the Remaking of World Order*. New York: Simon & Schuster.

Ilonszki, Gabriella (2008) 'From Minimal to Subordinate: A Final Verdict? The Hungarian Parliament 1990–2002', in David M. Olson and Philip Norton (eds), *Post-Communist and Post-Soviet Parliaments: The Initial Decade*. London: Routledge: 27–47.

Ilonszki, Gabriella and Michael Edinger (2008) 'MPs in Post-Communist and Post-Soviet Nations: A Parliamentary Elite in the Making', in David M. Olson and Philip Norton (eds), *Post-Communist and Post-Soviet Parliaments: The Initial Decade*. London: Routledge: 131–52.

Ingrao, Charles (1999) 'Understanding Ethnic Conflict in Central Europe: An Historical Perspective', *Nationalities Papers*, 27(2) (June): 291–318.

Independent International Commission on Kosovo (2000) *The Kosovo Report: Conflict, International Response, Lessons Learned*. Oxford: Oxford University Press.

International Commission on the Balkans (2005) *The Balkans in Europe's Future*, http://www.balkan-commission.org.

Ishiyama, John T. (1996) 'Electoral Systems Experimentation in the New Eastern Europe: The Single Transferable Vote and the Additional Member System in Estonia and Hungary', *East European Quarterly* 29 (4): 487–507.

Jacoby, W. (2004) *The Enlargement of the European Union and NATO: Ordering from the Menu in Central Europe*. Cambridge and New York: Cambridge University Press.

Jagodzinski, Andrzej (ed.) (2006) *The Visegrad Group: A Central European Constellation*. Bratislava: International Visegrad Fund.

Janos, Andrew (2000) *East Central Europe in the Modern World. The Politics of the Borderlands from Pre- to Post-Communism*. Stanford, CA: Stanford University Press.

Jasiewicz, Krzysztof (1998) 'Elections and Voting Behaviour' in: Stephen White, Judy Batt and Paul G. Lewis (eds), *Developments in Central and East European Politics 2*. London: Macmillan ,

Jasiewicz, Krzystof (2007) 'Citizens and Politics', in Stephen White, Judy Batt and Paul G. Lewis (eds), *Developments in Central and East European Politics 4*. Basingstoke: Palgrave Macmillan: 193–212.

Jaszi, Oskar (1923) 'Dismembered Hungary and Peace in Central Europe', *Foreign Affairs*, 2(2) (December): 270–81.

Jeszenszky, Geza (2006) 'The Origins and Enactment of the "Visegrad Idea"', in Andrzej Jagodziski (ed.), *The Visegrad Group: A Central European Constellation*. Bratislava: International Visegrad Fund: 60–2.

Jezermik, Bozidar (2004) *Wild Europe*. London: Saqi Books.

Johnson, S. and Loveman, G. (1995) *Starting Over in Eastern Europe: Entrepreneurship and Economic Renewal*, Boston, MA: Harvard Business School Press.

Jones, Erik (2002) *The Politics of Economic and Monetary Union: Integration and Idiosyncracy*. Lanham, MD: Rowman & Littlefield.

Jowitt, Kenneth (1992) *The New World Disorder*. Berkeley, CA: University of California Press.

Judah, Tim (2008) *Kosovo: What Everyone Needs to Know*. Oxford: Oxford University Press.

Judah, Tim (2009) *The Serbs*, 3rd edn, London and New Haven: Yale University Press.

Jungerstam-Mulders, Susanne (ed.) (2006) *Post-Communist EU Member States: Parties and Party Systems*. Aldershot: Ashgate.

Kaczynski, Jaroslaw (2012), 'Jaroslaw Kaczynski: mam poczucie, ze Lech Kaczynski zostal zamordowany' (interview), from http://wiadomosci. onet.pl/tylko-w-onecie/jaroslaw-kaczynski-mam-poczucie-ze-lech-kaczynski, 1,5093023, wiadomosc.html.

Kajnc, Sabina (2009) 'The Slovenian Presidency: Meeting Symbolic and Substantive Challenges', *Journal of Common Market Studies,* 47(1): 89–98.

Karpowicz, Ewa and Wlodzimierz Wesolowski (2002) 'Committees of the Polish Sejm in Two Political Systems', in David M. Olson and William E. Crowther (eds), *Committees in Post-Communist Democratic Parliaments: Comparative Institutionalization*. Columbus, OH: Ohio State University Press: 44–68.

Kask, Peet (1996) 'Institutional Development of the Parliament of Estonia', in David M. Olson and Philip Norton (eds), *The New Parliaments of Central and Eastern Europe*. London: Frank Cass: 193–212.

Katchanovski, Ivan (2006) *Cleft Countries: Regional Political Divisions and Cultures in Post-Soviet Ukraine and Moldova*. Stuttgart: Ibidem.

Keane, John (1988) *Democracy and Civil Society*. New York: Verso.

Kenney, Padraic (2002) *A Carnival of Revolution*. Princeton, NJ: Princeton University Press.

Khmelko, Irina (2012) 'Internal Organization of Post-Communist Parliaments over Two Decades: Leadership, Parties and Committees', in David M. Olson and Gabriella Ilonszki (eds), *Post-Communist Parliaments: Change and Stability in the Second Decade.* London: Routledge: 78–99.

Khmelko, Irina and Daniel J. Beers (2011) 'Legislative Oversight in the Ukrainian *Rada*: Assessing the Effectiveness of Parliamentary Committees', *Journal of Legislative Studies,* 17(4): 501–24

Kimmel, Michael S. (1990) *Revolution.* Philadelphia, PA: Temple University Press.

King, Charles (2000) *The Moldovans: Romania, Russia, and the Politics of Culture.* Stanford, CA: Hoover Institution Press.

Kiss, Csilla (2002) 'From Liberalism to Conservatism: The Federation of Young Democrats in Post-Communist Hungary', *East European Politics and Societies,* 16(3): 739–63.

Kitschelt, Herbert, Zdenka Mansfeldova, Radoslaw Markowski, and Gabor Toka (1999) *Post-Communist Party Systems: Competition, Representation and Inter-Party Cooperation.* Cambridge and New York: Cambridge University Press.

Koles, Sandor (2011) *Sharing the Experiences of Visegrad Cooperation in the Western Balkans and the Eastern Neighbourhood Countries.* Budapest: International Centre for Democratic Transition.

Konrad, Gyorgy (1983) *Antipolitics.* New York and London: Harcourt Brace Jovanovich.

Kopecky, Petr (2000) 'The Limits of Whips and Watchdogs: Parliamentary Parties in the Czech Republic', in Knut Heidar and Ruud Koole (eds), *Parliamentary Party Groups in European Democracies.* London: Routledge: 177–94.

Kopecky, Petr (2001) *Parliaments in the Czech and Slovak Republics: Party Competition and Parliamentary Institutionalization.* Aldershot and Burlington, VT: Ashgate.

Kopecky, Petr (2004) 'Power to the Executive! Changing Executive–Legislative Relations in Eastern Europe', *Journal of Legislative Studies,* 10(2–3) (Summer/Autumn): 142–53.

Kopecky, Petr (2007) 'Structures of Representation' in Stephen White, Judy Batt and Paul G. Lewis (eds), *Developments in Central and East European Politics 4.* Basingstoke: Palgrave Macmillan: 145–60.

Kopecky, Petr, and Cas Mudde (2000), 'Explaining Different Paths of Democratization: The Czech and Slovak Republics,' *Journal of Communist Studies and Transition Politics,* 16(3) (September): 63–84.

Kopecky, Petr and Maria Spirova (2011) 'Party Management and State Colonisation in Post-Communist Europe: the European Dimension', in Paul Lewis, and Radoslaw Markowski (eds), *Europeanising Party Politics? Comparative Perspectives on Central and Eastern Europe.* Manchester: Manchester University Press.

Kornai, Janos (1980) *Economics of Shortage,* Amsterdam: North-Holland.

Kornai, Janos (1992) *The Socialist System: The Political Economy of Communism.* Princeton, NJ: Princeton University Press.

Kornai, Janos (2012) 'Centralization and the Capitalist Market Economy', 1 February, from *Nepszabadsag* online, http://nol.hu/belfold/centralization_and_the_capitalist_market_economy.

Korosteleva, Elena *et al.* (eds) (2003), *Contemporary Belarus: Between Democracy and Dictatorship.* London: Routledge.

Kostadinova, Tatiana (2002) 'Do Mixed Electoral Systems Matter?: A Cross-National Analysis of their Effects in Eastern Europe', *Electoral Studies*, 21 (1) (March): 23–34.

Kostadinova, Tatiana (2003) 'Voter Turnout Dynamics in Post-Communist Europe', *European Journal of Political Research*, 42(6): 741–59.

Kostadinova, Tatiana (2009) 'Abstain or Rebel: Corruption Perceptions and Voting in East European Elections', *Politics & Policy*, 37(4): 691–714.

Kramer, M. (1997) 'Social Protection Policies and Safety Nets in East Central Europe: Dilemmas of the Postcommunist Transformation', in E. Kapstein and M. Mandelbaum (eds), *Sustaining the Transition: the Social Safety Net in Postcommunist Europe.* New York: Council on Foreign Relations.

Krasovec, Alenka and Tim Haughton (2011) 'Money, Organization and the State: the Partial Cartelization of Party Politics in Slovenia', *Communist and Post-Communist Studies*, 44(3) (September): 199–209.

Krasovec, Alenka and Haughton, Tim (2012) 'Election Briefing No. 69: Europe and the Parliamentary Elections in Slovenia December 2011', EPERN Election Briefing Series.

Krastev, Ivan (2003) 'Bringing the State Back Up', http://www.suedosteuropa-gesellschaft.com.

Krupavicius, Algis (2011) 'Lithuania', *European Journal of Political Research*, 50(7–8) 1045–57.

Kubik, Jan (1994) *The Power of Symbols Against the Symbols of Power.* University Park: Penn State University Press.

Kumar, Krishan (2001) *1989: Revolutionary Ideas and Ideals.* Minneapolis, MN: University of Minnesota Press.

Kundera, Milan (1984) 'The Tragedy of Central Europe', *New York Review of Books*, 26 April: 33–8.

Kuron, Jacek (1984) *Zlo, ktore czyni* [*The Evil of My Deeds*]. Warsaw: Niezalezna Oficyna Wydawnicza.

Kuzio, Taras (2000) 'Geopolitical Pluralism in the CIS: The Emergence of GUUAM', *European Security*, 9(2): 1–35.

Ladany J. and Szelenyi I. (2006) *Patterns of Exclusion: Constructing Gypsy Ethnicity and the Making of an Underclass in Transitional Societies of Europe.* Boulder, CO and New York: Columbia University Press.

Laki, M. and Szalai, J. (2006) 'The Puzzle of Success: Hungarian Entrepreneurs at the Turn of the Millennium', *Europe-Asia Studies*, 58(3) (May): 317–45.

Lampe, John (2000) *Yugoslavia as History: Twice There Was A Country*, 2nd edn. Cambridge and New York: Cambridge University Press.

LaPalombara, Joseph (2007) 'Reflections on Political Parties and Political Development, Four Decades Later', *Party Politics*, 13(2) (March): 141–54.

Lasswell, Harold D. (1986), 'Democratic Leadership,' in Barbara Kellerman (ed.), *Political Leadership*. Pittsburgh, PA: University of Pittsburgh Press.

Lawson, George, Chris Armbruster and Michael Cox (eds) (2010) *The Global 1989: Continuity and Change in World Politics*. Cambridge and New York: Cambridge University Press.

Lazarova, Daniela (2012) 'Head of STEM polling agency: Czechs are ashamed of their politicians', interview with Jan Jan Hartl, Czech Radio, 26 April 2012, http://www.radio.cz/en/section/panorama/head-of-stem-polling-agency-czechs-are-ashamed-of-their-politicians.

Leven, Bozena (2011), 'Avoiding Crisis Contagion: Poland's case', *Communist and Post-Communist Studies*, 44: 183–87.

Lewis, Paul G. (2000) *Political Parties in Post-Communist Eastern Europe*. London: Routledge.

Lewis, Paul and Mansfeldova, Zdenka (2006) *The European Union and Party Politics in Central and Eastern Europe*. Basingstoke: Palgrave Macmillan.

Lewis, Paul and Markowski, Radoslaw (2011) *Europeanising Party Politics? Comparative Perspectives on Central and Eastern Europe*. Manchester: Manchester University Press.

Lewis, Paul G. and Paul Webb (eds) (2003) *Pan-European Perspectives on Party Politics*. Leiden: Brill.

Liebich, André (1997) 'The Communists Reincarnated: Their Return in Russia and Eastern Europe,' *World Affairs*, 1 (1) (January–March).

Linek, Lukas and Zdenka Mansfeldova (2008) "The Parliament of the Czech Republic, 1993–2004", in David M. Olson and Philip Norton (eds), *Post-Communist and Post-Soviet Legislatures: Beyond Transition*. London: Routledge: 1–26.

Linek, Lukas and Stepan Pechacek (2007) 'Low Membership in Czech Political Parties: Party Strategy or structural determinants?', *Journal of Communist Studies and Transition Politics*, 23(2) (June): 259–75.

Linek, Lukas and Petra Rakusanova (2004) 'The More Parties Vote and the Bigger Their Majority is, the Less United They Are', in Zdenka Mansfeldova, David M. Olson, and Petra Rakusanova (eds), *Central European Parliaments: First Decade of Democratic Experience and Future Perspectives*. Prague: Czech Academy of Science: 102–19.

Linz, Juan J. and Alfred Stepan (1996) *Problems of Democratic Transition and Consolidation: Southern Europe, South America, and Post-Communist Europe*. Baltimore, MD: Johns Hopkins University Press.

Little, Alan and Laura Silber (1996) *The Death of Yugoslavia*, revised edn. Harmondsworth: BBC Books/Penguin.

Longley, Lawrence D. and Roger H. Davidson (eds) (1998) *The New Roles of Parliamentary Committees*. London: Frank Cass.

Lovenduski, J. and Woodall, J. (1987) *Politics and Society in Eastern Europe*. Basingstoke: Macmillan.

Lynch, Dov (2003) 'Separatist States and Post-Soviet Conflicts', in Andrew Wilson and Wendy Slater (eds), *The Legacy of the Soviet Union*. Basingstoke: Palgrave Macmillan: 61–82.

Macmillan, Margaret (2001) *Peacemakers: The Paris Conference of 1919 and its Aftermath*. London: John Murray.

Magocsi, Paul Robert (2010) *A History of Ukraine: The Land and its Peoples*, 2nd edn. Toronto: University of Toronto Press.

Mainwaring, Scott (1999) *Rethinking Party Systems in the Third Wave of Democratization*. Stanford, CA: Stanford University Press.

Mainwaring, Scott and Edurne Zoco (2007) 'Political Consequences and the Stabilization of Interparty Competition: Electoral Volatility in Old and New Democracies', *Party Politics*, 13(2) (March): 155–78.

Mair, Peter (2008) 'The Challenge to Party Government', *West European Politics*, 31(1–2) (January–March): 211–34.

Mair, Peter and Ingrid van Biezen (2001) 'Party Membership in Twenty European Democracies', *Party Politics*, 7(1) (January): 5–21.

Malova, Darina *et al.* (2010) *From Listening to Action? New Member States in the European Union*. Bratislava: Devin.

Malova, Darina and Deegan-Krause, Kevin (2000) 'Parliamentary Groups in Slovakia', in Knut Heidar and Ruud Koole (eds), *Parliamentary Party Groups in European Democracies*. London: Routledge: 195–213.

Malova, Darina and Ucen, Peter (2011) 'Slovakia', *European Journal of Political Research*, 50: 1118–29.

Mansfeldova, Zdenka (2012) 'Central European Parliaments Over Two Decades – Diminished Stability? Parliaments in Czech Republic, Hungary, Poland, and Slovenia', in David M. Olson and Gabriella Ilonszki (eds), *Post-Communist Parliaments: Change and Stability in the Second Decade*. London: Routledge: 13–31.

Mansfeldova, Zdenka and Petra Rakusanova (2008) 'Legislative Budgeting in the Czech Republic,' in Rick Stapenhurst, Riccardo Pelizzo, David M. Olson and Lisa von Trapp (eds), *Legislative Oversight and Budgeting: A World Perspective*. Washington, DC: World Bank: 279–92.

Mansfeldova, Zdenka, Jindriska Sylllova, Petra Rakusanova and Petr Kolar (2002) 'Committees of the Czech Chamber of Deputies of the Czech Republic,' in D.M. Olson and W. E. Crowther (eds), *Committees in Post-Communist Democratic Parliaments: Comparative Institutionalization*. Columbus, OH: Ohio State University Press: 69–92.

March, Luke (2005) *The Moldovan Communists: From Leninism to Democracy*. University of Strathclyde, Studies in Public Policy 405.

March, Luke and Graeme P. Herd (2006) 'Moldova between Europe and Russia: inoculating against the colored contagion?', *Post-Soviet Affairs*, 22 (4) (December): 349–79.

Marer, P. (2010) 'The Global Economic Crises: Impacts on Eastern Europe', *Acta Oeconomica*, 60(1): 3–33.

Markowski, Radoslaw and Zsolt Enyedi (2011) 'The Quality of Social, Partisan, and Governmental Representation', in Paul G. Lewis and Radoslaw Markowski (eds), *Europeanising Party Politics? Comparative Perspectives on Central and Eastern Europe*. Manchester: Manchester University Press.

Markowski, Radoslaw, and Joshua A. Tucker (2010) 'Euroscepticism and the Emergence of Political Parties in Poland', *Party Politics*, 16(4) (July): 523–48.

Marples, David (2006) 'Color Revolutions: The Belarus Case', in *Communist and Post-Communist Studies*, 39(3) (September): 351–64.

Marples, David R. (2009) 'Outpost of Tyranny? The Failure of Democratization in Belarus', *Democratization*, 16 (4) (August): 756–77.

Marten Board International (2004) (July) at http://www.martenboard.co.yu.

Martin, Roderick (2012) *Constructing Capitalisms*. Cambridge and New York: Cambridge University Press.

Marx, Karl (1962) *The Eighteenth Brumaire of Louis Bonaparte*. New York: International Publishers.

Mateju, Petr and Rehakova, Blanka (1997) 'Turning Left or Class Realignment? Analysis of the Changing Relationship between Class and Party in the Czech Republic 1992–1996', *East European Politics and Societies*, 11 (3): 501–42.

Mayhew, A. (2000) 'Enlargement of the European Union: An Analysis of the Negotiations with the Central and East European Candidate Countries', SEI Working Paper, No. 39, available at: http://home.aubg.bg/faculty/Didar/EUR406/MayhewEnlargementNegotiations.pdf.

Mazower, Mark (1998) *Dark Continent: Europe's Twentieth Century*. London: Penguin.

Mazower, Mark (2000) *The Balkans*. London: Weidenfeld & Nicolson.

McCormick, John (2002) *Understanding the European Union: A Concise Introduction*. Basingstoke: Palgrave Macmillan.

McFaul, Michael and Anders Aslund (eds) (2006) *Revolution in Orange: The Origins of Ukraine's Democratic Breakthrough*. Washington, DC: Carnegie Endowment.

Mendelski, Martin (2012) 'EU-Driven Judicial Reforms in Romania: A Success Story?' *East European Politics*, 28(1): 23–42.

Mentzel, Peter C. (2012) 'Nationalism, Civil Society, and the Revolution of 1989', *Nations and Nationalism,* 18(4) (October): 624–42.

Meyer-Sahling, Jan-Hinrik (2004) 'Civil Service Reform in Postcommunist Europe: The Bumpy Road to Depoliticisation,' *West European Politics*, 27(1) (January): 71–103.

Meyer-Sahling, Jan-Hinrik (2006) 'The Rise of the Partisan State? Parties, Patronage and the Ministerial Bureaucracy in Hungary,' *Journal of Communist Studies and Transition Politics*, 22(3) (September): 274–97.

Meyer-Sahling, Jan-Hinrik, and Tim Veen (2012) 'Governing the Post-Communist State: Government Alternation and Senior Civil Service Politicisation in Central and Eastern Europe', *East European Politics*, 28(1) (March): 4–22.

Michnik, Adam (1985) *Letters from Prison and Other Essays*. Berkeley, CA, and London: University of California Press.

Mike, Karoly (2007) 'An Unhappy Consensus: EU Membership and Party Collusion in Hungary', *World Political Science Review*, 3(4).

Milanovic, Branko (1998) *Income, Inequality and Poverty during the Transition from Planned to Market Economy*. Washington, DC: World Bank.

Milanovic, B. (1999) 'Explaining the Increase in Inequality during Transition', *Economics of Transition*, 7(2) (July): 299–341.

Millard, Frances (2004) *Elections, Parties, and Representation in Post-Communist Europe*. Basingstoke: Palgrave Macmillan.

Millard, Frances (2008) 'Executive-Legislative Relations in Poland, 1991–2005', *Journal of Legislative Studies*, 14(4): 367–93.

Millard, Frances (2011) 'Electoral-System Change in Latvia and the Elections of 2010', *Communist and Post-Communist Studies*, 44: 309–18

Mishler, William and Rose, Richard (2001) 'What Are the Origins of Political Trust? Testing Institutional and Cultural Theories in Post-Communist Societies', *Comparative Political Studies*, 34(1): 30–62.

Moghadam, V. (ed.) (1992) *Privatization and Democratization in Central and Eastern Europe and the Soviet Union: the Gender Dimension*. Helsinki: United Nations University.

Mole, Richard (2012) *The Baltic States from the Soviet Union to the European Union: Identity, Discourse and Power in the Post-Communist Transition of Estonia, Latvia and Lithuania*. London: Routledge.

Moore, Barrington (1966) *The Social Origins of Dictatorship and Democracy*. New York: Harper & Row.

Moraski, Bryon J. and Gerhard Loewenberg (1999) 'The Effect of Legal Thresholds on the Revival of Former-Communist Parties in East-Central Europe', *Journal of Politics*, 61(2): 151–70.

Moroney, Jennifer D. P., Taras Kuzio and Mikhail Molchanov (eds) (2002) *Ukrainian Foreign and Security Policy: Theoretical and Comparative Perspectives*. Westport, CT: Praeger.

Moser, Robert G. (1999) 'Electoral Systems and the Number of Parties in Post-Communist States', *World Politics*, 51(3): 359–84.

Mudde, Cas (2007) 'Civil Society', in S. White, J. Batt, and P. G. Lewis (eds) *Developments in Central and Eastern European Politics 4*, Basingstoke: Palgrave and Durham, NC: Duke University Press.

Munck, Gerardo and Jay Verkuilen (2002) 'Conceptualizing and Measuring Democracy: Evaluating Alternative Indices', *Comparative Political Studies*, 35(1): 5–34.

Myant, Martin, and Jan Drahokoupil (2012) 'International Integration, Varieties of Capitalism and Resilience to Crisis in Transition Economies', *Europe-Asia Studies*, 64(1): 1–33.

Nice, Alex (2012) 'Playing Both Sides: Belarus Between Russia and the EU', *DGAP Analyse*, no. 2, 19 March, https://dgap.org/de/think-tank/publikationen/dgapanalyse/playing-both-sides.

Nölke, Andreas and Arjan Vliegenthart (2009), 'Enlarging the Varieties of Capitalism: The Emergence of Dependent Market Economies in East Central Europe', *World Politics*, 61(4) (October): 670–702.

Norris, Pippa (2011) *Democratic Deficit: Critical Citizens Revisited*. Cambridge and New York: Cambridge University Press.

North, Douglass C. (1992) *Institutions, Institutional Change, and Economic Performance*. Cambridge and New York: Cambridge University Press.

O'Donnell, Guillermo and Philippe C. Schmitter (1986) *Transitions from Authoritarian Rule*, Baltimore and London: Johns Hopkins University Press.

O'Dwyer, Connor (2006) *Runaway State-Building: Patronage Politics and Democratic Development*. Baltimore, MD: Johns Hopkins University Press.

O'Dwyer, Conor and Schwartz, Katarina (2010) 'Minority Rights after EU Enlargement: A Comparison of Antigay Politics in Poland and Latvia', *Comparative European Politics*, 8(2): 220–43.

Olson, David M. (1993) 'Compartmentalized Competition: The Managed Transitional Election System of Poland', *Journal of Politics*, 55(2): 415–41.

Olson, David. M. (1994) *Democratic Legislative Institutions: A Comparative View*. Armonk, NY: M. E. Sharpe.

Olson, David M. (1999) 'From Electoral Symbol to Legislative Puzzle: The Polish Senat', in Samuel C. Patterson and Anthony Mughan (eds), *Senates: Bicameralism in the Contemporary World*. Columbus OH: Ohio State University Press: 301–33.

Olson, David M. and William E. Crowther (eds) (2002) *Committees in Post-Communist Democratic Parliaments: Comparative Institutionalization*. Columbus, OH: Ohio State University Press.

Olson, David M. and Gabriella Ilonszki (eds) (2012a) *Post-Communist Parliaments: Change and Stability in the Second Decade*. London: Routledge.

Olson, David M. and Gabriella Ilonszki (2012b) 'Two Decades of Divergent Post-Communist Parliamentary Development', in David M. Olson and Gabriella Ilonszki (eds), *Post-Communist Parliaments: Change and Stability in the Second Decade*. London: Routledge: 119–40.

Olson, David M. and Philip Norton (eds) (1996) *The New Parliaments of Central and Eastern Europe*. London: Frank Cass.

Olson, David M. and Philip Norton (eds) (2008a) *Post-Communist and Post-Soviet Legislatures: Beyond Transition*. London: Routledge

Olson, David M. and Philip Norton (2008b) 'Post-Communist and Post-Soviet Parliaments: Divergent Paths from Transition', in David M. Olson and Philip Norton (eds), *Post-Communist and Post-Soviet Legislatures: Beyond Transition*. London: Routledge: 153–85.

Orenstein, Mitchell A. (2001) *Out of the Red*. Ann Arbor, MI: University of Michigan Press.

Orenstein, Mitchell A., Stephen Bloom, and Nicole Lindstrom (2008) 'A Fourth Dimension of Transition', in Mitchell A. Orenstein, Stephen Bloom and Nicole Lindstrom (eds), *Transnational Actors in Central and East European Transitions*, Pittsburgh, PA: University of Pittsburgh Press: 1–18.

OSCE (2008) 'Belarus Parliamentary Elections 28 September 2008: OSCE/ODIHR Election Observation Mission Final Report', Warsaw: OSCE, Office for Democratic Institutions and Human Rights (28 November).

OSCE (2012) 'Republic of Croatia Parliamentary Elections 4 December 2011:

Limited Election Observation Mission Report', Warsaw: OSCE, Office for Democratic Institutions and Human Rights (3 February).

Ost, David (1990) *Solidarity and the Politics of Anti-Politics: Opposition and Reform in Poland Since 1968*, Philadelphia, PA: Temple University Press.

Ost, David (2005) *The Defeat of Solidarity: Anger and Politics in Postcommunist Europe*. Ithaca, NY: Cornell University Press.

Pacek, Alexander C., Grigore Pop-Eleches and Joshua A. Tucker (2009) 'Disenchanted or Discerning: Voter Turnout in Post-Communist Countries', *Journal of Politics*, 71 (2): 473–91.

Pavkovic, Alexander (2000) *The Fragmentation of Yugoslavia: Nationalism and War in the Balkans,* 2nd edn. Basingstoke: Palgrave Macmillan.

Pettai, Vello and Marcus Kreuzer (2001) 'Institutions and Party Development in the Baltic States', in Paul Lewis (ed.), *Party Development and Democratic Change in Post-Communist Europe: The First Decade*. London and Portland, OR: Frank Cass: 107–25.

Plasser, Fritz, Peter A. Ulram and Harald Waldrauch (1998) *Democratic Consolidation in East-Central Europe*. London: Macmillan.

Plecita-Vlachova, Klara and Stegmaier, Mary (2008) 'The Parliamentary Elections in the Czech Republic June 2006', *Electoral Studies,* 27(1): 179–84.

Polity IV Project (2012) *Political Regime Characteristics and Transitions, 1800–2010.* http://www.systemicpeace.org/inscr/inscr.htm.

Pollert, Anna (2003) 'Women, Work and Equal Opportunities in Post-Communist Transition', *Work, Employment and Society*, 17(2) (June): 331–57.

Pollert, Anna (2005) 'Gender, Transformation and Employment in Central Eastern Europe', *European Journal of Industrial Relations*, 11(2) (July): 213–30.

'Political Declaration 1 of 2010 (16 June) of the Hungarian National Assembly on National Cooperation' (2010), from http://www.mfa.gov.hu/NR/rdonlyres/1EC78EE5-8A4B-499C-9BE5-E5FD5DC2C0A1/0/Political_Declaration.pdf.

Pomorska, Karolina and Sophie Vanhoonacker (2012) 'Poland in the Driving Seat: A Mature Presidency in Turbulent Times', *Journal of Common Market Studies*, Vol. 50, *Special Issue: The JCMS Annual Review of the European Union in 2011* (September): 76–84.

Popescu, Nicu and Wilson, Andrew (2009) 'Moldova's Fragile Pluralism', in Michael Emerson and Richard Youngs (eds), *Democracy's Plight in the European Neighbourhood: Struggling Transitions and Proliferating Dynasties*. Brussels: CEPS: 92–102.

Pop-Eleches, Grigore (2010) 'Throwing Out the Bums: Protest Voting and Unorthodox Parties after Communism', *World Politics*, 62(2): 221–60.

Pop-Eleches, Grigore and Joshua Tucker (2013) 'Associated with the Past? Communist Legacies and Civic Participation in Post-Communist Countries', *East European Politics and Societies and Cultures*, 27(1) (February): 45–68.

Poulton, Hugh (1995) *Who are the Macedonians?* London: Hurst.

Pridham, Geoffrey (2005) *Designing Democracy: EU Enlargement and Regime Change in Post-Communist Europe*. Basingstoke: Palgrave Macmillan.

Pridham, Geoffrey (2008) 'Status Quo Bias or Institutionalisation for Reversibility? The EU's Political Conditionality, Post-Accession Tendencies and Democratic Consolidation in Slovakia', *Europe-Asia Studies*, 60(2) (June): 423–54.

Protsyk, Oleh (2005) 'Politics of Intra-Executive Conflict in Semi-Presidential Regimes in Eastern Europe,' *East European Politics and Society*, 19(2) (Spring): 1–20.

Przeworski, Adam (1991) *Democracy and the Market: Political and Economic Reforms in Eastern Europe and Latin America*. Cambridge and New York: Cambridge University Press.

Putnam, Robert D. (1993) *Making Democracy Work: Civic Traditions in Modern Italy*. Princeton, NJ: Princeton University Press.

Putnam, Robert (2000) *Bowling Alone. The Collapse and Revival of American Community*. New York: Simon & Schuster.

Radio Prague (2012) 'Czech Health Forum says government deserves a 'D' on health care', 31 May, http://www.radio.cz/en/section/news/news-2012-05-31.

Ramet, Sabrina P. (1991) *Social Currents in Eastern Europe: the Sources and Meaning of the Great Transformation*. Durham, NC: Duke University Press.

Rechel, Bernd (ed.) (2009) *Minority Rights in Central and Eastern Europe*. London: Routledge.

Regional Cooperation Council (2012) *2011–2012 Annual Report of the Secretary General of the Regional Cooperation Council on regional co-operation in South East Europe* (Sarajevo, 15 May).

Reschova, Jana and Zindriska Syllova (1996) 'The Legislature of the Czech Republic', in David M. Olson and Philip Norton (eds), *The New Parliaments of Central and Eastern Europe*. London: Frank Cass: 82–107.

Reynolds, Andrew (2011) *Designing Democracy in a Dangerous World*. Oxford: Oxford University Press.

Reynolds, Andrew, Ben Reilly and Andrew Ellis (2005) *Electoral System Design: The New International IDEA Handbook*, Stockholm: International IDEA.

Risse, Thomas (2003) 'The Euro: Between National and European Identity', *Journal of European Public Policy*, 10(4): 487–503.

Roberts, Andrew (2010) *The Quality of Democracy in Eastern Europe: Public Preferences and Policy Reforms*. Cambridge and New York: Cambridge University Press.

Roper, Stephen (2000) *Romania: The Unfinished Revolution*. London and New York: Routledge.

Rose, Richard (2002) 'A Bottom Up Evaluation of Enlargement Countries: New Europe Barometer 1', *Studies in Public Policy*, no. 364, Glasgow: Centre for Public Policy.

Rose, Richard (2004) 'Europe Expands, Turnout Falls: The Significance of the

2004 European Parliamentary Election', Stockholm: International Institute for Democracy and Electoral Assistance, available at www.idea.int/publications/voter_turnout_weurope/upload/Annex_Euro_Gap.pdf.

Rose, Richard (2009) *Understanding Post-Communist Transformation: A Bottom-up Approach*. London: Routledge.

Rose, Richard and William Mishler (1996) 'Representation and Leadership in Post-Communist Political Systems,' *Journal of Communist Studies and Transition Politics*, 12 (2) (June): 224–46.

Rose, Richard and William Mishler (1998) 'Negative and Positive Party Identification in Post-Communist Countries', *Electoral Studies*, 17(2): 217–34.

Rose, Richard, William Mishler and Christian Haerpfer (1998) *Democracy and Its Alternatives. Understanding Post-Communist Societies*. Baltimore, MD: Johns Hopkins University Press.

Rothschild, Joseph (1974) *East Central Europe between the Two World Wars*. Seattle, WA: University of Washington Press.

Rothschild, Joseph and Nancy M. Wingfield (2000) *Return to Diversity*, 3rd edn. New York: Oxford University Press.

Rupnik, Jacques (1990) 'Central Europe or Mitteleuropa?', *Daedalus*, 119(1) (Winter) : 249–78.

Rupnik, Jacques *et al.* (2012) 'Hungary's Illiberal Turn', *Journal of Democracy*, 23(3) (July): 132–7.

Sachs, Jeffrey (1993) *Poland's Jump to the Market Economy*. Cambridge, MA: MIT Press.

Safaei, Jalil (2012) 'Postcommunist Health Transitions in Central and Eastern Europe', *Economic Research International*, Article ID 137412.

Sanderson, Stephen K. (2010) *Revolutions. A Worldwide Introduction to Social and Political Contention*, 2nd edn. Boulder, CO, and London: Paradigm Publishers.

Sasse, Gwen (2009) 'The Politics of Conditionality: the Norm of Minority Protection before and after EU Accession', in Rachel Epstein and Ulrich Sedelmeier (eds), *International Influence beyond Conditionality: Postcommunist Europe after EU Enlargement*. London: Routledge.

Szczerbiak, Aleks and Monika Bil (2009) 'When in Doubt, (Re-)turn to Domestic Politics? The (Non-)impact of the EU on Party Politics in Poland', *Journal of Communist Studies and Transition Politics*, 25(4) (October): 447–67.

Schimmelfennig, F. and Sedelmeier, U. (2005) *The Europeanisation of Central and Eastern Europe*. Ithaca, NY: Cornell University Press.

Schmitter, Philippe (2011) 'Diagnosing and Designing Democracy in Europe', in Sonia Alonso, John Keane and Wolfgang Merkel (eds), *The Future of Representative Democracy*. Cambridge and New York: Cambridge University Press.

Schopflin, George (2006) 'After the Elections: Left and Right in Hungary', *Budapest Analyses*, 25 May, available online at www.budapestanalyses.hu/docs/En/Analyses_Archive/analysys_90_en.html.

Schopflin, George (2012) 'How to understand Hungary', 6 February, Open Democracy, 6 February, http://www.opendemocracy.net/george-sch%C3%B6pflin/how-to-understand-hungary.

Schopflin, George and Nancy Wood (eds) (1989) *In Search of Central Europe.* Oxford: Polity.

Schumpeter, Joseph A. (1976) *Capitalism, Socialism and Democracy*, 5th edn. London: Allen & Unwin.

Sedelius, Thomas (2006) *The Tug-of-War between Presidents and Prime Ministers: Semi-Presidentialism in Central and Eastern Europe.* Orebro, Sweden: Orebro Studies in Political Science.

Sedelmeier, Ulrich (2011) 'Europeanisation in New Member and Candidate States', *Living Reviews in European Governance*, 6(1), http://www. livingreviews.org/lreg-2011-1.

Sedelmeier, Ulrich (2012) 'Is Europeanisation through Conditionality Sustainable? Lock-in of Institutional Change after EU Accession', *West European Politics*, 35(1): 20–38.

Shugart, Matthew Soberg, and Martin P. Wattenberg (eds) (2001) *Mixed-Member Electoral Systems: The Best of Both Worlds*, Oxford: Oxford University Press.

Shvetsova, Olga (1999) 'A Survey of Post-Communist Electoral Institutions, 1990–1998', *Electoral Studies*, 18(3) (September): 397–409.

Sikk, Allan (2005) "How Unstable? Volatility and the Genuinely New Parties in Eastern Europe", *European Journal of Political Research*, 44(3) (May): 391–412.

Sikk, Allan (2011) 'Estonia', *European Journal of Political Research*, 50(7–8): 960–4 .

Sikk, Allan (2012) 'Newness as a Winning Formula for New Political Parties', *Party Politics*, 18(4): 465–86.

Silitski, Vitali (2005) 'Preempting Democracy: The Case of Belarus', *Journal of Democracy*, 16(4) (October): 83–97.

Simon, Maurice D. and David M. Olson (1980) 'Evolution of a Minimal Parliament: Membership and Committee Changes in the Polish Sejm', *Legislative Studies Quarterly*, 5 (May): 211–32.

Simonyi, Andras (2006) 'Visegrad Cooperation: A 15-Year-old Successor Story', in Andrzej Jagodzinski (ed.), *The Visegrad Group: A Central European Constellation.* Bratislava: International Visegrad Fund: 96–7.

Skocpol, Theda (1979) *States and Social Revolutions.* Cambridge and New York: Cambridge University Press.

Slomczynski, Kazmierz and Goldie Shabad (2012) 'Perceptions of Political Party Corruption and Voting Behavior in Poland', *Party Politics*, 18(6) (November): 897–917.

Smelser, Neil (1962) *A Theory of Collective Behavior.* New York: Free Press.

Smith, A., Stenning, A., Rochovska, A. and Swiatek, D. (2008) 'The Emergence of a Working Poor: Labour Markets, Neoliberalisation and Diverse Economies in Post-Socialist Cities', *Antipode*, 40(2) (March): 283–311.

Smith, David (2008) '"Woe from Stones": Commemoration, Identity Politics and Estonia's "War of Monuments"', *Journal of Baltic Studies*, 39(4): 419–30.

Smith, David, Artis Pabriks, Aldis Purs, and Thomas Lane (2002) *The Baltic States: Estonia, Latvia and Lithuania*. London and New York: Routledge.

Spendzharova, Aneta and Vachudova, Milada Anna (2012) 'Catching Up? Consolidating Liberal Democracy in Bulgaria and Romania after EU Accession', *West European Politics*, 35(1): 39–58.

Stan, Lavinia and Zaharia, Razvan (2011) 'Romania', *European Journal of Political Research*, 50(7–8): 1108–17.

Standing, Guy (1996) 'Social Protection in Central and Eastern Europe: A Tale of Slipping Anchors and Torn Safety Nets', in Gosta Esping-Andersen (ed.) *Welfare States in Transition*. Geneva/London: UNRISD/Sage.

Staniszkis, Jadwiga (1991) *The Dynamics of Breakthrough*. Berkeley, CA: University of California Press.

States News Service (Kyiv) (2011) 'President: Ukraine Considers its 2013 OSCE Chairmanship Good Opportunity to Contribute to Development of Democracy', 27 May.

Stefan, Laurentiu (2004) *Patterns of Political Elite Recruitment in Post-Communist Romania*. Bucharest: Ziua.

Stefan, Laurentiu, Sergiu Gherghina and Mihail Chiru (2012) 'We All Agree that We Disagree Too Much: Attitudes of Romanian MPs towards Party Discipline', *East European Politics*, 28(2) (June): 180–92.

Stewart, M. (2002) 'Deprivation, the Roma and "the Underclass"', in Chris Hann (ed.), *Postsocialism: Ideals, Ideologies and Practices in Eurasia*. London and New York: Routledge.

Stroem, Kaare (1998) 'Parliamentary Committees in European Democracies', *Journal of Legislative Studies*, 4(1) (Spring): 21–59.

Subtely, Orest (2009) *Ukraine: A History*, 4th edn. Toronto: University of Toronto Press.

Sudetic, Chuck (1998) *Blood and Vengeance: One Family's Story of the War in Bosnia*. New York: Norton.

Swain, N. (2011) 'A Post-Socialist Capitalism', *Europe-Asia Studies*, 63(9): 1671–95.

Szalai, Julia (1998) 'Women and Democratization: Some Notes on Recent Changes in Hungary,' in Jane S. Jaquette and Sharon L. Wolchik (eds), *Women and Democracy: Latin America and Central and Eastern Europe*. Baltimore, MD: Johns Hopkins University Press: 185–202.

Szczerbiak, Aleks (2012) *Poland Within the European Union: New Awkward Partner or New Heart of Europe?* London: Routledge.

Szczerbiak, Aleks and Sean Hanley (eds) (2006) *Centre-Right Parties in Post-Communist East-Central Europe*. London: Routledge.

Taggart, P. and Szczerbiak, A. (2009) (eds) *EU Enlargement and Referendums*. London: Routledge.

Tanner, Marcus (1998) *Croatia: A Nation Forged in War*. New Haven, CT Yale University Press.

Taras, Ray (ed.) (1998) *Postcommunist Presidents*. Cambridge and New York: Cambridge University Press.

Taras, Ray (2007) 'Executive Leadership', in Stephen White, Judy Batt and Paul G. Lewis (eds), *Developments in Central and East European Politics 4*. Basingstoke: Palgrave Macmillan: 127–44.

Tavits, Margit (2005) 'The Development of Stable Party Support: Electoral Dynamics in Post-Communist Europe', *American Journal of Political Science*, 49(2): 283–98.

Tavits, Margit (2008a) 'Party Systems in the Making: The Emergence and Success of New Parties in New Democracies', *British Journal of Political Science*, 38(1): 113–33.

Tavits, Margit (2008b) 'Policy Positions, Issue Importance, and Party Competition in New Democracies', *Comparative Political Studies*, 41(1): 48–72.

Taylor, Andrew J. (2005) '"We Are Not Asking You To Hug Each Other, But We Ask You To Co-exist": The Kosovo Assembly and the Politics of Co-existence', *Journal of Legislative Studies*, 11(1): 105–37.

Tilly, Charles (1978) *From Mobilization to Revolution*. Reading, MA: Addison-Wesley.

Tilly, Charles and Sidney Tarrow (2007) *Contentious Politics*. Boulder, CO, and London: Paradigm Publishers.

Tilly, Charles and Lesley J. Wood (2009) *Social Movements, 1768–2008*, 2nd edn. Boulder, CO, and London: Paradigm Publishers.

Tocqueville, Alexis de (1955) *The Old Regime and the French Revolution*. New York: Anchor.

Todorova, Maria (1997) *Imagining the Balkans*. Oxford: Oxford University Press.

Tokes, Rudolf (1996) *Hungary's Negotiated Revolution*. Cambridge and New York: Cambridge University Press.

Touraine, Alan (1983) *Solidarity: Poland 1980–81*. Cambridge and New York: Cambridge University Press.

Transparency International – Ceska republika (2011) 'Studie narodni integrity', Prague, December, downloaded from http://www.transparency.org/country#CZE_DataResearch_Reports.

Transparency International (2012) *Corruption Perceptions Index 2011*. www.transparency.org/whatwedo/pub/corruption_perceptions_index_2011.

Tucker, Joshua (2001) 'Economic Conditions and the Vote for Incumbent Parties in Russia, Poland, Hungary, Slovakia and the Czech Republic from 1990–1996', *Post-Soviet Affairs*, 17(4): 309–31.

Tucker, Joshua (2006) *Regional Economic Voting: Russia, Poland, Hungary, the Czech Republic, and Slovakia, 1990–1999*. Cambridge and New York: Cambridge University Press.

Tucker, Robert C. (1981), *Politics as Leadership*. Columbia, MO: University of Missouri Press.

2009/10 Hungarian Presidency (2010) (unpublished text), at http://www.visegradgroup.eu/documents/presidency-programs/2009-2010-hungarian-110412.

Tworzecki, Hubert (2002) *Learning to Choose: Electoral Politics in East-Central Europe*. Palo Alto, CA: Stanford University Press.

UNECE (United Nations Economic Commission for Europe) (2012), 'Share of Women among Government Ministers', at http://w3.unece.org/pxweb/quickstatistics/readtable.asp?qs_id=19 (accessed 8 June 2012).

UNU-WIDER (2008) UNU-WIDER World Income Inequality Database, Version 2.0c, May 2008. www.wider.unu.edu/research/Database/en_GB/database/.

Vachudova, Milada Anna (2005) *Europe Undivided: Democracy, Leverage and Integration after Communism*. Oxford: Oxford University Press.

Van Biezen, Ingrid (2003) *Political Parties in New Democracies*. Basingstoke: Palgrave Macmillan.

Van Biezen, Ingrid (2005) 'On the Theory and Practice of Party Formation and Adaptation in New Democracies', *European Journal of Political Research*, 44(1) (January): 147–74.

Van Biezen, Ingrid, Peter Mair and Thomas Poguntke (2012) 'Going, Going, Gone? The Decline of Party Membership in Contemporary Europe', *European Journal of Political Research*, 51(1) (January): 24–56.

Van der Brug, Wouter, Mark Franklin and Gabor Toka (2008) 'One Electorate or Many? Differences in Party Preference Formation between New and Established European Democracies', *Electoral Studies*, 27(4) (December): 589–600.

Vasaryova, Magda (2006) 'The Optimal Format for Regional Cooperation', in Andrzej Jagodzinski (ed.), *The Visegrad Group: A Central European Constellation*. Bratislava: International Visegrad Fund: 77–8.

Vassiliou, G. (2007) *The Accession Story: The EU from 15 to 25 Countries*. Oxford: Oxford University Press.

Verheijen, Tony (1999) 'The Civil Service System of Bulgaria: Hope on the Horizon,' in Verheijen and Alexander Kotchegura (eds), *Civil Service Systems in Central and Eastern Europe*. Cheltenham: Edward Elgar: 92–130.

Vermeersch, Peter (2006) *The Romani Movement: Minority Politics and Ethnic Mobilization in Contemporary Central Europe*. London and New York: Berghahn Books.

Vickers, Miranda and James Pettifer (2009) *The Albanian Question: Reshaping the Balkans*. London: Tauris.

Visegrad Insight (2012) 'Nobody Questions The Geopolitical Identity of the Region Anymore', 1: 42–4.

Vlachova, Klara (2001) 'Party Identification in the Czech Republic: Inter-party Hostility and Party Preference', *Communist and Post-Communist Studies*, 34(4): 479–99.

Vondra, Alexandr (2006) 'Visegrad Cooperation: How did it Start?', in Andrzej Jagodzinski (ed.), *The Visegrad Group: A Central European Constellation*. Bratislava: International Visegrad Fund: 79–80.

Wałęsa, Lech (2006) 'From Solidarnosc (Solidarity) to Cooperation and Integration', in Andrzej Jagodzinski (ed.), *The Visegrad Group: A Central European Constellation*. Bratislava: International Visegrad Fund: 81–3.

Wallace, Claire, Florian Pichler, and Christian Haerpfer (2012) 'Changing Patterns of Civil Society in Europe and America, 1995–2005: Is Eastern Europe Different?', *East European Politics and Societies and Cultures*, 26(1) (February): 3–19.

Waterbury, Myra A. (2010) *Between State and Nation: Diaspora Politics and Kin-State Nationalism in Hungary*. Basingstoke and New York: Palgrave Macmillan.

Way, Lucan (2003) 'Weak States and Pluralism: The Case of Moldova', *East European Politics and Societies*, 17(3): 454–82.

Way, Lucan (2005) 'Authoritarian State-Building and the Sources of Regime Competitiveness in the Fourth Wave: The Cases of Belarus, Moldova, Russia, and Ukraine,' *World Politics*, 57(2) (January): 231–61.

Way, Lucan (2006) 'Sources and Dynamics of Competitive Authoritarianism in Ukraine,' in Derek Hutcheson and Elena Korosteleva (eds), *The Quality of Democracy in Post-Communist Europe*. New York: Routledge.

Webb, Paul (2011) 'Political Parties, Representation and Politics in Contemporary Europe,' in Erik Jones, Paul Heywood, Martin Rhodes and Ulrich Sedelmeier (eds), *Developments in European Politics 4*. Basingstoke: Palgrave Macmillan: 65–80.

Webb, Paul and Stephen White (2007) 'Political Parties in New Democracies: Trajectories of Development and Implications for Democracy', in Paul Webb and Stephen White (eds) *Party Politics in New Democracies*. Oxford: Oxford University Press.

Wedel, Janine (1998) *Collision and Collusion: The Strange Case of Western Aid to Eastern Europe, 1989–1998*. New York: St Martin's Press.

Welsh, William (1980) 'The Status of Research on Representative Institutions in Eastern Europe,' *Legislative Studies Quarterly*, 5(2) (May): 275–308.

Welz, Christian and Timo Kauppinen (2005) 'Industrial Action and Conflict Resolution in the New Member States', *European Journal of Industrial Relations*, 11(1) (March): 91–105.

White, Stephen (1982) 'Some Conclusions', in Daniel Nelson and Stephen White (eds), *Communist Legislatures in Comparative Perspective*. London: Macmillan and Albany, NY: State University of New York Press: 191–5.

White, Stephen, Elena A, Korosteleva and John Lowenhardt (eds) (2005) *Postcommunist Belarus*. Lanham, MD: Rowman & Littlefield.

Whiteley, Paul F. (2011) 'Is the Party Over? The Decline of Party Activism and Membership Across the Democratic World', *Party Politics*, 17(1) (January): 21–44.

Whitmore, Sarah (2004) *State-Building in Ukraine: the Ukrainian Parliament, 1990-2003*. London: RoutledgeCurzon.

Wilson, Andrew (2005a) *Ukraine's Orange Revolution*. New Haven and London: Yale University Press.

Wilson, Andrew (2005b) *Virtual Politics: Faking Democracy in the Post-Soviet World*. New Haven and London: Yale University Press.

Wilson, Andrew (2007) 'The East Europeans: Ukraine, Belarus and Moldova', in Stephen White, Judy Batt and Paul G. Lewis (eds), *Central and East European Politics 4*. Basingstoke: Palgrave Macmillan: 90–109.

Wilson, Andrew (2009) *The Ukrainians: Unexpected Nation*, 3rd edn. New Haven and London: Yale University Press.

Wilson, Andrew (2011) *Belarus: The Last European Dictatorship*. New Haven and London: Yale University Press.

Wolchik, Sharon L. and Jane L. Curry (eds) (2011) *Central and East European Politics: From Communism to Democracy*, 2nd edn. Lanham, MD: Rowman & Littlefield.

Wolczuk, Kataryna (2002) *The Moulding of Ukraine: The Constitutional Politics of State Formation*. Budapest: Central European University Press.

World Bank (1996) *World Development Report 1996: From Plan to Market*. Oxford: Oxford University Press.

World Bank (2000) *Making Transition Work for Everyone: Poverty and Inequality in Europe and Central Asia*. Washington, DC: The World Bank.

World Bank (2002) *Transition, The First Ten Years: Analysis and Lessons for Eastern Europe and the Former Soviet Union*. Washington, DC: The World Bank.

World Bank (2012a) *World Development Report 2012: Gender Equality and Development*. Washington, DC: The World Bank.

World Bank (2012b) 'Worldwide Governance Indicators', at http://info.world-bank.org/governance/wgi/index.asp (accessed 4 June 2012).

Yekelchyk, Serhy (2007) *Ukraine: Birth of a Modern Nation*. Oxford: Oxford University Press.

Zajc, Drago (2004) 'Changing Functions of National Parliaments', in Zdenka Mansfeldova, David M. Olson, and Petra Rakusanova (eds), *Central European Parliaments: First Decade of Democratic Experience and Future Prospectives*. Prague: Czech Academy of Science: 60–75.

Zantovsky, Michael (2006) 'Visegrad between the Past and the Future', in Andrzej Jagodzinski (ed.), *The Visegrad Group: A Central European Constellation*, Bratislava: International Visegrad Fund: 84–5.

Zubek, Radoslaw (2008) 'Parties, Rules and Government Legislative Control in Central Europe: The Case of Poland', *Communist and Post-Communist Studies*, 41(2) (June): 147–61.

Zubek, Radoslaw (2012) 'Negative Agenda Control and Executive-Legislative Relations in East Central Europe, 1997–2008', in David M. Olson and Gabriella Ilonszki (eds), *Post-Communist Parliaments: Change and Stability in the Second Decade*. London: Routledge: 57–77.

Index

Printed in China